New Topics in Emerging Markets

Edited by Vito Bobek and Tatjana Horvat

Published in London, United Kingdom

New Topics in Emerging Markets
http://dx.doi.org/10.5772/intechopen.107812
Edited by Vito Bobek and Tatjana Horvat

Contributors
Van Anh Do, Sudeep Krishnan, Ulf Bosch, Isaac Ahinsah-Wobil, Silvana Dakduk, David Van der Woude, Camilo Alarcon Nieto, James Alic Garang, Olga Mezentceva, Vito Bobek, Vladislav Streltsov, Tatjana Horvat, Achraf Haddad, Bonginkosi A. Thango, Hakim Amira, Eleftherios Thalassinos, Stefan Bernat, Anna Sergeevna Khvorostyanaya

First published in London, United Kingdom, 2024 by IntechOpen
IntechOpen is the global imprint of INTECHOPEN LIMITED, registered in England and Wales, registration number: 11086078, 5 Princes Gate Court, London, SW7 2QJ, United Kingdom
Printed in Croatia

British Library Cataloguing-in-Publication Data
A catalogue record for this book is available from the British Library

Additional hard and PDF copies can be obtained from orders@intechopen.com

New Topics in Emerging Markets
Edited by Vito Bobek and Tatjana Horvat
p. cm.

This title is part of the Business, Management and Economics Book Series, Volume 14
Topic: Economics
Series Editor: Taufiq Choudhry
Topic Editor: Jaime Ortiz

Print ISBN 978-1-83769-132-6
Online ISBN 978-1-83769-133-3
eBook (PDF) ISBN 978-1-83769-134-0
ISSN 2753-894X

An electronic version of this book is freely available, thanks to the partial funding support of libraries working with Knowledge Unlatched. KU is a collaborative initiative designed to make high quality books Open Access for the public good. More information about the initiative and links to the Open Access version can be found at www.knowledgeunlatched.org

For EU product safety concerns:
IN TECH d.o.o., Prolaz Marije Krucifikse Kozulić 3, 51000 Rijeka, Croatia,
info@intechopen.com or visit our website at intechopen.com.

IntechOpen Book Series

Business, Management and Economics

Volume 14

Aims and Scope of the Series

This series will provide a comprehensive overview of recent research trends in business and management, economics, and marketing. Topics will include asset liability management, financial consequences of the financial crisis and covid-19, financial accounting, mergers and acquisitions, management accounting, SMEs, financial markets, corporate finance and governance, managerial technology and innovation, resource management and sustainable development, social entrepreneurship, corporate responsibility, ethics and accountability, microeconomics, labour economics, macroeconomics, public economics, financial economics, econometrics, direct marketing, creative marketing, internet marketing, market planning and forecasting, brand management, market segmentation and targeting and other topics under business and management. This book series will focus on various aspects of business and management whose in-depth understanding is critical for business and company management to function effectively during this uncertain time of financial crisis, Covid-19 pandemic, and military activity in Europe.

Meet the Series Editor

Prof. Choudhry holds a BSc degree in Economics from the University of Iowa, as well as a Masters and Ph.D. in Applied Economics from Clemson University, USA. In January 2006, he became a Professor of Finance at the University of Southampton Business School. He was previously a Professor of Finance at the University of Bradford Management School. He has over 80 articles published in international finance and economics journals. His research interests and specialties include financial econometrics, financial economics, international economics and finance, housing markets, financial markets, among others.

Meet the Volume Editors

Dr. Vito Bobek is a Professor of International Management at the University of Applied Sciences FH Joanneum, Graz, Austria; the Faculty of Economics and Business, University of Maribor, Slovenia; and the Faculty of Social Sciences, University of Ljubljana, Slovenia. He has published more than 500 units in his academic career and visited 22 universities worldwide as a visiting professor. He is a member of the editorial boards of six international journals. He has a long history in academia, consulting, and entrepreneurship. Among his previous functions, Dr. Bobek was a member of the Supervisory Board of KBM Infond Management Company Ltd, an advisor to the Minister of Economic Relations and Development, and a member of the Strategic Council of the Minister of Foreign Affairs of Slovenia.

Dr. Tatjana Horvat is an Associate Professor of Accounting and Auditing at the University of Primorska, Slovenia. She is a certified state internal auditor (licensed by the Ministry of Finance RS), a certified internal auditor for the business sector, and a certified accountant. At the Ministry of Justice of Slovenia, Dr. Horvat is a member of examination boards for court expert candidates and judicial appraisers in economy/ finance, valuation of companies, banking, and forensic investigation of economic operations/ accounting. At the leading business newspaper in Slovenia (Swedish ownership), Finance, she is the editor and head of the business, finance, tax-related papers, and educational programs. She has written more than 300 articles, papers, books, and manuals and was a guest at many international scientific and business conferences and universities.

Contents

Preface

The global landscape of economics and business continually evolves, with emerging markets playing an increasingly pivotal role in shaping the world's economic future. In this edited volume, *New Topics in Emerging Markets*, we delve into a diverse array of subjects that encapsulate the dynamism and complexity of these markets. We aim to provide a comprehensive and accessible exploration of critical issues in emerging markets for a general readership, offering insights into their challenges and opportunities.

Emerging markets, often characterized by rapid growth, changing demographics, and evolving business environments, are at the forefront of global economic discourse. Our contributors come from various academic and professional backgrounds, and their research spans a broad spectrum of topics, reflecting the multifaceted nature of emerging markets.

Chapter 1, "Hodrick-Prescott Filtering of Large Emerging Economies and Decoupling Hypothesis", begins by exploring economic trends in large emerging economies and the intriguing concept of decoupling. Are these economies becoming increasingly independent of their developed counterparts or are they still intricately linked to global economic cycles?

Chapter 2, "The Global Business Cycle within the New Commodities and the Financial Cycle: An Empirical Evidence Based on a Multivariate Unobserved Components Model (UCM)", delves into the intricate relationship between commodities and the global business cycle. As commodities become increasingly vital in today's interconnected world, understanding their impact on the worldwide economy is paramount.

Chapter 3, "Emerging Financial Markets in Ghana and Public Financial Management Crisis Uncertainties Amidst Debt Restructuring", uses Ghana's experience with emerging financial markets as a case study, shedding light on the challenges and uncertainties that arise during debt restructuring and their impact on public financial management.

Chapter 4, "How to Successfully Select the Best-Performing Bank Based on the Best Auditor's Choice Quality in Islamic and Conventional Banks?", explores the intricate process of selecting the best-performing bank, considering the quality of auditors in both Islamic and conventional banking systems.

Chapter 5, "Impacts of Board Quality on Financial Performance in Conventional and Participatory Banks during and after the Covid-19 Crisis: Evidence from Emerging and Developing Countries", investigates the role of board quality in influencing the financial performance of banks in emerging and developing countries during and after the COVID-19 pandemic, which disrupted global economies.

Chapter 6, "Causal Relationship Among Bank Capitalization, Efficiency, and Risk-Taking in ASEAN Commercial Banks", explores the intricate relationships among bank capitalization, efficiency, and risk-taking in ASEAN commercial banks, as banking stability and efficiency are essential to economic growth.

Chapter 7, "Policies for Improving the Efficiency of Innovative Clustering in an Emerging Market", discusses policies to enhance the efficiency of innovation clusters, which are hubs of creativity and entrepreneurship, in emerging markets.

Chapter 8, "Exploiting Technology during Pandemics in Sub-Saharan Africa", investigates how Sub-Saharan Africa leveraged technology to mitigate the impact of the COVID-19 pandemic.

Chapter 9, "Technological Adoption in Emerging Economies: Insights from Latin America and the Caribbean with a Focus on Low-Income Consumers", explores the phenomenon of technological adoption as a crucial driver of economic growth in Latin America and the Caribbean, focusing on low-income consumers.

Chapter 10, "Dynamics of Innovation Ecosystems: Orchestrating Actors and Interactions in Emerging Economies", uncovers the intricate dynamics of innovation ecosystems in emerging economies.

Chapter 11, "Perspective Chapter: eCommerce in the Web3 Era", provides insights into the intersection of e-commerce and the emerging Web3 world, which is spurring the rapid evolution of future commerce.

Chapter 12, "Fashion-Strategizing Leadership in Sports", explores the unique dynamics of leadership in the sports industry within emerging markets.

Chapter 13, "The Future of Education: Writing Exams in the Metaverse at South African Universities", explores the future of education in the Metaverse. Education is transforming, and South African universities are at the forefront of this change.

Chapter 14, "MNC Strategy in Contested Environments: Stay Put or Stay Foot?", examines multinational corporations' strategic decisions when faced with contested markets.

As you embark on this journey through *New Topics in Emerging Markets*, we hope you gain valuable insights into the intricacies, challenges, and opportunities that define these dynamic and rapidly evolving economies. Whether you are an academic, business professional, or simply an inquisitive reader, this volume offers a thought-provoking exploration of the issues shaping the future of emerging markets.

We would like to thank IntechOpen for allowing us to become the editors of this book. We appreciate that they believed we could provide the necessary knowledge and technical assistance. We together managed to find the other great colleagues who contributed to this volume. We thank each author for their valuable contributions that resulted in this book; it will be an asset to the professional community. We also thank our technical reviewers and colleagues at IntechOpen. We could not have done it without you.

Vito Bobek
Institute of International Management and Entrepreneurship,
University of Applied Sciences FH Joanneum,
Graz, Austria

Tatjana Horvat
Faculty of Management,
University of Primorska
Koper, Slovenia

Section 1

Economics of Emerging Markets

Chapter 1

Hodrick-Prescott Filtering of Large Emerging Economies and Decoupling Hypothesis

Olga Mezentseva

Abstract

The aim of this chapter is to summarize our researches about economic growth in large emerging economies: Russia, India, and China. There were launched back in 2014. Since the 2008 crisis, there has been speculation that large emerging economies have built up sufficient economic capacity and that emerging economies' economic cycles have become more independent of developed economies. However, our studies have shown that at the time of 2014–2015, the economic growth of large developing economies had too different qualitative characteristics to speak about the synchronization of economic cycles and confirm the decoupling hypothesis. In addition, we predicted a slowdown in China and extremely weak economic growth in Russia as early as 2014. However, the Russian-Ukrainian conflict and unprecedented anti-Russian sanctions artificially led to greater cooperation and communication between large emerging economies. Contrary to expectations, the Russian economy has shown its resilience, and economic ties between China and Russia, and India and Russia have strengthened. The main result of this research is that we have shown that, in addition to the indicator of economic growth, its qualitative characteristics are much more important. Until international cooperation occurs on a qualitative basis of economic growth, the decoupling hypothesis cannot be confirmed.

Keywords: geoeconomic fragmentation, Hodrik-Preskott filtering, economics cycle, decoupling hypothesis, output gap

1. Introduction

Global trade and integration are the main drivers of global economic growth. In the last decade, the global economy has faced a slowdown in economic growth and a decrease in the integration level, but global trade and integration have promoted a better flow of technology that ensures avoid gaps in economic development between developed and developing countries. Despite the fact that in the last 5 years the trend of globalization has changed to the trend of geoeconomic fragmentation, the issue of the effectiveness of creating economic unions has remained relevant, and only the point of view has changed. The presence of synchronization between the economic cycles of the countries of a geoeconomic union is a generally accepted indicator to determine the presence of integration and the efficiency of a geoeconomic union [1–5].

The large emerging economies: Russia, India, China (hereinafter—the "LEE") and their geoeconomic alliance is the object of our study. Russia, India, and China are emerging market countries. The role of emerging markets has grown significantly over the past few decades, and they are playing a significant role in the global economy [6]. Restrictive measures in China due to the coronavirus pandemic, as well as the lifting of restrictions, cause surges in resource prices around the world and peak loads in the global logistics system [7]. Kremer et al. [8] note that the decline in medium-term global growth reflects a slower rate of change in the progress of improving living standards in countries such as China and Korea. As a result, since the previous global crisis in 2008, there has been a debate about the separation of the economic development of emerging markets from developed markets, the so-called "decoupling hypothesis" [6, 9–11]. Before the 2008 crisis, most of the literature supported the decoupling hypothesis [12, 13]. Since the 2008 crisis, there have been many studies showing a reduction or disappearance of its effect [14, 15]. The trade wars between the United States and China also contribute against support for the decoupling hypothesis.

The topic of economic growth in the context of high risks of fragmentation of the global economy has great relevance. A number of researchers support the existence of spillover effects arising from alliances [12, 16], while others find no such evidence [17, 18].

In this paper, we investigated the output gaps of large emerging economies: Russia, India, and China. We chose the output gap as an indicator of the economic growth efficiency of national economies. We used the Hodrik-Preskott filtering method to isolate the output gap. Next, we conducted a spectral analysis to determine the degree of synchronization of economic cycles. A similar approach was taken by Papageorgiou et al. [4], and Frankel and Rose [2], etc., against European Union countries.

In the second part, we investigated the output gaps of LEE, having isolated it by the statistical method of Hodrik-Preskott filtering rather than by calculation one. This method allows us to determine positive and negative gaps between real and potential gross domestic product (GDP). We calculated output gaps in US dollars at 2015 prices, in local currency at constant prices, in US dollars at current prices, and in local currency at current prices. This allowed us to identify the inflationary component and the component related to the exchange rate of national currencies. We applied spectral analysis to determine the degree of synchronization of business cycles.

In the third part, we discussed statistical results of the study, and in the fourth part, we tried to find explanations for these results and make conclusions.

2. From globalization to geoeconomic fragmentation

Global trade and integration are the driving forces of global economic growth, but in the last decade, one of the main problems of the global economy has been a slowdown in economic growth and geoeconomic fragmentation that has replaced the trend of globalization. The main events that have led to increased geoeconomic fragmentation are those related to BREXIT; trade disputes between China and the United States, Russian invasion of Ukraine.

Trends in global investment have shifted to reshoring and friendshoring, resulting in a slowdown in technology transfer between developed and developing countries [19–21]. Under such conditions, China's economic growth will depend on the state of international trade [7]. At the same time, China accounts for a quarter of exports from Asia, and the removal of COVID restrictions in China causes positive spillover effects for countries with strong trade ties with it [22]. At the same time, the decline in medium-term global growth reflects a slowdown in the rate of improvement in living standards in countries such as China and Korea [8].

At the same time, while there are quite a lot of studies of the impact of China's economic situation on the global economy, in Russia there is a huge gap, which is further exacerbated by the closeness of Russian statistics.

After the introduction of anti-Russian sanctions, in particular the European hydrocarbon embargo, the economic and trade interaction between large developing economies has increased significantly. India and China account for 70% of Russian oil exports. Russia has increased oil supplies to India by 22 times. Russia completely redirected supplies of petroleum products from the European market to India and China. In 2022, Russia supplied China with a third of its total oil exports. Approximately 29% of the Russian budget is formed through energy trade with India and China. In fact, this speaks of the highest degree of integration of large emerging economies. However, we assume that such integration has no economic basis and is of an administrative nature. This has consequences in terms of the instability of such relations because such integration can also be stopped by administrative means. It is impossible to talk about high-quality and inclusive economic growth based on such integration.

3. Methods

3.1 Decoupling hypothesis

Prior to the 2008 crisis, there were many studies showing that emerging markets had sustained economic growth, had built up sufficient economic and technological capacity, and that their economic cycles had become more independent of those of developed countries—the decoupling hypothesis [23]. Since the 2008 crisis, however, developed countries have changed their monetary policy substantially and have become more focused on stimulating their productive forces. The trade wars between the United States and China, which began in 2018, allow us to talk about direct restrictions in the exchange of technology between the United States and China.

At the same time, China and other major developing countries are facing a slowdown in economic growth. As a result of these processes, emerging markets are facing capital outflows and devaluation of national currencies.

It is also important to distinguish between the issue of the synchronicity of economic cycles and the fragmentation of the economies of the global economy. From our perspective, the existence of the synchronicity of economic cycles is objective in nature. The synchronicity of economic cycles confirms the interaction of the economic systems of national economies and confirms the decoupling hypothesis. In addition, the fragmentation of economies can be caused by various geopolitical events, such as sanctions and various prohibitive measures that impede global trade and technology exchange. Now we see a trade war between the United States and China, anti-Russian sanctions, and an almost complete termination of free trade between Russia and the United States, Russia, and Europe. It is obviously a powerful geoeconomic fragmentation of the LEE. Nevertheless, whether their business cycles are synchronized remains a big question.

3.2 Hodrick-Preskott filtering method

Hodrick-Preskott filtering is a simple and straightforward method to extract the trend and the cyclic component of a time series. We considered the GDP data as a time series and, due to isolation of the cyclical component, determined the difference between actual and potential GDP or output gap, in other words.

By "trend," we mean a certain steady, systematic change over a long period. However, no matter how long the series is, we can never be sure that the trend is not just a part of a slow fluctuation. After having separated the trend from seasonal fluctuations, the remainder of the series is a function of cyclical fluctuations. Seasonal fluctuations are the easiest to detect, isolate, and study.

When defining a trend, we understand that any movement observed over a sufficiently long period can be smoothed. It means that, at least locally, the component corresponding to the trend can be expressed by a polynomial of time.

Thus, in our case, GDP is a trend and fluctuations around this trend [24, 25]:

$$y_t = y_t^g + y_t^c, \tag{1}$$

where y_t^g is a trend or structural component of the time series and y_t^c is the cyclical component of the time series.

We imposed a minimization condition on the cyclic component to obtain a smoothed series:

$$\sum_{t=0}^{\infty} \left(y_t^c\right)^2 + \lambda \sum_{t=0}^{\infty} \left[\left(y_{t+1}^g - y_t^g\right) - \left(y_t^g - y_{t-1}^g\right)\right]^2 \rightarrow min \tag{2}$$

where λ is a Lagrange multiplier. For annual data, $\lambda = 100$.

After elimination of the trend, we investigated the reminder of the series by spectral analysis methods.

3.3 Spectral analysis

To investigate the reminders of the time series, we applied spectral analysis techniques to check for correlations between time series members and to determine the period of major fluctuations in the reminders of the time series [26].

Suppose there is autocorrelation for any pair of values:

$$\rho_j = \frac{cov\left(u_t, u_{t-j}\right)}{\sigma^2}, \tag{3}$$

where ρ_j is the correlation between members of the time series after filtering by j,$cov\left(u_t, u_{t-j}\right)$ is the covariance between members of the time series after filtering by j,σ^2 is the dispersion of the rest of the time series.

The total sum of coefficients $\rho_0, \rho_1, \rho_2, \ldots$ is called the correlogram of the series. By determining the correlation of the other series gradually, without the components of the main trend, we can build a correlogram that allows us to graphically trace the interdependence between the members of the time series.

Then during studying of various kinds of periodic processes (we mean processes repeated over a certain period, including economic processes), it is best to decompose periodic functions describing these processes into trigonometric series. The simplest periodic functions are trigonometric functions $\sin x$ and $\cos x$. The period T of these functions is 2π.

The simplest periodic process is a simple harmonic oscillation described by a function:

$$y = A * sin\,(at + \varphi_0) \quad (4)$$

$$t \geq 0 \quad (5)$$

where A is the amplitude of the oscillation,

ω is the frequency,

φ_0 is the phase offset.

This kind of function (and its graph) is called a simple harmonic. The fundamental period of the function is $T = \frac{2\pi}{\omega}$, which means that one full oscillation occurs in the span of time $\frac{2\pi}{\omega}$. The denominator ω shows how many oscillations will occur within the time unit 2π.

Complex harmonic oscillation, which occurs as a result of applying a finite (or infinite) number of simple harmonics, is also described by the functions *sinx* and *cosx*. This way, a constant periodic function can be expressed with this system of Eqs. (6)–(8):

$$A = \frac{2}{\pi}\sum_{t=1}^{n} u_t,\ cos\ \frac{2\pi t}{\lambda}, \lambda = \frac{2\pi}{\alpha} \quad (6)$$

$$B = \frac{2}{\pi}\sum_{t=1}^{n} u_t,\ sin\ \frac{2\pi t}{\lambda} \quad (7)$$

$$S^2 = A^2 + B^2 = \frac{4}{n}\sigma^2\varpi(\lambda) \quad (8)$$

where u_t is a member of the time series after removing the trend:

λ is the wavelength;

S^2 is the intensity of the oscillations.

The graph of S^2 is dependence on the wavelength λ is called a periodogram.

4. Result

4.1 Hodrick-Preskott filtering application

We applied the Hodrick-Preskott filtering method to isolate the cyclic component of GDP. We took GDP data in US dollars at 2015 prices, in local currencies at constant prices, and in current prices in US dollars and local currencies. Thus, using different GDP data, we can not only identify the cyclical component but also analyze the contribution of local currency inflation and exchange rate to the result. In this case, it is worth noting that the exchange rate of the Chinese currency is not floating, as well as the rate of the Russian ruble is significantly affected by methods of administrative regulation such as "budget rule" and central bank interventions. Both the Russian and Chinese currencies are far from the free-floating exchange rate model.

Figure 1 shows the result of output gaps: Russia, India, and China calculated from GDP data in US dollars in 2015 prices. We believe that this calculation is cleared of the parameter of local currency inflation and the exchange rate and can be taken as a base. In addition, we logarithmized the original time series in order to bring it to an additive model. **Figure 1** shows that the cyclical component of economic growth looks different in all three countries.

For India, the constant random fluctuations around the GDP trend line are normal and reflect that the output gap is alternately positive and negative. It means that the economy works intensely and with a shortage of resources for a while, and then there is a period of recovery.

The output gap of all three countries in the base case is characterized by a period of positive values from 1999 to 2005. It is a period of rapid growth of emerging markets in the global economy. It means that economies have used their resources excessively and are now legitimately facing a slowdown in economic growth. The same situation was observed in Japan in the 1970s and 1980s, when rapid growth was replaced by the so-called lost decade. Today, we see a slowdown of the Chinese economy and almost zero economic growth in Russia.

However, in Russia, if we consider the basic version of the output gap calculation and the calculation in current prices in national currency, the picture is significantly different, and we see a huge negative effect associated with hyperinflation of the ruble and the instability of the national currency in the period from 1991 to 1999 (**Figure 2**) When analyzing economic cycles, we need to consider that emerging markets have no solid economic basis for market self-regulation. In addition, oftentimes in countries

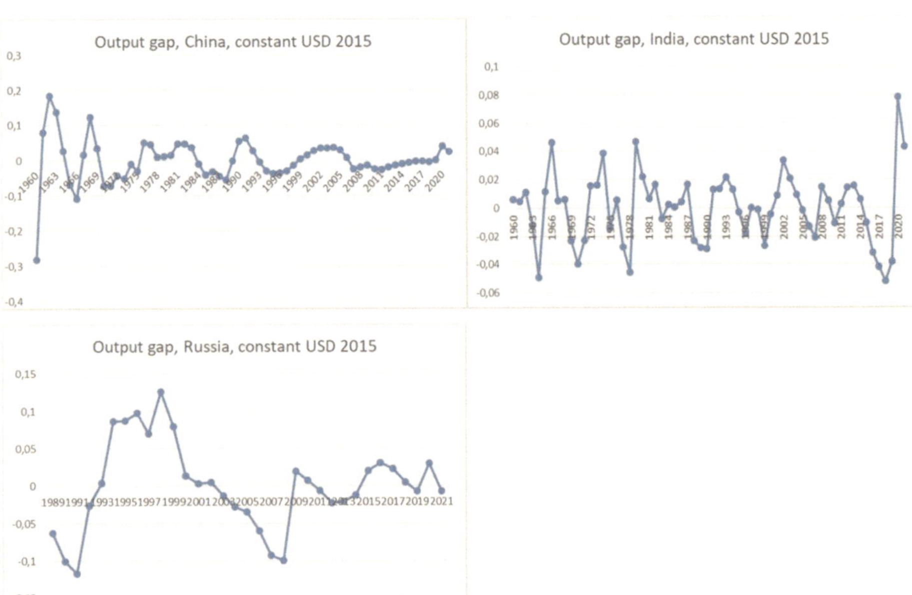

Figure 1.
Output gap.

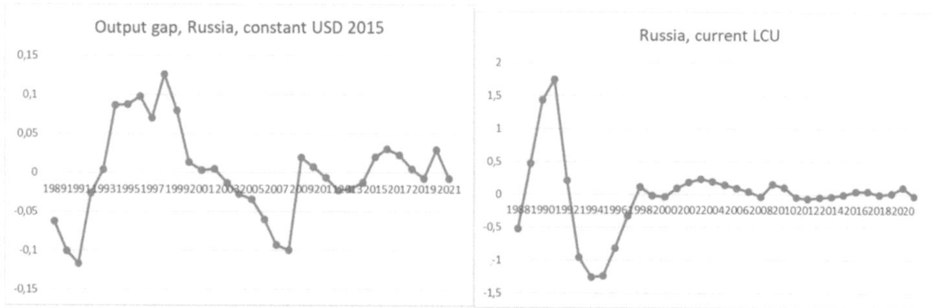

Figure 2.
Russian output gap in constant USD in 2015 year prices and in local currency.

such as China and Russia, economic regulation is performed by administrative methods, and the values of economic growth rates do not depend not only on the development of market mechanisms and the state of the economic environment but also on the level of government spending. This is why Russia has shown resistance to sanctions pressure, because after the 2008 crisis, Russia has been steadily replacing market mechanisms of regulation with administrative ones, which, when formally calculated, produce positive results, but the quality of such economic growth is left out of the picture.

However, we see an increase in the efficiency of the Russian economy in 2008, 2015, and 2020. In 2008, administrative regulation of the Russian economy was strengthened as a response to the global economic crisis, in 2015 as a response to the first wave of sanctions, and in 2020 in connection with the COVID pandemic. Such dynamics indicates the presence of a short-term effect from the replacement of market mechanisms of regulation with administrative ones. Then, when analyzing economic cycles and studying the degree of integration of countries, it is necessary to take into account the basis of this integration, whether integration is connected exclusively with administrative regulation.

Additionally, we calculated the impact of dollar inflation and inflation of the local currency, as shown in **Figures 3** and **4**, and found that the devaluation of the national currency gives a positive, but very short-term effect.

The third diagram shows the line reflecting the impact of inflation on economic growth for Russia in the period from 1991 to 1999, a period of sharp transition from administrative methods of regulation in Russia to the formation of a market economy. It is time when Russia faced huge negative effects associated with the devaluation of the ruble and hyperinflation. The excessive governmentalization of the Russian economy and the reliance on administrative methods of regulation today in the future may lead to the fact that the abrupt lifting of sanctions, for example, will be more disastrous than the sanctions themselves. Therefore, we can conclude that the dynamics of the output gap between countries is different, as well as the qualitative characteristics of economic growth, so we cannot confirm the synchronization of business cycles.

4.2 Spectral analysis

Next, after excluding the trend, we conducted an additional study of the remaining time series. **Figure 5** shows correlograms of the remaining time series of LEE countries' GDP.

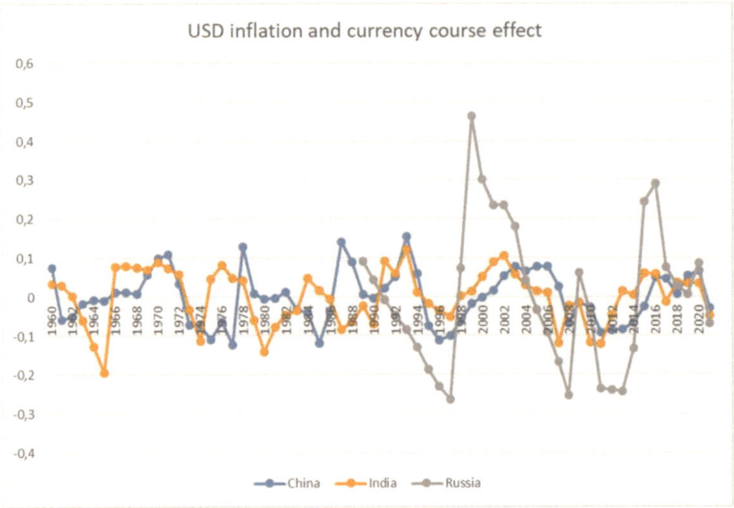

Figure 3.
Currency course effect.

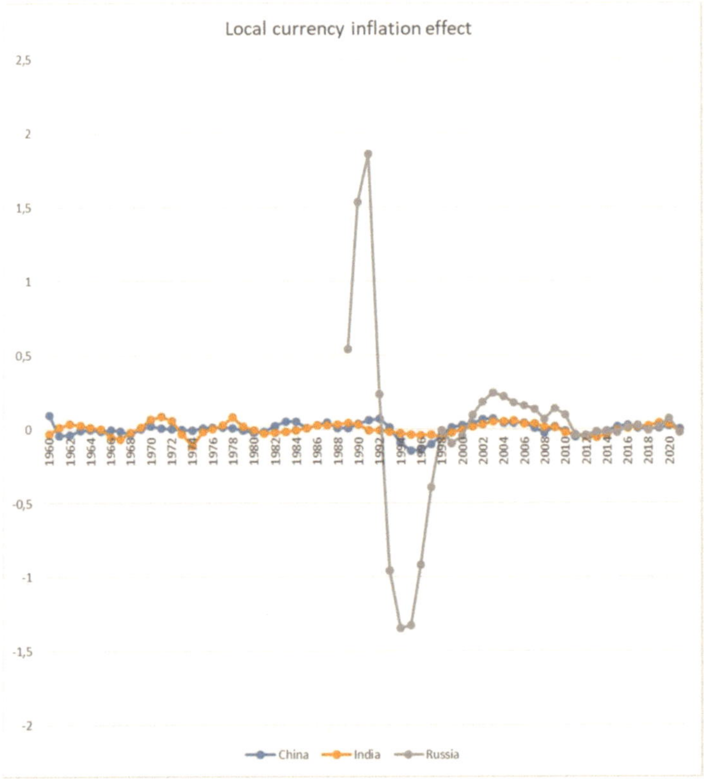

Figure 4.
Local currency inflation effect.

The highest dependence among the members of these series is: for India 8 and 9, and for Russia and China the diagram looks flat. Therefore, the graphs have different shape and nature, and there is not much correlation between them. As a result, the

DOI: http://dx.doi.org/10.5772/intechopen.112176

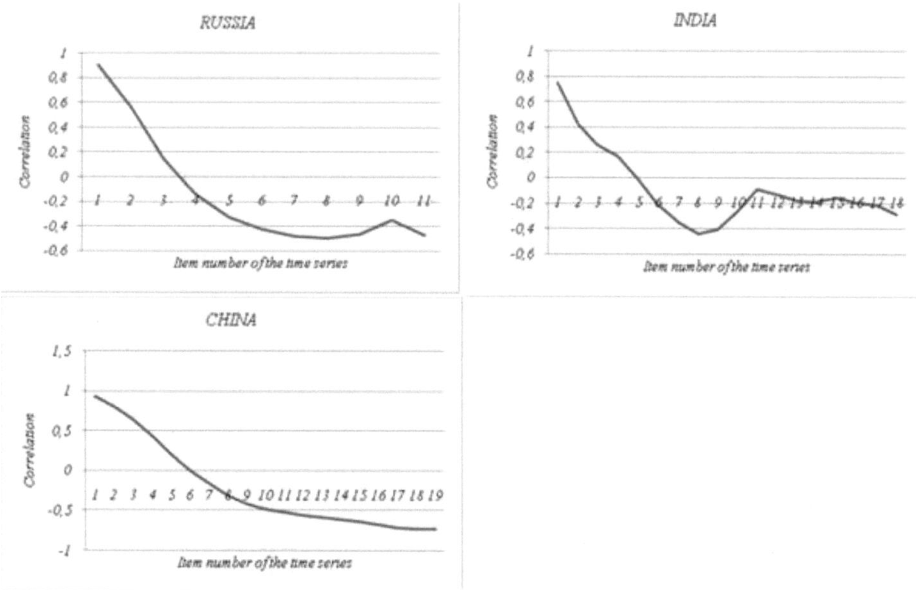

Figure 5.
Correlograms of the remaining time series of LEE countries' GDP.

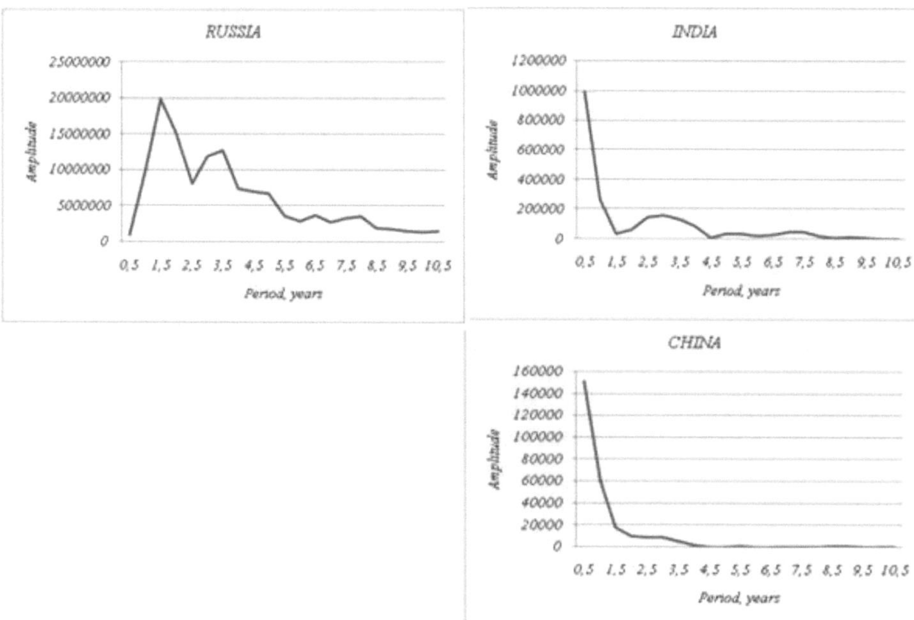

Figure 6.
Periodograms of the trend-less time series of lee countries' GDP.

most intense fluctuations in these remaining GDP time series are likely to be in the years when the elements of the time series have the highest correlation. To confirm this, we have shown periodograms of these LEE countries' GDP in **Figure 6**.

The periodograms show that in Russia, fluctuations around the basic trend occur at intervals of 1.5–2 years. It correlates with fluctuations in economic activity that is associated with capital markets. India and China reaffirm the conclusions we made in the previous section.

In general, the results show that the synchronization in the economic cycles of the countries is minimal, and we can find no confirmation of the decoupling hypothesis.

5. Discussion

Our study showed that LEE countries have different output gap dynamics, which does not allow us to confirm any significant level of synchronization in the economic cycles of LEE countries and, consequently, does not allow us to support the hypothesis of separation.

Despite it, our study agrees well with the existing research paradigm on the topic. Before the 2009 financial crisis, there was an environment of rapid growth in developing economies, especially Asian economies [6, 9, 10]. Most researchers have found in their research evidence of decoupling hypothesis and spillover effects [12, 13, 16]. However, the 2009 global crisis changed the trend [11] and studies began to show more and more evidence of the decoupling hypothesis and spillover effects after the 2009 crisis. Our study also indirectly supports the results of other researchers who noted a significant decrease in the decoupling effect after the 2009 crisis [14, 15].

We have also found that when considering the issue of economic growth, it is important to understand by what methods this economic growth is stimulated. It is impossible to talk about full-fledged economic integration and efficiency if only the methods of administrative regulation form the basis of economic growth.

6. Conclusion

We have conducted a study of the synchronization level of LEE countries' economic cycles. At the same time, two methods were used: Hodrick-Preskott filtering and spectral analysis. Thanks to the Hodrick-Preskott filtering we have found the multidirectional nature of the output gap dynamics of large emerging economies, which allowed us to conclude about the lack of synchronization of economic cycles and about the impossibility of supporting the decoupling hypothesis at present. Similar results were obtained by spectral analysis. Thus, the various alliances of major emerging economies currently have more geopolitical grounds than economic ones and are a manifestation of geoeconomic fragmentation rather than integration.

Author details

Olga Mezentseva
Online Business School of Financial Analytics, Romania

*Address all correspondence to: olgamezens@gmail.com

References

[1] Erdorf S, Heinrichs N. Co-movement of revenue: Structural changes in the business cycle. European Economic Review. 2011;**41**:761-770

[2] Frankel J, Rose A. The endogeneity of the optimum currency area criteria. The Economic Journal. 1998;**108**: 1009-1025

[3] Imbs J. Trade, finance, specialization, and synchronization. Review of Economics and Statistics. 2004;**86**(3): 723-734

[4] Papageorgiou T, Michaelides PG, Milios JG. Business cycles synchronization and clustering in Europe (1960–2009). Journal of Economics and Business. 2010; **62**:419-470

[5] Bäurle G, Burren D. Business cycle accounting with model consistent expectations. Economics Letters. 2011; **110**:18-19

[6] Kose MA, Otrok C, Prasad E. How much decoupling? How much converging? Finance and Development. 2008;**45**(2):36-40

[7] Aiyar S, Chen J, Ebeke C, Garcia-Saltos R, Gudmundsson T, Ilyina A, et al. Geoeconomic Fragmentation and the Future of Multilateralism. Staff Discussion Note 2023/001. Washington, DC: International Monetary Fund; 2023. Available from: https://www.imf.org/en/Publications/Staff-Discussion-Notes/Issues/2023/01/11/Geo-Economic-Fragmentation-and-the-Future-of-Multilateralism-527266

[8] Kremer M, Willis J, Yang Y. Converging to convergence. In: Eichenbaum MS, Hurst E, editors. NBER Macroeconomics Annual. Vol. 36. Chicago: University of Chicago Press; 2022. pp. 337-412

[9] Felices G, Wieladek T. Are emerging market indicators of vulnerability to financial crises decoupling from global factors? Journal of Banking and Finance. 2012;**36**(2):321-331

[10] Kawai M, Petri PA. Asia's role in the global economic architecture. Contemporary Economic Policy. 2014;**32**(1):230-245

[11] Yeyati EL, Williams T. Emerging economies in the 2000s: Real decoupling and financial recoupling. Journal of International Money and Finance. 2012; **31**(8):2102-2126

[12] Dooley M, Hutchison M. Transmission of the U.S. subprime crisis to emerging markets: Evidence on the decoupling-recoupling hypothesis. Journal of International Money and Finance. 2009;**28**(8):1331-1349

[13] Gilenko E, Fedorova E. Internal and external spillover effects for the BRIC countries: Multivariate GARCH-in-mean approach. Research in International Business and Finance. 2014;**31**:32-45

[14] Dimitriou D, Kenourgios D, Simos T. Global financial crisis and emerging stock market contagion: A multivariate FIAPARCH-DCC approach. International Review of Financial Analysis. 2013;**30**:46-56

[15] Wälti S. The myth of decoupling. Applied Economics. 2012;**44**(26): 3407-3419

[16] Das DK. Another perspective on globalization. Journal of International Trade Law and Policy. 2010;**9**(1):46-63

[17] Tsheola J. South Africa in gear: 'A better life for all' or a zero-sum game of

globalization? GeoJournal. 2002;**57**(1-2): 79-92

[18] Tsheola J. South Africa's form of globalisation: A continental posture paradox for insertion and dependence. Political Geography. 2002;**21**(6):789-811

[19] Alfaro L, Chanda A, Kalemli-Ozcan S, Sayek S. FDI and economic growth: The role of local financial markets. Journal of International Economics. 2004;**64**(1):89-112. DOI: 10.1016/S0022-1996(03)00081-3

[20] Javorcik B. Does foreign direct investment increase the productivity of domestic firms? In search of spillovers through backward linkages. American Economic Review. 2004;**94**(3):605-627. DOI: 10.1257/0002828041464605

[21] Kose MA, Prasad E, Rogoff K, Wei S-J. Financial Globalization: A Reappraisal. IMF Staff Papers. 2009;**56**(1):8-62. Available from: https://www.jstor.org/stable/40377798

[22] Srinivasan K, Helbling T, Peiris SJ. Asia's Easing Economic Headwinds Make Way for Stronger Recovery. Washington, DC, USA: IMF Blog; 2023. Available from: https://www.imf.org/en/Blogs/Articles/2023/02/20/asias-easing-economic-headwinds-make-way-for-stronger-recovery [Accessed: February 20, 2023]

[23] Chkili W, Nguyen DK. Exchange rate movements and stock market returns in a regime-switching environment: Evidence for BRICS countries. Research in International Business and Finance. 2014;**31**:46-56

[24] Hodrick R, Prescott EC. Postwar business cycles: An empirical investigation. Journal of Money, Credit, and Banking. 1997;**29**(1):1-16

[25] Tsyplakov A. An introduction to state modeling. Quantile. 2011;**9**:1-24

[26] Kendall M, Stuart A. The Advanced Theory of Statistics. London: Charles Griffin & Company limited; 1966

Chapter 2

The Global Business Cycle within the New Commodities and the Financial Cycle: An Empirical Evidence Based on a Multivariate Unobserved Components Model (UCM)

Hakim Amira and Eleftherios Thalassinos

Abstract

The recent analysis focused on gold and energy as hedge fund and channel for the cyclicity of the economic system. Within the occurrence of the prominent crisis, the financial cycle became a nexus relation with the real sphere. The aim of this chapter is to investigate the impact of the commodities and the stock market on the global business cycle within filtering based on HP and Band Pass filter for the period Q1–1984 to Q4–2020. We review the literature on the business cycle, commodities, and financial cycle research. We find which HP trend is close to the estimated trend of global GDP based on a multivariate UC model. We provide a Band-Pass filter to examine the upswing and downswing commodities cycle as well as the financial cycle. We construct a multivariate unobserved component model that includes the gold price, the crude oil price, and the financial cycle as the independent component within the model. The estimation of the model found that oil has a lag impact on the fluctuation of the business cycle, it reacts as an impulsion for the crisis, compared to the gold and the global financial cycle which reacts simultaneously with the trend of the global business cycle.

Keywords: global business cycle, financial cycle, gold, oil, filtering, multivariate UCM

1. Introduction

The vulnerability of financial stability toward any risk might arise shed light on the linkage between global demand and financial stability as a key factor that influences the economic system and the trend of the business cycle. Studying the business cycle is the top macroeconomic topic which is interlinked for any economic and non-economic issue that might arise. The concept of the business cycle is a macroeconomic concept based on different definitions with reference to the context referred to, such as the macroeconomic variables investment, inflation, consumption, GDP, and production. Within this study, we will refer to the business cycle within the GDP. Schumpeter [1] is initiating the concept of the business cycle through the innovation cycle in the economy as "innovation clusters". The long cycle in the economy is complemented by Mensch [2], Haustein and Neuwirth [3], Van Duijn [4], and Kleinknecht [5] by further empirical studies.

Clarke et al. [6] pointed out an increase in the number of critical innovations during the recovery of the long cycles. Singer [7] has complemented the theory of the long cycle by finding that the trade gaps between standardized and innovative products follow a deteriorating trend. The application of these studies in the commodities economy has brought important literature with different approaches. The fluctuation of the long cycle and the commodities have lay an important role in the variation of the intensity of use of productive inputs, where the commodities such as precious metals and energy have played a relevant role. For the expansion phase, the expanding demand for precious metals drags prices upwards. Respectively in the new period of stagnation, the intensity of demand drops as well as the prices of precious metals. It is by analogy applying to the energy sector as well as the financial market. Studying the long cycle of commodities and the financial cycle and their connection to the global economic dynamics is an area to be more and more explored, as these sectors are open for more interconnected development.

Within this context, this chapter is novel as it might contribute to an area of limited research, which is less studied by combining the commodities market and the financial market. The macroeconomic impact of the commodities on the business cycle has been studied in isolation or within the monetary policy but not in conjunction with the standards of the business cycle. Studying the interlink of the commodities and the business cycle is a big literature with different empirical approaches, studies, and theoretical focusing on detecting the breaks of the time series components.

Therefore, decomposing and forecasting the business cycle within the commodities and the stocks frame can be efficient for policy decisions and the synchronization of the interference and the trade-off between the concerned targeted policies. The business cycle is considered as the main framework for the evaluation of the economic system in general and the policymakers. We attempt to interlink the financial sector and commodities with the business cycle to give a more-clear overview about the economic system in general. The interdependence between the business cycle and the financial cycle was with a prominent literature taking the credit gap and house prices as a reference for the financial sector [8–11].

Within our study, we are referring to the stock prices for the financial cycle. Several literatures treat the stock market and the commodities apart for the interlink with the business cycle of the economy. The study of the volatility of the business cycle allows for more vulnerability toward any economic and extra-economic shocks such as the buoyant of the stock market and the pro-cycle of the commodities.

Within this chapter, we aim to investigate the impact of the energy commodity e.g., the crude oil, and the non-energy commodity e.g., the gold and the financial cycle on the global business cycle. It is a univariate unobserved component model followed by an extension to the multivariate model using the commodities and the financial cycle to decompose the macroeconomic aggregates. The eventual connection between the long cycle of the commodities and the financial cycle with the economic cycle considers the further relationship between the business cycle and the demand for the essential commodities selected as well as the proxies of the financial cycle. In economic theory, the long cycle classified with different groups basic on different factors to study the cyclicity of the economy for different horizons: the business cycle (2–8 years), the Kitchin cycle (3–5 years), the Juglar cycle (7–11 years), the Kuznet swings (15–25 years), the medium term business cycle, and long economic cycle wave or the Kondratiev wave (K-wave) currently recognized with the period of 45–60 years [12]. Within this study, the chosen period is 36 years, quarterly data, dated from 1984-Q1 to 2020-Q4 studying the global business cycle.

The chapter is structured as follows: In the first section, we decompose the trend of the commodities cycle using the filtering approach. The second section is dedicated to analyzing the financial cycle for the selected global assets. The third section is devoted to the modeling using the univariate and multivariate approach for the Unobserved Components Model. The fourth section presents the estimation of the model and reports our numerical results. The last section contains a discussion of further policy recommendations and concluding remarks.

2. Related literature

Our study constructs on an extended literature, which is focus on the business cycle, the financial cycle, the energy commodities such as oil, and the non-energy commodities such as gold.

The interlink between the financial sphere and the real sphere within the economic activity, shed the light to any macroeconomic or monetary policy is conducted. Several documented studies highlight the interaction of the financial cycle and the business cycle within the occurrence of the multi-type of crisis. Helbling et al. [13] provide an analysis of the interlink between the credit market and the global business cycle naming that credit shocks play an important role in shaping the US business cycle. Drehmann et al. [14] provide a justification on the finding of the prior studies that financial cycles are longer and more ample than business cycles. Claessens et al. [10] report that there are strong links between different phases of business cycles and financial cycles. Recessions associated with financial disruption tend to be longer and deeper than other recessions and recoveries associated with rapid growth in credit and house prices are often stronger. Gerdrup et al. [15] and Detken et al. [16] argue that the average length of the financial cycle is around four times that of the business cycle.

In the same perspective Borio [8] argues that the financial cycle and the business cycle are find out within three properties. The financial cycle is most parsimoniously described in terms of credit and property prices, it has a much lower frequency than the traditional business cycle (2–8 years), its peaks are closely associated with the financial crisis, and it helps to detect financial distress risk in real-time. Stremmel [17], and Stremmel and Zsamboki [18] argue that the financial cycle is less synchronized in tranquil periods and more synchronized in a period of common financial stress. Gorton and Ordonez [19] show that not all credit booms are followed by financial crises. Schüler et al. [20] find that financial cycles exhibit higher amplitude and persistence than business cycles. Rünstler and Vlekke [21] find out that the financial cycle is heterogeneous across European countries having a much longer and more ample financial cycle. The link between the business cycle, the movement in dividends, stock prices have been studied extensively in the macroeconomic and asset pricing literature such as in the works of Lucas [22] and Blanchard [23].

Rangvid [24] finds that the stock price-output ratio is a predictor of expected US stock returns. Cooper and Priestley [25] argue that the output gap has in-ample and out-of-ample predictive power for stock returns in the US and other G7 countries. From the same perspective, Vivian and Wohar [26] analyze whether the US output gap predicts the return of portfolio formed on size and value. Gold is a traded asset globally as an alternative investment class to the ordinary portfolio comprising stocks and bonds. Baur and McDermott [27] argue that gold is a stabilizing factor for the financial system since it minimizes losses for market participants and portfolio managers in the event of negative market shocks. Beaudry et al. [28] argue that the metaphor of profit-driven by fluctuation called gold rushes provides a period of economic boom associated with expenditure aimed at securing a claim near a new found vein of gold.

Pierdzioch et al. [29] found that the international business cycle has out-of-ample predictive power for gold price fluctuations. Apergis and Eleftheriou [30] found that the business cycle asymmetrically affects gold returns, while these returns respond stronger during the recessionary than booming phases of the cycle. Within the same perspective applying to several types of precious metals such as gold, silver and platinum, Kucher and McCoskey [31] found that the co-integrating relationships between precious metal prices are not stable over time with significant shifts in the price relation around business cycle peaks and during recessions. Within the last decade, after the oil shocks and petroleum crisis, the constraint of adjustment within the capital market has probably less influenced by the size and level of stock trading which for some countries targeted their policies for the optimum arrangements for their portfolios. For the policy economic makers, they have to take their decisions on the volume and pricing of oil with the desired level of oil revenues and their use (consumer goods, investment goods, and financial investments). The interlink between oil as a main key for the financial sphere and the real sphere has been documented in several studies on the impact of the volatility of pricing oil on the business cycle. The oil is acting as the hedge fund for several investments, the interlink with the cyclicity of the economic system as a source of the business cycle is a topic for a prominent literature review.

Hamilton [32] is shedding light on oil as a source of the business cycle in the case of the US, by finding out that an increase in oil is leading to a recession in the US. The volatility of oil prices such as an increase has a positive effect on the output of the exporting countries [33]. The prominent works by Estrella and Hardouvelis [34], Estrella and Mishkin [35], Chauvet and Potter [36], Nyberg [37], and Ng [38] studying the impact of oil price shocks on business cycle fluctuations, by modeling the probability of the recession and the Probit and Logit models as binary dependent variable models. The main result of these models is identifying the term spread and stock market returns as useful predictors of US recessions. Michael [39] found that shocks of the oil price explain the reduced fraction of the real GNP growth and inflation variance in US and Japan. Sadorsky [40] found that oil price volatility shocks have asymmetric effects on the market activity. From a different empirical approach Elder and Serletis [41] argued that oil price volatility has a negative and statistically significant impact on several measures of investment, durable consumption, and aggregate output.

Moreover, using a GARCH-in mean empirical method, Elder and Serletis [41] found that the volatility in oil price shocks has a negative and statistically significant effect on different measures of investment, durable consumption, and aggregate output. Jo [42] showed the negative effect of oil price uncertainty shock on world industrial production using a quarterly vector autoregressive model with stochastic volatility in mean. In the same perspective, [43] use the oil supply and demand shocks to estimate the US dividend yields components. Using a measure oil market uncertainty Yin and Feng [44] studied the dynamic relationship between oil market uncertainty and international business cycles, the authors have found that oil market uncertainty has a linear leading effect on international business cycles. Pönkä and Zheng [45] studied the role of oil prices in forecasting the Russian recession period using a Probit model. The author suggests that fluctuations in nominal oil prices are useful predictors of the Russian business cycle, with the term spread turning out to be the most powerful predictor of future recessions.

Our contribution to the literature by summing up the three sources of international business cycles such as the financial cycle, the gold and the oil on the trend of the international business cycle, is the use of the Unobserved Component Model Univariate and Multivariate based on the significant studies of Polbin [46], Grant and Chan [47], and Yoon [48].

3. The business cycle and the commodity

The Schumpeter theory Schumpeter [1] brings an overview of the business cycle, the trend of an economic system. According to Schumpeter [1], the business cycle is a sum of perpetual economic cycles or an overlapping cycle. His main theory is focusing on the business cycle within the process of creative destruction, for which the introduction of innovation boosts investment opportunities and creates economic growth and at the same time decay in the obsolete sector of production. This process is containing an expansion phase and a recession phase where the economy assimilates the innovation across sectors. The commodity prices are involved in the same perspective regarding the demand. Within the expansion phase, the competition for commodities product such as gold and energy tend to increase their prices compared to manufacturing goods, the introduction of innovation as imitation reduces the opportunities for investment to obtain economic rent, decreasing the demand for commodities. Schumpeter is among the economists who reject the frame that the decline in prices might be a result of a slow-down in terms of output and growth, as he explains that within the great recession (1878–1896) for the case of the falling of price due to a decline in the production of gold which result in profit squeeze and the decrease of the investment. From the same perspective as Schumpeter, for the economic phase of the commodities and the manufactured good on the business cycle, we find Prebisch [49], Singer [50], as well as Ocampo [51] and Ocampo and Parra [52] as prominent literature studying the commodities prices and the business cycles.

According to IMF five years ahead forecast for 2017, the expected long-term growth boosted by the boom of the commodity price has been revised down from 4 to 3%. The boom in the commodities prices has an increasing effect in the short run on the real GDP by raising the value and production and lifting the demand for ancillary goods and services. An increase in the investment in the resource sector, such as metal or energy, may raise the potential output, which in turn boosts the financial resource for the investment in the other sector. However, in the long term, commodities boosting growth is a controversial question. According to Corden [53], the positive term trade and income shock associated with the commodity boom shift production out of non-commodity tradable and into the non-tradable service sectors with lower productivity. The global economic crisis starting in 2012 was the result of the boom in commodity prices characterized by unprecedented magnitude and duration, as the price reached the highest level in history, this phase was characterized as a phase of mineral boom. In fact, within the depression of the global economy after the subprime crisis, which slow down the demand for the commodity price, however, the recover for the price was surprisingly fast and the world economy experienced a boom in commodity prices which might be seen as a continuation of 2004–2008. The upswing demand in commodity lifts the resilience of the growth performance of major developing countries and producers' countries. Within the several literatures, it is tempting to believe that there are causality links between the business cycle in terms of output and commodities.

Among many econometric approaches such as the SVAR, UC, and VECM, prove the biased data with low-frequency movement. Fernald [54] noted that low-frequency movement in an hour per capita may bias the VAR model with long-run restriction. Differencing removes the low-frequency movement from the data [55]. In opposite Hamilton [56] affirms that differencing a bounded series may involve misspecification issues by suggesting a filtering approach prior to the estimation model [57]. However, Gospodinov et al. [58] found that filtering the data prior to the estimation removes necessary information to identify these stocks using long-run restrictions.

Within our study, we aim to estimate the model of the Univariate and Multivariate Unobserved Component Model using the HP filtering data and the Band-Pass filtering data. Filtering data, through the selected filters, with a filter window such that cycles are generated at such frequencies. The decomposition method isolates major fluctuations in the deviation of a macroeconomic variable, such as the GDP, around its trend through a combination of detrending procedures and smoothing techniques [59]. Within the literature, determining the long wave is also based on the filtering approach, such as in Baxter and King [60] and Christiano and Fitzgerald [61], the time series is considered as a summation of different frequencies and the filtering approach consists to determine the filter coefficients so as to isolate specific frequencies and to show the course of the pre-specified frequency component in the time domain. The choice of both filters is mentioned in the next section.

4. The HP filter

The Hodrick-Prescott filter has been the common use of filtering approach in many documented works studying the cyclicity of the economic system. Our first part of the study will study the real GDP and the trend through the HP filter. The trend of the data series $\{y_t\}, t = 1, \ldots, T$, is the solution $\{x_t\}$ of the following minimization:

$$\sum_{t=1}^{T} (y_t - x_t)^2 + \lambda \sum_{t=3}^{T} (\Delta^2 x_t)^2 \tag{1}$$

T is the sample size and Δ denote the difference operator. y_t is the log of real GDP and * is the potential or unobserved level

$$\Delta y_t^* = \Delta y_{t-1}^* + \varepsilon_{0,t},\ \varepsilon_{0,t} \sim N(0, \sigma_0^2) \tag{2}$$

$$y_t = y_t^* + \varepsilon_{1,t},\ \varepsilon_{1,t} \sim N(0, \sigma_1^2) \tag{3}$$

$$\Delta x_t = x_t - x_{t-1} \text{ and } \Delta^2 x_t = \Delta x_t - \Delta x_{t-1} = x_t - 2x_{t-1} + x_{t-2} \tag{4}$$

The first component in Eq. (1) measures the error $y_t - x_t$, the second component measures the smoothness of the trend. $\Delta^2 x_t, \lambda \geq 0$ is a regularization or smoothing parameter (or a turning parameter) that controls the trade-off between the size of the error and the smoothness of the trends. Eq. (1) is penalized the least square problem, penalizing the smoothness of its solution. The solution of the Eq. (1) is denoted as $x^{hp}(\lambda) \in R^T$. It is common to calibrate the variance error term so that their ratio is equal $\lambda = 1600$, which correspond to a business cycle of 8 year, for quarterly data is not always appropriate.

Within our study we refer to the minimization of Eq. (1) to find the value of λ. **Figure 1** denotes the real global GDP, shown in red and the trend shown in blue. At a further step later in the model we ask which HP trend is close to the estimated trend of global GDP from the multivariate UC model. The search for λ in Eq. (1) is limited to positive integers. We find that the HP trend with $\lambda = 540{,}000$ minimizes Eq. (1).

Figure 2 shows the global GDP from 1984 to the fourth quarter of 2020, which is our sample data in the study and the trend using the HP filter. Based on that filtering

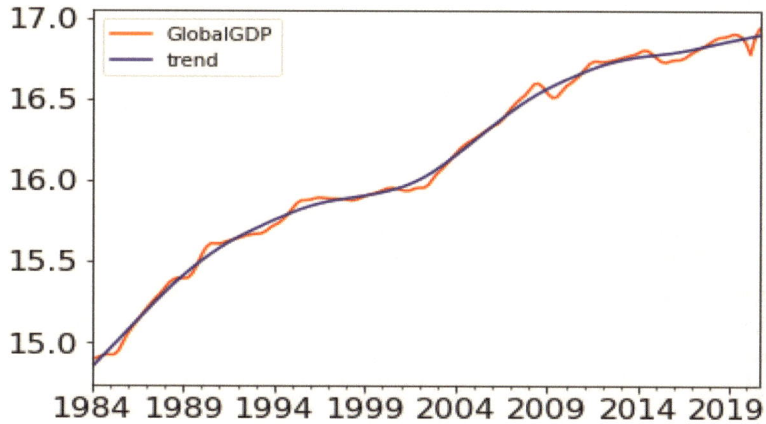

Figure 1.
Global real GDP and the estimated smoothed trend, 1984:Q1–2020:Q4. The red line shows the global real GDP, and the blue line is the estimated smoothed trend. Source: Own study.

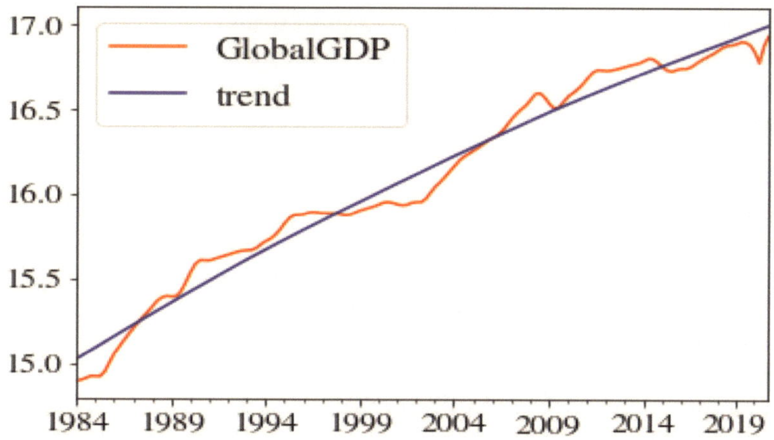

Figure 2.
The estimated smoothed trend and HP trend with $\lambda = 54000$ of global GDP. Source: Own study.

we have 6 downswings, 1984–1986, 1993–1996, 2001–2004, 2008–2012, 2015–2018, and 2020 and 4 upswings, 1987–1992, 1997–2000, 2005–2007, 2013–2014. The analyzed swings are short as the data sampled cycle is for 36 years, we have an average of 4 years of upswings and 3 years of downswings. We can understand from this figure, considering the second petroleum shock and the Asiatic, the Mexican, the Russian crisis and the subprime crisis, that we have an average of 4 years of upswing and an average downswing of about 3 years, for a total average cycle length of 7 years. The presence of several crises and monetary shocks impulsion as well as the petroleum shock are bringing down this average.

In order to reframe the trend of the global GDP with a close trend to the smoothed estimated trend in **Figure 2**, we calculate the value of λ based on the minimization of the Eq. (1). The blue line shows the HP trend with a smoothing parameter equal to 400,000. Making a comparison between **Figures 1** and **2** for the trends we can understand that both trends are not identical, which we can affirm that a standard choice of $\lambda = 16000$ for quarterly data is not appropriate to show the real trend.

5. The financial cycle

Within the literature, the financial cycle proxies are with several definitions such as the house-pricing asset, the interest rate, the stock market, and the exchange rate. The literature review opts for several approaches to measure the financial cycle within the connectedness with the business cycle. Drehmann et al. [14] propose two approaches to measure the financial cycle such as the turning point analysis and the Band-Pass filter using five financial variables such as the credit, the credit to GDP ratio, property price, equity price, and an aggregate asset price index, the study distinguishes a short term financial cycle and a medium-term financial cycle. Borio [8] recommended the use of credit and property price as the interlink between credit and saving and investment to measure the volatility and the cyclicity of the financial cycle.

Gorton and He [62] used real estate as collateral for credit and property price fluctuations affecting the credit and induce pro-cyclicality of credit and real estate price. The credit to GDP is considered as leverage measure in the macroeconomic context and an indirect indicator of the absorptive capacity of the financial system [63]. Regarding the stock market price, there is a controversial debate about a measure for the financial cycle. Drehmann et al. [14] argued that share prices do not fit as a proxy component of the financial cycle because they exhibit comparatively higher volatility at short-term frequencies and co-move far less with the other series. However, Schüler et al. [64] find that share price creates important common cyclicality with credit and residential price, while Tölö et al. [65] claimed that stock returns are considered as an early indicator warning of crisis.

In the same perspective of a combined measure Drehmann et al. [14], and Stremmel [17], use various financial measures such as the credit-to-GDP ratio, credit growth, and the ratio of house price to income. Drehmann et al. [14], Stremmel [17], Aglietta and Brand [66], Merler [67], Galati et al. [68], Schüler et al. [20] stress that despite there is no consensus on the best measure of the financial cycle that a composite financial cycle exploiting the co-movement of credit growth and house price is the best indicator of the systemic banking crisis.

The main goal of this chapter is to investigate the interconnectedness of the financial cycle and the global business cycle and not to provide a more developed measure of the financial cycle. Therefore, we opt on the chapter for using one indicator and not the

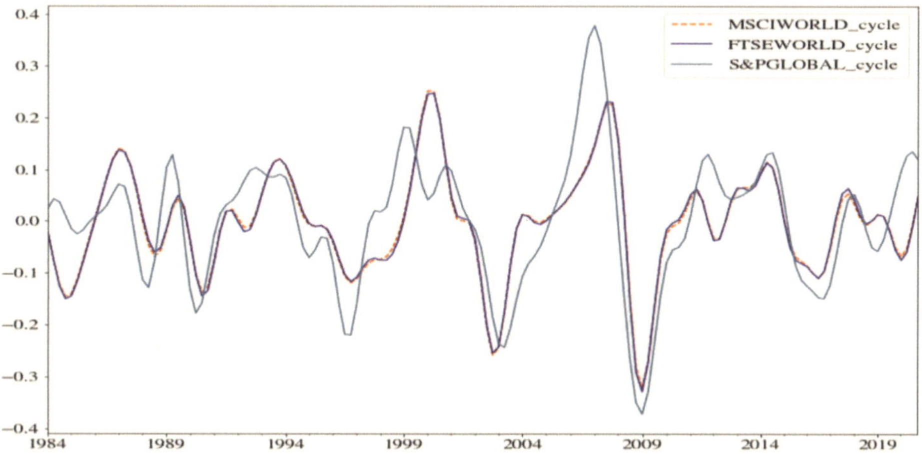

Figure 3.
The cycle of each global asset apart obtained by band-pass filter. Source: Own study.

composite variables such as the asset price indicator of three global assets such as the MSCI, S&P, and the FTSE. To measure the financial cycle, we construct an index of the combined three global assets based on the variable proposed by the literature such as the aggregate asset price index, all the series are normalized to Q1 1984, and in logs. As a first step, we use the filter band pass to filter the data and remove the low-frequency movement. We build the combined index of the financial cycle indicator by taking the average of the three filtered time series of the weighted stock prices. **Figure 3** plots the cycle of each global asset apart obtained by the Band-Pass filter.

The blue line in **Figure 3** shows the FTSE world cycle, the green line shows the S&P world cycle, and the red dotted line shows the MSCI world cycle. For the MSCI and the FTSE, they follow the same trend with the same peaks, we can discern 4 peaks in 1990, 2000, 2008, and 2015 implying a peak-to-peak average cycle of 5 years. After the Asiatic and the Russian crisis, there are three peaks, 2000, 2008, and 2015, implying two cycles of 8 years from peak to peak. Regarding the S&P, they keep the same trend as the MSCI and FTSE with a lag of two years. There are short periods of cyclical movement within these cycles. **Figure 4** shows the financial cycle for the global stock market based on the selection of three global assets with a Band Pass filter.

Figure 3 shows the financial cycle for the global economy based on the variable of the aggregate stock market returns for the main global asset. Based on that filtering approach we have four upswings, 1990, 2000, 2007, and 2014, and four downswings, 1991, 2003, 2009, 2016. The dipper downswing is in 2009, corresponding to the subprime crisis, as it is the biggest crash for the stock market compared to the other financial crisis.

6. The commodities trend: gold and energy

Gold and energy are interlinked to the financial system as a payment system and investment. The integration of the volatility of both commodities influences the business cycle within the demand and the investment. Using the band pass filter, we are aiming at removing the low frequencies of data. **Figure 5** shows the data for real non-oil commodity prices such as the gold price and the oil commodity price such as crude oil.

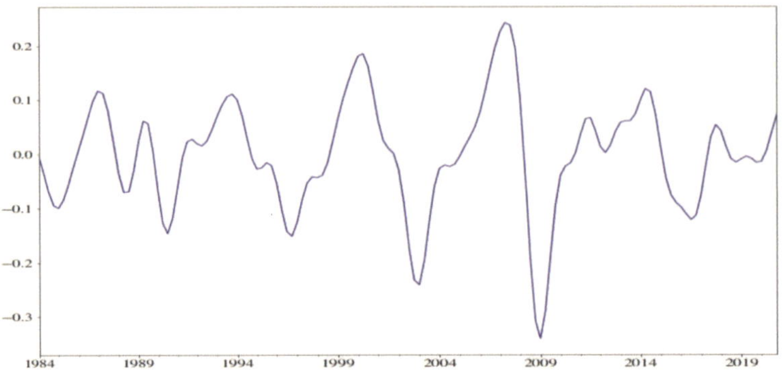

Figure 4.
The financial cycle for the global stock market. Source: Own study.

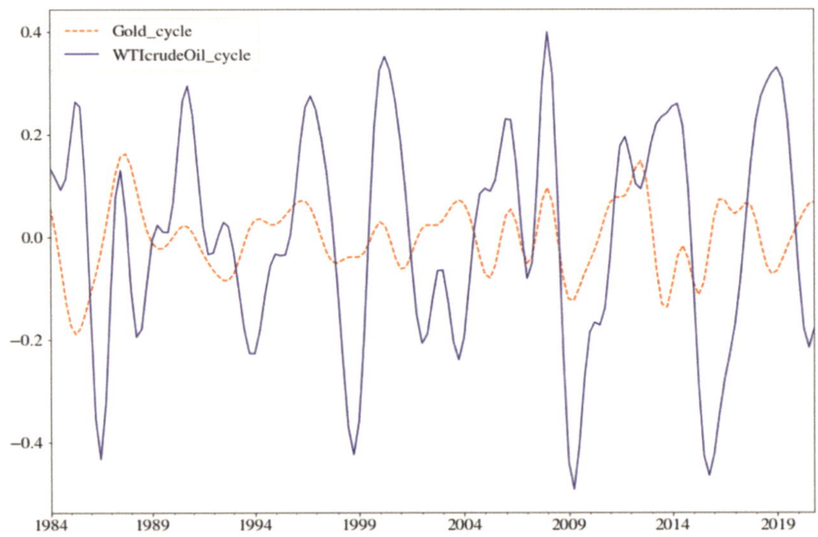

Figure 5.
The cycle of the gold price and the crude oil price with band pass filter. Source: Own study.

The blue line shows the cycle of the crude oil, and the dashed red line shows the cycle of the gold price.

For the energy crude oil, according to **Figure 5**, we can discern eight peaks, 1986, 1990, 1997, 2001, 2006, 2008, 2012, 2014, implying a peak-to-peak average cycle length of around 5 years. However, related to the gold we realize that the number of peaks is different to the crude oil. We can discern four peaks, 1984, 1994, 2004, 2014, implying a peak-to-peak average cycle length of around 10 years.

7. The model

The Basic Unobserved Components Models GDP and Inflation.

The UC model is based on studying or capturing the prior trend about each component based on the approach of Structural Time Series (STs) developed by Engle [69], Gersch and Kitagawa [70], Harvey and Todd [71], and Harvey [72], or through the ARIMA model based on Box et al. [73], Burman [74], Hillmer and Tiao [75], Bell and Hillmer [76], Maravall and Pierce [77]. Most of the model-based approaches use a linear assumption with different statistical features specified for each model. In Clark [78], all shocks to the component of the UC model are assumed to be orthogonal. Morley & Nelson [79] found that the orthogonality assumption results in the over identification for UC models, the authors pointed out that in the UC model within constant growth rate and a cyclical component followed the AR(2) process, the correlation between the trend and cycle is estimable and the resulting negative estimate of the correlation leads to a substantially more volatile trend estimate and less volatile cycle estimate. Oh and Zivot [80] find out that based on the given AR(2) specification for the cyclical component suggest two feasible cases of the exact identification, the first, the trend shock and the cycle shock are allowed to be correlated but the trend growth rate shock is independent of the other two shocks and they are refereeing to this case as the trend-cycle; the second, the trend growth rate shock and the cycle shock are allowed to be correlated but the trend shock is independent from the other two shocks and they are referring to this case as the drift-cycle case.

The literature review studying the trend of the GDP within the UC model is diversified and based on different models within different statistical approaches. Morley & Nelson [79] found that within the feature data of the US, the dataset does not contain a sufficient amount of variation in the long-run growth rate. Ma and Wohar [81] estimate a multivariate UC model of output, consumption and investment with common trends and common cycles. Yoon [48] found in the case of US real GDP a sequence of mostly negative shocks, rather than a few extraordinarily large ones, are responsible for the change in the US real GDP trend. Morley & Nelson [79] showed that the difference between widely used trend-cycle decomposition such as in Beveridge and Nelson's [82] decomposition and Watson [83] Unobserved Component Model is entirely due to one restriction imposed in the UC model, the correlation between the innovations to the trend and the cycle is assumed to be zero.

Without this restriction, Morley & Nelson [79] found that the two trend-cycle decomposition are identical, and both approaches yield to output gap estimated are noisy and small in amplitude. The filtering approach before the estimation is a well-recognized step in any econometric model dedicated to decomposing the data. The well-used filter HP [84, 85] for decomposition is often criticized as it might bring a biased result for the decomposition of the data, among others [84–88] while others affirm that the use of HP filter by removing the low-frequency movement in the data might lead to poor model fit and forecasts. Morley & Nelson [79] find out that the estimating of the US output gap using the correlated UC model is close to zero, however, by using the HP filter the corresponding estimate is as large as 3%.

To overcome the black box character of filtering and the lack of a proper statistical model for filters limit the importance of the filtering approach in terms of detecting the cases in which the filter is not appropriate for the series at hand, which brings as the main statistical overview that there is no systematic procedure to overcome the filter inadequacies. Filtering yields an estimator of the unobserved component. Within this part, we will focus on the Univariate Component model. The Univariate UC model [78], makes a distinction between "the smooth trend" and "the irregular trend" models. The developed setup of the Clark [78] model is as follows:

$$y_t = \tau_t + c_t + \varepsilon_t \tag{5}$$

$$\tau_t = \tau_{t-1} + d_{t-1} + w_t, w_t \sim i.i.d.N\left(0, \sigma_w^2\right) \tag{6}$$

$$d_t = d_{t-1} + u_t, u_t \sim i.i.d.N\left(0, \sigma_u^2\right) \tag{7}$$

$$c_t = \phi_1 c_{t-1} + \phi_2 c_{t-2} + v_t, v_t \sim i, i, d.N\left(0, \sigma_v^2\right) \tag{8}$$

where τ_t, c_t, and ε_t represent trend, cyclical, and seasonal components respectively. In Eq. (6) the trend component captures the productivity shocks that tend to have a permanent effect on the GDP. The trend component follows a random walk with a drift (d_t). The trend and seasonal components are modeled by linear dynamic stochastic processes, which depend on disturbances. The drift (d_t) follows another random walk as the trend and the cycle. The components are not deterministic, they are formulated to be allowed to change over time. The disturbances driving the components are independent of each other. The cyclical component captures the business cycle features of a time series and corresponds to deviations of the actual output from its long run or potential level. Within that model, we are referred to the stationary AR (2) process to model the cyclical component. There is a variety of stochastic specifications of the cycle component that can be considered. ε_t are the seasonal component of the model and they represent the seasonal effect at time t that is associated with season S. The trend component τ_t is modeled as a random walk process, $N\left(0, \sigma_w^2\right)$ refers to normally independently distributed series with mean zero and variance σ^2. The disturbance series is serially independent and mutually independent of all other disturbance series related to y_t. w_t, u_t, and v_t are innovation to trend, trend growth rate, and cycle respectively. The model is rewritten as follows:

$$y_t = H\xi_t + \varepsilon_t$$

$$\xi_t = F\xi_{t-1} + \eta_t, \eta_t \sim i.i.d.N(0, Q)$$

$$H = (1\ 1\ 0\ 0)\ \xi_t = (\tau_t \quad c_t \quad c_{t-1} \quad d_{t.})$$

$$F = \begin{pmatrix} 1 & 0 & 0 & 1 \\ 0 & \phi_1 & \phi_2 & 0 \\ 0 & 1 & 0 & 0 \\ 0 & 0 & 0 & 1 \end{pmatrix} Q = \begin{pmatrix} \sigma_w^2 & \sigma_{wu} & \sigma_{wv} & 0 \\ \sigma_{wu} & \sigma_u^2 & \sigma_{uv} & 0 \\ \sigma_{uv} & \sigma_{uv} & \sigma_v^2 & 0 \\ 0 & 0 & 0 & 0 \end{pmatrix}$$

The generalized UC model univariate estimated by a variant of the Kalman Filter. The UC models are developed based on parametric models which are very close to AR, MA, or ARIMA model popularized by Box and Jenkin [89].

8. The extension: the multivariate unobserved component model

The unobserved component model is among the feature econometric models to detrend the cyclicity of economic activities. We are referring to our modeling of the Multivariate Unobserved Components Model to the model of Polbin [46] as he developed a model of Multivariate Unobserved Components for the growth, consumption and investment with a common growth and cyclical components, the oil price. Within this model, we are referring to the same methodology as in the proposed model. We use macroeconomic variables such as the GDP y_t, the consumption c_t, the investment

I_t, and the inflation Inf_t. We use as commodities energy such as the crude oil price p_t and the gold such as the price of gold per ounce g_t, and the financial cycle through the price of three global Assets A_t, which is a set of three global assets such as the FTSE, the SP and the MSCI. The macroeconomic variables, $z_t \in \{y_t, c_t, I_t, Inf_t\}$, are with an independent permanent component, $\bar{z}^{nb}$, for oil price, gold price and financial asset price respectively, with a permanent component determined by $\beta^z p_t$, $\alpha^z g_t$, and $\sigma^z A_t$, oil price, gold price, and financial assets respectively; an independent transitory component $\tilde{z}^{nb}$ of the oil price, the gold price and financial asset respectively; and transitory component $\tilde{z}^{b}$ determined by oil price, gold price and financial assets respectively. The parameter β^z, α^z, and σ^z are the long-term elasticity of the macroeconomic variables z_t with respect to the oil price, the gold price and the financial assets price respectively.

$$y_t = \bar{y}^{no} + \beta^y p_t + \tilde{y}^{no} + \tilde{y}^{o} + \bar{y}^{ng} + \alpha^y g_t + \tilde{y}^{ng} + \tilde{y}^{g} + \sigma^y A_t + \tilde{y}^{nA} + \tilde{y}^{A} + \bar{y}^{nA} \tag{9}$$

$$c_t = \bar{c}^{no} + \beta^c p_t + \tilde{c}^{no} + \tilde{c}^{o} + \bar{c}^{ng} + \alpha^c g_t + \tilde{c}^{ng} + \tilde{c}^{g} + \sigma^c A_t + \tilde{c}^{NA} + \tilde{c}^{A} + \bar{c}^{nA} \tag{10}$$

$$I_t = \bar{I}^{no} + \beta^I p_t + \tilde{I}^{no} + \tilde{I}^{o} + \bar{I}^{ng} + \alpha^I g_t + \tilde{I}^{ng} + \tilde{I}^{g} + \sigma^I A_t + \tilde{I}^{NA} + \tilde{I}^{A} + \bar{I}^{nA} \tag{11}$$

$$\begin{aligned} Inf_t = {} & \overline{Inf}^{no} + \beta^{Inf} p_t + \tilde{Inf}^{no} + \tilde{Inf}^{o} + \overline{Inf}^{ng} + \alpha^{Inf} g_t + \tilde{Inf}^{ng} + \tilde{Inf}^{g} + \sigma^{Inf} A_t \\ & + \tilde{Inf}^{NA} + \tilde{Inf}^{A} + \overline{Inf}^{nA} \end{aligned} \tag{12}$$

It is assumed that the growth rates of the permanent components such as the oil price the gold and the financial asset share the common path as follow:

$$\begin{pmatrix} \bar{y}_t^{nb} \\ \bar{c}_t^{nb} \\ \bar{I}_t^{nb} \\ \overline{Inf}_t^{nb} \end{pmatrix} = \begin{pmatrix} 1 \\ \lambda b^c \\ \lambda b^I \\ \lambda b^{Inf} \end{pmatrix} \mu_t^b + \begin{pmatrix} \bar{y}_{t-1}^{nb} \\ \bar{c}_{t-1}^{nb} \\ \bar{I}_{t-1}^{nb} \\ \overline{Inf}_{t-1}^{nb} \end{pmatrix}, \text{b} = \text{o, g, and A} \tag{13}$$

λb^c, λb^I, λb^{Inf} are loading parameters for the common growth rate components. It is assumed that the long-run growth μ_t^b the random walk of oil price, gold prices and financial assets price are as follow:

$$\mu_t^b = \mu_{t-1}^b + u_t^b,\ u_t^b \sim \mathcal{N}\left(0, \sigma_{u^b}^2\right) \tag{14}$$

The oil price, the gold price, and the financial asset prices are described by a random walk process.

$$\begin{pmatrix} p_t \\ g_t \\ A_t \end{pmatrix} = \begin{pmatrix} p_{t-1} \\ g_{t-1} \\ A_{t-1} \end{pmatrix} + \begin{pmatrix} \eta_t^b \\ \eta_t^b \\ \eta_t^b \end{pmatrix},\ \eta_t^b \sim \mathcal{N}\left(0, \sigma_{\eta^b}^2\right) \tag{15}$$

The independent transitory of the variables $\tilde{z}^{nb}$ shares a common transitory component q_t^b described by the AR(2) as follow:

$$q_t^b = \rho_1 q_{t-1}^b + \rho_2 q_{t-2}^b + \varepsilon_t^b, \varepsilon_t^b \sim \mathcal{N}\left(0, \sigma_{\varepsilon^b}^2\right) \tag{16}$$

The model is based on stochastic disturbances in Eq. (5). γ^c, γ^I, and γ^{Inf} are loading parameters for the transitory components. $\tilde{y}_t^{nbi}$, $\tilde{c}_t^{nbi}$, $\tilde{I}_t^{nbi}$, and $\tilde{Inf}_t^{nbi}$ are idiosyncratic transitory components for the GDP, the consumption, the investment, and the inflation respectively.

$$\begin{pmatrix} \tilde{y}_t^{no} \\ \tilde{y}_t^{ng} \\ \tilde{y}_t^{nA} \end{pmatrix} = \begin{pmatrix} q_t^o \\ q_t^g \\ q_t^A \end{pmatrix} + \begin{pmatrix} \tilde{y}_t^{noi} \\ \tilde{y}_t^{ngi} \\ \tilde{y}_t^{nAi} \end{pmatrix} \tag{17}$$

$$\tilde{c}_t^{nb} = \gamma^c q_t^b + \tilde{c}_t^{nbi} \tag{18}$$

$$\tilde{I}_t^{nb} = \gamma^I q_t^b + \tilde{I}_t^{nbi} \tag{19}$$

$$\tilde{Inf}_t^{nb} = \gamma^{Inf} q_t^b + \tilde{Inf}_t^{nbi} \tag{20}$$

The idiosyncratic transitory component for the macroeconomic variables is described by AR(1) process as follow:

$$\begin{cases} \tilde{y}_t^{nbi} = \zeta_b^y \tilde{y}_{t-1}^{nbi} + \xi_t^y, \xi_t^y \sim \mathcal{N}\left(0, \sigma_{\xi^y}^2\right) \\ \tilde{c}_t^{nbi} = \zeta_b^c \tilde{c}_{t-1}^{nbi} + \xi_t^c, \xi_t^c \sim \mathcal{N}\left(0, \sigma_{\xi^c}^2\right) \\ \tilde{I}_t^{nbi} = \zeta_b^I \tilde{I}_{t-1}^{nbi} + \xi_t^I, \xi_t^I \sim \mathcal{N}\left(0, \sigma_{\xi^I}^2\right) \\ \tilde{Inf}_t^{nbi} = \zeta_b^{Inf} \tilde{Inf}_{t-1}^{nbi} + \xi_t^{Inf}, \xi_t^c \sim \mathcal{N}\left(0, \sigma_{\xi^{Inf}}^2\right) \end{cases} \tag{21-24}$$

The dynamic of the transitory component of the macroeconomic variables $\tilde{z}^{nb}$ determined by the oil price, the gold price and the financial assets are described as follows:

$$\tilde{y}_t^b = \psi_b^y \tilde{y}_{t-1}^b + \theta_b^y \eta_t \tag{25}$$

$$\tilde{c}_t^b = \psi_b^c \tilde{c}_{t-1}^b + \theta_b^c \eta_t \tag{26}$$

$$\tilde{I}_t^b = \psi_b^I \tilde{I}_{t-1}^b + \theta_b^I \eta_t \tag{27}$$

$$\tilde{Inf}_t^b = \psi_b^{Inf} \tilde{Inf}_{t-1}^b + \theta_b^{Inf} \eta_t \tag{28}$$

θ^y, θ^c, θ^I, and θ^{Inf} are the shocks sensitivity parameters for GDP, consumption, investment, and inflation respectively. These shocks parameters are negative, as the actual macroeconomic variables take time to adapt to their permanent level, and are instantaneously changed by the oil price shock, the gold price shock, and the financial assets shock.

$\beta^y + \theta_b^y$, $\alpha^y + \theta_b^y$, and $\sigma^y + \theta_b^y$ are the short-run elasticities of the GDP to the oil price, the gold price, and the financial assets price.

$\beta^c + \theta_b^c$, $\alpha^c + \theta_b^c$, and $\sigma^c + \theta_b^c$ are the short-run elasticities of the consumption to the oil price, the gold price, and the financial assets price.

$\beta^I + \theta_b^I$, $\alpha^I + \theta_b^I$, and $\sigma^I + \theta_b^I$ are the short-run elasticities of the investment to the oil price, the gold price, and the financial asset price.

$\beta^{Inf} + \theta_b^{Inf}$, $\alpha^{Inf} + \theta_b^{Inf}$, and $\sigma^{Inf} + \theta_b^{Inf}$ are the short-run elasticities of the investment to the oil price, the gold price, and the financial assets price.

9. Estimation results

Within this section, we report the cycle estimates and other parameters of interest under the multivariate unobserved component model by the maximum likelihood method using the Kalman filter. In a second step, we proceed to calculate the c and Beta parameters for the trend, cycle, and seasonal parameters using LLT and State Space model using as instruments the gold, energy, and the financial cycle.

The parameters' estimates for the likelihood estimator are shown in **Table 1**. All the parameters are statistically significant. Global consumption and global inflation are significantly negatively determined by the oil, the gold and the financial cycle, which is confirming the expected result compatible with the theory, as a higher price of commodities have a negative impact on the consumption and enhances the inflation which leads to affecting the global economy negatively. In opposite global investment is significantly positively determined by the oil, the gold, and the financial cycle as the oil, the gold are used as hedge funds by the investors as well as the trading of the stock market which promotes the global economy and affects the cyclicity of the global business cycle within the peak. The long-run global investment elasticity of the global output is the highest equal to 0.119. This is confirming that the three determinants are used as a hedge fund for the investors and the payment system and are consistent with the capital channel of the global system, which means that the commodities are distributed mainly for investment other than consumption. **Figure 6**a–d shows the trend of the global business cycle within the Multivariate Unobserved Components model. The time lag of one period for the global GDP has not pronounced an impact on the cyclicity of the global business cycle, which might be explained as the

Dependent Variable: GLOBALGDP				
Method: LIML / K-Class				
Sample (adjusted): 1984Q2 2020Q4				
Included observations: 147 after adjustments				
Covariance type: K-Class				
Constant added to instrument list				
Variable	Coefficient	Std. Error	t-Statistic	Prob.
GLOBALGDP(−1)	0.959091	0.055487	17.28497	0
GLOBALCONSUMPTION	−0.06819	0.088511	−0.77039	0.9423
GLOBAL_INVESTMENT	0.119578	0.149275	0.801058	0.9244
GLOBALCPI	−0.00811	0.006946	−1.16793	0.9448
R-squared	0.998838	Mean dependent var		16.11314
Adjusted R-squared	0.998813	S.D. dependent var		0.57896
S.E. of regression	0.019945	Sum squared resid		0.056886
Durbin-Watson stat	0.793426	LIML min. Eigenvalue		1

The estimate of the generalized UC model for the global GDP. The estimation result of the generalized UC model is reported. The sample period is 1984:Q 1–2020:Q4. Within the estimation, we are limiting to the standard format of the multivariate unobserved model using the maximum likelihood estimator with the Kalman filter. Source: Own study.

Table 1.
Result maximum likelihood estimator with Kalman filter for multivariate unobserved model of the global GDP.

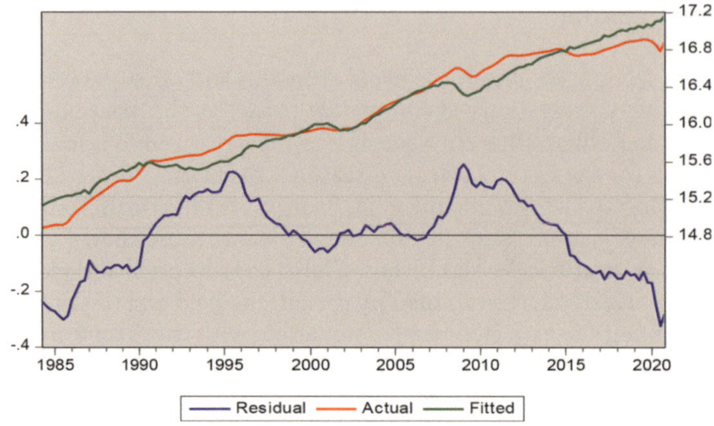

(a)

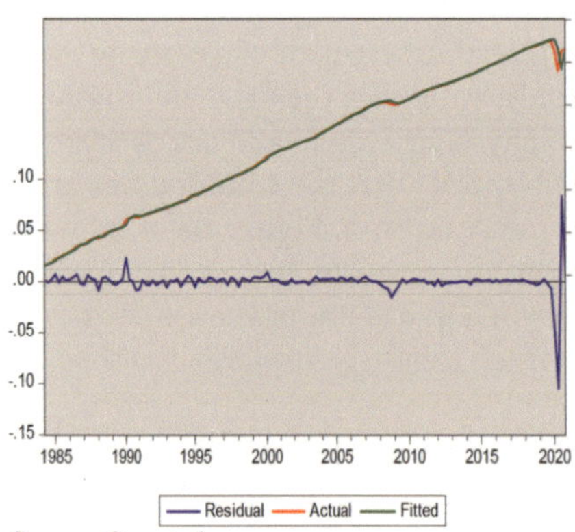

Source: *Own study.*

(b)

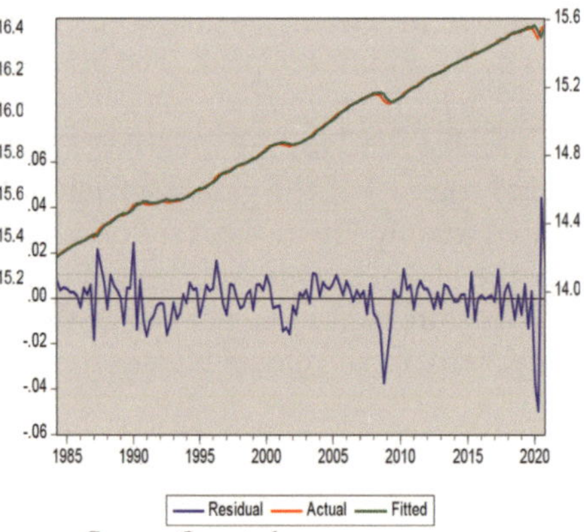

Source: *Own study.*

(c)

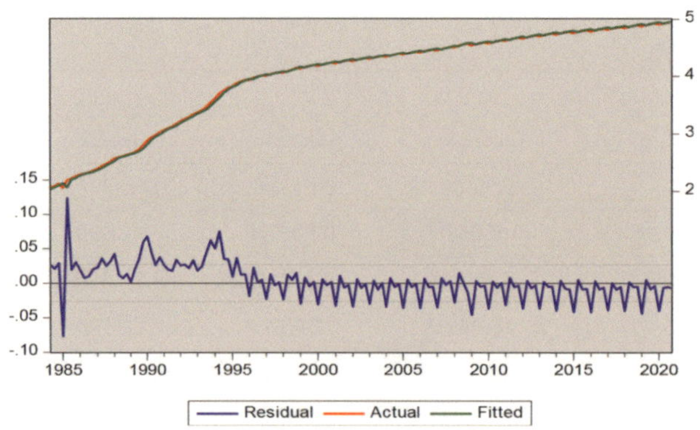

(d)

Figure 6

a. the residual, actual, and fitted estimation of global GDP with maximum likelihood estimator. b. the residual, actual, and fitted estimation of global consumption with maximum likelihood estimator. c. the residual, actual and fitted estimation of global investment with maximum likelihood estimator. d. the residual, actual and fitted estimation of global inflation with maximum likelihood estimator. Source: Own study.

deterministic commodities influence the upswing and downswing of the business cycle. However, basic on the filtering data, it is confirmed that oil has a lag impact on the fluctuation of the business cycle, it reacts as an impulsion for the crisis, compared to the gold and the global financial cycle which react simultaneously with the trend of the global business cycle.

Related to the investment, the inflation, and the consumption the related graph will show the univariate unobserved component model for each variable determined by the oil, the gold, and the financial cycle. According to the main result, we can consider that the determinant oil, gold, and financial cycle was a passive influencer for the global cycle of investment, consumption, and inflation. It is in opposite to the theory; however, it can be explained economically that the macroeconomic aggregate is an endogenous aggregate of the fluctuation of the commodities and not the opposite. However, related to the global business cycle, the commodities are reacting as an intermediary between the global business cycle and the investment, consumption, and inflation. Our result confirms that the long-run relationship between commodities and the business cycle is influenced by the economic condition. The relationship between gold and the financial cycle is stable with significant shifts during peak and recession.

10. Conclusion

This chapter uses a Multivariate Unobserved Component Model to determine the impact of the commodities and the financial cycle on the global business cycle. It shed light on the cyclicity of the unobserved components as a determinant of the business cycle using the filtering approach Band-Pass filter. One distinctive feature of our research is that it combines the financial and non-financial markets as the realm of economic systems to examine the cyclicity of the business cycle.

Our model produces several implications, which are discussed in the chapter. We use the maximum likelihood estimator with the Kalman filter to estimate the model. The main results show that oil has a lag impact on the fluctuation of the business cycle, it reacts as an impulsion for the crisis, compared to the gold and the global financial cycle which reacts simultaneously with the trend of the global business cycle. Our results are in accordance with the prominent literature treating the energy as an impulsion for any upswing or downswing within the cyclicity of the business cycle. Within the recent reframing of the economic system and the interconnectedness of the real and the financial spheres, the gold and the stock market are acting as hedge funds and as investment reacts simultaneously with the trend of the global business cycle. Our study might bring new features that the energy is acting as a hedge fund rather than just a consumption creating a combined business cycle with prominent expectations of their fluctuations.

Author details

Hakim Amira[1*] and Eleftherios Thalassinos[2,3]

1 ISIGK, University of Kairouen, Tunisia

2 University of Piraeus, Greece

3 Department of Insurance and Risk Management, Faculty of Economics, Management and Accountancy, University of Malta, Malta

*Address all correspondence to: hkmamira@gmail.com

References

[1] Schumpeter J. BUSINESS CYCLES. A Theoretical, Historical and Statistical Analysis of the Capitalist Process. Second. ed. New York: McGraw-Hill; 1939

[2] Mensch G. Stalemate in Technology: Innovations Overcome the Depressions. New York: Ballinger; 1979

[3] Haustein H-D, Neuwirth E. Long waves in world industrial production, energy consumption, innovations, inventions, and patents and their identification by spectral analysis. Technological Forecasting and Social Change. 1982;**22**:53-89

[4] Van Duijn JJ. The Long Wave in Economic Life. Boston: George Allen and Unwin; 1983

[5] Kleinknecht A. Innovation Patterns in Crisis and Prosperity. London: Palgrave Macmillan, UK; 1987

[6] Clarke N, Freeman C, Soete L. Long waves, inventions and innovations. Futures. 1981;**13**:308-322

[7] Singer HW. Beyond terms of trade: Convergence/divergence and creative/ uncreative destruction. Zagreb International Review of Economics and Business. 1998;**1**(1):13-25

[8] Borio C. The financial cycle and macroeconomics: What have we learnt? Journal of Banking & Finance. 2014;**45**: 182-198

[9] Borio C, Disyatat P, Juselius M. Rethinking potential output: Embedding information about the financial cycle. Oxford Economic Papers. 2016;**69**: 655-677

[10] Claessens S, Kose MA, Terrones ME. How do business and financial cycles interact? Journal of International Economics. 2012;**87**:178-190

[11] Rabanal P, Taheri S. Financial Factors: Implications for Output Gaps. International Monetary Fund; 2015

[12] Grinin L, Korotayev A, Tausch A. Economic Cycles, Crises, and the Global Periphery. Springer International Publishing; 2016

[13] Helbling T, Huidrom R, Kose MA, Otrok C. Do credit shocks matter? A global perspective. European Economic Review. 2011;**55**:340-353

[14] Drehmann M, Borio C, Tsatsaronis K. Characterising the Financial Cycle: don't Lose Sight of the Medium Term! Bank for International Settlements; 2012

[15] Gerdrup K, Kvinlog AB, Schaanning E. Key Indicators for a Countercyclical Capital Buffer in Norway - Trends and Uncertainty. Norges Bank; 2013 Staff Memo No. 13

[16] Detken C, Weeken O, Alessi L, Bonfim D, Boucinha M, Castro C, et al. Operationalising the Countercyclical Capital Buffer: Indicator Selection, Threshold Identification and Calibration Options. ESRB Occasional Paper No. 5. European Systemic Risk Board; 2014

[17] Stremmel, H., 2015. Capturing the Financial Cycle in Europe. ECB Working Paper Series No 1811

[18] Stremmel, H., Zsamboki, B., 2015. The Relationship between Structural and Cyclical Features of the EU Financial Sector. ECB Working Paper No. 1812

[19] Gorton G, Ordoñez G. Good Booms, Bad Booms. NBER Working Paper 22008; 2016

[20] Schüler YS, Hiebert P, Peltonen T. Coherent Financial Cycles for G-7 Countries: Why Extending Credit Can Be an Asset. ESRB; 2017 Working Paper Series No. 2017/43

[21] Rünstler G, Vlekke M. Business, housing, and credit cycles. Journal of Applied Econometrics. 2018;**33**:212-226

[22] Lucas RE. Asset prices in an exchange economy. Econometrica. 1978;**46**:1429

[23] Blanchard OJ. Output, the stock market, and interest rates. The American Economic Review. 1981;**71**: 132-143

[24] Rangvid J. Output and expected returns. Journal of Financial Economics. 2006;**81**:595-624

[25] Cooper I, Priestley R. Time-varying risk premiums and the output gap. The Review of Financial Studies. 2009;**22**: 2801-2833

[26] Vivian A, Wohar ME. The output gap and stock returns: Do cyclical fluctuations predict portfolio returns? International Review of Financial Analysis. 2013;**26**:40-50

[27] Baur DG, McDermott TK. Is gold a safe haven? International evidence. Journal of Banking & Finance. 2010;**13**: 1886-1898

[28] Beaudry P, Collard F, Portier F. Gold rush fever in business cycles. Journal of Monetary Economics. 2011;**58**:84-97

[29] Pierdzioch C, Risse M, Rohloff S. The international business cycle and gold-price fluctuations. The Quarterly Review of Economics and Finance. 2014; **54**:292-305

[30] Apergis N, Eleftheriou S. Gold returns: Do business cycle asymmetries matter? Evidence from an international country sample. Economic Modelling. 2016;**57**:164-170

[31] Kucher O, McCoskey S. The long-run relationship between precious metal prices and the business cycle. The Quarterly Review of Economics and Finance. 2017;**65**:263-275

[32] Hamilton JD. Oil and the macro-economy since world war II. Journal of Political Economy. 1983;**91**:228-248

[33] Berument MH, Ceylan NB, Dogan N. The impact of oil Price shocks on the economic growth of selected MENA countries. The Energy Journal. 2010;**31**: 149-176

[34] Estrella A, Hardouvelis GA. The term structure as a predictor of real economic activity. The Journal of Finance. 1991;**46**:555-576

[35] Estrella A, Mishkin FS. Predicting U.S. recessions: Financial variables as leading indicators. The Review of Economics and Statistics. 1998;**80**:45-61

[36] Chauvet M, Potter S. Forecasting recessions using the yield curve. Journal of Forecasting. 2005;**24**:77-103

[37] Nyberg H. Dynamic probit models and financial variables in recession forecasting. Journal of Forecasting. 2010; **29**:215-230

[38] Ng ECY. Forecasting US recessions with various risk factors and dynamic probit models. Journal of Macroeconomics. 2012;**34**:112-125

[39] Michael MH. Structural change and the macroeconomic effects of oil shocks: empirical evidence from the United States and Japan. Journal of International Money and Finance. 1993:587-606

[40] Sadorsky P. Oil price shocks and stock market activity. Energy Economics. 1999;**21**:449-469

[41] Elder J, Serletis A. Oil Price uncertainty. Journal of Money, Credit and Banking. 2010;**42**:1137-1159

[42] Jo S. The effects of oil Price uncertainty on global real economic activity. Journal of Money, Credit and Banking. 2014;**46**:1113-1135

[43] Chortareas G, Noikokyris E. Oil shocks, stock market prices, and the U.S. dividend yield decomposition. International Review of Economics & Finance. 2014;**29**:639-649

[44] Yin L, Feng J. Oil market uncertainty and international business cycle dynamics. Energy Economics. 2019;**81**: 728-740

[45] Pönkä H, Zheng Y. The role of oil prices on the Russian business cycle. Research in International Business and Finance. 2019;**50**:70-78

[46] Polbin A. Multivariate unobserved component model for an oil-exporting economy: The case of Russia. Applied Economics Letters. 2021;**28**: 681-685

[47] Grant AL, Chan JCC. Reconciling output gaps: Unobserved components model and Hodrick–Prescott filter. Journal of Economic Dynamics and Control. 2017;**75**:114-121

[48] Yoon G. Locating change-points in Hodrick–Prescott trends with an application to US real GDP: A generalized unobserved components model approach. Economic Modelling. 2015;**45**:136-141

[49] Prebisch R. The Economic Development of Latin America and its Principal Problems. United Nations; 1950

[50] Singer HW. The distribution of gains between investing and borrowing countries. The American Economic Review. 1950;**40**:473-485

[51] Ocampo J. New developments in trade theory and LDCs. Journal of Development Economics. 1986;**22**: 129-170

[52] Ocampo JA, Parra M. Returning to an Eternal Debate: The Terms of Trade for Commodities in the Twentieth Century. United Nations Publications; 2003

[53] Corden WM. Booming sector and Dutch disease economics: Survey and consolidation. Oxford Economic Papers, New Series. 1984;**36**:359-380

[54] Fernald JG. Trend breaks, long-run restrictions, and contractionary technology improvements. Journal of Monetary Economics. 2007;**54**: 2467-2485

[55] Gubler M, Hertweck MS. Commodity price shocks and the business cycle: Structural evidence for the U.S. Journal of International Money and Finance. 2013;**37**:324-352

[56] Hamilton JD. Time Series Analysis. Priceton University Press; 1994

[57] Canova F, Ferroni F. Multiple filtering devices for the estimation of cyclical DSGE models: Multiple filtering devices for DSGE estimation. Quantitative Economics. 2011;**2**:73-98

[58] Gospodinov N, Maynard A, Pesavento E. Sensitivity of impulse responses to small low-frequency Comovements: Reconciling the evidence

on the effects of technology shocks. Journal of Business & Economic Statistics. 2011;**29**:455-467

[59] Goldstein J. Long Cycles: Prosperity and War in the Modern Age. New Haven: Yale Univ. Press; 1988

[60] Baxter M, King RG. Measuring business cycles: Approximate band-pass filters for economic time series. The Review of Economics and Statistics. 1999;**81**:57-593

[61] Christiano LJ, Fitzgerald TJ. The band pass filter. International Economic Review. 2003;**44**:435-465

[62] Gorton GB, He P. Bank credit cycles. Review of Economic Studies. 2008;**75**: 1181-1214

[63] Schularick M, Taylor AM. Credit booms gone bust: Monetary policy, leverage cycles, and financial crises, 1870–2008. American Economic Review. 2012;**102**:1029-1061

[64] Schüler, Y.S., Hiebert, P., Peltonen, T.A., 2015. Characterising the Financial Cycle: A Multivariate and Time-Varying Approach. ECB Working Paper No. 1846

[65] Tölö E, Laakkonen H, Kalatie S. Evaluating indicators for use in setting the countercyclical capital buffer. International Journal of Central Banking. 2018;**14**:61

[66] Aglietta M, Brand T. La stagnation séculaire dans les cycles financiers de longue période. In: L'economie Mondiale 2016. Paris; 2015

[67] Merler S. Squaring the Cycle: Financial Cycles, Capital Flows and Macroprudential Policy in the Euro Area. Brussels: Bruegel; 2015

[68] Galati G, Hindrayanto I, Koopman SJ, Vlekke M. Measuring financial cycles in a model-based analysis: Empirical evidence for the United States and the euro area. Economics Letters. 2016;**145**:83-87

[69] Engle RF. Estimating structural models of seasonality. In: Seasonal Analysis of Economic Time Series. Washington, D.C.: U.S. Dept. of Commerce - Bureau of the Census; 1978. pp. 281-297

[70] Gersch W, Kitagawa G. The prediction of time series with trends and Seasonalities. Journal of Business & Economic Statistics. 1983;**1**:253

[71] Harvey AC, Todd PHJ. Forecasting economic time series with structural and Box-Jenkins models: A case study. Journal of Business & Economic Statistics. 1983;**1**:299

[72] Harvey AC. Forecasting, Structural Time Series ModeLs and the Kalman Filter. Cambridge: Cambridge University Press; 1989

[73] Box GEP, Hillmer SC, Tiao GC. Analysis and modeling of seasonal time Serie. In: Seasonal Analysis 0/Economic Time Senes. Washington, D.C.: U. 8. Dept. of Commerce - Bureau of the Census; 1978. pp. 309-334

[74] Burman JP. Seasonal adjustment by signal extraction. Journal of the Royal Statistical Society. Series A (General). 1980;**143**:321

[75] Hillmer SC, Tiao GC. An ARIMA-model-based approach to seasonal adjustment. Journal of the American Statistical Association. 1982;**77**:63-70

[76] Bell WR, Hillmer SC. Issues involved with the seasonal adjustment of

economic time series. Journal of Business & Economic Statistics. 1984;**2**:291

[77] Maravall A, Pierce DA. A prototypical seasonal adjustment model. Journal of Time Series Analysis. 1987;**8**: 177-193

[78] Clark PK. The cyclical component of U. S. Economic activity. The Quarterly Journal of Economics. 1987;**102**:797

[79] Morley, J.C., Nelson, C.R., Eric Zivot, 2003. Why are the Beveridge-Nelson and Unobserved-components decompositions of GDP so different? The Review of Economics and Statistics 85, 235–243

[80] Oh, K., Zivot, E., 2006. The Clark Model with Correlated Components.

[81] Ma J, Wohar ME. An unobserved components model that yields business and medium-run cycles. Journal of Money, Credit and Banking. 2013;**45**: 1351-1373

[82] Beveridge S, Nelson CR. A new approach to decomposition of economic time series into permanent and transitory components with particular attention to measurement of the business cycle. Journal of Monetary Economics. 1981;7:151-174

[83] Watson MW. Univariate detrending methods with stochastic trends. Journal of Monetary Economics. 1986;**18**:49-75

[84] Hodrick RJ, Prescott EC. Post-war U.S. business cycles: An empirical investigation. Journal of Money, Credit and Banking. 1997;**28**:1-16

[85] Hodrick RJ, Prescott EC. Postwar U.S. business cycles: An empirical investigation. Journal of Money, Credit and Banking. 1980;**29**(1): 1-16

[86] Baştürk N, Çakmakli C, Ceyhan SP, Van Dijk HK. Posterior-predictive evidence on us inflation using extended new Keynesian Phillips curve models with non-filtered data. Journal of Applied Econometrics. 2014;**29**: 1164-1182

[87] Canova F. Bridging DSGE models and the raw data. Journal of Monetary Economics. 2014;**67**:1-15

[88] Morley J, Piger J. The asymmetric business cycle. The Review of Economics and Statistics. 2012;**94**:208-221

[89] Box GEP, Jenkin G. Time Series Analysis, Forecasting and Control. San Francisco: Holden-Day; 1970

Section 2

Financial System in Emerging Markets

Chapter 3

Emerging Financial Markets in Ghana and Public Financial Management Crisis Uncertainties Amidst Debt Restructuring

Isaac Ahinsah-Wobil

Abstract

Ghana's financial markets and the associated challenges, with a particular focus on the impact of debt restructuring on the country's public financial management, and its potential implications for Ghana's overall economic development. This paper will begin with a brief overview of the financial market structure in Ghana, followed by a discussion of the implications of debt restructuring for the country's public financial management. It will then discuss current and potential policy measures that could be implemented to promote financial market development in the country, before concluding with an examination of the prospects for financial market development in Ghana. This chapter aims to investigate the current challenges facing emerging financial markets in Ghana and the public financial management uncertainties arising from debt restructuring. It seeks to identify potential solutions to the country's current financial market and public financial management issues, examine the potential implications of these issues on the country's economic development, and provide a review of the current policy measures and their potential effectiveness.

Keywords: banking, financial, crisis, markets, emerging

1. Introduction

In recent years, financial markets have been emerging in Ghana as a result of various economic and financial reforms. This includes the development of private sector banks, the liberalization of exchange rates, the deregulation of interest rates, and the introduction of Treasury bills. In addition, the country has seen an increase in cross-border investments and the emergence of venture capitalists [1]. This paper examines the implications of these emerging financial markets for Ghana and the public financial management crisis it faced in 2022. It looks at the challenges posed by the country's debt restructuring process, which has been complicated by the fiscal crisis and the uncertain economic outlook. It also examines the prospects for a sustainable financial system in the country, drawing on the experiences of both regional and international investors. Ghana has recently been faced with a major public financial management crisis, due to a combination of factors, including declining oil and gold prices, the depreciation of the local currency and massive debt accumulation. In response, the Ghanaian government, in collaboration with the International Monetary Fund (IMF), has implemented several fiscal reforms and instituted a debt restructuring process. This has been further complicated by the uncertain global economic outlook, which has limited both the availability of external financing and the government's ability to effectively manage fiscal resources. The fiscal crisis in Ghana is part of a wider challenge facing many African economies and is linked to the broader context of debt sustainability and the need for improved financial oversight and transparency [2]. The country's financial markets have been relatively small and underdeveloped, with a small number of participants and limited depth and liquidity. Despite this, recent years have seen a significant rise in the importance of these markets and growing flows of capital. Private sector banks have grown in number and foreign investors have become increasingly involved. Furthermore, the Ghanaian government has taken steps to improve the regulatory environment, including the introduction of a financial sector recovery program and the development of an online platform to facilitate direct lending by banks [3].

The emergence of these financial markets has helped to provide the country with increased access to capital and has provided the government with additional channels to manage its debt and reduce its exposure to financial crisis risks. However, there are still significant uncertainties surrounding the stability of Ghana's financial sector. An important challenge is a potential for a liquidity crisis, as a result of insufficient levels of capital and borrowing capacity. Furthermore, the increasing global focus on debt transparency and risk assessment has placed pressure on the government to ensure that debt restructuring takes place in a responsible and transparent manner. Ghana has presented both opportunities and challenges for the country. On the one hand, it has enabled the government and the private sector to access more capital and better manage their debt. On the other hand, it has created uncertainty about the sustainability of the financial system and posed significant challenges to the debt restructuring process [4]. As Ghana continues to grapple with its public financial management crisis, it is important that the government is able to effectively manage the risk posed by the financial markets and ensure that the country's financial system remains stable and sustainable. Financial markets play an important role in the economic development of a country, and their current development is of great importance to Ghana. Ghana's financial markets have recently emerged, and they are faced with numerous challenges which could have a significant impact on the country's public financial management and debt restructuring strategies [5].

Financial markets have always been an important part of any economy, and their role in the development of Ghana is no exception. Financial markets play a major role in helping to allocate funds efficiently, allowing macro-economic demands and supply to interact in a plan that is profitable to both individuals and businesses alike. In Ghana, a number of domestic and international financial markets have been established, ranging from the world-renowned international stock markets, to the more obscure and recently-established domestic investments [6].

The concept of financial markets in Ghana dates back to the early twentieth century, when the British Gold Coast was established and the Bank of Ghana was established in 1957. The Bank of Ghana would become the main regulator of the financial markets in Ghana, and would be responsible for setting the interest rates, controlling the money supply and issuing credit. Prior to the 1950s, Ghana was heavily reliant on the cocoa bean for its economic growth and development. This agricultural commodity provided most of the income for the country and its people. However, the 1950s saw a shift away from the reliance on cocoa to the emergence of financial markets, which started to provide a more reliable stream of income and capital to the nation. One of the most important financial markets in Ghana is the Ghana Stock Exchange, which was established in 1990 [7]. The Ghana Stock Exchange is the largest and most liquid of all the financial markets in Ghana, and it plays an important role in the nation's economy by allowing businesses to list their securities and attract private investments. The Ghana Stock Exchange has been successful in helping to attract foreign capital to the nation, as a result of which international financial institutions such as the World Bank and International Monetary Fund have provided the country with much needed credit. In addition to the Ghana Stock Exchange, other financial markets have sprung up such as the Ghana Investment and Securities Exchange, the Ghana Securities Exchange, the Ghana Commodities Exchange, and the Ghana Derivatives Exchange [8].

2. Discussion

Financial markets highlight an important role in the development of Ghana's economy, and the resulting economic gains of such markets are numerous. The main economic gains of the financial markets include:

- Increased liquidity of the capital markets in Ghana, which allows for more efficient capital allocation and better pricing of investments.

- Better access to global markets, which can attract foreign capital and help create a more competitive market.

- Improved confidence in the economy, which can help attract tourists and foreign investments.

- Increased foreign investment, which can help improve the living standards of the people.

- Greater transparency and oversight, which can help reduce market volatility and ensure market integrity and investor protection.

- Improved access to credit and financial services, which can help improve the safety of savings, reduce transaction costs, and increase access to capital.

Financial markets are an integral part of any economy, and their role in the development of Ghana is no exception. Ghana's financial markets have been instrumental in helping to provide the nation with much-needed capital, liquidity, and access to foreign capital. As a result, the economic gains of these markets are numerous, including the improved allocation of capital, improved investor confidence, increased foreign investments, and better access to credit and financial services [9]. With the help of financial markets, Ghana is well-positioned to continue its economic development and improve the living standards of its citizens.

2.1 Financial market structure and challenges in Ghana

The financial market of Ghana is a segment of the larger economy and plays an integral role in driving economic growth, development, and stability in the country.

Ghana's economy is heavily reliant on external sources of capital, such as foreign aid and external borrowing, and thus the management of these funds and the functioning of the domestic financial market are of utmost importance. A thorough understanding of the structure and challenges of the financial market in Ghana is thus necessary to maintain a healthy and sustainable economy. The financial market of Ghana is composed of traditional financial intermediaries such as banks, non-banking financial institutions, microfinance institutions, insurers, and other non-banks. These institutions are regulated by the Bank of Ghana, the central bank of Ghana, to ensure the soundness, efficiency, and stability of the system. Furthermore, the Bank of Ghana plays an active role in the regulation of the capital and money markets of Ghana, as well as overseeing the activities of the non-bank financial intermediaries [10].

Despite the presence of the Bank of Ghana's regulatory role, various challenges hinder the effective functioning of the financial market in Ghana. These challenges can be categorized broadly into three main areas: deficient financial infrastructure, financial inclusion, and liquidity risks. Firstly, the structure of the financial market in Ghana suffers from limited infrastructure, which hinders the ability of the banks and other financial intermediaries to operate efficiently and effectively. The lack of efficient payment systems, poor access to financial technology, and inadequate capital markets infrastructure all impede the efficient flow of money and the allocation of credit. As a result, there is a lack of access to capital and resources, which can act as a major constraint on the growth of the market. Financial inclusion is also a major challenge in Ghana. Notably, the country has an extremely large unbanked population, with around 43% of the population estimated to be unbanked. This is due to various factors, such as access to capital, poverty, and a lack of basic financial literacy. To ensure that all citizens have access to the financial market, the government and the regulators encourager greater financial inclusion and that efforts must be made to educate the population about financial services and products.

Finally, liquidity risks are a major challenge for the Ghanaian financial market. The market is characterized by low liquidity and a lack of long-term resources, leading to a reliance on short-term money markets. This poses significant risks, as the market can be vulnerable to sudden changes in liquidity, which can cause rapid and significant downturns in the economy. The structure of Ghana's financial market is thus hampered by various challenges, which affect its ability to provide the efficient credit and capital allocation needed for economic growth and stability. To counter this, the government and the regulators must continue to work to improve the infrastructure of the financial system, promote financial inclusion and provide access to credit to all citizens, and promote long-term resources and enhanced liquidity. Ghana has experienced a turbulent economic landscape in recent years. Economic difficulties have been compounded by several factors, including rising global commodity prices, political uncertainty and an overvalued exchange rate. These issues have highlighted the need for Ghana to undertake a successful debt restructuring program. Furthermore, the banking sector in particular has suffered from a difficult operating environment and the need for reform processes has become increasingly apparent.

2.2 Financial market structure

The financial market structure (FMS) in Ghana is characterized by a relatively large banking sector, comprising 31 banks, 3 non-bank financial institutions and 5 microfinance institutions (MFI's). Furthermore, the country is served by a non-bank financial system including savings and loans companies, merchant banks, and insurance and finance houses. The banking sector is governed by the Bank of Ghana (BOG), which is responsible for formulating and implementing monetary and banking regulations. The BOG also serves as the primary regulator and supervisor of the banking sector. The banking sector has experienced a period of consolidation in recent years, with the number of banks decreasing from 37 in 2001 to 31 in 2017. The decreasing number of banks has led to an increased concentration of banking assets in the larger financial institutions. There is also a trend of increasing ownership of banking assets within the banking sector, which could result in a lack of competition and higher prices for banking services [11].

The capital market in Ghana is relatively underdeveloped and is characterized by a low level of activity and limited access to finance from the capital markets. The number of listed companies on the Ghana Stock Exchange (GSE) is also low. As of July 2017, the GSE had a total of 43 listed companies, which is one of the lowest levels for a capital market in Sub-Saharan Africa.

2.3 Challenges in Ghana's debt restructuring

Ghana's debt restructuring has been hampered by several challenges. These include:

1. Unclear debt reporting: The lack of clarity over the country's debt burden has hampered the ability of the government to make well-informed decisions on debt restructuring. Much of the data on public debt is not reported consistently and the lack of transparency has hindered the ability of the authorities to make progress in debt restructuring [12].

2. Political risks: Political uncertainty in Ghana has posed a challenge to the success of a debt restructuring programme. The lack of political consensus on the terms of a debt restructuring deal has created further delays and hindered progress in this area.

3. Lack of market access: Ghana has limited access to international capital markets and this has restricted the country's ability to raise funds or restructure its debt. This is compounded by a lack of creditor confidence due to several external shocks and political uncertainty in recent years.

4. Limited capacity: The government of Ghana has limited capacity to implement a successful debt restructuring programme, due to a lack of technical expertise in debt restructuring and a lack of financial resources. This has hindered the ability of the authorities to negotiate the terms of a restructuring deal with creditors.

2.4 Future of banks in Ghana

The banking sector in Ghana has experienced a period of turbulence in recent years. The sector is characterized by a lack of competition, due to a decreasing number of banks and increasing concentration of assets in the larger financial institutions. Furthermore, the sector has been affected by a difficult operating environment, with high non-performing loans (NPLs) and cost-income ratios.

However, the outlook for the banking sector in Ghana is likely to be positive. There is an expectation that the consolidation of the sector will result in a more efficient banking system. Furthermore, the implementation of a successful debt restructuring programme should result in improved financial conditions, and promote a more favorable operating environment. The implementation of a regulatory reform agenda should also improve the efficiency and stability of the banking sector [12]. The Bank of Ghana has undertaken several reforms in recent years, which should reduce concentration risk and increase competition. In addition, technological advances in the banking sector, such as mobile banking and the use of artificial intelligence, should improve the efficiency and quality of service offerings from banks in the country. The financial market structure and challenges in Ghana's debt restructuring and the future of banks in Ghana have been highlighted in this paper. It has been demonstrated that Ghana has a relatively large banking sector, which has experienced a period of consolidation in recent years. Furthermore, Ghana's debt restructuring has been hampered by several challenges, including political risks and limited market access. Despite these challenges, the outlook for the banking sector in Ghana is positive, with several regulatory reforms being undertaken and technological advances potentially improving the efficiency and quality of bank services.

2.5 Impact of debt restructuring on public financial management in Ghana

Debt restructuring is a key component of the economic and financial landscape in Ghana. Recently, the country has been engaged in several debt restructuring agreements with various creditors, as part of its effort to address its sovereign debt. The impact of these agreements on the public financial management system in Ghana is largely dependent on the specific terms and conditions of each agreement. Nonetheless, debt restructuring can have a range of serious implications for the fiscal stance of the government and the general state of public finances. One major impact of debt restructuring on public financial management in Ghana is the effect on the fiscal stance of the government. Debt restructuring agreements can often involve the restructuring of debt payments and the lengthening of repayment periods, which can free up short-term resources for the government. This can then be used by the government to finance increased spending or provide greater tax relief. Debt restructuring can also have a significant impact on the liquidity and solvency of the government. If the payments of debt are restructured in a way that reduces liabilities in the short term, then this can provide the government with greater liquidity and solvency, allowing it to borrow at more favorable interest rates and increasing its ability to finance projects and activities.

Furthermore, debt restructuring can also affect the ability of the government to access credit in the future. If the terms of the restructuring agreement are not favorable, this can lead to an increase in the cost of borrowing, which can make it difficult for the government to secure financing for its operations and projects. Moreover, the renegotiated terms often come with strings attached, such as the imposition of reforms or austerity measures, which can negatively affect the quality of public services and the economy as a whole. Finally, it is important to note that debt restructuring can also have a negative impact on investor confidence, as creditors may be reluctant to lend to a government that has restructured its debt. This can lead to an increased cost of borrowing for the government, further reducing its ability to finance operations, and can also reduce foreign direct investment in the country.

Overall, debt restructuring can have both positive and negative impacts on public financial management in Ghana. On the positive side, it can provide the government with greater liquidity and solvency, enabling it to access credit at lower interest rates and free up short-term resources for public spending. On the negative side, it can lead to an increased cost of borrowing, reduce investor confidence, and require the government to adhere to certain conditions and reforms. Therefore, it is important to carefully assess the potential impacts of debt restructuring before furthering any agreements. Debt restructuring is the process of renegotiating loans, or restructuring the repayment schedule so as to reduce the payments and/or interest rates paid on them. It has become a critical tool for managing debt in order to mitigate the consequences of debt overhang. In Ghana, debt restructuring has been used as a means of regaining fiscal discipline and reducing fiscal deficits.

2.6 Impact on credit worthiness and fiscal discipline

Debt restructuring can have a major impact on Ghana's creditworthiness and fiscal discipline. The country's debt has increased significantly since 2008, when the government implemented a Debt Relief Programme. This programme enabled Ghana to reduce its debt to GDP ratio from 97.8% to 79.2% by 2011. Despite this reduction, however, Ghana has experienced a series of debt restructurings since 2008, which have led to an increase in the country's debt burden. The restructuring of these debts has eroded the country's creditworthiness and fiscal discipline. Debt restructuring has also had an impact on the country's fiscal sustainability. A number of studies have found that debt restructuring can reduce fiscal sustainability, especially when debt restructuring is used to reduce the principal of a loan. This reduction in principal leads to a reduction in the financial sustainability of the loan, as the debt servicing costs are reduced. In addition, debt restructuring can also lead to a reduction in the interest rate of a loan, which can lead to a further reduction in the sustainability of the loan.

2.7 Impact on public financial sustainability

Debt restructuring can also have a major impact on the public sector's financial sustainability. It has been argued that debt restructuring can reduce public expenditure by freeing up resources that can be used for other purposes. In addition, debt restructuring can increase public sector revenues by improving the country's creditworthiness and helping to attract foreign investments. Moreover, debt restructuring can help to reduce the public sector's debt burden by reducing the cost of servicing the debt.

In conclusion, debt restructuring has had a significant impact on public financial management in Ghana. It has reduced the country's creditworthiness and fiscal discipline, as well as its public sector's financial sustainability. In addition, it has helped to reduce the country's debt burden and free up resources for other purposes. However, it is important to note that debt restructuring should not be used as a substitute for sound economic policy and long-term fiscal discipline.

2.8 Potential implications for economic development in Ghana

The implications of Ghana's financial market structure and debt restructuring on the country's economic development are numerous and complex. On one hand, a well-functioning financial market can provide the necessary resources for economic growth and job creation. On the other, a less-than-optimal system could reduce access to capital and resources, resulting in limited economic activity and thus, limited economic growth. Furthermore, debt restructuring agreements can have both positive and negative implications for economic development in Ghana. The positive implications of a well-functioning financial market and effective debt restructuring on economic development in Ghana include improved access to capital and resources, increased investor confidence, increased employment, and increased economic growth. Specifically, improved access to capital allows businesses to expand and grow, potentially creating more jobs and leading to a rise in economic activity. Furthermore, increased investor confidence increases the chances of foreign direct investment, which can bring with it additional capital and resources that can be used to further drive economic growth. On the other hand, the negative implications of a deficient financial market and ineffective debt restructuring on economic development in Ghana include reduced access to capital and resources, decreased investor confidence, reduced employment, and hampered economic growth. Specifically, limited access to capital reduces the opportunities for businesses to invest and grow, leading to reduced economic activity and fewer employment opportunities. Additionally, decreased investor confidence can lead to a decreased influx of foreign direct investment, further reducing access to capital and resources, and thus, economic activity.

Ghana has experienced significant economic development in the past few decades, and its economy is expected to continue to progress in the future. The potential implications for economic development in Ghana are vast and will have a profound effect on the nation's economic growth and well-being. One of the most important implications is the potential for increased access to health care, education, and financial services. Access to quality health care and education can help to lift people out of poverty, improve productivity and economic growth, and ultimately, lead to a better quality of life. Additionally, increased access to financial services can help to stimulate economic development, as it allows people to borrow money to invest in businesses, purchase goods and services, and start new businesses that may have an economic impact.

Second, the potential implications of economic development in Ghana include the development of infrastructure. Ghana currently has a strong road network and is in the process of developing additional roads, electricity grids, and telecommunications networks. This infrastructure development can provide the foundation for further economic growth and the expansion of businesses, as it will help facilitate the movement of goods, services, and people, as well as the sharing of information. Furthermore, the development of this infrastructure will lead to increased access to international markets and greater economic stability and prosperity.

Third, economic development can have a positive impact on Ghana's business environment. The development of a strong and vibrant business sector can lead to increased investment, employment, and economic growth. This can be accomplished through the liberalization of the market and the removal of bureaucratic impediments, such as excessive regulation, that hinder the development of businesses. This can lead to a greater number of small and medium-sized enterprises (SMEs), which are often the most dynamic and innovative in any economy. This can help improve the lives of people in Ghana and create more jobs and opportunities.

Possibility of banks in Ghana collapsing amidst debt restructuring and uncertainties in financial markets: The financial stability of Ghana is dependent on the banking sector. The banking sector is one of the major sources of foreign capital in the economy and it is largely responsible for the stability and growth of the economy. However, with the current debt restructuring and uncertainties in financial markets, there is a risk of banks collapsing in Ghana. Ghana is an emerging market economy that has managed to achieve high growth rates in the past decade which is the result of prudent macroeconomic policies and a sound legal framework. The country's Gross Domestic Product (GDP) has been growing steadily, with a peak of 7.6% growth in 2017. In 2019, real GDP growth was estimated to reach 8.8%, driven by strong performance in the services, industry and agriculture sectors. The country's nominal GDP was estimated at $57 billion in 2019.

However, the economy has been facing several challenges in the recent past. The country has been facing rising inflation, declining currency, and increasing debt levels, which have had a major impact on the banking sector and the economy as a whole.

The banking system in Ghana plays a major role in the economy, and is the backbone of the financial system. Recently, the country has been through several rounds of economic turmoil and the banking sector has been at the center of the turbulence. As a result, observers have been speculating on the potential collapse of banks in Ghana and the potential implications for the economy and the people of Ghana.

At the end of 2019, there were 32 commercial banks operating in the country, including foreign-owned banks. The banking sector has been facing several challenges over the past few years. The sector has been affected by high levels of bad debt, falling profitability and rising costs. In addition, the sector has been plagued by inadequate capitalization, weak corporate governance and a lack of transparency.

The Ghanaian economy has been facing a severe economic crisis over the past few years. This crisis has been triggered by several factors, including rising inflation, declining currency, and increasing debt levels. The crisis has had a major impact on the banking sector, as well as the wider economy. In an effort to address the economic crisis, the government of Ghana requested assistance from the International Monetary Fund (IMF). In 2016, the Ghanaian government and the IMF signed a three-year Extended Credit Facility (ECF) Program, with the aim of restoring macroeconomic stability, reducing poverty, and promoting private sector-led growth. Under the program, the IMF provided $918 million in financing and policy advice.

Given the challenging economic situation in Ghana, there is a possibility that some banks could collapse if the country's economic situation does not improve. The banking sector has been facing several challenges in recent years, including inadequate capitalization, weak corporate governance, and a lack of transparency. In addition, the sector is facing rising non-performing loans and increasing costs. These factors could potentially lead to the collapse of some banks in the country.

The IMF program in Ghana is aimed at restoring macroeconomic stability, reducing poverty, and promoting private sector-led growth. The program has been successful in restoring stability, however, it is likely that the program will not be able to address the underlying causes of the banking sector's decline, such as weak corporate governance and a lack of transparency.

The collapse of banks in Ghana could have major implications for the economy and the people of Ghana. Banks play an essential role in the economy, providing vital financial services to businesses and individuals. If banks collapse, it could lead to a disruption of the financial system, leading to job losses and reduced economic activity. In addition, it could lead to a significant increase in poverty levels as people may not have access to the financial services they need.

The main cause of financial instability in Ghana is the increasing debt burden. As of December 2019, total public debt of Ghana was estimated at 75.3% of the GDP. This is among the highest in Africa and the rising debt burden has increased the risk of the banking system becoming vulnerable. In addition, the government has adopted policies that have resulted in the weak fiscal position of the country. This has led to poor fiscal discipline and fiscal deficit, which have been exacerbated by the lack of diversification of the economy.

In addition, there are several other underlying factors that have contributed to the instability of the banking sector in Ghana. These include the increasing reliance on foreign currency loans, the high levels of non-performing loans, and weak corporate governance. These have increased the vulnerability of the banking sector to risks such as interest rate and liquidity shocks.

The global financial crisis of 2022 and its aftermath had a lasting impact on financial markets around the world. This has led to a situation of market volatility, with the uncertainty of the economic and financial outlook making investing difficult. This has become more evident in the last couple of years, with the uncertainty surrounding the Russain-Ukraine war, COVID and other geopolitical tensions resulting in a lack of investor confidence. This has further weakened the banking sector in Ghana, as investors are increasingly cautious about investing in the country due to the risks of market instability.

The banking sector in Ghana is highly exposed to the risk of collapse due to the rising debt burden and the uncertainty in global financial markets. The rising debt burden has increased the vulnerability of the banking sector to risks such as interest rate and liquidity shocks. In addition, the uncertainty in global financial markets and the weak corporate governance have increased the risk of default, as investors are increasingly reluctant to invest in the country. This has resulted in a decrease in the availability of credit and a decrease in investment. Another challenge for banks in Ghana is the high level of non-performing loans, which has resulted in a decrease in the profitability of banks. This has resulted in an increase in the risk of insolvency and a decrease in the availability of capital. The banking sector in Ghana is highly exposed to risks such as an increase in debt, uncertainty in global financial markets, and weak corporate governance. These risks have increased the possibility of banks in Ghana collapsing amidst debt restructuring and uncertainties in financial markets. As such, it is important for the government to take measures to address the underlying causes of financial instability and incentivize investors to invest in the banking sector. This will help to reduce the risk of bank collapse and ensure the stability of the banking sector in Ghana.

Finally, increased economic development in Ghana can lead to the development of the nation's natural resources, such as its oil reserves. The development of these resources can provide an important source of revenue, create economic growth, and help to reduce poverty. Furthermore, it can also lead to an increase in foreign investment, which can be used to create more jobs and further economic development.

3. Conclusion

In conclusion, economic development in Ghana can have a profound effect on the nation's economic growth and well-being. Increased access to health care, education, and financial services can help to reduce poverty, while infrastructure development and the development of the business sector can provide the foundation for further economic growth and the expansion of businesses. Additionally, increased economic development can lead to the development of the nation's natural resources, providing an important source of revenue and creating economic growth that can reduce poverty and create new jobs.

Overall, it is essential that the government and the regulators take steps to ensure the efficient and effective functioning of the financial market in Ghana in order to promote economic development. This includes strengthening the infrastructure of the financial system, promoting greater financial inclusion and access to credit, and promoting long-term resources and improved liquidity. Additionally, the government must ensure that all debt restructuring agreements are undertaken with the utmost due diligence, as this can have serious implications on the fiscal stance of the government and the overall economic development of the country.

Author details

Isaac Ahinsah-Wobil
Swiss School of Business and Management, Geneva, Switzerland

*Address all correspondence to: peacewalkghana@yahoo.com

References

[1] Sulaiman LO. Effect of financial liberalization on economic growth in developing countries: The Nigerian experience. International Journal of Economics. 2012

[2] Bank, W. Reviving Urban Development the Importance of Freetown for the National Economy. Sierra Leone Economic Update; 2018

[3] Ceyla Pazarbasioglu AG. Digital Financial Services. World Bank; 2020

[4] Barry M. The crisis of Ghana's public financial management: Causes and remedies. In: Paper Presented at the 41st Annual Conference of the International Association for Research in Income and Wealth. The University of Zimbabwe; 2013

[5] Aboagye M. Emerging financial markets in Ghana and their role in financial inclusion. Journal of International Development and Economics. 2015;**2**(2):41-50

[6] Akintoye A. Macro-economic leading indicators of construction contract prices. International Journal of Construction Management. 2010

[7] Anthony Kyereboah-Coleman KF-T. Impact of Macroeconomic Indicators on Stock Market Performance: The Case of the Ghana Stock Exchange. Emerald Group Publishing Limited; 2008

[8] Guermond V. Whose money? Digital remittances, mobile money and fintech in Ghana. Cogent Social Sciences. 2021

[9] Owusu-Mireku E. Reshaping public financial management in Ghana: A systemic approach to debt restructuring. International Journal of Public Administration and Policy. 2017;**1**(1):1-14

[10] Achimugu P, Thompson K. Financial restructuring and Ghana's debt sustainability. African Development Review. 2012;**24**(3):372-387

[11] Mensah EK. An analysis of emerging financial markets and their impact on Ghana's public financial management. International Journal of Financial Research. 2018;**9**(2):212-223

[12] The IMF's Approach to Debt Restructuring in Ghana. International Monetary Fund. 2021. Available from: https://www.imf.org/en/News/Articles/2021/04/29/pr21423-imf-approach-debt-restructuring-ghana

Chapter 4

How to Successfully Select the Best-Performing Bank Based on the Best Auditor's Choice Quality in Islamic and Conventional Banks?

Achraf Haddad

Abstract

Prior research looked at the impact of external audit quality (EAQ) on financial performance (FP) subsequent to the certification of the financial statements, which means after the external auditor's choice (EAC). However, in this research, I chose the EAC as a proxy for the EAQ to study the results of the EAC quality before the external auditor (EA) appointment on FP in the most well-known bank types, namely conventional and Islamic banks. This paper aims to minimize the EAC problem, overcome the choice risks, and solve the choice ambiguity between conventional and Islamic banks that exists in the literature. The first datum was collected from 180 conventional banks (CBs), while the second datum was composed from 180 Islamic banks (IBs). By using random and fixed effects, we investigated cylindrical panel data to parse the link between EAC quality and FP during the period (2010–2022). Hence, we inferred that the EAC quality ameliorated the IBs' FP but lowered that of the CBs.

Keywords: conventional banks (CBs), Islamic banks (IBs), external auditor (EA), external auditor choice (EAC), external audit quality (EAQ), financial performance (FP), agency theory, comparative study

1. Introduction

The progressive reading has shown that the EAC is considered a central governance mechanism around which several other mechanisms and stakeholders are correlated [1]. Banks' shareholders appoint a renowned audit corporation and choose a reputable EA to obtain sufficient assurance that presents a good report quality. Generally, the best EAC in management control is increasingly becoming an obligation in the banking system to strengthen internal governance, which exposes managers to disciplinary forces inside and outside the bank. Besides, banks can be companies in other banks or subsidiaries in multinational bank groups; thus, they manage high capital and are forced to allocate it more efficiently. In practice, the EAC can threaten managers who benefit from their positions and act according to their interests without considering those of shareholders. This will subsequently cause suspicious consequences that can negatively influence the banks' FP.

Moreover, external governance represents stakeholders' control, with the markets allowing the completion of internal governance [2]. Among these mechanisms that are part of external governance, we cite the financial market, the market for goods and services, the labor market for managers, EA, etc. Hence, external audits address the importance of the EAC to the EAQ. According to Caprio and Levine [3], the possible sources of banks' external governance are fourfold. These sources are creditors, shareholders, governments, and competitive discipline in product and service markets. To evaluate the EAQ, we chose the EAC as an external governance mechanism to meet the expectations of shareholders and creditors [4]. Nevertheless, all competitive external audit mechanisms may urge managers to behave opportunistically since the impact of substitutability leads to information asymmetry between the mechanisms or between managers and investors within the same bank. Audit opinion shopping was extensively studied in accounting research. Many firms are committed to opinion shopping by influencing or even manipulating their auditor's decision to obtain the estimated opinion [5]. Therefore, the accumulation of these acts will destroy the process of creating FP and weaken the audit's protective effect on investors.

The banks' control policy that complies with standards of good governance practices requires the disclosure of reliable information that is relevant, intelligible, and accurate to promote performance, maintain stability, and reflect the banks' real situation [6]. However, several empirical studies explored the effect of the EAQ on earnings management, FP evolution, financial handling, and banks' accounting restatements [7–15]; since the appearance of such financial and accounting phenomena created a paradox and confirmed that the theoretical foundations for selecting the EA differ from the real and practical criteria. Because there are no studies that discussed the standard basis on which the banks select their auditors and the effects of the EAC on the banks' FP, we took the initiative to resolve this issue by focusing on the two famous bank types, namely Islamic banks and conventional banks.

Before studying the difference between the detailed effects of the EAC within conventional and Islamic banks, it seems appropriate to, first, draw the readers' attention to the fact that an overview of the literature on the EAC sheds light on two separate lines of research: the effect of the EAC on governance quality [16–22] and the impact of the EAC on FP [13, 23–27]. **Figure 1** schematizes the link between the EAC and FP measurements in the presence of endogenous and exogenous factors that can create practical flows that lead to altering the EAC or influencing FP.

The financial audit that is conducted by a BIG4 auditor has a major effect on other internal governance mechanisms. Therefore, an independent external audit plays a crucial role in maintaining stakeholders' confidence in financial reports and contributes to reducing agency costs [28, 29]. Shareholders aim to curb agency costs, optimize the FP, increase owners' dividends, gain the confidence of the financial markets, and protect the interests of current and potential investors. It is a complicated, multidimensional relationship where the shareholders control the auditor and the auditor controls the managers. An auditor's conspiracy with the officers will result in a conflict of interest between the shareholders and the officers. When shareholders discover this complicity, the auditor risks losing their bank fees.

Although the recent financial crises stem from the decline in the banks' FP, a noticeable increase is found in the practice of earnings management and the reporting of fictitious false FP levels, originating in most cases from false reporting and the lack of external audit transparency [18, 21, 30–32]. The banks' EAC may alter the

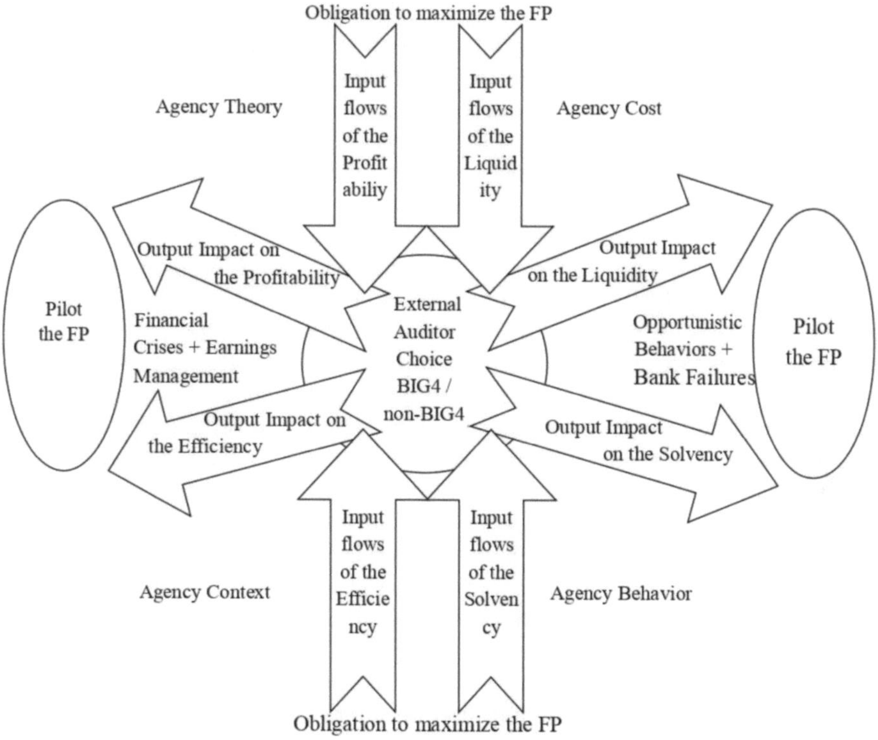

Figure 1.
Explanation of possible effects movements between EAC and FP.

relevance of the audit engagement and ensure the financial statements' reliability. The Subprime scandal affected the stakeholders' trust through the financial information included in the auditors' reports. It destroyed financial reports users' trust, which raises the question of the auditors' honesty and independence and whether audit quality enhances the quality of disclosed information [33]. Kassem and Higson [34] concluded that EAs are liable for assessing corruption risks. Yet, external audit regulators could not clearly define their role. Moreover, Mohammad and Ahmed [35] proved that big audit corporations have no considerable impact on financial reporting quality.

Following the 2007 governance scandal, many multinational banks failed, and governments bailed out many financial institutions, whether in developed or undeveloped countries around the world. Because of the revival of interest in CBs and the credit governance problems, the false disclosure results and the FP swelling were transformed into toxic interest gains. The discussed gap originates from their bad EAC and the decline of their EAQ. It all depends on the bank's audit policy goal. Indeed, the EAC quality can make a radical change (positive/negative) through the integration of a constructive/destructive vision, the implementation of an efficient/deficient monitoring system, and the introduction of a good/bad transparency policy, whether in conventional or Islamic banks. However, because banks worked within an agency financial framework, financial reality showed many complicated details and opposite results from the expectations of the EAC. Furthermore, in the literature on IBs' governance, not many papers tackled the subject of EAC [36–38] because, in IBs, there are other substitutable mechanisms like the Charia Supervisory Board and religion standards, where this mechanism has lost some of its importance.

At this stage, given that prior research on the impact of EAC on FP revealed inconsistent findings and EAC showed different and inclusive impacts on the association with banks' FP and that none of them has compared these impacts in conventional and Islamic banks, we examined whether the EAC provides indications on the development or the fall separately on the Islamic or conventional banks' FP. Furthermore, because the failure of banking transactions becomes imperative and occurs regardless of the bank type, we invested in this virgin field. Moreover, since the results evaluating the EAC's effect on the FP of conventional and Islamic banks are mixed, we tried to solve the ambiguity problem, find an effective solution to this contradiction, and definitively answer our comparative hypothesis. Based on the governance literature of Islamic and conventional banks, the criticisms of previous research showed that the EAC's impacts on conventional and Islamic FP are different. Some countries where banks applied international accounting standards also met international auditing standards. Other countries adopted local accounting and auditing standards. However, a third class of countries implemented specific sectoral accounting and auditing standards. Because there is no unique standard that organizes the external audit function [16], our explanatory paper aims to examine the link between the EAC and selected FP measures. This method will remain valid and useful in future studies in case the samples or contexts change.

With all this huge momentum of critics and challenges on the EAC on the IBs' FP and especially on the CBs' FP, financial literature may benefit from our study in many ways. From a practical perspective, our study improves how the EAC controls FP policy and determines the bank's fate. Indeed, our second practical contribution is to provide economic agents with the most serious bank type when choosing their EAs and in which bank type the EAC internal restrictions can force the EAQ and oblige the EA to respect their obligations towards the bank. Theoretically, we demonstrated that the banks' FP is a dependent variable of the impact generated by EAC which is a strategic process that leads either to the financial sustainability of the Islamic or/and conventional bank or to its exposure to unbearable financial shocks.

As an implication, this study will contribute to the disclosure quality of bank accounting information. Second, our research helps banks detect the weaknesses of the accounts' certification on the FP of such a bank type and correct possible threats resulting from the wrong EAC. Third, this study can help banks ameliorate their EAC quality, support the strengths and opportunities that promote the effectiveness of financial reporting, and maximize their FP via the EAC's generated impact. Fourth, our study also helps banks' investors choose the most efficient bank.

The present work is organized as follows: Section 2 provides a literature survey of structural differences between the impacts of EAC on the FP of Islamic and conventional banks. Section 3 exposes our methodology, tools, and data. Section 4 contains empirical results. Section 5 concludes the paper.

2. Litterature review

2.1 External audit choice

There are different techniques through which the EAC could be demonstrated (independence, audit tenure, auditor size, auditor experience, BIG4, etc.) [39–42].

The best choice is measured by qualification, sufficient training, and experience. The annual report's quality is regarded as the most important tool for monitoring the EAC [4, 18]. For the firm's transparency and accountability obligations towards the stakeholders [13], a lot of detailed information should normally be mentioned in the annual report. This information mainly concerns the operational risk level, financial parameters' evolution, significant errors, and the tests' extent carried out to assess the assets' value at market value. There are different techniques through which the EAC could be demonstrated (independence, audit tenure, auditor size, auditor experience, BIG4, etc.) [39–42]. The best choice is measured by qualification, sufficient training, and experience. The annual report's quality is regarded as the most important tool for monitoring the EAC [4, 18].

For the corporation's transparency and accountability obligations towards its stakeholders, a lot of detailed information should normally be mentioned in the annual report [13]. It mainly concerns the operational risk level, financial parameters' evolution, significant errors, and the tests' extent carried out to evaluate the assets' value at market value. This information could go beyond EA's technical functions, but it contains all financial measures and adjustments to all assistants' interests [43]. The approval or rejection of accounting data is not a simple control process; it requires a lot of vigilance and professionalism to extract the errors of the mismanagement of any bank, which also depends mainly on the EAC's effectiveness. In this sense, Kamolsakulchai [44] showed a strong and positive link between the quality of audits and the quality of financial reporting, as determined by an unqualified audit opinion. This indicates that financial reporting was prepared according to generally accepted accounting standards.

The main limitations of the EAC effectively contributed to little transparency in audit procedures, the absence of large databases (Big Data) containing official figures, and the dearth of in-depth studies that illustrate the real hurdles of global regulation and the profession's dynamism. In reality, there is an insufficiency of practical explanations that represent unique standards to judge the EAC's quality. External audits as well as the audit control authorities could not clearly define the EA's role [34]. The visibility issue is fundamental not only for academic researchers but also for regulators and global rating agencies to appreciate and evaluate the EA's efforts. Ideal oversight requires the auditor's ability to judge difficult times with consistency, vigilance, and transparency, as well as their resistance to pressure and conflict from leaders [45, 46]. Otherwise, the EAC will have doubts about the EA's independence. The greater the auditor's financial dependence, the greater the pressure on their responsibilities to interfere with their duties. Conversely, the more the EA's independence improves, the richer the audit quality. As a result, the EAQ maintains good surveillance. This leads to supporting the bank's profitability, creating more liquidity, repaying more liquidity, and contributing to a rational use of resources that is normally positively reflected in wealth creation.

However, previous empirical studies resulted in controversial outcomes on the effect of competition between auditors operating in similar audit markets. Regulators discovered that little competition in the audit market is likely to curb the EAQ, while its strengthening promotes auditor independence and improves the EAQ, even though other researchers reported the opposite. More specifically, Fujiao [47] studied the impact of competition between EAQ in the audit market on the EAQ. He stated that competition negatively reflects the auditee-auditor relationship. The competition considerably modifies the EAC that moderates the EAQ provided to the customers by providing non-audit services (NAS) by the agent. However, EAC, measured by competition, has a positive moderating impact on the inverse association between the NAS provision and the EAQ. He also discovered that EAC indirectly affects EAQ through increased auditor independence. In conclusion, he declared that weak internal control, such as continuity notices (favorable or unfavorable) and financial restatements, determines the EAQ.

Likewise, Brooks et al. [48] came to the conclusion that the EAQ increases in parallel with the mandates' length due to a learning effect and decreases with recent audit mandates due to a surety effect. When the link effect dominates the learning effect during the service period, the EAQ decreases as a result of the decrease in the audit team's independence. The EAQ change grows with EAC, BIG4 auditors, and specialist auditors. Also, Elad [49] noted that the auditors' training has a partial effect on the intentional reduction of their responsibilities related to the preparation of accounting records and financial statements since this facilitates the audit procedure judgment. However, the auditors' training does not affect the detection of fraud, the financial statements' reliability, and the usefulness of decisions.

Indeed, to evaluate the risk of sudden and recent changes in control approaches applied by the chosen audit firms, Kutum [50] tested the extent of applying the risk audit approach to business by non-BIG4 auditors, as well as its pros, cons, and consequences, particularly in three countries, which are the United Kingdom, America, and Canada. As measurement parameters, our paper relies on four alleged advantages for large companies, which are, respectively, the informational content of audit reports, the consistency of audit practices with audit manuals worldwide, the auditors' awareness of risks, and audit effectiveness. During the period of collecting information, the author considered the contextual factors affecting non-BIG auditors' choices. The results showed that non-BIG4 auditors in the three countries adopted firms' risk auditing. First, this approach helps auditors better understand their customers, promotes audit efficiency, and facilitates the audit risk management process. Second, risk control makes it easier to follow the general trend of non-BIG4 auditors and the accounting standards applied within each country.

Nevertheless, other studies that analyzed the EAC effect on the banks' FP revealed the opposite. It turned out that big audit corporations are the best known. They have higher expertise [46, 51], are more able to appreciate the situation's complexity [39, 52], are more independent [53, 54], and are more competent [45, 55] than others because they no longer have to worry about their reputation. Moreover, they are more cautious about significant legal sanctions [56]. According to this current, the certification of multinational banks by this type of auditor is not tainted by manipulation, omissions, or falsification. In addition, big auditors will be more likely to maintain the audit's credibility than small audit corporations by resisting accounting and financial pressures when negotiating their fees. The various EAC approaches proved that the services provided by BIG4 audit are distinctive and provide better services suited to their customers' needs compared to those of other firms because they are less involved in fraudulent acts. In this sense, Watts and Zimmerman [57], Chan et al. [58], and Firth [59] found that auditors who are involved in bad accounting manipulations lose their reputations.

Based on its experience, Ernst and Young reported in 2003 that the audit committees' power was stronger than that of EAs in the studied institutions. However, big audit firms better recognize how to interact with banks' committees. Indeed, they know how to rise above difficulties, solve problems, and communicate solutions. To do so, Ernst and Young indicated that a detailed assessment of the guidelines would help audit committees adopt more efficient operating procedures. To improve the discussed correlation, Baumann and Erlend [60] noticed that banks disclosing more information on their profits and FP have higher funds ratios. This reserve provides greater protection against the probability of unexpected losses. In conclusion, thanks to their good EAC, banks that improve their publishing processes increase their FP because they build stakeholder confidence by attracting new investments [61, 62]. A good EAC positively influences the governance quality and, consequently, the equity book value.

Returning to the accounting literature, the audit firms' classification started as BIG6s, then as BIG5s, and then as BIG4s, which currently represent a basic benchmark related to control quality worldwide [63]. For example, Francis et al. [64] found that on average, 50% of the audit services costs were granted to leading corporations in the audit market, whereas only 22% of these services were entrusted to small firms. Besides, the most developed sectors in America are audited by BIG5 firms. Thus, the sample was distributed according to the audit firms: 14 companies for Arthur Andersen, 5 companies for Deloitte & Touche, 16 companies for Ernest & Young, 9 companies for KPMG, and 19 companies for PricewaterhouseCoopers. Moreover, Jeff et al. [65] confirmed that, generally, investment banks are oriented towards BIG4 auditors mainly for insurance and trust reasons. This proves that the choice between BIG4 firms and second-level firms is not based on actual quality that reflects their fundamental independence but rather on a preference limited to their perceived quality based mainly on structural choices.

According to international auditing standards, before expressing an opinion, the EA must comply with accounting standards, the bank's operating principles, and good governance rules. Because the communication of FP information in conventional and Islamic banks is very delicate, these banks call on the big audit firms as part of their stakeholders - shareholders, creditors, and investors - who are looking for reliable and relevant FP information. This helps to monitor the leaders' behavior, protect their interests, and evaluate their decisions [4]. The fundamental role of a good EAC is to curb the information asymmetry between both holders and users of FP information. In the event of financial manipulation, the EAs assume responsibility for their actions and the results of the fake FP information. The truly independent EA always tends to reduce FP information asymmetry. However, since qualified auditors are more likely to behave in compliance with standards, boosting the banks' FP depends on the EAC's activeness and their ability to discover inappropriate accounting practices, limit managers' opportunistic behavior, detect moral hazard problems that threaten the shareholders' interests, and cover managers' revenue manipulation [66, 67]. The EAs generate a fundamental role as bank supervisors if they guarantee that depositors are informed about the encountered financial difficulties that may affect the bank's FP and lead to a bank panic. In this case, their role is still focused on strengthening deposit protection so that depositors have fewer incentives to monitor the bank [68, 69]. The published report consistently reflects the various aspects of a bank's operations with or without reserves [44].

Because all audit missions must be carried out in secrecy to protect property rights and to respect the banks' private information, the information covers the protection of their customers' particularities in front of their competitors and also agrees with the accounting methods' conservatism. Indeed, Steven et al. [70] stated that in firms audited by experienced auditors, the managers' discretionary power is weak. It is recognized that all practices, experience, and professional audit training in various fields that are acquired over time increase the error detection levels in financial statements [71–74]. In the same sense, Chia et al. [75] noticed that the companies audited by BIG4 record lower rates of earnings management than other companies. Moreover, given the BIG4s' reputation in the global financial market, Cahan and Zhang [76] reported that big audit corporations are more attentive to litigation risk compared to smaller ones. Similarly, other academics explored the link between the EAQ and the earnings management level. They noticed that the institutions audited by BIG4 auditors recorded low rates of earnings management [25, 26]. From the same perspective, Lee and Vivek [77] studied the link between discretionary accruals and the litigation risks of private firms audited by BIG6 versus firms audited by non-BIG6. They concluded that the former managed fewer discretionary accruals than the latter since they avoided the risk of losing their reputation on the market. In the Korean context, Jeong et al. [78] demonstrated that companies that have certified accounts by state-appointed auditors recorded a higher level of abnormal accruals than firms audited by freely chosen auditors. Furthermore, Hasan et al. [18] examined the moderating impact of audit quality on financial reporting quality, i.e., real earnings management, in Malaysian companies. They recorded that audit quality plays an important role in restricting real earnings management practices.

Moreover, Houqe et al. [79] revealed that compliance with ethical principles leads to a positive and significant effect on the BIG4s' choice. Thus, all the countries' control variables are positively linked to the BIG4's choice. Yet, by controlling both company and country factors, the probability of hiring a quality auditor is enhanced by the company's ethical values. Yet, the impact of the company's ethical values on the auditor's choice remains significant and positive when the control variables in the country are included in the model. So, the indicators of the companies' ethical values have additional explanatory power for controlling countries. In conclusion, the EAC indirectly improves the relationship between companies' compliance with ethical standards and financial information quality.

As for the impact of EAC that results in the EAQ on FP, Teoh and Wong [26], Becker et al. [30], and Krishnan [25] noted that the EAQ and the results quality announced by the companies audited by BIG4s are more reliable compared to the results of firms audited by non-BIG4s [13, 80]. The BIG4s' resources are greater than those owned by small firms [81], so as to maintain their reputation and ensure accounting and financial information quality. Indeed, the perceived independence of BIG4 firms is positively correlated with a competitive environment [82]. Consequently, BIG4s certify more credible financial statements compared to the financial statements audited by other auditors [25, 30]. Moreover, Hamed et al. [83] showed the existence of an insignificant correlation between EA quality proxies and ROA. They also noted that the audit fee has a positive and significant relationship with Tobin's Q. Yet, EAs' rotation has an insignificant correlation with Tobin's Q. Indeed, Ezejiofor et al. [24] examined the impact of audit quality on the FP of bank deposits in Nigeria between 2009 and 2016. Their results showed the existence of a significant correlation between audit quality and deposits' FP. Furthermore, Rahman et al. [13] found that BIG4s have a positive and significant correlation with firms' FP. Even more, Ziaee [5] found that EAQ could affect companies' FP. Similarly, Muotolu et al. [84] revealed that BIG4 positively and significantly affects Nigerian banks' FP. To avoid the deposits' management, the researchers suggested that Nigerian banks be audited by one of the BIG audit firms. In the same context, Ado et al. [23] showed that auditor size positively and significantly affected the ROA. Moreover, they concluded that auditor independence had more power over the FP than auditor size.

The discussion of the EAC effect on the IBs' FP is not very extensive in the literature given the delimitation of the IBs' networks worldwide [85]. A few studies have previously assessed whether the EAC really affects or contributes to the growth of the IBs' FP [86–89]. According to Quttainah et al. [89], IBs support the risk of losing all or some of their investments since they use contracts like Murabaha, Musharakah, and Mudarabah. Without the Charia audit, IBs rely on the same auditing standards used by their competitors [12]. However, according to some researchers, an independent external audit system is very important in IBs since it ensures management supervision and develops a healthy culture within the organization adapted to the nature of their risks [87]. In Indonesia, for example, the central bank regulations require the presence of an independent EA within the Indonesian IBs. The auditing of the financial statements is obligatorily entrusted to competent personnel. Furthermore, the Indonesian central bank is forcing IBs to appoint an accounting firm registered in its system of recognized independent auditors who must put the enhancement of the IBs' FP at the top of their priorities [88]. To reach this goal, by obligation, the EA should disclose much information in their report, such as equitable ownership of the board's members, compensation policy, board meetings, internal fraud, charity funds allocation, rooting symptoms, etc. Therefore, the EAs deal with inappropriate accounting treatment, failures in the risk management system and internal control, obstacles that prevent the creation of FP, fraud, and manipulation of charges and products, which add to operational management weaknesses.

From the history of previous research that has explored this theme, we estimated the following hypotheses:

Hypothesis 1:

Hypothesis 1-1: The EAC positively impacted the FP of conventional and Islamic banks.

Hypothesis 1-2: The EAC negatively impacted the FP of conventional and Islamic banks.

Hypothesis 1-3: The EAC positively impacted the CBs' FP and negatively affected the IBs' FP.

Hypothesis 1-4: The EAC negatively impacted the CBs' FP and positively affected the IBs' FP.

2.2 Control variables

We selected control variables that focus on the factors that best explain the measures of FP. In order to achieve our research objective, we chose four commonly used parameters that, we believe, can shed light on the FP of both conventional and Islamic banks. These variables consist of the age, size, type, and inflation of the banks.

2.2.1 Bank size

In a contractual environment, while the financial system remains stable, individuals who seek personal gains focus on taking advantage of agency relationships. The bank's size plays a crucial role in determining the nature of financial streams and informational content beyond its financial policy, regardless of the specific bank type. In situations that deviate from the norm, like conflicts of interest or information imbalances, opportunistic individuals in governance tend to focus on specific factors such as net result, FP, cash flow, dividends, etc., in order to maximize their profits. For instance, Bhushan [90] claimed that executives in big companies were pressured into deliberately making errors. The purpose of earnings management is either to deceive shareholders by presenting unreal and distorted results that reflect the achievement of predetermined objectives, or to underestimate actual results. In both cases, the directors have control over financial information. Skinner and Sloan [91] support this idea by stating that banks that do not accurately predict and analyze their FP based on rational accounting choices will face negative consequences in their results and profits. Consequently, they concluded that the size of a bank is negatively associated with its FP. Existing literature provides numerous studies illustrating the natural relationship between bank size and FP. **Table 1** demonstrates several diverse studies that utilized bank size in similar research.

Previous research	Context	Period	Impact class	Conclusions
Jemric and Vujcic [92]	Croatia	1995–2000	Negative impact/FP	There is a clear relationship between the size of banks and their FP measures. Smaller banks tend to be more efficient because they have a lower number of non-performing loans. On the other hand, larger banks only demonstrate effectiveness when it comes to generating profits through large-scale sales.
Salas and Saurina [93]	Spain	1985–1997	Positive impact/FP	FP measures, especially non-performing loans, were significantly influenced by the banks' size.
Jonathan and Nghia [94]	South Asian region.	1990–2003	Positive impact/FP	Big CBs are bigger than big IBs. Regardless of the type of bank, there is a clear and significant connection between bank size and effectiveness. In fact, larger banks have demonstrated higher levels of profitability compared to their smaller counterparts.
Shamsher et al. [95]	21 countries of the OIC[1]	1990–2005	Not significant impact/FP	The average cost scores of both large and small banks in each bank type are not significantly different. However, big banks have effectively managed their profits compared to their profitability. Additionally, there are no noticeable disparities in the profitability of banks with varying assets and cash flows. Although the costs of big IBs are slightly more efficient than those of big CBs, the benefits of large CBs are more effective.
Manthos, and Nikolaos [96]	EU countries[2]	1994–2005	Positive impact/FP	The banks' efficiency was enhanced by external factors and the investment environment, including the size of the banks.
Hussein and Charif [97]	UAE	1996–2005	Positive impact/FP	Large banks are more effective than small ones.
Alharthi [98]	MENA region	2005–2012	Positive impact/FP	Big CBs outperformed smaller CBs in terms of performance. Additionally, accepting loans brought benefits that enhanced their efficiency. Concerning IBs, effectiveness is higher in large IBs compared to their smaller counterparts.
Ulussever [27]	16 countries	2005–2011	Negative impact/FP	The size of banks has a significant and negative impact on the values of IBs, but it does not have a significant impact on the FP of CBs.

[1]OCI, Organization of the Islamic Conference.
[2]Bulgaria, Czech, Estonia, Hungary, Latvia, Lithuania, Poland, Romania, Slovakia, and Slovenia.

Table 1.
The contradictory findings of some studies regarding the association between FP and the size of banks.

According to the legitimacy theory, as a firm grows larger, it becomes more accountable legally, socially, and politically to both the law and its stakeholders [99]. Consequently, as financial operations become more complex, the flow of financial information expands and financial complexities increase [100]. Moreover, as big banks focus on serving their customers [101], their size negatively impacts their FP. In fact, as the bank grows, bureaucratic obstacles start to hinder its FP.

After exposing the necessary theoretical foundations, our hypotheses were formulated as follows:

Hypothesis 2:

Hypothesis 2-1: Bank size affects the FP of conventional and Islamic banks.

Hypothesis 2-2: Bank size ameliorates the FP of conventional and Islamic banks.

Hypothesis 2-3: Bank size affects the CBs' FP and ameliorates the IBs' FP.

Hypothesis 2-4: Bank size ameliorates the CBs' FP and affects the IBs' FP.

2.2.2 Bank age

Age was commonly used in literature as a variable for control, particularly in studies examining its influence on various bank parameters. Yet, the research results regarding the relationship between a bank's age and its FP were varied and inconclusive. This inconsistency motivated us to investigate and clarify the true correlation between these two variables. One prevailing belief is that regardless of the type of bank, the level of seniority can impact the quality of services and restrict the authority of auditors due to the presence of friendly connections and conflicts of interest. This hinders auditors from adhering to good governance standards and obstructs efforts to enhance FP and generate value. Another existing viewpoint elucidated the restricted growth of the Islamic banking sector, with studies revealing that the industry remains confined and primarily localized in certain regions due to various reasons. Additionally, the slow spread of the Islamic banking sector can be attributed to the limited support from the government and the low demand for investment, all while adhering to the Profit and Loss Sharing (PLS) technique [102]. Moreover, the lack of liquidity in the secondary markets has hindered the growth of the IBs, although there have been gradual improvements over time [103, 104]. The reason for the different conclusions of previous studies is explained by the fact that Islamic banks are concentrated in certain regions more than others, as stated by Samad [105]. However, it should be noted that the funding model has evolved over time, leading to the

Previous research	Context	Period	Impact class	Conclusions
Kraft and Tirtiroglu [106]	Croatia	1994–1995	Positive impact/ FP	Regardless of whether banks are owned by private institutions or the government, those that recently intervened in the monetary market showed less efficiency compared to older banks. Yet, the new banks have achieved higher profitability than their older counterparts.
Jemric and Vujcic [92]	Croatia	1995–2000	Negative impact/ FP	The effectiveness of the new banks is superior to that of the old banks. This can be attributed to the poor quality of the old banks' portfolio, which primarily comprised inefficient investments, ineffective products, and unprofitable services. Additionally, the old banks faced higher expenses in terms of personnel and assets than the new banks.

Previous research	Context	Period	Impact class	Conclusions
Shamsher et al. [95]	21 countries of the OIC[1]	1990–2005	Negative impact/ FP	The new banks were able to attain greater profitability compared to the old banks. The old banks gained valuable insights from their experiences, which helped them avoid various risks and safeguard themselves against fraudulent activities and manipulation. It is evident that the primary focus for the new CBs is to maximize their profits, due to the challenges they currently face. In order to achieve this goal, they need to entice customers who are currently with other banks. Therefore, their strategy involved offering higher interest rates to the customers of the old CBs, while bargaining elevated profit rates with the old IBs' customers.
Filip et al. [107]	Macedonia	2008–2011	Positive impact/ FP	The banks' outdated nature had a negative effect on capital requirements, suggesting that increasing capital would stimulate the provision of additional liquidity over time to compensate for the fall in profitability.

[1]OIC, Organization of the Islamic Conference

Table 2.
The contradictory findings of some studies regarding the association between FP and the age of banks.

expansion of the banking network to new regions. **Table 2** reveals the uncertainty regarding the impact of the banks' age on their FP.

In general, international banking networks view Islamic products as a chance for investment and profit, according to Siddiqui [108]. As time has passed, the Islamic banking model has evolved from a basic system of depositing funds to a more complex investment-focused system that emphasizes value creation. As the demand for Islamic products grew, shareholders were motivated to focus on creating flexible products that tailored to their customers' needs. In addition, they developed derivative products and innovative services that mirrored those offered by conventional banks, allowing them to tap into new markets [109].

From what we have already seen, the most suitable hypotheses are the following:

Hypothesis 3:

Hypothesis 3-1: Bank age ameliorates the FP of Islamic and conventional banks.

Hypothesis 3-2: Bank age affects the FP of Islamic and conventional banks.

Hypothesis 3-3: Bank age ameliorates the CBs' FP and affects the IBs' FP.

Hypothesis 3-4: Bank age affects the CBs' FP and ameliorates the IBs' FP.

2.2.3 Bank type

The objective of our study is to conduct a study that examines the different effects of flows on FP, and by distinguishing between different types of banks, we can consider the unique characteristics of each type. This segmentation of banks can be determined by factors such as the field, sector, or type of activity. The specific characteristics of different bank types are important in monitoring their economic and financial indicators, particularly governance. This interdependence between different criteria allows researchers to distinguish between the unique effects of conventional and Islamic banks, taking into account their inherent traits. However, specialization in

Previous research	Context	Period	Impact class	Conclusions
Cornett et al. [110]	16 countries[1]	1989–2004	Negative impact/FP	They showed that the FPs of private and public banks decreased greatly during the time of the study. In countries where public participation in bank capital is high, banks recorded low FP. In contrast, private banks generated higher profitability and efficiency than public banks.
Farazi et al. [111]	MENA region	2001–2008	Positive impact/FP	Most of the listed banks are private; however, the number of publicly listed banks is limited. In both cases, the listed banks generated higher interest margins compared to the unlisted banks because of their smaller balance sheets. The authors explained this statement by citing the application of very strict governance standards by the listed banks despite the exorbitant listing costs.

[1] *The countries highlighted are India, Bangladesh, China, Hong Kong, Malaysia, Indonesia, Macao, Nepal, Pakistan, South Korea, Philippines, Singapore, Thailand, Sri Lanka, Taiwan, and Vietnam.*

Table 3.
The contradictory findings of some studies regarding the association between FP and the type of banks.

banking allows for a narrower market and allows multiple competing banks to divide the available customer base in order to control the banks' overall FP (**Table 3**).

Based on the previous researches, the possible hypotheses are:

Hypothesis 4:

Hypothesis 4-1: Bank type affects the FP of conventional and Islamic banks.

Hypothesis 4-2: Bank type ameliorates the FP of conventional and Islamic banks.

Hypothesis 4-3: Bank type affects the CBs' FP and ameliorates the IBs' FP.

Hypothesis 4-4: Bank type ameliorates the CBs' FP and affects the IBs' FP.

2.2.4 Country inflation

The finance literature extensively examined the effect of inflation on the FP of CBs. However, this aspect was not widely covered in Islamic finance literature. Despite operating under a specific regime, some research indicates that Islamic banks may not be affected by inflation's impact on their FP. Additionally, the finance literature observed that IBs are not affected by the interplay of inflation, interest rates, and traditional banks' financial policies. The connection between inflation and typical bank fees is not substantial as IBs do not engage in interest-based practices. In the context of inflation, IBs maintain stability and experience an increase in their return rate [112].

Prior studies found a positive correlation between inflation and banks' FP, regardless of the type of bank. However, recent research showed that changes in inflation have no impact on the profitability of banks, specifically the income costs of both CBs and IBs [113, 114]. On the other hand, other recent studies by Bashir [115], Bennaceur and Omran [100], and Saeed [116] demonstrated that inflation increases debt costs and decreases the value of banks. **Table 4** highlights selected previous research that investigated the impact of inflation on banks' FP.

The exposed literature leads us to pose the following hypotheses:

Hypothesis 5:

Hypothesis 5-1: Country inflation affects the FP of Islamic and conventional banks.

Previous research	Context	Period	Impact class	Conclusions
Bennaceur and Omran [100]	Middle East and North Africa countries	1989–2005	Negative impact on the FP	The decrease in deposits indicated the observed growth, suggesting that banks suffered the full burden of inflation. If banks fail to foresee inflation, they will have difficulty controlling the adjustment of their interest rates, resulting in faster growth of management fees compared to income. Consequently, inflation will have a detrimental impact on banks' FP policies.
Fahad [113]	Bangladesh	2008–2012	Negative impact on the FP	Inflation has a significant negative impact on IBs' FP, despite their prohibition of interest in their transactions and exchange of goods and services.
Rashwan and Ehab [117]	12 countries[1]	2009–2014	Not significant impact/FP	The increase in inflation had a significant impact on the net interest margin and non-interest costs for banks. When inflation rates rise, banks are able to reduce their expenses not related to interest and increase their net interest margin. As a result, both conventional and Islamic banking models experienced a significant improvement in their operating income thanks to inflation.
Rashwan and Ehab [117]	12 countries	2009–2014	Positive impact on the FP	The banks in the sample have absorbed the entire burden of inflation, which can be seen through the decrease in deposit rates. Even though inflation is not foreseen, the delay in adjustment led to an increase in spending that outpaced income. Consequently, inflation had detrimental effects on the efficiency and profitability of the banks.

[1]Egypt, Pakistan, Bangladesh, Saudi Arabia, Kuwait, Qatar, Iraq, United Arab Emirates, Sudan, Turkey, Bahrain, and Jordan.

Table 4.
The contradictory findings of some studies regarding the association between FP and inflation.

Hypothesis 5-2: Country inflation ameliorates the FP of Islamic and conventional banks.
Hypothesis 5-3: Country inflation affects the CBs' FP and ameliorates the IBs' FP.
Hypothesis 5-4: Country inflation ameliorates the CBs' FP and affects the IBs' FP.

3. Methodological aspects

Given the lack of an exhaustive and up-to-date database that integrates all conventional and Islamic banks' information worldwide and their FP evolution, the generalization of the impacts resulting from the comparative results remains a challenge. Moreover, there are no big data sets that contain BIG4s and non-BIG4s EA characteristics worldwide, nor is there an exhaustive list of their clients. Furthermore, the correlation between the EAC and the banks' FP is generally subject to regional and behavioral rules with no constant or compliant impacts since they are dependent on law systems that differ from one country to another as well as people's behaviors that differ from one person/stakeholder to another. Because of the scientific gap between the theoretical cumulation and the unfounded exceptions to the empirical reality, maximizing the bank's FP means the selection of a good EAC and the selection of a good bank type based on a good EAC in the case of comparative studies. This remains an open debate for arbitration. That is why we insisted on using a demonstrative approach. First, we present the data collection. Next, we describe the search variables. Finally, we show the models to be estimated.

3.1 Data collection

From two financial institutions populations (3822 conventional financial institutions and 794 Islamic financial institutions), we chose two samples of banks that are located in 56 countries[1] whose banking systems integrate conventional as well as Islamic banks during the period (2010–2022). Based on qualitative and quantitative filtration criteria, we excluded specific, mutated, non-banking institutions and banks for which data is not available and added non-purely conventional or Islamic banks. Afterward, we filtered the remaining banks for each type until each CB had its Islamic counterpart in the same country. Therefore, we obtained two smaller sample sizes than those of the original populations. The cited conditions led us to eliminate 3642 conventional financial institutions and 514 Islamic financial institutions to end up with two equal samples, made up of 180 banks each.

3.2 Variables to be tested

3.2.1 Endogenous variables

To explain FP, we used four measures. **Table 5** displays the chosen ratios as well as their symbols.

FP measurement	Measurement	IBs' rating	CBs' rating
Profitability ratio	Marginal Profit/Total Revenues Onuonga [118]; Salem et al. [85]	LnMPTRi	LnMPTRc
Efficiency ratio	Operating result/Average Total Assets Osama et al. [119]; Haddad et al. [120]	NLTAi	NLTAc
Liquidity ratio	Net Loans/Total Assets Lartey et al. [121]; Salem et al. [85]	ORATAi	ORATAc
Solvency ratio	Total Loans/Total Deposits Tandelilin et al. [122]; Haddad et al. [123]	LnTLTDi	LnTLTDc

Table 5.
Endogenous variables details.

[1] Saudi Arabia (9/9), Pakistan (8/8), Iran (8/8), Malaysia (7/7), Afghanistan (6/6), Bahrain (6/6), Qatar (6/6), Kuwait (6/6), United Kingdom (5/5), United Arab Emirates (5/5),Sudan (5/5), Yemen (5/5), Turkey (5/5), Bahamas (4/4), Jordan (4/4), Egypt (4/4), Singapore (4/4), Morocco (4/4), Iraq (4/4), Switzerland (4/4), Bangladesh (4/4), Indonesia (4/4), Kazakhstan (3/3), Algeria (3/3), Tajikistan (3/3),Germany (3/3), Brunei Darussalam (3/3), Senegal (3/3), Philippines (3/3), Ireland (3/3), Oman (3/3), USA (2/2), France (2/2), Mauritania (2/2), Libya (2/2), India (2/2), Tunisia (2/2), Luxembourg (2/2), Guinea (2/2), Nigeria (2/2), Lebanon (2/2), Australia (2/2), Sri Lanka (1/1), South Africa (1/1), Russia (1/1), Niger (171), Canada (1/1), Mali (1/1), Thailand (1/1), Djibouti (1/1), Gambia (1/1), Denmark (1/1), Albania (1/1), Italy (1/1), Kenya (1/1), and Somalia (1/1).

3.2.2 Exogenous variable

EAC was symbolized by the EA size. With reference to the previous studies, the main independent variable is described in **Table 6** as follows:

EAC measurement	IBs' rating	CBs' rating
Binary variable: 1: If the conventional/Islamic bank assigned one of the BIG4 firms as EAC 0: if not Houqe et al. [79]; Nafli [1]; Jiang et al. [80]; Salem et al. [85]	EAC performed by IB (EACi)	EAC performed by CB (EACc)

Table 6.
Explanatory variable details.

3.2.3 Control variables

Referring to the literature, the most widely used control variables that may correlate with the banks' FP are bank type, bank age, bank size, and inflation. **Table 7** summarizes the details of the variables' list.

Control variable	Measurement	IBs' rating	CBs' rating
Bank size	Logarithm of the total assets of conventional/Islamic bank Rashid and Jabeen [124]; Salem et al. [85]	LnBSizei	LnBSizec
Bank age	Age of the conventional/Islamic bank from the start date Jemric and Vujcic [92]; Filip et al. [107]	LnBAgei	LnBAgec
Bank type	This variable can take 3 forms: 1. if the bank is commercial 2. if the bank is of investment 3. if the bank is universal Kim and Rasiah [125]; Charles et al. [126]	BTypei	BTypec
Country inflation	The average of annual inflation rate of all countries by sample Fisseha [127]; Rashwan and Ehab [117]	LnCInflationi	LnCInflationc

Table 7.
Control variables details.

3.3 Models to be estimated

Before moving on to estimation, we present our formal models, one list is specific to CBs and the other relates to IBs. As it appeared in **Table 8**, we ordered the proposed models as follows.

Bank type Association type	IBs' models	CBs' models
Association between profitability and EAC	LnMPTRiit = β0 + β1EACiit + β2BTypeiit + β3LnBAgeiit + β4LnBSizeiit + β5LnCInflationiit + εit	LnMPTRcit = α0 + α1EACcit + α2BTypecit + α3LnBAgecit + α4LnBSizecit + α5LnCInflationcit + εit
Association between efficiency and EAC	NLTAiit = β0 + β1EACiit + β2BTypeiit + β3LnBAgeiit + β4LnBSizeiit + β5LnCInflationiit + εit	NLTAcit = α0 + α1EACcit + α2BTypecit + α3LnBAgecit + α4LnBSizecit + α5LnCInflationcit + εit
Association between liquidity and EAC	ORATAiit = β0 + β1EACiit + β2BTypeiit + β3LnBAgeiit + β4LnBSizeiit + β5LnCInflationiit + εit	ORATAcit = α0 + α1EACcit + α2BTypecit + α3LnBAgecit + α4LnBSizecit + α5LnCInflationcit + εit
Association between solvency and EAC	LnTLTDiit = β0 + β1EACiit + β2BTypeiit + β3LnBAgeiit + β4LnBSizeiit + β5LnCInflationiit + εit	LnTLTDcit = α0 + α1EACcit + α2BTypecit + α3LnBAgecit + α4LnBSizecit + α5LnCInflationcit + εit

Table 8.
The equivalent models to be estimated.

4. Analysis of the comparative impacts between conventional and Islamic banks

4.1 Individual impacts analysis

To bridge the problem of evaluation and comparison between the Islamic and conventional FP levels via the EAC effect, it is necessary to first solve the comparison ambiguity of individual effects on each FP measure to see if the EAC individual effects are the same or different among FP measures. Since EAC can have a positive impact or negatively affect the banks' FP, it all depends on the bank type and their financial situation. First, we checked each model's EAC effects significance. Second, we established a comparative study of the impacts resulting from similar models. Finally, we compared the predicted signs with the actual signs. In what follows, **Tables 15-22** in the appendices include the findings of equivalent regressions for two bank types.

Returning to the list of tables in the indexes, we noticed that for each bank type, the estimates gave different individual coefficients that varied from one model to another according to the sign and significance of each FP measure. This implies that the individual effects are heterogeneous. In addition, with regard to the similar separate impacts of CBs and IBs on the same FP measures, the same models also recorded variable impacts according to sign and significance. Therefore, we cannot rely on these preliminary results to make a definitive comparative decision. We must advance the decision rule even further by bringing the divergent signs together. The solution requires the grouping of the separate EAC impacts given by a similar modeling technique.

4.2 Combined impacts analysis

To avoid the detailed EAC ambiguity effects on the FP of each bank type, we followed a more developed analysis process. We started by grouping the individual EAC impacts and each control variable on each FP measure. Then, we compared the close effects of the independent variable in each IB model with the similar close effects of the independent variable in each CB model.

4.2.1 Differential analysis between the impacts of the EAC on the FP of conventional and Islamic banks

According to **Table 9**, choosing a BIG4 auditor to verify and certify the CBs' financial statements presented a brake force that restricted their FP. This effect reflects the lack of professionalism, independence, or qualifications of the regional BIG4s' executive managers, accountants, or auditors. Although the presence of experts favorably preoccupied the CBs' profitability, the effect of the designation of a BIG4 on other CBs' FP indicators showed the opposite. This explains why, even if the EA is qualified and stimulates the CBs' profitability, there are other stronger internal factors that fill in the other measures. This scenario casts doubt on the reasons for the creation of wealth and profits as well as the dividend destination. But, above all, it shows that the BIG4 weakened and reduced the CBs' liquidity. CBs' managers and internal auditors broke down BIG4 choices and sometimes blocked their work, and vice versa. Instead of becoming a transparency certificate for economic agents and insurance of the accounting information's quality for financial statements' users, it turned out that the BIG4 appointment resulted in the demotivation of staff and the destruction of all purification initiatives of the big CBs' accounting documents. In our case, the BIG4 choice showed that the BIG4 negatively fulfilled almost all the FP measures except for profitability. This result explains why BIG4s' auditors hide the bad realities of their audited CBs by following a strong counseling approach. Hence, this leads us to confirm that in our conventional sample, the BIG4s auditors allowed the publication of the CBs' reports without reservations. However, in most selected countries, listed CBs have to publish their audited annual reports by internationally renowned and reputable BIG4s. However, choosing the big names does not mean maintaining audit quality and providing consistent information that reflects the CBs' reality. Along with the lack of effectiveness and solvency, CBs' commercial reputation does not provide assurance for their depositories and investors. Also, the lack of transparency in liquidity management does not protect owners' rights. The harmony between the bank's size and the auditors' size and independence is only a cover that hides several financial difficulties, many conflicting relationships, and many opportunistic behaviors between the CBs' managers. Consequently, over time, the shareholders will lose their control powers over their holdings in the bank capital to new share and bond buyers through an adverse selection transfer.

Contrary to what happened in the CBs, the certification of the IBs' financial statements by an independent, well-known, and international BIG4 auditor marked a positive effect on their FP. BIG4s' choice should normally draw the attention of those in charge to the sources of weaknesses in IBs' FP, account for the reasons for the bad IBs' financial situation, and solve the internal networks of conflicts of interest or conscious manipulations. This act generated a deposit for the various stakeholders to

Variables	LnMPTRc/ LnMPTRi	NLTAc/ NLTAi	ORATAc/ ORATAi	LnTLTDc/ LnTLTDi	Cumulative effect	Decision
EACc	+*	—	-*	-*	—	H1-1 rejected, H1-2 rejected, H1-3 rejected, H1-4 accepted
EACi	+*	-*	+*	—	+	

Table 9.
Summary of the close effects of the EAC on the FP of conventional and Islamic banks.

maintain compliance with Charia standards and to audit listed IBs. In fact, the large and listed IBs audited by BIG4s, including specialists in Fikh Al-Mouamalat and Islamic Charia, reflected the credibility and good quality of their financial statements in their users' eyes, especially the shareholders and donors. From the recorded results, we drew two conclusions. First, we stressed the basic IBs' EAC principles and the Islamic model's characteristics on the EAQ and the FP. Second, the total EAC impact on the IBs' FP is the combination of the individual EAC impacts on several IBs' factors. This does not happen haphazardly but is caused by the ethical culture advantage, which is inspired by Islamic Charia standards. IBs' Islamic culture played a fundamental and significant role in improving the efficiency of the external audit process. This demonstrated that in IBs, the accounting and financial information verified by a BIG4 auditor is much more accredited and credible than that published by local or smaller auditors. Consequently, the EAC is a principal tool for continuous assessment of the IBs' governance systems, which promote the internal control process, the detection of specific opportunistic behavior, and the management of financial, operational, liquidity, and profitability risks.

4.2.2 Differential analysis between the impacts of control variables on the FP of conventional and Islamic banks

To understand the difference between the effects of control variables on the FP for each bank type, we also regrouped the individual effects of each bank type on the FP measures. The aim of this step is to obtain purely combined effects for each bank model. Then, we moved on to the total comparative analysis between the combined EAC effects on all conventional and Islamic FP measures and drew the necessary conclusions.

4.2.2.1 Bank size

According to **Table 10**, the close effect of the CBs' size weakened their FPs and, more precisely, their efficiency and liquidity. This implies that for CBs that become exceptionally large, their size negatively affects their FP because of the bureaucracy, the transactions' complexity, and the huge number of branches. This result means that despite their enormous sizes, the CBs were limited in their ability to produce, manage, or market these ranges of services through their multiple subsidiaries. Moreover, this indicates that the FP speed and the scale of transformation of the asset values at these banks are very slow and insufficient to create growth. Our CBs' sample generally used a poor policy of managing their product and service lines and a poor orientation to launch new competitive products, to practice the scale sale commercial policy, or to order their business priorities. Indeed, our results showed that the CBs developed in a badly controlled way and exceeded their threshold sizes. Therefore, any extension beyond the optimal size or that exceeds the possible localization limit on the financial market has the opposite

Variables	**LnMPTRc/ LnMPTRi**	**NLTAc/ NLTAi**	**ORATAc/ ORATAi**	**LnTLTDc/ LnTLTDi**	**Cumulative effect**	**Decision**
LnBSizec	—	–*	–*	+*	—	H2-1 rejected, H2-2 accepted, H2-3 rejected, H2-4 rejected
LnBSizei	–*	+*	+*	+*	+	

Table 10.
Summary of the close effects of the bank size on the FP of conventional and Islamic banks.

consequences. There are other reasons that may be at the origin of the obtained results, given the expansion of large CBs' branches or the presence of financial corruption centers within large CBs' groups. Among these, we cite the poor control of the financial information process, the management of accounting results, the misuse of resources, the handling of expenses, revenues and provisions, and uncontrollable governance structures. All these reasons caused the explicit and implicit dwindling of the CBs' FP.

On the contrary, **Table 10** gives an inverse combined effect. Indeed, the increase in IBs' size was reached according to income, profits, assets, and employees; all these are important to increase their efficiency, liquidity, and solvency, despite the strong competition that negatively weighs on their profitability. Large IBs have good cost management policies and abilities. Thus, effective big sales management and efficient big asset management automatically generate excess liquidity. Besides, large IBs can produce cheaper goods than small CBs because they can spread their fixed costs over a greater number of services and achieved more learning and cumulative experience. Also, since we worked on a large IBs' sample, their size encouraged them to raise their assets and their capital base, as this would re-enhance their efficiency after a financial crisis period. Moreover, as Mule et al. [128] revealed, a unit change in firm size in terms of return on equity leads to a rise in its FP. Even more, the positive association between IBs' size and FP stems from the IBs that implemented greater differentiation and a variety of services compared to their conventional counterparts. The IBs have succeeded in relaunching specialization strategies that are likely to be concurrently provided to their customers. Therefore, this is why the IBs' size generated a strengthening effect on efficiency, liquidity, and solvency at a time when the IBs' size negatively influenced their profitability.

4.2.2.2 Bank age

Referring to **Table 11**, the CBs' age significantly improved all their FP measures. As a result, the longer the CBs were created and advanced in time, the more efficient they became. In our case, the CBs' experience offered them the ability not only to resist variations in FP parameters but also to acquire the necessary skills to avoid risky events and serious financial transactions that might impact their FP. Besides, seniority enabled the CBs to plan a harmonious internal audit scheme for their FP, leaving the fewest gaps between the different measures. Older banks went through difficult situations and learned many lessons that seriously affected their FP in the past, especially during the financial crises periods. Thus, aged CBs prepared advance planning and risk management programs for all their FP measures. Hence, they estimate the evolution of each FP measure so as to correct, improve, and maximize it daily. During the period of our study, CBs showed that they gained immunity through seniority, so they are vaccinated against financial shocks. They also amended the sudden factors that might act negatively on FP and benefited from opportunities to maximize their profitability, efficiency, liquidity, and solvency. In addition, the older CBs enjoy a solid reputation that

Variables	LnMPTRc/ LnMPTRi	NLTAc/ NLTAi	ORATAc/ ORATAi	LnTLTDc/ LnTLTDi	Cumulative effect	Decision
LnBAgec	+*	+*	+*	+*	+	H3-1 accepted, H3-2 rejected, H3-3 rejected, H3-4 rejected
LnBAgei	+*	+*	−*	+*	+	

Table 11.
Summary of the close effects of the bank age on the FP of conventional and Islamic banks.

could help them mobilize their resources to implement appropriate business strategies that allow them to guarantee their sustainability and their FP continuity.

The same table showed that the combined effect of the IBs' age recorded a driving and significant influence on their profitability, efficiency, and solvency. However, our sample includes some recent IBs, so their combined impact on the IBs' FP is positive. The IBs' experiences, measured by the bank's age, resulted in the last stage in the accumulation of profitability, efficiency, and solvency. However, the individual negative impact on the IBs' liquidity is accounted for by the mismanagement and under exploitation of liquidity reserves. Also, the older the IBs, the more they can develop a reputation in the credit market with other banks, the more they control their expenses, and the more gradually they shrink the information asymmetry with borrowers in the event of their existence through the guidance policy that builds on the reputation of their credit history. As a result, new IBs are riskier than old ones. The latter, being older, become more famous and well-known to lenders, and are therefore more capable of developing longer relationships and making the most profitable, efficient, and solvent investment choices that can create more wealth for the IBs. Furthermore, when partners request funding for investments, the old IBs' risks are easier and faster to assess by stakeholders than the evaluation of recent IBs' risks.

4.2.2.3 Bank type

Referring to **Table 12**, the CBs' segmentation by specialization into three types weakens their FPs. More precisely, with reference to the most commonly used classification and segmentation into commercial banks, investment banks, and universal banks, CBs' profitability, efficiencies, and solvency are depleted. The economic phenomenon we are talking about indicates that the CBs' customers will be divided into several divisions of the same sector. This policy does not meet the forecast axes; it contradicts the planning and limits the choices, opportunities, and fields of activities facing the banks' decision-makers. This orientation also costs the CBs extra expenses that make them lose money due to competition. This constraint type causes the creation of many nodes with financial problems. Therefore, the strong rivalry in the market for goods and services creates financial difficulties, which consequently lead to a decrease in CBs' FP. If we adopt the cost function as the first criterion to evaluate CBs, we retain the intermediation approach, where bank products are loans, direct and indirect commissions, and other income-generating assets. Our findings reveal that the presence of competition between CBs reduces both their profitability and efficiency levels, which results in a drop in FP as a whole.

Similarly, **Table 12** shows that the IBs' specialization within the same sector causes a drop in their FP. But unlike CBs, in this case, the IBs focus on specific customer niches in particular had a negative impact on their liquidity and, to a lower degree, their profitability and efficiency due to the reduction in the scope of banks' practice

Variables	LnMPTRc/ LnMPTRi	NLTAc/ NLTAi	ORATAc/ ORATAi	LnTLTDc/ LnTLTDi	Cumulative effect	Decision
BTypec	–*	–*	—	–*	—	H4-1 accepted, H4-2 rejected, H4-3 rejected, H4-4 rejected
BTypei	—	—	–*	+*	—	

Table 12.
Summary of the close effects of the bank type on the FP of conventional and Islamic banks.

within the same sub-sector. The inadmissible impact is explained by several reasons, such as sharing the same commercial or investment activity between several Islamic competitors, who themselves compete with other conventional competitors in the financial market and the capital market. This confirms that IBs operate under financial stress, which leads to their isolation and suffering with regard to financial flows. Besides, sharing the IBs' customers among several specialists makes it possible to represent a problem in marketing their products insofar as the customers' number is always limited. IBs' clients are retained by religious convictions and are not overly motivated by financial interests, as in the instance of CBs. Furthermore, sectoral specialization is oriented towards specific activities that require a high development cost and a diversification of their services to face their competitors' pressures and gain an advantage over them. Attracting more customers and maximizing FP, specifically profitability and liquidity, always remains a limited probability since the chosen commercial policy is limited to a few products. Moreover, IBs suffer from a shortage of product and service diversity, which can attract more customers and increase their business margins. Indeed, IBs retain the Islamic finance principle; they are not allowed to earn additional products through the mobilization of additional sources. This attitude is the result of operational failure and poor management efficiency, which are seriously reflected in their profitability and, more precisely, in their liquidity.

4.2.2.4 Country inflation

Referring to **Table 13**, about the combined effect of inflation on the CBs' FP, we pointed out that all FP measures suffered a significant decline. As presented in **Table 14**, since the average inflation over the entire period was not stable, it dwindled between several peaks where positive inflation (9.52% in 2012, 8.56% in 2015, 7.09% in 2017, 7.35% in 2018, 8.46% in 2019, 9.48% in 2021, and 9.96% in 2022) was followed by deflation, and so on (7.26% in 2011, 8.12% in 2013, 6.73% in 2014, 6.22% in 2016, and 7.26% in 2020). However, following the Subprime crisis, we noticed two phenomena: a recessionary shock that resulted in a lasting opening of the output gap because of the unstable national inflation rates; followed by deflationary rates that led the CBs to seek historical inflation levels. The quick inflation variation in all the countries explained that whatever the region, the CBs' activities had unique consequences and that the conventional banking system is sensitive to inflation. When inflation increases, resource deposits and loan demand fall. Consequently, the CBs' benefits undergo a reduction, which is reflected in their efficiency and liquidity and, in the end, in their solvency. Moreover, since the deflation periods are limited, the inflation return filled new investments given the rise in commodity prices and investment costs (2012, 2015, 2017, 2019, 2021, and 2022). Our results underline the sharp deterioration of CBs' FP and justify the old conventional products' weaknesses.

Variables	LnMPTRc/ LnMPTRi	NLTAc/ NLTAi	ORATAc/ ORATAi	LnTLTDc/ LnTLTDi	Cumulative effect	Decision
LnCInflationc	−*	+*	−*	−*	—	H5-1 accepted, H5-2 rejected, H5-3 rejected, H5-4 rejected
LnCInflationi	−*	+*	−*	−*	—	

Table 13.
Summary of the close effects of inflation on the FP of conventional and Islamic banks.

Year	**2010**	**2011**	**2012**	**2013**	**2014**	**2015**	**2016**	**2017**	**2018**	**2019**	**2020**	**2021**	**2022**
Average inflation rate	8.41%	7.26%	9.52%	8.12%	6.73%	8.56%	6.22%	7.09%	7.35%	8.46%	7.26%	9.48%	9.96%

Source: World Bank.

Table 14.
Evolution of the average inflation rate.

Therefore, relying on new unconventional instruments as a supplement to the practice of monetary policy to create new revenues that are primarily focused on price stability can be an efficient solution to maintaining FP continuity. As such, the obligation to reduce large variations in the interest rate is clear. Taking the broad view that prevailed before and following the Subprime crisis, inflation was the most important factor that triggered a huge rise in interest rates. In an unstable economic framework with significant financial shocks, it was necessary to plan FP growth according to inflation rates on relatively stable trajectories using the functions that would allow CBs to minimize the variances of inflation and maximize their FP.

Returning to **Table 14**, despite the price deflation between 2010 and 2011, this variable had an unfavorable effect on the IBs' FP. Like CBs, between 2010 and 2022, the obtained combined effect implies that the rise in inflation froze all measures of IBs' FP due to the sharp rise in prices by designing the investment costs, especially in 2012, 2015, 2017, 2019, 2021, and 2022. Indeed, we worked over a stable economic decade without a crisis, whereas inflation remains a variable that evolves dependently on the prices' variation on the markets of goods and services. Given the average rates, the period immediately after the Subprime financial crisis showed specific characteristics similar to those of the second half. This difference reflected rational and significant consequences in this situation. Therefore, we advocated the hypothesis of the transfer of difficulties between the financial market and other market types. Since Islamic finance forbids the practice of all kinds of interest, usury, and Riba, the IBs' activities are essentially based either on techniques practicing potential investment based on the principle of sharing of products and losses, such as Mucharaka and Mudaraba, or on the exchange of real products, such as Murabaha and Ijara. Anyway, the impact of inflation on these financial instruments had no great influence on their historical values. However, inflation has an indirect effect on the IBs' FP. Optimal arbitrage is now more in favor of IBs activity volume. Inflation results in a swelling of the value of exchangeable products and raw materials necessary for investments. In other words, it slows down the initiative and the speed of investment, which significantly deteriorates the IBs' profitability and liquidity and creates subsequent efficiency and solvency problems. Finally, the main distinction in the IBs' FP measures is accounted for by the higher activity variance, an original phenomenon of the great moderation in prices that happened in 2012, 2015, 2017, 2018, 2019, 2021, and 2022. This inflationary rise created volatility and instability in all IBs' FP indicators.

5. Conclusion

From the empirical results, we concluded that the evaluation of the breach in BIG4 legitimacy as well as its impacts on the Islamic and conventional banks' FP should be performed by the most appropriate chartered accountants. The latter have the right to do so given their expertise in the domain of bank financial statements' certification, especially by CBs' stakeholders and, to a lower degree, by IBs' investors. Therefore, the lack of substantial impacts generated by the EAC quality on some CBs' FP measures means that the added value of BIG4 is low or nil. In other words, no difference is found between choosing a BIG4 or a non-BIG4. Consequently, the BIG4s lost the reason for their advantage within the CBs. This justifies two conclusions. First, most of the CBs' EAC are not efficient. Second, since they represent an external governance mechanism, the BIG4 fail to effectively fulfill their obligations according to the general norms. This is what explains and improves their inability to respect good audit standards and to support CBs' liquidity, efficiency, and even solvency. The main question at this level is whether to put at stake the validity of the reports surrounding the audit function, the CBs' transparency, and the credibility of the selected BIG4. But this does not prevent the fact that IBs' EAC weakness also deeply affects a part of their efficiency. Therefore, what is available is that the banking governance systems, specifically CBs, suffered mainly from systematic failures that focused for a long time on improving the perceived EAQ independently of the actual quality [129].

Indeed, because of the managers' preferences and the owners' expectations rather than the assessment of the discussed financial situation, which is especially determined by the FP measures, the EAC will be taken subjectively. In general, these shortcomings in the EA impact can be linked to the recording of accounting and financial data, the weaknesses of the banks' governance structure, the shortage of EA behavior recognition, and the lack of exhaustive knowledge of the BIG4 accountants. This finding is precisely due to the false BIG4 reputation.

Based on the above, the present paper represents a better understanding of the difference between the weight of the EAC within the CBs and the weight of the EAC within the IBs. We discovered that the EAC can lead not only to the EAQ which constitutes a tool for stimulating banks' FP, but can also be a filling factor for banks' FP. In a paradigm of contractual efficiency, this situation leads us to investigate the audit process at the heart of conflicts of interest and agency problems that characterize the banks' governance in general and the CBs' governance in particular and which come from the likelihood that the EAs have more or less recourse to external funding sources. Thus, a qualified EAC should logically meet a demand for handling agency conflicts intended to minimize contractual costs and maintain a balanced governance system. Consequently, our reflection will make it possible to be precisely located at the heart of the audit process to resolve the financial issues and rectify the internal and external weaknesses that may affect the EAC at the beginning and at the end of their regular control process.

EAC for IBs and specifically for CBs is not only a way to ensure management and accounting documents but also provides the usual EA tools to continuously improve collective FP, ameliorate security, and develop control efficiency [130, 131]. Moreover, the EAC for conventional or Islamic banks is not identical. In some countries, the banks applied international accounting and auditing standards; in another category of countries, they adopted local standards; and in some other countries, they implemented sector-specific standards. For these reasons, international banks should try to develop a contemporary system that helps them make a good EAC for banks and that eludes them from similar scenarios. There are many alternatives based on internal control and the auditor's reputation, but we aim to establish an original system based on EAC progress and FP planning. Implementing a new and original approach to EAC must be done by adopting a comprehensive, clear, and detailed evaluation vision of the conventional and Islamic banks' FP. Kuhn [132] stated that scientific revolutions are considered non-cumulative development episodes because an older and incompatible paradigm can be replaced as a whole or in part by a new paradigm. Our contribution in this area is the proposal of a new governance approach called "Dynamic EAC By Objective"; the objective, in our case, is the amelioration of conventional/Islamic banks' FP. This system can be defined as a series of dynamic audit procedures organized in a parallel structure to classical organizational bank control. However, the limitation of our study is that our results might be changed in future research if the latter uses other ratios or another couple of banks.

A. Appendices

LnMPTRtc	Coefficient	Std. Err.	Z	P > |z|	[95% Conf. Interval]		Decision
AuditQualitytc	0.4424734	0.0820987	5.39	0.000***	0.2815628	0.603384	H1 accepted
LnBankSizetc	−0.0624853	0.0847836	−0.74	0.461	−0.228658	0.1036874	H4 rejected
LnBankAgetc	0.3078381	0.0418379	7.36	0.000***	0.2258374	0.3898389	H3 accepted
BankTypetc	−0.070767	0.0301271	−2.35	0.019**	−0.1298151	−0.0117189	H2 accepted
LnInflationtc	−0.2450715	0.0280158	−8.75	0.000***	−0.2999816	−0.1901615	H5 accepted
Constant	2.198415	0.3147353	6.98	0.000	1.581545	2.815285	—

** *Correlation is significant at the 5%.*
*** *Correlation is significant at the 1%.*

Table 15.
Results of the impacts of EAC on the CBs' profitability.

LnMPTRti	Coefficient	Std. Err.	Z	P > |z|	[95% Conf. Interval]		Decision
AuditQualityti	0.6347444	0.0829376	7.65	0.000***	0.4721897	0.797299	H1 accepted
LnBankSizeti	−0.9601464	0.1532855	−6.26	0.000***	−1.26058	−.6597124	H4 accepted
LnBankAgeti	0.2752722	0.039679	6.94	0.000***	0.1975028	0.3530416	H3 accepted
BankTypeti	−0.0313351	0.0400925	−0.78	0.434	−0.1099149	0.0472448	H2 rejected
LnIInflationti	−0.3242184	0.0310019	−10.46	0.000***	−0.384981	−0.2634557	H5 accepted
Constant	3.998581	0.355863	11.24	0.000	3.301102	4.696059	—

*** *Correlation is significant at the 1%.*

Table 16.
Results of the impacts of EAC on the IBs' profitability.

NLTAtc	Coefficient	Std. Err.	Z	P > |z|	[95% Conf. Interval]		Decision
AuditQualitytc	−0.036531	0.0472186	−0.77	0.439	−0.1290777	0.0560157	H1 rejected
LnBankSizetc	−0.8258304	0.0634519	−13.02	0.000***	−0.9501938	−0.701467	H4 accepted
LnBankAgetc	0.3171886	0.0384162	8.26	0.000***	0.2418943	0.392483	H3 accepted
BankTypetc	−0.2333826	0.0478806	−4.87	0.000***	−0.3272268	−0.1395384	H2 accepted
LnInflationtc	0.2884913	0.0250897	11.50	0.000***	0.2393164	0.3376662	H5 rejected
Constant	−3.082779	0.1823059	−16.91	0.000	−3.440092	−2.725467	—

*** *Correlation is significant at the 1%.*

Table 17.
Results of the impacts of EAC on the CBs' efficiency.

NLTAti	Coefficient	Std. Err.	Z	P > |z|	[95% Conf. Interval]		Decision
AuditQualityti	−0.0031633	0.0011864	−2.67	0.008***	−0.0054887	−0.0008379	H1 rejected
LnBankSizeti	0.0131012	0.0035907	3.65	0.000***	0.0060635	0.0201388	H4 rejected
LnBankAgeti	0.0097473	0.0006949	14.03	0.000***	0.0083854	0.0111092	H3 accepted
BankTypeti	−0.0005261	0.0007872	−0.67	0.504	−0.002069	0.0010169	H2 rejected
LnInflationti	0.0024923	0.0005908	4.22	0.000***	0.0013343	0.0036503	H5 rejected
Constant	−0.0433005	0.0075409	−5.74	0.000	−0.0580803	−0.0285207	—

******Correlation is significant at the 1%.***

Table 18.
Results of the impacts of EAC on the IBs' efficiency.

ORATAtc	Coefficient	Std. Err.	Z	P > |z|	[95% Conf. Interval]		Decision
AuditQualitytc	0.0247045	0.016348	1.51	0.02**	−0.007337	0.056746	H1 accepted
LnBankSizetc	−0.0531223	0.0195569	−2.72	0.007***	−0.0914531	−0.0147915	H4 accepted
LnBankAgetc	0.0279316	0.008736	3.20	0.001***	0.0108093	0.0450539	H3 accepted
BankTypetc	−0.0145894	0.009461	−1.54	0.123	−0.0331327	0.0039538	H2 rejected
LnInflationtc	−0.0712712	0.007126	−10.00	0.000***	−0.0852379	−0.0573046	H5 accepted
Constant	0.7539894	0.0597384	12.62	0.000	0.6369042	0.8710746	—

***Correlation is significant at the 5%.*
****Correlation is significant at the 1%.*

Table 19.
Results of the impacts of EAC on the CBs' liquidity.

ORATAti	Coefficient	Std. Err.	Z	P > |z|	[95% Conf. Interval]		Decision
AuditQualityti	0.0148074	0.0119677	1.24	0.086*	−0.0086489	0.0382637	H1 accepted
LnBankSizeti	0.2938356	0.025406	11.57	0.000***	0.2440408	0.3436305	H4 rejected
LnBankAgeti	−0.0507484	0.0083239	−6.10	0.000***	−0.067063	−0.0344338	H3 rejected
BankTypeti	−0.0647458	0.0088427	−7.32	0.000***	−0.0820771	−0.0474144	H2 accepted
LnInflationti	−0.0495386	0.00707	−7.01	0.000***	−0.0633954	−0.0356817	H5 accepted
Constant	0.2335224	0.0638224	3.66	0.000	0.1084329	0.358612	—

**Correlation is significant at the 10%.*
****Correlation is significant at the 1%.*

Table 20.
Results of the impacts of EAC on the IBs' liquidity.

LnTLTDtc	Coefficient	Std. Err.	Z	$P > \lvert z \rvert$	[95% Conf. Interval]		Decision
AuditQualitytc	−0.0336292	0.0292968	−1.15	0.061*	−0.0237914	0.0910498	H1 rejected
LnBankSizetc	0.129404	0.025043	5.17	0.000***	0.0803206	0.1784873	H4 rejected
LnBankAgetc	0.0293781	0.0145626	2.02	0.044**	0.0008358	0.0579203	H3 accepted
BankTypetc	−0.0674065	0.0136172	−4.95	0.000***	−0.0940958	−0.0407172	H2 accepted
LnInflationtc	−0.0806047	0.0117335	−6.87	0.000***	−0.1036019	−0.0576076	H5 accepted
Constant	−0.3079346	0.0751069	−4.10	0.000	−0.4551415	−0.1607278	—

**Correlation is significant at the 10%.*
****Correlation is significant at the 5%.*
****Correlation is significant at the 1%.*

Table 21.
Results of the impacts of EAC on the CBs' solvency.

LnTLTDti	Coefficient	Std. Err.	Z	$P > \lvert z \rvert$	[95% Conf. Interval]		Decision
AuditQualityti	0.0283128	0.1567669	0.18	0.857	0.3355703	0.2789447	H1 rejected
LnBankSizetc	1.886044	0.139794	13.49	0.000***	1.612053	2.160035	H4 rejected
LnBankAgeti	0.2530683	0.0379865	6.66	0.000***	0.3275205	0.1786161	H3 accepted
BankTypeti	−0.1369333	0.0398734	−3.43	0.001***	−0.2150838	−0.0587827	H2 accepted
LnInflationti	−0.2710539	0.0429241	−6.31	0.000***	−0.3551837	−0.1869241	H5 accepted
Constant	−2.852438	0.3140807	−9.08	0.000	−3.468025	−2.236851	—

****Correlation is significant at the 1%.*

Table 22.
Results of the impacts of EAC on the IBs' solvency.

Classification

JEL classification: E42, E52, F37, G20, G29, G30, G33, G39, G40

Author details

Achraf Haddad[1,2]

1 Doctor of Financial and Accounting Methods, Tunisia

2 Faculty of Economic Sciences and Management of Sfax, The Laboratory of Governance, Finance, and Accounting, Tunisia

*Address all correspondence to: achraf.haddad2015@gmail.com

References

[1] Nafli O. Impact of the external audit quality and corporate governance on the Tunisian company' financial performance of before and after the 2011 revolution. International Journal of Accounting and Financial Reporting. 2019;**9**(3):34-58

[2] Halme L. Bank corporate governance and financial stability. In: Halme L et al., editors. Financial Stability and Central Bank: Selected Issues for Financial Safety Nets and Market Discipline. London: Center for Central Banking Studies. Bank of England; 2000. pp. 32-70

[3] Caprio G, Levine R. Corporate governance of banks: Concepts and international observations. In: Litan RE, Pomerleano M, Sundarajan V, editors. Financial Sector Governance: The Roles of the Public and Private Sectors. USA: Brookings Institution Press; 2002. pp. 17-49

[4] Alhadab M, Clacher I. The impact of audit quality on real and accrual earnings management around IPOs. The British Accounting Review. 2018;**50**(4):442-461

[5] Ziaee M. The effect of audit quality on the performance of listed companies in Tehran stock exchange. International Letters of Social and Humanistic Sciences. 2014;**21**:36-43. DOI: 10.18052/www.scipress.com/ILSHS.21.36

[6] Barth J, Caprio G, Levine R. Bank regulation and supervision: What works best ? Journal of Financial Intermediation. 2004;**13**(2):205-248

[7] Alves S. The impact of audit committee existence and external audit on earnings management: Evidence from Portugal. Journal of Financial Reporting and Accounting. 2013;**11**(2):143-165. DOI: 10.1108/JFRA-04-2012-0018

[8] Francis JR, Yu MD. Big 4 office size and audit quality. The Accounting Review. 2016;**84**(5):1552. DOI: 10.2308/accr.2009.84.5.1521

[9] Inaam Z, Khamoussi H. Audit committee effectiveness, audit quality and earnings management: A meta-analysis. International Journal of Law and Management. 2016;**58**(2):179-196. DOI: 10.1108/IJLMA-01-2015-0006

[10] Khalil M, Ozkan A. Board independence, audit quality and earnings management: Evidence from Egypt. Journal of Emerging Market Finance. 2016;**15**(1):84-118. DOI: 10.1177/0972652715623701

[11] Lopes AP. Audit quality and earnings management: Evidence from Portugal. Athens Journal of Business & Economics, Athens Institute for Education and Research (ATINER). 2018;**4**(2):179-192. DOI: 10.30958/ajbe.4.2.4

[12] Quttainah MA, Cocco J, Al-Zufairi A. The determinants of theeffectiveness of corporate governance at Islamic banks. International Journal of Business Governance and Ethics. 2017;**12**(2):174-196

[13] Rahman MM, Meah MR, Chaudhory NU. The impact of audit characteristics on firm performance: An empirical study from an emerging economy. Journal of Asian Finance, Economics and Business. 2019;**6**(1):59-69

[14] Yasser S, Soliman MS. The effect of audit quality on earnings Management in Developing Countries: The case of Egypt. International Research Journal of Applied Finance. 2016;**9**(4):216-231. Available from: https://www.scienceope

n.com/document_file/4250c67b-08a9-4291-854c-3d4ccc7dd845/API/31-56.pdf

[15] Boulila Taktak N, Mbarki I. Board characteristics, external auditing quality and earnings management: Evidence from the Tunisian banks. Journal of Accounting in Emerging Economies. 2014;**4**(1):79-96. DOI: 10.1108/JAEE-10-2011-0046

[16] Abdallah AAN, Hassan MK, McClelland PL. Islamic financial institutions, corporate governance, and corporate risk disclosure in Gulf Cooperation Council countries. Journal of Multinational Financial Management. 2015;**31**:63-82

[17] Eli A, Yanling G, Gilad L. Auditor independence and the cost of capital before and after Sarbanes–Oxley: the case of newly issued public debt. European Accounting Review. 2010;**19**(4):633-664

[18] Hasan S, Kassim M. The impact of audit quality, audit committee and financial reporting quality: Evidence from Malaysia. International Journal of Economics and Financial Issues. 2020;**10**(5):272-281

[19] Hassan SU, Farouk MA. Audit quality and financial performance of quoted cement firms in Nigeria. European Journal of Business and Management. 2014;**6**(28):73-82

[20] Mustapha UA, Mohd Rashid NN, Lateef SA, Bala AA. The effect of corporate governance attributes on audit quality in Nigeria. International Journal of Recent Technology and Engineering. 2019;**8**(4):4882-4886

[21] Piot C, Janin R. External auditors, audit committees and earnings management in France. European Accounting Review. 2007;**16**(2):429-454

[22] Wang Q, Wong TK, Xia L. State ownership, the institutional environment and auditor choice: Evidence from China. Journal of Accounting and Economics. 2008;**46**(1):112-134

[23] Ado AB, Rashid N, Mustapha UA, Ademola LS. The impact of audit quality on the financial performance of listed companies in Nigeria. Journal of Critical Reviews, 2020;**7**(9):37-42. DOI: 10.31838/jcr.07.09.07

[24] Ezejiofor RA, Erhirhie FE. Effect of audit quality on financial performance: Evidence from deposit money banks in Nigeria. International Journal of Trend in Scientific Research and Development. 2018;**2**(6):1235-1244

[25] Krishnan CV. Does Big6 auditor industry expertise constrain earnings management? Accounting Horizons. 2003;**19**(1):1-16

[26] Teoh SH, Wong TJ. Perceived auditor quality and earnings response coefficient. The Accounting Review. 1993;**68**(2):346-367

[27] Ulussever T. A comparative analysis of corporate governance and bank performance: Islamic banks with conventional banks. Research Journal of Business and Management (RJBM). 2018;**5**(1):34-50

[28] Imhoff EA. Accounting quality, auditing, and corporate governance. Accounting Horizons. 2003;**17**(s–1):117-128

[29] Jensen MC, Meckling WH. Theory of the firm: Managerial behavior, agency costs and ownership structure. Journal of Financial Economics. 1976;**3**(4):305-360

[30] Becker CL, Defond ML, Jiambalvo J, Subramanyam KR. The effect of audit

quality on earnings management. Contemporary Accounting Research. 1998;**15**(1):1-24

[31] European Commission. Audit Policy: Lessons from the Crisis. The International Auditing and Assurance Standards Board; European Commissioner for Internal Market and Services; European Commission BERL 10/034 B - 1049. Brussels, Belgium. 2010. Available from: https://www.ifac.org/_flysystem/azure-private/meetings/files/6090_0.pdf

[32] Gul FA, Sun SYJ, Judy SLT. Audit quality, earnings, and the Shanghai stock market reaction. Journal of Accounting, Auditing, and Finance. 2003;**18**(3): 411-427

[33] Barlaup K, Iren Drønen H, Stuart I. Restoring trust in auditing: Ethicaldiscernment and the Adelphia scandal. Managerial Auditing Journal. 2009;**24**(2):183-203

[34] Kassem R, Higson AW. External auditors and corporate corruption: Implications for external audit regulators. American Accounting Association. 2016;**10**(1):1-10

[35] Mohammad AJ, Ahmed DM. The impact of audit committee and external auditor characteristics on financial reporting quality among Malaysian firms. Research Journal of Finance and Accounting. 2017;**8**(13):9-16

[36] Karim RAA. The independence of religious and external auditors: The case of Islamic banks. Accounting, Auditing and Accountability. 1990; **3**(3):34-44

[37] Mollah S, Zaman M. Charia supervision, corporate governance and performance: Conventional vs Islamic banks. Journal of Banking &Finance. 2015;**58**(C):418-435. DOI: 10.1016/j.jbankfin.2015.04.030

[38] Pomeranz F. The zccounting and auditing organization for Islamic financial institutions. Journal of International Accounting Auditing and Taxation. 1997;**6**(1):1-7

[39] Alzoubi ESS. Audit quality, debt financing, and earnings management: Evidence from Jordan. Journal of International Accounting Auditing and Taxation. 2018;**30**:69-84

[40] Chia-Ah E, Karlsson J. The Impact of Extended Audit Tenure on Auditor Independence. Umea, Sweden: Umea School of Business; 2010

[41] Lin JW, Hwang MI. Audit quality, corporate governance, and earnings management: A meta-analysis. International Journal of Auditing. 2010; **14**(1):57-77

[42] Lisa MG, Andrea SK, Molly M, Teri LY. Understanding the relation between financial reporting quality and audit quality. Auditing: A Journal of Practice & Theory. 2016;**35**(4):1-22

[43] Humphrey H, Loft A, Woods M. The global audit profession and the international financial architecture: Understanding regulatory relationships at a time of financial crisis. Accounting, Organizations and Society. 2009;**34**(6–7):810-825

[44] Kamolsakulchai M. The impact of the audit committee effectiveness and audit quality on financial reporting quality of listed company in stocks exchange of Thailand. Review of Integrative Business and Economics Research. 2015;**4**(2):328-341

[45] Commerford BP, Hermanson DR, Houston RW, Peters MF. Real earnings

management: A threat to auditor comfort? Auditing: A Journal of Practice & Theory. 2016;**35**(4):39-56

[46] Gunn JL, Paul N. Michas auditor multinational expertise and audit quality. The Accounting Review. 2018; **93**(4):203-224

[47] Fujiao X. Competition, Auditor Independence and Audit Quality. Manoa: University of Hawaii; 2017. DOI: 10125/51624

[48] Brooks LZ, Cheng CS, Johnston J, Reichelt KJ. When does audit quality start to decline in firm audit tenure? - An international analysis. 2011. Available from: https://ssrn.com/abstract=1933488. 10.2139/ssrn.1933488

[49] Elad FL. The Impact of Audit Education on the Audit Expectation Gap Evidence from Civilekonom Students in Sweden. Karlstad, Sweden: Karlstad Business Scool, Karlstad University; 2017 Available from: http://www.diva-portal.org/smash/get/diva2:1114221/FULLTEXT01.pdf

[50] Kutum I, Fraser I, Hussainey K. The application of business risk audit methodology within non-Big-4 firms. Journal of Financial Reporting and Accounting. 2015;**13**(2):226-246. DOI: 10.1108/JFRA-03-2014-0015

[51] Kanagaretnam K, Lee J, Lim CY, Lobo GJ. Relation between auditor quality and corporate tax aggressiveness: Implications of cross-country institutional differences. Auditing: A Journal of Practice & Theory. 2016;**35**(4):105-135. DOI: 10.2308/ajpt-51417

[52] Zhang Y, Zhou J, Zhou N. Audit committee quality, auditor independence, and internal control. Journal of Accounting and Public Policy. 2007;**26**:300-327

[53] Sarowar H, Kenichi Y, Monroe GS. The relationship between audit team composition, audit fees, and quality. Auditing: A Journal of Practice & Theory. 2017;**36**(3):115-135

[54] Simnett R, Ken TT. Twenty-five-year overview of experimental auditing research: Trends and links to audit quality. Behavioral Research in Accounting. 2018;**30**(2):55-76

[55] Chukwunedu OS, Okafor GO, Ofoegbu GN. The effect of joint audit on audit quality- the perceptions of accountants. In: Auditors and Accounting Academics at AAFA 2015 Conference in Mauritius. African Accounting and Finance Association 2015 Conference; Mauritius. 2015. DOI: 10.13140/RG.2.1.2695.6009

[56] Gul FA. Size of audit fees and perceptions of auditors' ability to resist management pressure in audit conflict situations. Abacus. 1991;**27**(2):162-172

[57] Watts RL, Zimmerman JL. Agency problems, auditing and the theory of the firm: Some evidence. Journal of Law and Economics. 1983;**26**(3):613-633

[58] Chan P, Ezzamel M, Gwilliam D. Determinants of audit fees for quoted UK compagnies. Journal of Business Finance and Accounting. 1993;**20**(6): 765-786

[59] Firth M. The provision of non audit services by accounting firms to their audit clients. Contemporary Accounting Research. 1997;**14**(2):1-21

[60] Baumann U, Erlend N. Disclosure, volatility and transparency-an empirical investigation into the value of bank disclosure. Frbny Economic Policy Review. 2004;**10**(2):31-45

[61] Benjamin PC, Richard CH, Richard WH. The effect of real earnings

management on auditor scrutiny of Management's other financial reporting decisions. The Accounting Review. 2018; **93**(5):145-163

[62] Chou J, Nataliya Z, Bohui Z. Does auditor choice matter to foreign investors? Evidence from foreign mutual funds worldwide. Journal of Banking and Finance. 2014;**46**(1):1-20

[63] De–Angelo LE. Auditor size and audit quality. Journal of Accounting and Economics. 1981;**3**(3):183-199

[64] Francis K, Dechun. The pricing of national and city-specific reputations for industry expertise in the US audit market. The Accounting Review. 2005; **80**(1):113-136

[65] Jeff PB, Khurana IK, Raman KK. Do the Big4 and the second–tier firms provide audits of similar quality ? Journal of Accounting Public Policy. 2010;**29**(4): 330-352

[66] Athula E, Perera H, Sujatha P. Towards a framework to analyse the role of accounting in corporate governance in the banking sector. Journal of Applied Management Accounting Research. 2009;**7**(2):21-40

[67] Whittington R, Margheim L. The effects of risk, materiality, and assertion subjectivity on external auditors' reliance on internal auditors. Journal of Practice and Theory. 1993;**12**(1):50-64

[68] Niinimaki JP. Inter-temporal diversification in financial intermediation. Journal of Banking and Finance. 2001;**25**(5):965-991

[69] Zulkafli A, Fazilah AS. Corporate governance and performance of banking firms: Evidence from Asian markets. In: Hirschey M, John K, Makhija AK, editors. Issues in Corporate Governance and Finance Advances in Financial Economics. Vol. 12. Bingley: Emerald Group Publishing Limited; 2007. pp. 49-74. DOI: 10.1016/S1569-3732(07)12003-X

[70] Steven B, Krishnan J, Yang JS. Auditor industry specialization and earnings quality. Journal of Practice and Theory. 2003;**22**(2):71-97

[71] Gramling A, Stone DN. Audit firm industry expertise: A review and synthesis of the archival literature. Journal of Accounting Literature. 2001; **20**:1-29

[72] Hammersley JS. Pattern identification and industry-specialist auditors. The Accounting Review. 2006; **81**(2):309-336. Available from: https://www.jstor.org/stable/4093141

[73] Hubbard AA. Experience and error frequency knowledge as potential determinants of audit expertise. Accounting Review. 1991;**66**(2):218-239

[74] Ira S, Michael DS, Ray WO. What do industry-specialist auditors know? Journal of Accounting Research. 1999;**37**(1):191-208

[75] Chia YM, Lapsley I, Lee HW. Choice of auditors and earnings management during the Asian financial crisis. Managerial Auditing Journal. 2007;**22**(2):177-196

[76] Cahan SF, Zhang W. After Enron: Auditor conservatism and ex–Andersen clients. The Accounting Review. 2006;**81**(1):49-82

[77] Lee HY, Vivek M. The effect of the private securities litigation reform act of 1995 on accounting discretion of client managers of Big6 and non–Big6 auditors. A Journal of Practice and Theory. 2003; **22**(1):93-108

[78] Jeong SW, Jung K, Lee SJ. The effect of mandatory auditor assignment and non-audit service on audit fees: Evidence from Korea. International Journal of Accounting. 2005;**40**(3):233-248

[79] Houqe MN, Zijl TV, Dunstan K, Karim W. Corporate ethics and auditor choice–international evidence. Research in Accounting Regulation. 2015;**27**(1): 57-65

[80] Jiang J, Wang I, Wang KP. Big N auditors and audit quality: New evidence from quasi-experiments. The Accounting Review. 2019;**94**(1):205-227

[81] Chung R, Firth M, Kim J-B. Auditor conservatism and reported earnings. Accounting and Business Research. 2003;**33**(1):19-32. DOI: 10.1080/00014788.2003.9729629

[82] Gul FA. Bankers' perceptions of factors affecting auditor independence. Accounting, Auditing and Accountability Journal. 1989;**2**(3):40-51

[83] Hamed S, Rohaida B, Siti ZAR, Mohamed AE. The impact of audit quality on firm performance: Evidence from Malasia. In: The 1st World Virtual Conference on Social and Behavioral Sciences 2015, 28–30 Jun, 2015. Kuala Iumpur, Malaysia: Skudai Johor, Universiti Teknologi Malaysia; 2015 Available from: http://www.akademiabaru.com/wvsocial/temp/acc4.pdf

[84] Muotolu C, Nwadialor EO. Effect of audit quality on the financial performance of deposit money banks in Nigeria. International Journal of Trend in Scientific Research and Development. 2019;**3**(2):923-932

[85] Salem R, Usman M, Ezeani E. Loan loss provisions and audit quality: Evidence from MENA Islamic and conventional banks. The Quarterly Review of Economics and Finance. 2021; **79**:345-359. DOI: 10.1016/j.qref.2020.07.002

[86] Abdelsalam O, Dimitropoulos P, Elnahass M, Leventis S. Earningsmanagement behaviors under different monitoring mechanisms: The case ofIslamic and conventional banks. Journal of Economic Behavior & Organization. 2016;**132**:155-173

[87] Chapra MU, Ahmed H. Corporate Governance in Islamic Financial Institutions. Jeddah: Islamic Development Bank, Islamic Research and Training Institute; 2002. pp. 1-85

[88] Darmadi S. Corporate governance disclosure in the annual report: An exploratory study on Indonesian islamic banks. Humanomics. 2013;**29**(1):4-23

[89] Quttainah MA, Song L, Wu Q. Do Islamic banks employ less earnings management? Journal of International Financial Management and Accounting. 2013;**24**(3):203-233

[90] Bhushan R. An informational efficiency perspectives on the post–earnings annoucement drift. Journal of Accounting and Economics. 1999;**18**(1): 45-65

[91] Skinner DJ, Sloan RG. Earnings surprises, growth expectations and stock returns or don't let an earnings torpedo sink your portfolio. Review of Accounting Studies. 2002;**7**(2):289-312

[92] Jemric I, Vujcic B. Efficiency of banks in Croatia: A DEA approach. Comparative Economic Studies. 2002;**44** (2–3):169-193

[93] Salas V, Saurina J. Credit risk in two institutional regimes: Spanish commercial and savings banks. Journal

of Financial Services Research. 2002;**22**(3):203-224

[94] Jonathan W, Nghia N. Financial liberalisation, crisis and restructuring: A comparative study of bank performance and bank governance in south east asia. Journal of Banking and Finance. 2005;**29**(8–9):2119-2154

[95] Shamsher M, Hassan T, Bader MKI. Efficiency of conventional versus islamic banks: International evidence using the stochastic frontier approach (SFA). Journal of Islamic Economics, Banking and Finance. 2008;**4**(2):107-130

[96] Manthos DD, Nikolaos IP. Determinants of bank efficiency: Evidence from a semi–parametric methodology. Managerial Finance. 2009; **35**(3):260-275

[97] Hussein HA, Charif H. Multiple approaches in performance assessment of UAE commercial banks. International Journal of Islamic and Middle Eastern Finance and Management. 2011;**4**(1): 74-82

[98] Alharthi M. The Determinants of Efficiency, Profitability and Stability in the Banking Sector: A Comparative Study of Islamic, Conventional and Socially Responsible Banks. UK: University of Plymouth; 2016. Available from: http://hdl.handle.net/10026.1/5324

[99] Patten DM. Exposure, legitimacy and social disclosure. Journal of Accounting and Public Policy. 1991;**10**(4):297-308

[100] Bennaceur S, Omran M. The effects of bank regulations, competition and financial reforms on MENA banks' profitability. Emerging Markets Review. 2011;**12**(1):1-20. DOI: 10.1016/j.ememar.2010.08.002

[101] Benston GJ, Hanweck GA, Humphrey DB. Scale economies in banking, a restructuring and reassessement. Journal of Money, Credit and Banking. 1982;**14**(4):435-455

[102] Ascarya A. The lack of profit–and–loss sharing financing in Indonesia's Islamic banks revisited. In: Conference: 10th Annual International Symposium on the Analytic Hierarchy Process 2009, at Katz Graduate School of Business. Pittsburgh, Pennsylvania, USA: University of Pittsburgh; 2009. pp. 70-98. DOI: 10.13033/isahp.y2009.087

[103] Iqbal Z. Islamic financial systems. Finance and Development. 1997;**34**(2): 42-45

[104] Zaher TS, Hassan MK. A comparative literature survey of islamic finance and banking. Financial Markets, Institutions and Instruments. 2001;**10**(4):155-199

[105] Samad A. Performance of interest free islamic banks vs interest-based conventional banks of Bahrain. IIUM Journal of Economics and Management. 2004;**12**(2):1-25

[106] Kraft E, Tirtiroglu D. Bank efficiency in Croatia: A stochastic–frontier analysis. Journal of Comparative Economics. 1998;**26**(2):282-300

[107] Filip F, Vesna M, Kiril S. Corporate governance and bank performance: Evidence from Macedonia. In: Proceedings of 16th international students' conference, Faculty of Economics and Administrative Sciences. Izmir: Ege University; 2013. pp. 76-99. Available from: https://mpra.ub.uni-muenchen.de/id/eprint/46773

[108] Siddiqui A. Financial contracts, risk and performance of Islamic banking. Managerial Finance. 2008;**34**(10):680-

694. Available at:. DOI: 10.1108/03074350810891001

[109] Olivier P, Krassimira G. Islamic finance at the crossroads of chemists. Financial Economics Review. 2008;**92**: 197-213

[110] Cornett MM, McNutt JJ, Tehranian H. Corporate governance and earnings management at large US bank holding companies. Journal of Corporate Finance. 2009;**15**(4):412-430

[111] Farazi S, Feyen E, Rocha R. Bank ownership and performance in the Middle East and North Africa region. Review of Middle East Economics and Finance. 2011;**9**(2):1-51. DOI: 10.1515/rmeef-2012-0025

[112] Cihak M, Hesse H. Islamic banks and financial stability: An empirical analysis. Journal of Financial Services Research. 2010;**38**(2–3):95-113

[113] Fahad NU. An econometric analysis on financial performance of commercial banks in Bangladesh: A comparative study. Journal of Business Studies. 2014; **8**:33-50

[114] Gul S, Irshad F, Zaman K. Factors affecting bank profitability in Parkistan. The Romanian Economic Journal. 2011; **14**(39):61-87

[115] Bashir AHM. Assessing the performance of Islamic banks: Some evidence from the middle east. Topics in Middle Eastern and North African Economies. 2001;**3**.
Available from: https://api.semanticscholar.org/CorpusID:12832951

[116] Saeed MS. Bank–related, industry–related and macroeconomic factors affecting bank profitability: A case of the United Kingdom. Research Journal of Finance and Accounting. 2014;**5**(2):42-50

[117] Rashwan MH, Ehab H. Comparative efficiency study between Islamic and traditional banks. Journal of Finance and Economics. 2016;**4**(3):74-85

[118] Onuonga SM. The analysis of profitability of Kenya's top six commercial banks: Internal factor analysis. American International Journal of Social Science. 2014;**3**:94-103

[119] Osama MAH, Naser MAG, Ahmed MEG. Financial performance and compliance with basel III capital standards: Conventional vs islamic banks. The Journal of Applied Business Research. 2013;**29**(4):1031-1048

[120] Haddad A, El Ammari A, Bouri A. Comparative study of ambiguity resolution between the efficiency of conventional and Islamic banks in a stable financial context. International Journal of Economics and Financial, Issues. 2019;**9**:111-129

[121] Lartey VC, Antwi S, Boadi EK. The relationship between liquidity and profitability of listed banks in Ghana. International Journal of Business and Social Science. 2013;**4**(3):48-56

[122] Tandelilin E, Kaaro H, Mahadwartha PA, Supriyatna P. Corporate governance, risk management and bank performance: Does type of ownership matter ?. EADN working paper No. 34. 2007

[123] Haddad A, El Ammari A, Bouri A. Comparative study between solvencies of Islamic and conventional banks in a financial stable period: Evidence from heterogeneous countries. International Journal Financial Services Management. 2021;**11**(1):50-74

[124] Rashid A, Jabeen S. Analyzing performance determinants: Conventional vs islamic banks in

Pakistan. Borsa Istanbul Review. 2016;**16**(2):92-107

[125] Kim PK, Rasiah D. Relationship between corporate governance and bank performance in Malaysia during the pre and post Asian financial crisis. European Journal of Economics. Finance and Administrative Sciences. 2010;**21**(1): 39-63

[126] Charles CW, Florian H, Marie H. A theory of Bank liquidity requirements. Columbia Business School Research Paper No. 14-39. 2015. Available from: https://ssrn.com/abstract=2477101. 10.2139/ssrn.2477101

[127] Fisseha FL. Meta analysis on the determinants of commercial bank's profitability: A conceptual framework and modelling. European Scientific Journal. 2015;**11**(19):323-351

[128] Mule KR, Mukras MS, Nzioka OM. Corporate size, profitability and market value: An econometric panel analysis of listed firms in Kenya. European Scientific Journal. 2015;**2015**:1857-7431

[129] Jackson AB, Moldrich M, Roebuck JK. Audit-firm tenure and the quality of financial reports. Contemporary Accounting Research. 2008;**19**(4): 637-660

[130] Jensen MC. The modern industrial revolution, exit and the failure of internal control system. Journal of Finance. 1993;**48**(3):831-880

[131] Letza S, Kirkbride J, Sun X, Smallman C. Corporate governance theorizing: Limits, critics and alternatives. International Journal of Law and Management. 2008;**50**(1):17-32

[132] Kuhn TS. The structure of scientific revolutions, international encyclopedia of unified science. Enlarged, Foundations of the Unity of Science. 1970;**2**(2):1-210

Chapter 5

Impacts of Board Quality on Financial Performance in Conventional and Participatory Banks during and after the Covid-19 Crisis: Evidence from Emerging and Developing Countries

Achraf Haddad

Abstract

Going back to the governance literature, we found two equates on the correlation between the bank board and financial performance (FP). Firstly, we noticed that, in previous studies, the impacts of board quality on the financial performance of conventional and participatory (Islamic) banks were mixed, unstable, and sometimes contradictory. Secondly, we noticed a total absence of comparative studies showing the importance of the impact of the board composition quality on the financial performance of conventional and Islamic banks during and after the covid-19 crisis. To clarify the ambiguity, in this study, we compared in depth the impact of the board of directors (BOD) on the FP in the two cited bank types. FP measures and board quality determinants are collected from 30 countries. The data concern 112 banks of each type that have published their reports regularly. Panel regressions were used to solve the ambiguity of the board quality's impact on the FP of conventional and participatory banks in the agency theory framework during the period (2019–2022), giving us 448 observations in each subsample. Empirical results showed that the BOD negatively affects the FP of conventional banks (CBs), while that of participatory banks (PBs) has an ambiguous impact on their FP.

Keywords: conventional banks (CBs), participatory banks (PBs), board of directors (BOD), financial performance (FP), corporate governance, comparative study, agency theory

1. Introduction

According to the financial approach, the board of directors (BOD) is considered the most important mechanism of an integrated governance system to resolve conflicts of interest and opportunistic decisions between shareholders and executives. Although the internal control system includes the main governance actors, the BOD is responsible for the effectiveness of other governance mechanisms in the banking system. It coordinates three levels of interest: shareholders, leaders, and other stakeholders.

Empirical studies dealing with the relationship between the BOD and the banks' financial performance (FP) have considered this mechanism an internal control system that helps the leaders to solve agency conflicts between managers and shareholders [1, 2], effectively monitor managers and reduce agency costs [3], and protect shareholders' interests [4, 5]. This current research represents another noticeable finding in the literature, as these researchers have interpreted the board determinants as part of agency theory.

Two factors explain the comparison between the impacts of participatory and conventional banks (CBs) on their FP. The first is the scientific factor, which is manifested by the multiplicity of board definitions in the literature and the differences in their main roles in the current and previous scientific approaches. As far as this factor is concerned, some researchers proved that the board is responsible for the periodic evaluation of the bank's performance, the managers' control, and the follow-up of its plans, the fixation of its remuneration, as well as establishing disclosure systems for all banking information [6]. Others concluded that the board must also ensure compliance with banking standards. None of the shareholders or officers has the right to use their authority to change the decisions made by the board's vote in their interest [7]. Indeed, to allow the BOD to be an effective control mechanism in financial institutions, [2] suggested the following conditions:

1. The free access of board members to reliable and relevant accounting information and not only to the information imposed on them by the officer;

2. A board size of seven to eight members is relatively small and sufficient to be more effective and cannot be influenced or controlled by the leader's authority;

3. Holding a significant number of the firm's shares by the executive creates a convergence of interests with the shareholders; and

4. The separation between the director's and the board chairman's duties to ensure the effectiveness of supervision exercised by the board.

Nevertheless, referring to the participatory banks (PBs) literature, the Islamic board concept, in its classic form, does not exist. Rather, it is used as a control mechanism to adapt the classical banking control system to that of Islamic banking so as to facilitate its integration into highly developed financial and stock markets. Because the financial world operates according to a financial policy based on globalization and competition, and because the board's importance differs from one bank model to another, the divergence can implicitly generate different impacts, which can generate the same impact, but at a lower level, or it can automatically give the same impact in another financial model that reduces or improves the board's quality and consequently the PBs' efficiency. Regardless of non-valued movements or decisions taken outside the Islamic rules, the board constitution in the Islamic banking community is filled by not only the sectoral constitutional norms but also by the provisions of the Islamic norms. For this reason, previous studies considered the variation of these effects within a closed governance system whose components are complementary. In this framework, Ulussever [8] compared the effect of board quality on the FP of participatory and conventional banks during the period 2005–2011 in 16 countries. The results revealed that the ROA and the ROE are significantly higher in IBs than in their conventional counterparts. Specifically, the results revealed that the board size and independence of IBs are positively correlated with the ROA, confirming that these variables have very meaningful impacts on the IBs' governance structure and very significant impacts on their FP. However, in their conventional counterparts, board independence negatively affected the ROE. The results of the other variables such as the board size and the CEO duality, revealed that there is no significant relationship between the ROA and the Tobin Q.

The second factor that motivated us to study this topic is the technical factor. This factor deals with the structural differences between the CBs' board importance and quality and that of PBs. Consequently, these differences influence the type and degree of the resulting impacts from the board's determinant of each bank model on their FP. The criticism of previous research revealed that the countries that adopted an Islamic banking system alongside the conventional system did not simultaneously apply the same regulatory laws and international conventional/Islamic accounting and auditing standards. Besides, their provisions are not similarly administered and controlled in all regions as they are not addressed to the same customer categories. In some countries, PBs operate under a traditional system that is inconsistent with the Islamic principles of good governance practices of the PBs' board; this is considered a flagrant override of the Charia principles. In the opposite form, we find that the CBs operate under a financial system based on Charia standards, which is also very common in practice. Moreover, PBs located outside the Islamic countries' areas and the banks belonging to the non-Islamic original countries' subsidiaries do not necessarily apply the same board control standards. Conversely, it is not evident that all CBs located in Islamic countries adopt Islamic governance standards and that all CBs located in non-Islamic areas ignore the application of Charia standards in their subsidiaries. This debate is very complicated; it depends on the banks' individual reasoning in each sample, case by case. Therefore, this factor created typical differences between the board structures of conventional and Islamic banks, which translated into disagreements on their FPs' impacts. Everything depends on the bank's activity and the magnitude of its financial objectives. Whatever the bank type, the more the gap between the board's determinants increases, the more the impacts on their FP differ.

Furthermore, based on the theoretical knowledge, since the results of previous studies separately analyzing the impact of the BOD's effects on the FP of conventional or participatory banks are mixed, comparative studies between these impacts in the agency theory framework are nonexistent. Also, all of the previous studies were carried out before, during, or after the subprime crisis. However, no study has analyzed or compared the trends in these impacts during and after the covid-19 health crisis. The first goal of this study is to determine the type of causality between the BOD and the FP of each bank type in an economically unstable period. The second objective of this study is to solve the comparison ambiguity between the impacts of the boards' quality on the FP of conventional and participatory banks (Islamic banks) in the agency theory framework and overcome previous unclear and inconclusive results *via* the selection of the bank type that has the best board quality that has the best impact on their FP during and after the covid-19 crisis in emerging and developing countries. The third objective is to help stakeholders find out which bank type performs best *via* its board quality in a crisis situation.

The theoretical contribution that was highlighted in this work is to call for a comprehensive and exhaustive revision of the governance theory, which not only interests the banks' board side but also concerns all the governance mechanisms within conventional and participatory banks. Our first practical contribution is the discovery of a new board system applicable in both stable and unstable financial contexts. This board has to be objective, dynamic, strategic, and able to improve the governance quality of Islamic and conventional banks. The second practical contribution is to put into perspective an original, integrated, and multidisciplinary evaluation approach involving different perspectives and knowledge of boards in conventional and participatory banks, starting with maximizing the FP goal.

The remainder of the paper is organized as follows: Section 2 reviews previous research on this topic and the study hypotheses. Section 3 describes the employed methodology, the data sources, the variables, and the models' specifications. Empirical results are presented in Section 4. Finally, Section 5 contains concluding remarks.

2. Literature review

2.1 Theoretical background and hypotheses: board determinants

In previous studies, the trend in research was to study separately, either the impact of BOD on CBs' FP or the impact of BOD on PBs' FP. However, this study aims to compare these two impacts and specify which board type has a greater effect on FP although their conclusions are not unified. For this reason, our work aims to address an explanation of the evolution of Islamic and conventional banks' performance proportionate to the change in the BOD structure in the specific financial context of covid-19 in emerging and developing countries. The banking governance literature has identified several determinants of BOD. Yet, to avoid econometric problems arising from the unavailability of observations from one of the samples, I have included only four determinants of board composition effectiveness: size, rooting of the board chairman, independence of the board members, and the number of meetings held.

2.1.1 Board size

In the banking governance literature, the impact of board size on banks' FP was largely addressed by several studies [9–17]. Nevertheless, previous research has not yet yielded a unified result, which is why this question remains unanswered [9]. At this stage, the most pressing question concerns the optimal number of directors to better control the managers' activities and subsequently improve the banks' performance. However, previous studies failed to determine the ideal number of directors. Practically, we noticed that the evidence of the board size impact on CBs is inconclusive [18], while work on the board size of PBs is almost nonexistent.

In some studies, the correlation between board size and FP revealed the existence of an intermediate approach named the "neutralist approach" [9, 18, 19].

A lot of research has established a positivist vision about the fundamental role of the board size as a stimulator of FP [13, 20–32]. The board's size enhanced its ability to monitor and improve banks' FP. As a result, as the number of directors increases, so does the ability to harmonize instruments and mobilize resources to guard against risks. The small board easily suffers from the leaders' influence more than the large one does because it has a variety of experiences belonging to the different administrators [33]. The addition of more members creates more interaction between them and provides a favorable ground for encouraging directors to pursue their interests and make mistakes. The impact of such a work environment can lead to an inappropriate climate full of agency relationships, conflicts of interest [34], and financial statement fraud [35].

Although some researchers found that the more board members there are, the higher the bank's FP, other studies found that a small board is more effective at improving a bank's FP. These researchers argue that the number of directors is negatively related to abnormally high profitability because the board's size minimizes managerial incentives to destroy the bank's value and its FP [2, 10, 36–50]. Moreover, large boards are less effective according to the criteria of coordination, control, and decision-making flexibility [2, 37]. Also, boards with fewer directors have more effective control than large boards with supervisory challenges because of communication difficulties [43]. Similarly, a small board provides a better control function, while boards with large sizes tend to control the general manager [2]. Besides, within this same stream, Rashidah and Fairuzana [51] confirmed that there is a positive relationship between the board size and the propensity to manage the outcome.

Our proposal focuses on conventional and participatory banks, in which the board size has a greater effect on the bank's value regardless of its type [52]. Given the dependent and independent contradictory results, the meaning of our basic assumptions essentially depends on the consideration of board size in an agency context as a principal proxy, which allows us to signal the effect of conflicting relationships on FP.

After a rich exposure to the literature concerned with the relationship between the FP and the board size, we propose the following suggestion:

Hypothesis 1: The board size.

Hypothesis 1.1: The board size has a negative effect on the FP of conventional and participatory banks during and after the covid-19 crisis in emerging and developing countries.

Hypothesis 1.2: The board size has a positive effect on the FP of conventional and participatory banks during and after the covid-19 crisis in emerging and developing countries.

Hypothesis 1.3: The board size has a negative effect on the CBs' FP, but it has a positive effect on the PBs' FP during and after the covid-19 crisis in emerging and developing countries.

Hypothesis 1.4: The board size has a positive effect on the CBs' FP, but it has a negative effect on the PBs' FP during and after the covid-19 crisis in emerging and developing countries.

2.1.2 Board chairman's rooting: automatic mandate renewal

Previous research has attempted to demonstrate the board's effectiveness and its impact on the CBs' FP [28, 32, 53, 54], while others have shown the opposite [17, 45, 55–59]. However, in PBs the subject of rooting is not yet widely treated. This may be due to the weakness of the board effect or because of its limited power as a governance mechanism. Theoretically, rooting means the occupation of the same post by a manager after the end of their first fixed-term contract. It is manifested in two methodical forms leading to the same results: either through the CEO duality or by the same person as the board chairman; or the same person who is designed as the board chairman will exceed his first contract or will automatically renew his mandate without verifying the conditions of his independence.

The opinions of previous studies already carried out on CBs' samples are divergent. Moreover, the empirical results did not confirm whether the duality/rooting generates a clear impact or, if this impact is real, whether it has a positive or negative impact on the banks' FP. Based on the trend of the previous results highlighted in this area, we predict the following hypothesis:

Hypothesis 2: The rooting of the board chairman.

Hypothesis 2.1: There is a positive relationship between the rooting of the board chairman and the FP of conventional and participatory banks during and after the covid-19 crisis in emerging and developing countries.

Hypothesis 2.2: There is a negative relationship between the rooting of the board chairman and the FP of conventional and participatory banks during and after the covid-19 crisis in emerging and developing countries.

Hypothesis 2.3: There is a positive relationship between the rooting of the board chairman and the CBs' FP, but this relationship is negative in the PBs' case during and after the covid-19 crisis in emerging and developing countries.

Hypothesis 2.4: There is a negative relationship between the rooting of the board chairman and the CBs' FP, but this relationship is positive in the PBs' case during and after the covid-19 crisis in emerging and developing countries.

2.1.3 Board independence

The literature on the relationship between board independence and FP is also inconclusive. Independent directors' impact on banks' FP presented several non-uniformities [12, 16, 18, 19, 60–64].

The first stream found a positive effect of board independence on the FP [27, 36, 65–72], as this would lead to better monitoring, broad expertise, and better protection of the rights of minority shareholders [73]. According to agency theory, outside directors reduce agency problems between shareholders and executives by protecting shareholder interests and reducing opportunistic managerial behavior [42]. This prevents the executive director from making mistakes and prevents him from making false choices in the adverse selection of dependent administrators [74]. Board members are directly elected by shareholders to represent their interests [75]. Besides, independent directors are appointed to the board to control executive directors, protect minority shareholders, and maximize FP [76]. In other words, outside directors ensure that executives pursue policies that are consistent with shareholders' interests as intended, because if the number of independent directors increases, the propensity to manage the result decreases [77]. Independent members on the boards of conventional and Islamic banks are often perceived as a sign of transparency and voluntary governance quality improvement. According to this approach, the presence of independent directors on banks' boards is an additional mechanism of governance aimed at mitigating behavioral and moral hazards among stakeholders, protecting shareholders' interests, creating value, fostering control independence, resolving business problems, limiting their exposure to risk, and improving their institutions' FP [36, 78]. Moreover, external directors are more qualified with a high level of expertise, and experience and ensure the best execution of their tasks compared to boards dominated by simple employees [79].

However, another discordant explanatory approach stipulated that external directors were not able to understand the complexity of the banks' activities. They considered outside directors unable to carry out their stakeholder control, detect the opportunistic managers' behavior, and monitor the overruns against the sense of increased performance. Moreover, within this argument, some researchers found that the presence of foreign directors on the board has a negative and significant effect on banks' FP [17, 31, 32, 45, 80–83]. Independent directors with conflicting interests lead to poor governance practices, as the situation favors the appearance of conflict between the board and managers [73] leading to a decline in performance [84]. Also, Minton et al. [85]; Beltratti and Stulz [36], and Adams [86] found that the financial expertise of the independent directors of commercial banks is negatively related to the variations of their values. They went through financial troubles, which led to a decrease in the banks' FP.

In financial institutions, we recorded that many studies were done on one of two banking models, but not many supported the comparative approach. Several studies highlighted the effect of board composition and its impact on the CBs' FP [17, 18, 87]. However, the literature review showed that few studies have focused on the independence degree of PBs' boards since it is not a primary governance quality mechanism.

Theoretically, according to agency theory, board independence is both an index of transparency and a success factor in mitigating excessive risks. The independent directors, who are known to be vigilant, curb conflicts of interest, and at the same time stimulate bank growth. Empirically, the results report mixed conclusions, depending on contextual factors and sampling specifications. Previous research has yielded different results, according to which the correlation between board independence and FP depends on the absence and/or presence of other contingent factors.

As shown in the literature review, it is generally accepted that the independence of the BOD is a very important factor in determining the type of correlation between the quality of the board-generating effect, the optimal number of independent directors, and the objective of maximizing the banks' FP. They are expected to be more effective in monitoring operational, strategic, and decision-making activities in conventional or Islamic banks. Therefore, they have benefited from more freedom from any managerial influence, especially the CEO, to avoid conflict situations. Based on the previous selective studies, we formulated our third research hypothesis in the following form:

Hypothesis 3: The proportion of the board's independent directors.

Hypothesis 3.1: There is a positive relationship between the proportion of the board's independent directors and the FP of conventional and participatory banks during and after the covid-19 crisis in emerging and developing countries.

Hypothesis 3.2: There is a negative relationship between the proportion of the board's independent directors and the FP of conventional and participatory banks during and after the covid-19 crisis in emerging and developing countries.

Hypothesis 3.3: There is a positive relationship between the proportion of the board's independent directors and the CBs' FP, but the same relationship is negative in the PBs' case during and after the covid-19 crisis in emerging and developing countries.

Hypothesis 3.4: There is a negative relationship between the proportion of the board's independent directors and the CBs' FP, but the same relationship is positive in the PBs' case during and after the covid-19 crisis in emerging and developing countries.

2.1.4 Meetings held by the board of directors

Based on the literature review, several studies have identified the importance of the frequency of board meetings as a determinant able to influence governance quality in one way or another in different contexts [88–92] or as a performance control parameter [9, 11, 17, 93].

The effect added by this governance mechanism led us to distinguish two groups of previous studies. The majority of the proposals put forward by the researchers opt for a large number of meetings so that the BOD can effectively carry out its monitoring role [32, 43, 89, 93, 94]. However, there are other researchers who have founded a current based on their opposite results [31, 88, 90, 95]. In contrast, an intermediate stream has established coordination among governance mechanisms to determine whether the quality of one mechanism affects or enhances the quality of the other [9, 89, 92]. These researchers found no correlation.

Contrary to studies that considered board meetings' number in CBs, the studies discussing the effect of board meetings' number on FP in PBs are almost nonexistent. The results of the impact of the board meeting on the FP are mixed.

From the foregoing, it appears that the frequency of board meetings plays a very important role in the FP of both participatory and conventional banks. We draw the following hypothesis from the foregoing:

Hypothesis 4: The frequency of board meetings.

Hypothesis 4.1: There is a negative relationship between the frequency of board meetings and the FP of conventional and participatory banks during and after the covid-19 crisis in emerging and developing countries.

Hypothesis 4.2: There is a positive relationship between the frequency of board meetings and the FP of conventional and participatory banks during and after the covid-19 crisis in emerging and developing countries.

Hypothesis 4.3: There is a negative relationship between the frequency of board meetings and the CBs' FP, but this relationship is positive in the PBs' case during and after the covid-19 crisis in emerging and developing countries.

Hypothesis 4.4: There is a positive relationship between the frequency of board meetings and the CB' FP, but this relationship is negative in the PBs' case during and after the covid-19 crisis in emerging and developing countries.

3. Research methodology

3.1 Methodological aspects

3.1.1 Data collection

Two samples were taken from two reference populations, which are made up of 683 participating financial institutions and 2974 conventional financial institutions. The selection of banks is made in 30 countries,[1] whose banking systems include Islamic and conventional banks, over the period 2019–2022. However, we have

[1] Algeria (3,3), Bahrain (6,6), Bangladesh (4,4), Canada (1,1), Egypt (4,4), France (2,2), India (2,2), Indonesia (4,4), Jordan (4,4), Kazakhstan (3,3), Kuwait (6,6), Lebanon (2,2), Luxembourg (2,2), Malaysia (7,7), Nigeria (2,2), Oman (3,3), Pakistan (8,8), Qatar (6,6), Saudi Arabia (9,9), Senegal (3,3), Singapore (4,4), South Africa (1,1), Sri Lanka (1,1), Sudan (5,5), Thailand (1,1), Tunisia (2,2), Turkey (5,5), United Arab Emirates (5,5), United Kingdom (5,5), and USA (2,2).

excluded all specific financial institutions subject to specific regulations[2]. The observations chosen are all purely conventional or participatory banks. Moreover, due to difficulties in collecting information on FP and BOD, we excluded banks marked with missing data. We also ignored the mutated banks and conventional banks that added Islamic services. These restrictions led us to eliminate 571 participatory financial institutions and 2862 conventional financial institutions. Thereafter, we equalized the two samples on the basis of the qualitative and quantitative filtering criteria (equality of the samples, type of activity, similarity of the country of origin, and width of the bank) to finally obtain 112 banks in each sample.

3.1.2 Measurement of variables to be tested

3.1.2.1 Endogenous variables

In this subsection, we present the FP measures. The main variable to explain was represented by four dependent variables: profitability, efficiency, liquidity, and solvency. **Table 1** shows the parameters we worked on, the symbols, and the respective reports.

3.1.2.2 Exogenous variables

Throughout the remaining part of this work, banks' FP is explained by four BOD determinants. Referring to the review of the previous literature, the predominantly independent variables were described in **Table 2** as follows:

3.1.2.3 Measurements of additional explanatory variables

Table 3 displays the list of control variables supported by some previous studies that employed the same variables and their measures.

FP parameter	Rating for CBs	Rating for PBs	Measurement	Previous studies
Profitability	Pc	Pi	Marginal Profit/ Total Revenues	Sujan et al. [96]; Atyeh et al. [97]; Ogbeide and Akanji [98]; Haddad et al. [99]; and Asare et al. [18].
Liquidity	Lc	Li	Net Loans/ Total Assets	Olson and Zoubi [100]; Onakoya and Onakoya [101]; Al-Hares et al. [102]; and Haddad et al. [103].
Efficiency	Ec	Ei	Operating Result /Average Total Assets	Olson and Zoubi [100]; Onakoya and Onakoya [101]; Ola and Suzanna [104]; and Haddad et al. [105].
Solvency	Sc	Si	Total Loans/ Total Deposits	Olson and Zoubi [100]; Onakoya and Onakoya [101]; Ola and Suzanna [104]; and Haddad et al. [106]

Table 1.
Description of variables to explain.

[2] We excluded insurance companies, micro-credit companies, indirect finance companies, financing windows, and mixed conventional and Islamic banks and conventional banks that have Islamic windows and vice versa.

Heading	Rating for CBs	Rating for PBs	Measurement	Previous studies
Board Determinant	Board size of CB (BOARDSc)	Board size of PB (BOARDSi)	The number of executive directors in the BOD.	Joenoes and Rokhim [14]; Bawaneh [9]; Hermuningsih et al. [13]; and Bansal and Singh [17].
	Rooting of the board chairman or accumulation of the post of CEO and the board chairman (BO-ARDCRc)	Rooting of the board chairman or accumulation of the post of CEO and the board chairman (BO-ARDCRi)	Binary variable: 1: if the CEO also holds the post of board chairman of the bank or the board chairman exceeded the mandate 0: if not.	Al-Hawary [53]; Mollah and Zaman [45]; Hsu et al. [57]; and Bansal and Singh [17].
	Board independence: presence of external directors in the BOD (BOARDIc)	Board independence: presence of external directors in the BOD (BOARDIi)	Number of external executive directors who are not related to any professional/family relationship, nor the bank nor the executives.	Mollah and Zaman [45]; Li & Roberts [61]; Asare et al. [18]; and Bansal and Singh [17].
	Number of meetings held by the CB's board (BO-ARDMc)	Number of meetings held by the PB's board (BO-ARDMi)	Number of meetings held by the BOD in a year.	El-Maude et al. [11]; Eluyela et al. [93]; Bawaneh [9]; and Bansal and Singh [17].

Table 2.
Description of the explanatory variables.

Control Variable	Rating for CBs	Rating for PBs	Measurement	Previous studies
Bank type	TYc	TYi	Variable with three forms: 1. For commercial bank 2. For investment bank 3. For universal bank.	Cornett et al. [107]; Kim and Rasiah [108]; and Charles et al. [109].
Bank Age	AGc	AGi	Age of conventional/participatory bank for each year.	Kraft and Tirtiroglu [110]; Jemric and Vujcic [111]; and Filip et al. [112].
Bank size	SIc	SIi	Logarithm of book value of total assets of conventional/participatory bank at the end of each year.	Delis and Papanikolaou [113]; Al-Hawary [53]; and Rashid and Jabeen [114].
Inflation	INFc	INFi	Annual inflation rate in the country of origin of the conventional/participatory bank.	Gul et al. [115]; Rashwan and Ehab [116]; and Tugba et al. [117].

Table 3.
Description of control variables.

3.1.3 Presentation of models to estimate

In this subsection, we aim to detail and symbolize the basic models that will allow us to answer the questions already mentioned in the theoretical part. Also, it is necessary to present the standard models to reassess the FP several times, and each time the dependent variable will be changed according to the estimates of the conventional or participatory financial institutions. In what follows, as it appears in

Model Type	Conventional models of multiple regressions	Participatory models of multiple regressions
Association between profitability and board quality.	$LnPtc = \alpha_0 + \alpha_1 LnBOARDSc + \alpha_2 BOARDCRc + \alpha_3 LnBOARDIc + \alpha_4 LnBOARDMc + \alpha_5 TYc + \alpha_6 LnAGc + \alpha_7 LnSIc + \alpha_8 LnINFc + \varepsilon t$	$LnPti = \beta_0 + \beta_1 LnBOARDSi + \beta_2 BOARDCRi + \beta_3 LnBOARDIi + \beta_4 LnBOARDMi + \beta_5 TYi + \beta_6 LnAGi + \beta_7 LnSIi + \beta_8 LnINFi + \varepsilon t$
Association between efficiency and board quality.	$Etc = \alpha_0 + \alpha_1 LnBOARDSc + \alpha_2 BOARDCRc + \alpha_3 LnBOARDIc + \alpha_4 LnBOARDMc + \alpha_5 TYc + \alpha_6 LnAGc + \alpha_7 LnSIc + \alpha_8 LnINFc + \varepsilon t$	$Eti = \beta_0 + \beta_1 LnBOARDSi + \beta_2 BOARDCRi + \beta_3 LnBOARDIi + \beta_4 LnBOARDMi + \beta_5 TYi + \beta_6 LnAGi + \beta_7 LnSIi + \beta_8 LnINFi + \varepsilon t$
Association between liquidity and board quality.	$Ltc = \alpha_0 + \alpha_1 LnBOARDSc + \alpha_2 BOARDCRc + \alpha_3 LnBOARDIc + \alpha_4 LnBOARDMc + \alpha_5 TYc + \alpha_6 LnAGc + \alpha_7 LnSIc + \alpha_8 LnINFc + \varepsilon t$	$Lti = \beta_0 + \beta_1 LnBOARDSi + \beta_2 BOARDCRi + \beta_3 LnBOARDIi + \beta_4 LnBOARDMi + \beta_5 TYi + \beta_6 LnAGi + \beta_7 LnSIi + \beta_8 LnINFi + \varepsilon t$
Association between solvency and board quality.	$LnStc = \alpha_0 + \alpha_1 LnBOARDSc + \alpha_2 BOARDCRc + \alpha_3 LnBOARDIc + \alpha_4 LnBOARDMc + \alpha_5 TYc + \alpha_6 LnAGc + \alpha_7 LnSIc + \alpha_8 LnINFc + \varepsilon t$	$LnSti = \beta_0 + \beta_1 LnBOARDSi + \beta_2 BOARDCRi + \beta_3 LnBOARDIi + \beta_4 LnBOARDMi + \beta_5 TYi + \beta_6 LnAGi + \beta_7 LnSIi + \beta_8 LnINFi + \varepsilon t$

Table 4.
Approximation of models to be estimated related to conventional and participatory banks.

Table 4, we have moved to the exhibition of adequate models best suited to our data while explaining the meaning of all the constitutive variables.

4. Results and discussion

4.1 Interpretation of the comparative results between the board quality effects on the financial performance measures of the conventional and participatory banks

Before judging the impacts of board quality, we should estimate the separate impacts provided by the board determinants and the effects generated by the other control variables on the FP measures. To do this, we established multiple linear models.

4.1.1 Analogical study of the depth of the significant effects of board quality on the financial performance measures

To correctly determine the individual significance of the variables, we referred to the student statistic. When the estimated statistic's probability is less than one of the reference significance thresholds, we select the variable in question. Otherwise, the effect of the variable is considered insignificant. As shown in the appendix, **Tables A1–A8** illustrate the impacts of board quality on different FP measures. This list summarizes the coefficients of the different explanatory variables estimated by the model for each sample.

The BOD may have a positive or negative influence on the bank's FP, depending on the situations encountered. So far, we have checked the significance of the variables that explain the BOD quality in each model. In the next step, we established a comparative study of the impact between similar models, which highlights the importance of the board in their existence. Finally, we drew a comparison between the preestablished signs (expected) and the signs already found.

From the foregoing, the mono-analysis already carried out shows an ambiguity in the hypotheses' confirmation or assertion from a single FP measure. Also, not all tested variables revealed important and significant effects on performance measures. The resolution of the incompatibility of the signs led us to establish a state of reconciliation between the effects specific to the determinants that are specific to each bank type.

4.1.2 Differential analysis between the board impacts on the financial performance of conventional and participatory banks

To better appreciate the depth of the difference in board effects on the FP of each bank type, we grouped the individual impacts of each board-related variable on the FP for each bank type. Then, we proceeded to the comparative analysis between the combined impacts of the BOD on each FP measure relative to the CBs' group and the combined effects of the BOD on each FP measure of the PBs' group. **Tables 5–8** illustrate the reconciliation results specific to CBs with their Islamic competitors.

4.1.2.1 Board size

According to **Table 5**, if the reasonable composition is not balanced based on the criteria of the number and quality of directors, during and after the covid-19 crisis, the board size has a negative influence on the CBs' FP [36, 37, 41, 47, 48, 50]. This is valid if the board members did not satisfy the independence and competence conditions. A large board destroys its effectiveness due to the loss of responsibility and coordination among its members, which encourages directors to pursue their own interests. Besides, boards composed of a large number of directors favor opportunistic behavior and the power of dominance among directors. These acts are transformed into conflicts of interest and coalitions [2, 43]. Large boards encourage members to push managers to maximize board spending as well as their remunerations. Such pressure directly affects the FP of banks because of additional expenses [36]. This type of conduct results in the exclusion of the minority shareholders' interests.

Similarly, the same Table shows that, during and after the covid-19 crisis, the combined impact of board size in the framework of PBs negatively affected their FP [10, 45]. As a result, in PBs, boards made up of a large staff deteriorated their FP. This makes it difficult to supervise members and provide more human capital to advise

Variable	LnPc/LnPi	Ec/Ei	Lc/Li	LnSc/LnSi	Cumulative Effect	Decision
LnBOARDSc	–❁	–❁	+	–❁	—	H_{11} accepted but H_{12}, H_{13} and H_{14} rejected
LnBOARDSi	–❁	+❁	–❁	–❁	—	

Notes: + = positive impact, – = negative impact, and ❁ = significant impact.

Table 5.
Summary of the board size impacts on the FP of conventional and Islamic banks.

managers. The effect of many directors negatively affected mainly liquidity and solvency, which shows that the board extension within PBs results from decisions that provoke unfavorable financial flaws in FP. This situation may be due to several reasons. First, the lack of sufficient training among some administrators on Fikh Al Mouamalat can generate decisions far from the Charia law. Next, as the number of directors increases, so does the proportion of conflicts between board members. Moreover, consistent scientific knowledge can create ambiguity in the process of financial reporting between a large board and the Charia committee members. This type of relationship ended up developing information asymmetry, limiting transparency, and monopolizing decisions independently of the Charia committee. Indeed, within the PBs, a large board favors the guidance of the right to vote against the policies adopted by the Charia committee related to the liquidity and recovery of the PBs' credits. Finally, given the auxiliary role of the PBs' board as a complementary governance mechanism, there is excessive intervention by board members in the decision-making process, confirmation of investments, and distribution of loans to customers. On the one hand, the excess generates an imbalance in the control procedure; on the other hand, the intervention of the new members causes FP volatility.

4.1.2.2 Rooting of the board chairman

According to **Table 6**, during and after the covid-19 crisis, the effect on the board chairman's reliance on the CBs' FP was negative [17, 45, 55–59]. In the framework of agency theory, such an impact can be interpreted according to the context. All other things being equal, mandate votes are renewed by the general assembly, and if there is no cumulation between the CEO and board chairman positions, this situation is considered beneficial for the bank's continuity, provided that it has good financial indicators justifying the legal progress of the mandate. Conversely, if the CEO also serves as the board chairman, or if he/she finds the opportunity to automatically renew his/her mandate, or if he/she exploits the shortcomings of the governance system for his/her own benefit, the extension is considered unfavorable because it is not justified. Since our CBs' sample is heterogeneous, the intention to renew a mandate for rooting exists in some banks. This impact was confirmed by the collective effect of the duality on the CBs' efficiency and liquidity. Moreover, the warranted prolongation of the mandate also exists in other types of CBs. This was demonstrated by the dominant effect of the variable "BOARDCRc" on the CBs' profitability and solvency, but its impacts are not considerable.

However, during and after the covid-19 crisis, **Table 6** identified a positive cumulative association between the rooting of the board chairman and the PBs' FP [28, 32, 53, 54]. According to the results, liquidity is a central axis for evaluating PBs. Although the creation of liquidity is linked to investments, and the former directors, in the majority of cases, held a proportion of the bank's capital, the establishment and

Variable	LnPc/LnPi	Ec/Ei	Lc/Li	LnSc/LnSi	Cumulative Effect	Decision
BOARDCRc	+	–❁	–❁	+	—	H_{24} accepted but H_{21}, H_{22} and H_{23} rejected
BOARDCRi	—	+❁	+❁	+	+	

Notes: + = positive impact, – = negative impact, and ❁ = significant impact.

Table 6.
Summary of the impacts of the rooting of the board chairman on FP of conventional and Islamic banks.

maximization of business relations are correlated mainly with the seniority of the board chairman. The more the world of the board chairman is renewed, the more he/she gains experience and the more he/she masters the situation and the reality of the bank. Besides, large PBs are often built by family businesses or widely-owned companies. Also, the choice of profitable investments, the extension of projects, and the opening of several economic sectors require useful experience, good control of the economic environment, a high level of consciousness, and sufficient intelligence to help him/her predict the level of investment risk and avoid challenges and confusions of legal rules and transaction jurisprudence.

4.1.2.3 Board independence

Returning to the conclusions drawn from **Table 7**, during and after the covid-19 crisis, the cumulative effect on the various measures of FP showed that the presence of independent members on the CBs' boards threatens the banks' FP [17, 31, 32, 80–83]. Independent directors influenced the voting power in making important decisions related to recruitment, compensation, dividend policy, and the appointment and removal of officers. The key factor that determines the ideal board composition is the ability to provide competent individual/collective oversight of risk-taking activities and better stakeholder control. Besides, executive directors typically have valuable information about the banks' activities. However, our CBs' sample consists of a group of large and publicly traded banks. The selection of qualified people who meet both independence and competence criteria is very difficult. Nevertheless, governance issues related to agency relationships are directly correlated to FP or one of its determinants, such as profit, expense, or revenue. Risk-taking is an obligation of the "Control" function; it remains a questionable necessity as CBs market a very complex range of products and encompasses a mosaic of incoherent governance mechanisms.

However, in the case of PBs, during and after the covid-19 crisis, board independence had a positive combined effect on FP [27, 36, 65, 66, 68, 69, 71, 72]. This effect originates from the centralization of power. It reflects the authority to release specific information given by the BOD's executive directors. Also, in PBs, this result is due to work sharing between several committees, the decentralization of decision-making power, and the planning procedure for the FP objectives. In fact, an external director specializing in Islamic banking has a stimulating and positive impact on profitability and efficiency. This can have an insignificant impact on profitability, liquidity, and solvency because he/she has a good skill that provides him/her with the ability to understand and master the true situation of the bank. Moreover, nonexecutive directors are, in most cases, prohibited from holding additional positions and related

Variable	LnPc/ LnPi	Ec/ Ei	Lc/ Li	LnSc/ LnSi	Cumulative Effect	Decision
LnBOARDIc	—	–❁	—	+	—	H_{34} accepted but H_{31}, H_{32} and H_{33} rejected
LnBOARDIi	+❁	—	+❁	+❁	+	
Notes: + = positive impact, – = negative impact, and ❁ = significant impact.						

Table 7.
Summary of the board independence impacts on FP of conventional and Islamic banks.

activities on the boards of several PBs. As a result, they objectively follow the control process to keep their positions.

4.1.2.4 Number of board meetings

As shown in **Table 8**, during and after the covid-19 crisis, the analysis of the impacts corresponding to the number of board meetings on the CBs' FP revealed a fuzzy combinatorial effect [9, 89, 92]. A high number of board meetings has a positive impact on the CBs' liquidity and solvency as their liquidity levels improve through many board meetings. The board is legally authorized to hire, fire, and compensate officers for fraud, manipulation, or results/earnings' management. Also, the BOD is responsible for auditing financial reliability, verifying compliance with regulations, and reducing asymmetric information between shareholders and managers. Besides, the BOD oversees the operational, strategic, and financial decisions of the bank. However, all these responsibilities require an optimal number of meetings to cover all discussions, occupy all complex operations, view all detailed records, and frame all the problems and challenges of departments. To do this, the more the directors meet, the more they ensure that managers pursue strategies that follow the shareholders' interests, and the directors ensure smooth running, evaluation, and correction. This scene is valid for all financial transactions and records of the CBs' availability, even if the directors have decreased the annual number of meetings due to mutual control or because of the strong pressure exerted by all stakeholders on the board members. Nevertheless, in cases of profitability, the decision parameters are reversed insofar as profitability depends on several external, partially controllable factors, such as the deposit rate, the investor credit rate, and the consumption credit rate at the end of the year. Similarly, the decision rule is reversed in the case of an assessment of bank profitability since it depends on the economic environment and the macroeconomic factors that must be well controlled. In general, the decrease in the number of board meetings generates more freedom to make arbitrary decisions and judgments and gives managers the space to plan performance diligence, manage the results, choose investments that are more or less profitable, agree to variable-rate loans, change interest rates, change monetary practices, misapply policies, etc. As a result, these practices open up the space for information asymmetry between board directors and foster conflicts of interest between other governance mechanisms and between stakeholders in general.

Contrary to our prediction, according to **Table 8**, within the PBs, during and after the covid-19 crisis, the association of the different effects relative to the impact of board meetings on the FP generated an overall negative effect [31, 88, 90, 95]. Depending on the case, this impact can be justified by one of three reasons. First, it is caused by the deliberate and intentional weakness at the board level for the benefit of another substitute mechanism, such as the Audit Committee, the Charia Committee,

Variable	LnPc/LnPi	Ec/Ei	Lc/Li	LnSc/LnSi	Cumulative Effect	Decision
LnBOARDMc	−❁	−❁	+❁	−❁	Neutral effect	Blurred effect
LnBOARDMi	−❁	—	+	+	—	H_4 rejected

Notes: + = positive impact, — = negative impact, and ❁ = significant impact.

Table 8.
Summary of the board meetings impacts on FP of conventional and Islamic banks.

the Nominating Committee, the Compensation Committee, and the Executive Committee. Second, the undesirable effect is caused by a radical failure in the PBs' policies regarding meetings. This is due to the bad choice of meeting times, inefficient treatment of the problems of earnings management, asset appointments and dismissals, opportunistic behaviors, and personal interests. Third, the administrators made many decisions discordant with the general policy followed by the PBs and contradictory with those taken by the Charia Committee. They did not have the necessary competence to take decisions in conformity with the Charia norms. Whatever the official policy adopted by the bank, the number of meetings affects the PBs' FP in two ways. In quantitative terms, the limited number of meetings reflects a lack of awareness of internal control issues, management control, financial fraud, and accounting falsification. In qualitative terms, a small meeting number does not allow members to discuss the reliability of financial information, verify the degree of compliance with Islamic audit regulations, maintain good governance, and establish necessary mechanisms to reduce the asymmetry of information between shareholders and executives to ensure the investors' interests and the PBs' FP.

4.2 Discussion

The board size had a combined negative and statistically significant impact on the FP of both conventional and participatory banks during and after the covid-19 crisis, thus confirming the first hypothesis. In this comparative study between FPs, the concerning impact limited the comparison's extent. It can add more information to stakeholders, as it can neutralize the comparison between the FPs of two types of banks based solely on this criterion. This impact corroborates the work of [43, 118]. During and after the covid-19 crisis, a large number of directors on the board improved their expertise. However, in an agency framework, it increases potential conflicts and presents a more significant potential for disagreement and lack of coordination in management decisions [47, 119, 120].

In accordance with the literature predictions, the duality has a negative and significant combined impact on the CBs' FP during and after the covid-19 crisis; for this reason, the second hypothesis was accepted [17, 119, 121]. However, in the case of PBs, the duality had a positive and statistically significant combined effect on the PBs' FP during and after the covid-19 crisis. For this reason, the second hypothesis was rejected [53, 122]. In the agency theory framework, this result joins the literature that denounces management duality by causing abuse of the leader's power. Indeed, some authors, such as [2, 5] stipulate that this accumulation of functions decreases agency costs through, for example, the ambiguity of responsibilities, the impartiality of control, the imbalance of power, the conflicts of interest, the asymmetry of information, etc., and weakens the board's effectiveness and thus reduces FP.

As for the percentage of independent directors on the board, during and after the covid-19 crisis, this variable generated a negative and significant combined impact on the CBs' FP that led to the rejection of the third hypothesis [17, 64, 123]. However, in the PBs' framework, the overall impact of the same variable generated a positive and significant impact on their FP during and after the covid-19 crisis, which led us to accept the third hypothesis [124]. In the agency context, independent directors are not able to understand the complexity of the bank's activities, resolve agency conflicts, and fulfill their main role, namely the managers' discipline. This result was proved by several authors, such as [125, 126]. In this case, we can estimate that the control role of the manager in the CBs is attributed to the central banks that represent the regulatory and supervisory authorities, which enact several prudential rules to be observed by all CBs and ensure their application.

Regarding the differences between the combined impacts of the boards' meetings on FPs, we found that the overall impacts of the CBs' board meetings were ambiguous during and after the covid-19 crisis. This result is due to the unclear trend of all the impacts on their FP [9]. For this reason, I cannot draw a conclusive result either by accepting or rejecting the provided hypothesis in the case of CBs. However, in the PBs' framework, during and after the covid-19 crisis, the compound impact of the PBs' board meetings on their FP is negative [11, 127]. Therefore, the global result is not conclusive and does not allow users of financial information to make a useful comparative decision.

The filtration of the obtained impacts allowed us to only take the impacts resulting from two board determinants on the banks' FP: the CEO/Chairman duality and the boards' independence. The comparative report of these two determinants showed that during and after the covid-19 crisis, duality and independence deteriorated the CBs' FP, while on the other hand, they increased the PBs' FP.

5. Conclusion

From the results, we noticed that the combined impact of the BODs on the CBs' FP reduced their FP during and after the covid-19 crisis. Besides, the presence of a nonsignificant composite impact, particularly of the CBs' board meetings on the FP, provides the failure of this determinant to stage their role in a behavioral decision attitude. Independent of the bank type, the board is responsible for planning policies and making the best decisions. Jointly, line managers are required to improve the FP and maximize banks' profits; however, the lack of credibility and feasibility of the board's quality affected the CBs' FP. As a result, this finding leads to the conclusion that there are one or more substitutable determinants/mechanisms of the lost impact or that there is a complete failure of the governance system that requires revision.

In the context of participatory financial institutions, governance theories are not fully developed. The literature lacks integration of strategic considerations into the guidelines of the BOD. Moreover, empirically, although the sum of the cumulative impacts of the different BOD determinants on the PBs' FP is preferable to that relating to CBs, their impact on FP remains unclear during and after the covid-19 crisis. To overcome the problems related to the impact of the board's quality on the PBs' FP, we proposed the creation of a unified international academy of accounting, finance, and governance specialized in teaching the Islamic sciences of control, audit, and operating practices. The purpose of this body is to train scientifically, theoretically, and practically qualified executives not only to perform the traditional duties of a banker (accountant, financier, and auditor) and to comply with Islamic standards but also to introduce a radical change that aims to improve the products and services' quality in PBs and to continuously drive the creation and improvement of FP.

To avoid some negative impacts and the ambiguity of other impacts on FP, the BOD must first and foremost consider the processes' complexity with uncertainties, process discussions, techniques, and decision-making in its authority position to optimally monitor resources. For this gap, we proposed an innovative auditing system that is relevant not only for governing the board but is also very useful for other governance mechanisms: Dynamic governance by objective (DGBO). This is an intelligent information system that is formed by a large and detailed informational fiber. This system adapts simultaneously to all other systems of governance for all types of banks, while the traditional technical system is limited to the analysis and nervous interpretation of data. The set of two systems forms an instant mechanism for sending alerts once there are overruns. The introduction of a momentary double-checking system pushes the controlling actors to establish systemic coordination of the interdependent tasks to ensure the quality of the accounting documents and avoid errors. If fraud and falsification exist, they will be detected by the intelligent system. The new approach to governance is based on a decentralized vision and is too focused on control as its reason, which is data at a very advanced level. This model ensures the coordination of actions through the collective regulation of interorganizational dimensions and the

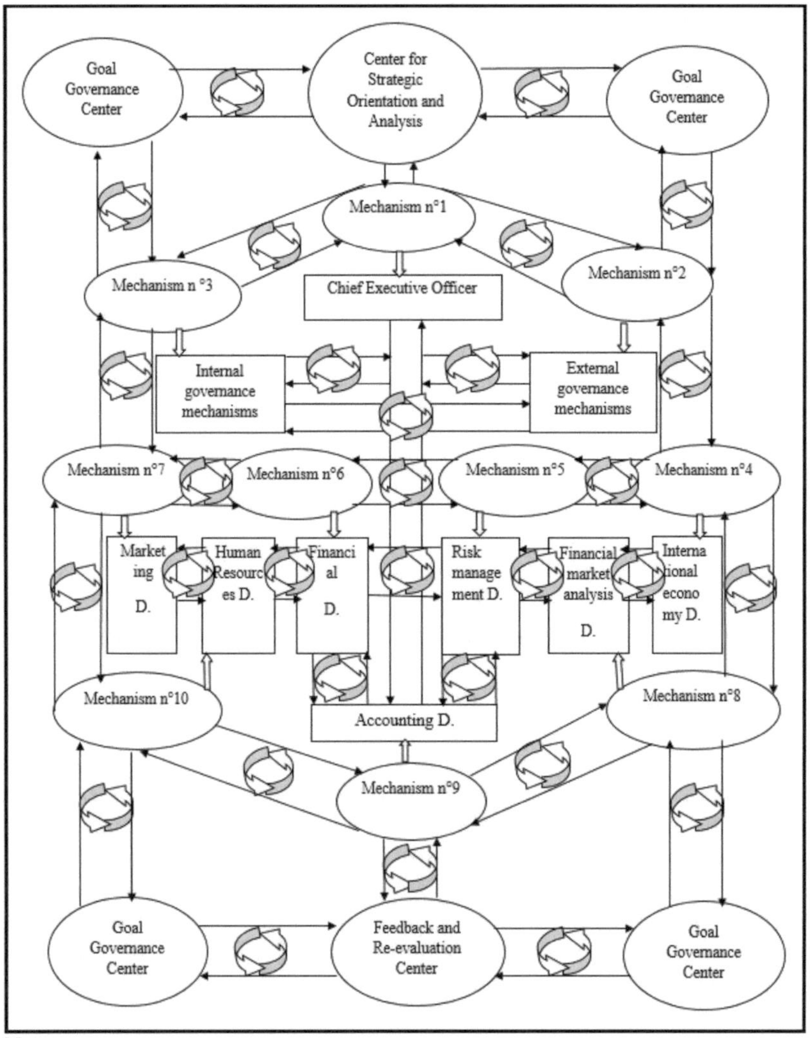

Notes:
: exchange of information, data, accounting documents and decisions
: relative control relationship between management and / or department and governance mechanisms
: intersection between dynamic behavioral governance flows and opportunistic behavior flows

Figure 1.
Simplified organizational structure of an objective governance system.

integration of interprofessional processes that cannot be established by summation or discrimination.

The constituent bodies of an objective regulatory system shall exchange their information, figures, documents, instruments, activities, records, and financial statements, usually in two reciprocal directions. As displayed in **Figure 1**, the new system is composed of an exchange network for incoming data and another network in the reverse direction. In these centers, all the data and information fibers collected by the specialists in the areas of internal control, management control, and auditing are collected and filtered to identify frauds, manipulations, misappropriations, conflicts of interest, and moral behaviors. After clustering, the center that detects the manipulation, fraud, challenge, or abnormal behavior, the fiber directs the data to the nearest referral center to make the necessary corrections and then reorients the new corrected data and related information into the correct meaning according to the objectives fixed in advance. All this program is prepared through an information system that is established according to the bank type and its particularities. Our alternative governance system is as follows:

Like all scientific research, our study is not exempt from limitations. First, the main limitation is using only four proxies to measure board quality because it ignores much of the board's impact on banks' FP in both bank types. The adopted board proxies in the present study could be augmented with the addition of other variables such as executive directors' specialization, executive directors' reputation, executive directors' tenure, executive directors' sex, and executive directors' expertise. Second, using a limited number of FP measures may not capture all the impacts issued by the boards. Therefore, despite the large sample sizes, we cannot draw thorough generalizations from our comparative results. Moreover, although the sample sizes are important, expanding the sample sizes and the countries' numbers tends to minimize the probability of errors, maximize the accuracy of the banks' estimates, and increase the generalizability of the comparative results.

Appendices

LnPc	Coefficient	Std. Err.	Z	P > |z|	[95% Conf. Interval]	
LnBOARDSc	−.4250975	.1177521	−3.61	.000***	−.6558874	−.1943076
BOARDCRc	.0199997	.0573994	0.35	.728	−.0925011	.1325005
LnBOARDIc	−.0362331	.0349907	−1.04	.300	−.1048137	.0323474
LnBOARDMc	−.542087	.0646165	−8.39	.000***	−.668733	−.415441
TYc	.0771252	.0655637	1.18	.239	−.0513773	.2056277
LnAGc	.3560312	.0444134	8.02	.000***	.2689826	.4430799
LnSIc	.3086841	.11053	2.79	.005***	.0920493	.5253188
LnINFc	−.2208978	.0402224	−5.49	.000***	−.2997322	−.1420635
Constant	3.600837	.3567324	10.09	.000	2.901654	4.30002

*** *Correlation is significant at the 1%.*

Table A1.
Regression results of board impacts on CBs' profitability.

LnPi	Coefficient	Std. Err.	Z	P > |z|	[95% Conf. Interval]	
LnBOARDSi	−.2258192	.1247032	−1.81	.070*	−.0185946	.470233
BOARDCRi	−.0304139	.0760295	−0.40	.689	−.179429	.1186011
LnBOARDIi	.0283029	.0490483	0.58	.004***	.1244357	.06783
LnBOARDMi	−.0792698	.0460498	−1.72	.085*	−.1695257	.0109861
TYi	.2171499	.0522316	4.16	.000***	.1147778	.319522
LnAGi	.2108591	.0596759	3.53	.000***	.0938965	.3278217
LnSIi	−.4366414	.2311491	−1.89	.059*	−.8896853	.0164026
LnINFi	−.5308617	.0509122	−10.43	.000***	−.6306477	−.4310756
Constant	3.201927	.5702389	5.62	.000	2.08428	4.319575

Correlation is significant at the 10%.* ***Correlation is significant at the 1%.*

Table A2.
Regression results of board impacts on PBs' profitability.

Ec	Coefficient	Std. Err.	Z	P > |z|	[95% Conf. Interval]	
LnBOARDSc	−.4034392	.1541054	−2.62	.009***	−.7054803	−.1013981
BOARDCRc	−.2044307	.0665404	−3.07	.002***	−.3348476	−.0740138
LnBOARDIc	−.3385383	.0602644	−5.62	.000***	−.4566544	−.2204223
LnBOARDMc	−.2001578	.0680429	−2.94	.003***	−.3335194	−.0667962
TYc	.1072601	.0679662	1.58	.001***	−.0259513	.2404714
LnAGc	.2722857	.071187	3.82	.000***	.1327617	.4118096
LnSIc	−.6239381	.1124029	−5.55	.000***	−.8442438	−.4036325
LnINFc	−.3353558	.0493592	6.79	.000***	.2386136	.432098
Constant	−2.00778	.4745786	−4.23	.000	−2.937937	−1.077623

****Correlation is significant at the 1%.*

Table A3.
Regression results of board impacts on CBs' efficiency.

Ei	Coefficient	Std. Err.	Z	P > |z|	[95% Conf. Interval]	
LnBOARDSi	.0124856	.0024575	5.08	0.000***	.0076691	.0173022
BOARDCRi	.0014518	.001415	1.03	0.001***	−.0013214	.0042251
LnBOARDIi	−.0010896	.0011001	−0.99	0.322	−.0032457	.0010665
LnBOARDMi	−.001975	.0013519	−1.46	0.144	−.0046248	.0006748
TYi	.0012718	.0009673	1.31	0.189	−.0006242	.0031677
LnAGi	.0073942	.001096	6.75	.000***	.005246	.0095423
LnSIi	.0122375	.0048068	2.55	.011***	.0028165	.0216586
LnINFi	−.0006461	.0012217	0.53	.597	−.0017485	.0030407
Constant	−.0599947	.011775	−5.10	.000	−.0830733	−.0369162

****Correlation is significant at the 1%.*

Table A4.
Regression results of board impacts on PBs' efficiency.

Lc	Coefficient	Std. Err.	Z	P > |z|	[95% Conf. Interval]	
LnBOARDSc	.0055105	.0258944	0.21	.831	−.0452415	.0562625
BOARDCRc	−.0346359	.0144743	−2.39	.017**	−.0630051	−.0062667
LnBOARDIc	−.0104435	.0104218	−1.00	.316	−.0308699	.0099829
LnBOARDMc	.0748228	.0115973	6.45	.000***	.0520925	.0975531
TYc	−.0114669	.012047	−0.95	.341	−.0350786	.0121448
LnAGc	.0381463	.0104971	3.63	.000***	.0175724	.0587202
LnSIc	−.0725111	.0216542	−3.35	.001***	−.1149526	−.0300696
LnINFc	−.0846695	.0110867	−7.64	.000***	−.1063991	−.0629399
Constant	.6602716	.0862141	7.66	.000	.4912951	.8292481

** *Correlation is significant at the 5%.* *** *Correlation is significant at the 1%.*

Table A5.
Regression results of the board impacts on CBs' liquidity.

Li	Coefficient	Std. Err.	Z	P > |z|	[95% Conf. Interval]	
LnBOARDSi	−.0647014	.0266515	−2.43	.015**	−.1169374	−.0124654
BOARDCRi	.0290831	.0121164	2.40	.018**	.0053353	.0528308
LnBOARDIi	.0027745	.0144338	0.19	.000***	−.0255152	.0310642
LnBOARDMi	.0095326	.0121374	0.79	.432	−.0142563	.0333215
TYi	.0127265	.0129126	0.99	.004***	.0380348	.0125819
LnAGi	−.0208915	.0117612	−1.78	.076*	−.043943	.00216
LnSIi	.2445306	.0341898	7.15	.000***	.1775197	.3115415
LnINFi	−.0200158	.0112233	−1.78	.075*	−.0420131	.0019815
Constant	.2448671	.0955678	2.56	.010	.0575576	.4321766

* *Correlation is significant at the 10%.* ** *Correlation is significant at the 5%.* *** *Correlation is significant at the 1%.*

Table A6.
Regression results of the board impacts on PBs' liquidity.

LnSc	Coefficient	Std. Err.	Z	P > |z|	[95% Conf. Interval]	
LnBOARDSc	−.0839261	.0403352	−2.08	.037**	−.1629815	−.0048707
BOARDCRc	.0056781	.0167608	0.34	.735	−.0271724	.0385286
LnBOARDIc	.0119223	.0154934	0.77	.442	−.0184442	.0422888
LnBOARDMc	.0542974	.0186937	2.90	.004***	.0176584	.0909364
TYc	−.1263987	.0213637	−5.92	.000***	−.1682707	−.0845267
LnAGc	−.0388244	.0161149	−2.41	.016**	−.0704091	−.0072397
LnSIc	−.0500508	.0304722	−1.64	.001***	−.1097752	.0096737
LnINFc	−.196619	.0177722	−11.06	.000***	−.2314519	−.1617862
Constant	.6580049	.1015307	6.48	.000	.4590084	.8570014

** *Correlation is significant at the 5%.* *** *Correlation is significant at the 1%.*

Table A7.
Regression results of the board impacts on CBs' solvency.

LnSi	Coefficient	Std. Err.	Z	P > |z|	[95% Conf. Interval]	
LnBOARDSi	−1.078232	.2612626	−4.13	.000***	−1.590297	−.5661666
BOARDCRi	.0157862	.0735698	0.21	.830	−.1284079	.1599802
LnBOARDIi	.358276	.0948083	3.78	.000***	.1724552	.5440968
LnBOARDMi	.0942325	.0748859	1.26	.208	−.0525411	.2410061
TYi	−.0163018	.0599326	−0.27	.786	−.1337676	.1011641
LnAGi	−.0016083	.0488283	−0.03	.974	−.09731	.0940934
LnSIi	.0953078	.151482	0.63	.529	−.2015914	.3922071
LnINFi	−.2130698	.0584814	−3.64	.000***	−.3276912	−.0984484
Constant	1.901046	.6527903	2.91	.004	.6216002	3.180491

***Correlation is significant at the 1%.*

Table A8.
Regression results of the board impacts on PBs' solvency.

Author details

Achraf Haddad[1,2]

1 Doctor of Financial and Accounting Methods, Tunisia

2 The Laboratory of Governance, Finance, and Accounting, Faculty of Economic Sciences and Management of Sfax, Tunisia

*Address all correspondence to: achraf.haddad2015@gmail.com

References

[1] Charreaux G. The positive theory of the agency: Positioning and contributions. Review of Industrial Economics. 2000;**92**(2–3):193-214. Available from: https://www.persee.fr/doc/rei_0154-3229_2000_num_92_1_1046

[2] Jensen MC. The modern industrial revolution, exit and the failure of internal control system. Journal of Finance. 1993; **48**(3):831-880. DOI: 10.1111/j.1540-6261.1993.tb04022.x

[3] Choe H, Lee BS. Korean bank governance reform after the Asian financial crisis. Pacific–Basin Finance Journal. 2003;**11**(4):483-508. DOI: 10.1016/S0927-538X(03)00051-9

[4] Fama EF. Agency problems and the theory of the firm. Journal of Political Economy. 1980;**88**(2):288-307. Available from: https://www.jstor.org/stable/1837292

[5] Fama EF, Jensen MC. Separation of ownership and control. Journal of Law & Economic. 1983a;**26**(2):301-325. Available from: https://www.jstor.org/stable/725104

[6] Nam S-W, Nam IC. Corporate Governance in Asia: Recent Evidence from Indonesia, Republic of Korea, Malaysia, and Thailand. Asian Development Bank Institute. Indonesia, Republic of Korea, Malaysia, and Thailand: Tokyo Research Paper; 2004. Available from: https://www.adb.org/sites/default/files/publication/159384/adbi-corp-gov-asia.pdf

[7] Cattrysse J. Reflections on corporate governance and the role of the internal auditor. Master in Internal Auditing, Roularta Media Group. 2005:1-66. DOI: 10.2139/ssrn.485364

[8] Ulussever T. A comparative analysis of corporate governance and bank performance: Islamic banks with conventional banks. Research Journal of Business & Management. 2018;**5**(1): 34-50. DOI: 10.17261/Pressacademia.2018.815

[9] Bawaneh S. Impact of corporate governance on financial institution's performance: A board composition case. Asian Economic & Financial Review. 2020;**10**(1):54-63. DOI: 10.18488/journal.aefr.2020.101.54.63

[10] Elgadi E. Assessing the Financial Performance of Islamic Banking: The Case of Sudanese Banks. Ph.D. thesis. University of East London, Business and Law. London: UEL Research Repository 2019 Powered by Haplo; 2016. DOI: 10.15123/PUB.5373

[11] El-Maude JG, Bawa AB, Shamaki A. Effect of board size, board composition and board meetings on financial performance of listed consumer goods in Nigeria. International Business Research. 2018;**11**(6):1-10. DOI: 10.5539/ibr.v11n6p1

[12] Harris M, Raviv A. A theory of board control and size. Review of Financial Studies. 2008;**21**(4):1797-1832. DOI: 10.1093/rfs/hhl030

[13] Hermuningsih S, Kusuma H, Cahyarifida RA. Corporate governance and firm performance: An empirical study from Indonesian manufacturing firms. The Journal of Asian Finance, Economics & Business. 2020;**7**(11): 827-834. DOI: 10.13106/jafeb.2020.vol7.no11.827

[14] Joenoes MZ, Rokhim R. Does foreign board increase the company's

performance? The evidence from Indonesia. Journal of Economics, Business, & Accountancy Ventura. 2019; **22**(2):213-222. DOI: 10.14414/jebav.v22i2.1449

[15] Pathan S. Strong boards, CEO power and bank risk–taking. Journal of Banking & Finance. 2009;**33**(7): 1340-1350. DOI: 10.1016/j.jbankfin.2009.02.001

[16] Shawtari FA, Mohamad MHS, Rashid HMA, Ayedh AM. Board characteristics and real performance in Malaysian state-owned enterprises (SOEs). International Journal of Productivity and Performance Management. 2017;**66**(8):1064-1086. DOI: 10.1108/IJPPM-12-2015-0188

[17] Bansal D, Singh S. Does board structure impact a firm's financial performance? Evidence from the Indian software sector. American Journal of Business. 2022;**37**(1):34-49. DOI: 10.1108/AJB-08-2020-0125

[18] Asare N, Muah P, Frimpong G, Anyass IA. Corporate board structures, financial performance and stability: Evidence from banking markets in Africa. Journal of Money and Business. 2022. DOI: 10.1108/JMB-12-2021-0071

[19] Borlea SN, Achim MV, Mare C. Board characteristics and firm performances in emerging economies: Lessons from Romania. Economic Research-Ekonomska Istraživanja. 2017; **30**(1):55-75. DOI: 10.1080/1331677X.2017.1291359

[20] Adams RB, Mehran H. Is corporate governance different for bank holding companies? FRBNY Economic Policy Review. 2003;**9**(1):123-142. Available from: https://www.newyorkfed.org/medialibrary/media/research/epr/03v09n1/0304adampdf.pdf

[21] Adams RB, Mehran H. Bank board structure and performance: Evidence for large bank holding companies. Journal of Financial Intermediation. 2012;**21**(2): 243-267. DOI: 10.1016/j.jfi.2011.09.002

[22] Battaglia F, Gallo A. Risk governance and Asian bank performance: An empirical investigation over the financial crisis. Emerging Markets Review. 2015; **25**(C):53-68. DOI: 10.1016/j.ememar.2015.04.004

[23] Belkhir M. Board of directors' size and performance in the banking industry. International Journal of Managerial Finance. 2009;**5**(2):201-221. DOI: 10.1108/17439130910947903

[24] Choi DW, Velikova N, Lee S. Influence of corporate governance on financial performance among alcohol beverage firms. Journal of Quality Assurance in Hospitality & Tourism. 2021;**22**(4):425-446. DOI: 10.1080/1528008X.2020.1802389

[25] Dalton DR, Daily CM, Johnson JL, Ellstrand AE. Number of directors and financial performance: A meta–analysis. Academy of Management Journal. 1999; **42**(6):674-686. DOI: 10.2307/256988

[26] Lim S, Matolcsy Z, Chow D. The association between board composition and different types of voluntary disclosure. European Accounting Review. 2007;**16**(3):555-583. DOI: 10.1080/09638180701507155

[27] Merendino A, Melville R. The board of directors and firm performance: Empirical evidence from listed companies. Corporate Governance: The International Journal of Business in Society. 2019;**19**(3):508-551. DOI: 10.1108/CG-06-2018-0211

[28] Naushad M, Malik SA. Corporate governance and bank performance: A

study of selected banks in GCC region. Asian Social Science. 2015;**11**(9):226-234. DOI: 10.5539/ass.v11n9p226

[29] Wasiuzzaman S, Gunasegavan UN. Comparative study of the performance of Islamic and conventional banks: The case of Malaysia. Humanomics. 2013; **29**(1):43-60. DOI: 10.1108/08288661311299312

[30] Yung MF. The Relationship between Corporate Governance and Bank Performance in Hong Kong. Master dissertation paper. China: Auckland University of Technology; 2009. Available from: https://orapp.aut.ac.nz/bitstream/handle/10292/739/YungMF.pdf?sequence=4&isAllowed=y

[31] Khatib SFA, Nour A-NI. The impact of corporate governance on firm performance during the covid-19 pandemic: Evidence from Malaysia. Journal of Asian Finance, Economics & Business. 2021;**8**(2):943-952. DOI: 10.13106/jafeb.2021.vol8.no2.0943

[32] Mititean P. Is the financial performance affected by board characteristics during covid-19? Evidence from the energy industry. Oradea Journal of Business and Economics. 2022;7(special):100-110. DOI: 10.47535/1991ojbe149

[33] Gary SW, Gleason AE. Board structure, ownership, and financial distress in banking firms. International Review of Economics & Finance. 1999; **8**(3):281-292. Available from: http://www.sciencedirect.com/science/article/pii/S1059-0560(99)00026-X

[34] Yoshikawa T, Phan PH. The performance implications of ownership-driven governance reform. European Management Journal. 2003;**21**(6): 698-706. DOI: 10.1016/j.emj.2003.09.013

[35] Beasley MS. An empirical analysis of the relation between the board of director composition and financial statement fraud. The Accounting Review. 1996;**71**(4):443-465. Available from: www.jstor.org/stable/248566

[36] Beltratti A, Stulz RM. The credit crisis around the globe: Why did some banks perform better? Journal of Financial Economics. 2012;**105**(1):1-17. DOI: 10.1016/j.jfineco.2011.12.005

[37] Cheng S. Board size and the variability of corporate performance. Journal of Financial Economics. 2008; **87**(1):157-176. DOI: 10.1016/j.jfineco.2006.10.006

[38] Cornett MM, Gayane H, Palia D, Hassan T. The impact of the manager–shareholder conflict on acquiring bank returns. Journal of Banking & Finance. 2003;**27**:103-131. DOI: 10.1016/S0378-4266(01)00210-2

[39] De-Andres P, Azofra V, Lopez F. Corporate boards in OECD countries: Size, composition, functioning and effectiveness. International Review. 2005;**13**(2):197-210. DOI: 10.1111/j.1467-8683.2005.00418.x

[40] Eisenberg T, Sundgren S, Wells MT. Larger board size and decreasing firm value in small firms. Journal of Financial Economics. 1998;**48**(1):35-54. Available from: https://scholarship.law.cornell.edu/facpub/393

[41] Fanta AB, Kemal KS, Waka YK. Corporate governance and impact on bank performance. Journal of Finance & Accounting. 2013;**1**(1):19-26. DOI: 10.11648/j.jfa.20130101.12

[42] Jensen MC, Meckling WH. Theory of the firm: Managerial behavior, agency costs and ownership structure. Journal of

Financial Economics. 1976;**3**(4):305-360. DOI: 10.1016/0304-405X(76)90026-X

[43] Lipton M, Lorsch JW. A modest proposal for improved corporate governance. Business Lawyer. 1992; **48**(1):59-77. Available from: https://www.jstor.org/stable/40687360

[44] Mak YT, Kusnadi Y. Size really matters: Further evidence on the negative relationship between board size and firm value. Pacific–Basin Finance Journal. 2005;**13**(3):301-308. DOI: 10.1016/j.pacfin.2004.09.002

[45] Mollah S, Zaman M. Charia supervision, corporate governance and performance: Conventional vs Islamic banks. Journal of Banking &Finance. 2015;**58**(C):418-435. DOI: 10.1016/j.jbankfin.2015.04.030

[46] Singh M, Davidson WN. Agency costs, ownership structure and corporate governance mechanisms. Journal of Banking & Finance. 2003;**27**(5):793-816. Available from: Http://www.sciencedirect.com/science/article/pii/S0378-4266(01)00260-6

[47] Staikouras C, Staikouras P, Agoraki MEK. The effect of board size and composition on European bank performance. European Journal of Law and Economics. 2007;**23**(1):1-27. DOI: 10.1007/s10657-007-9001-2

[48] Wang J, Chen M-H, Fang C-Y, Tian L. Does board size matter for Taiwanese hotel performance? Agency theory or resource dependence theory. Cornell Hospitality Quarterly. 2017; **59**(4):317-324. DOI: 10.1177/1938965517735906

[49] Yermack D. Higher market valuation of companies with a small board of directors. Journal of Financial Economics. 1996;**40**(2):185-211. DOI: 10.1016/0304-405X(95)00844-5

[50] Duppati G, Rao NV, Matlani N, Scrimgeour F, Patnaik D. Gender diversity and firm performance: Evidence from India and Singapore. Applied Economics. 2019;**52**(14):1553-1565. DOI: 10.1080/00036846.2019.1676872

[51] Rashidah AR, Fairuzana HMA. Board, audit committee, culture and earnings management: Malaysian evidence. Managerial Auditing Journal. 2006;**21**(7):783-804. DOI: 10.1108/02686900610680549

[52] Mersland R, Strom OR. Performance and governance in microfinance institutions. Journal of Banking & Finance. 2009;**33**(4):662-669. DOI: 10.1016/j.jbankfin.2008.11.009

[53] Al-Hawary SIS. The effect of governance banks on the banking performance of Jordanian commercial banks: Tobin's model Q "an applied study". International Journal of Finance & Economics. 2011;**71**:34-47. Available from: www.researchgate.net/publication/289782208_The_effect_of_banks_governance_on_banking_performance_of_the_Jordanian_commercial_banks_Tobin's_Q_model_an_applied_study

[54] Chang K, Lee J, Shim H. CEO duality and firm performance: Does economic policy uncertainty mediate the relation? International Review of Finance. 2019;**19**(4):877-891. DOI: 10.1111/irfi.12193

[55] Adams BR, Ferreira D. A theory of friendly boards. Journal of Finance. 2007;**62**(1):217-250. DOI: 10.1111/j.1540-6261.2007.01206.x

[56] Durgavanshi SS. Impact of Corporate Governance Practices on New

Topics in Emerging Markets Financial Performance of Microfinance Institutions in India. Thesis, USA: Tufts University, The Fletcher School of Law and Diplomacy; 2014. pp. 1-37. Available from: https://dl.tufts.edu/concern/pdfs/dr26z842z

[57] Hsu S, Lin S-W, Chen W-P, Huang J-W. CEO duality, information costs, and firm performance. The North American Journal of Economics & Finance. 2021;**55**(C):101011. DOI: 10.1016/j.najef.2019.101011

[58] Mihaela O, Bogdan-Narcis F, Paula-Andrea T. Corporate governance influence on banking performance: An analysis on Romania and Bulgaria. Scientific Annals of Economics and Business, Sciendo. 2018;**65**(3):317-332. DOI: 10.2478/saeb-2018-0020

[59] Wijethilake C, Ekanayake A. CEO duality and firm performance: The moderating roles of CEO informal power and board involvements. Social Responsibility Journal. 2020;**16**(8):1453-1474. DOI: 10.1108/SRJ-12-2018-0321

[60] Chen Y, Wang Y, Lin L. Board network, independent directors' governance and executive incentives. China Journal of Accounting Research. 2012;**7**(2):101-118. DOI: 10.1016/j.cjar.2013.09.002

[61] Li M, Roberts H. Does mandated independence improve firm performance? Evidence from New Zealand. Pacific Accounting Review. 2018;**30**(1):92-109. DOI: 10.1108/par-01-2017-0004

[62] Linck, J. S., Netter, J. M., &, Yang, T. (2008). The determinants of board structure. Journal of Financial Economics, 87(2), 308-328. doi:10.1016/j.jfineco.2007.03.004.

[63] Nguyen BD, Nielsen KM. The value of independent directors: Evidence from sudden deaths. Journal of Financial Economics. 2010;**98**(3):550-576. DOI: 10.1016/j.jfineco.2010.07.004

[64] Terjesen S, Couto EB, Francisco PM. Does the presence of independent and female directors impact firm performance? A multi-country study of board diversity. Journal of Management & Governance. 2016;**20**(3):447-483. DOI: 10.1007/s10997-014-9307-8

[65] Andres P, Vallelado E. Corporate governance in banking: The role of the board of directors. Journal of Banking and Finance. 2008;**32**(12):2570-2580. DOI: 10.1016/j.jbankfin.2008.05.008

[66] Beltratti A, Stulz RM. Why did Some Banks Perform Better during the Credit Crisis? A Cross–country Study of the Impact of Governance and Regulation. Working paper No. 15180. NBER Working Papers from National Bureau of Economic Research, Inc. Columbus, OH: The Ohio State University; 2009. Available from: http://www.nber.org/papers/w15180.pdf

[67] Bozec R, Dia M. Board structure and firm technical efficiency: Evidence from Canadian state-owned enterprises. European Journal of Operational Research. 2005;**177**(3):1734-1750. DOI: 10.1016/j.ejor.2005.10.001

[68] Erkens DH, Hung M, Matos P. Corporate governance in the 2007-2008 financial crisis: Evidence from financial institutions worldwide. Journal of Corporate Finance. 2012;**18**(2):389-411. DOI: 10.1016/j.jcorpfin.2012.01.005

[69] Fahlenbrach R, Stulz RM. Bank CEO incentives and the credit crisis. Journal of Financial Economics. 2011;**99**(1):11-26. DOI: 10.1016/j.jfineco.2010.08.010

[70] Fama EF, Jensen MC. Agency problems and residual claims. The Journal of Law & Economics. 1983b;**26** (2):327-349. DOI: 10.1086/467038

[71] Kallamu BS. Ownership structure, independent directors and firm performance. E3 Journal of Business Management & Economics. 2016;**7**(1): 19-28 Available from: Http://e3journals.org/cms/articles/1453866629_10.18685_EJBME-15-012.pdf

[72] Liu Y, Miletkov MK, Wei Z, Yang T. Board independence and firm performance in China. Journal of Corporate Finance. 2015;**30**:223-244. DOI: 10.1016/j.jcorpfin.2014.12.00

[73] Zahra SA, Pearce JH. Board composition from a strategic contingency perspective. Journal of Management Studies. 1992;**29**(4): 411-438. DOI: 10.1111/j.1467-6486.1992.tb00672.x

[74] Zahra SA, Pearce JA. Determinants of board directors' strategic involvement. European Management Journal. 1990; **8**(2):164-173. DOI: 10.1016/0263-2373(90)90082-H

[75] Tarek RG, Mohamed GA. Corporate governance of UAE financial institutions: A comparative study between conventional and Islamic banks. Journal of Applied Finance & Banking. 2016;**6**(5):119-160. Available from: Http://www.scienpress.com/Upload/JAFB%2FVol%206_5_7.pdf

[76] Brown P, Beekes W, Verhoeven. Corporate governance, accounting and finance: A review. Journal of Accounting & Finance. 2011;**5**(1):96-172. DOI: 10.1111/j.1467-629X.2010.00385.x

[77] Klein A. Audit committee, board of director characteristics and earnings management. Journal of Accounting & Economics. 2002;**33**(3):375-400. DOI: 10.1016/S0165-4101(02)00059-9

[78] Booth JR, Cornett MM, Tehranaian H. Boards of directors, ownership and regulation. Journal of Banking & Finance. 2002;**26**(10):1973-1996. DOI: 10.1016/S0378-4266(01)00181-9

[79] Macey JR, O'Hara M. The corporate governance of banks. Federal Reserve Bank of New York Economic Policy Review. 2003;**9**(1):91-107. Available from: https://www.newyorkfed.org/medialibrary/media/research/epr/03v09n1/0304mace.pdf

[80] Adams BR, Ferreira D. Strong managers, weak boards? CESifo Economic Studies. 2009;**55**(3–4): 482-514. DOI: 10.1093/cesifo/ifp023

[81] Adnan MA, Htay SNN, Rashid HMAB, Meera AKM. A panel data analysis on the relationship between corporate governance and bank efficiency. Journal of Accounting, Finance & Economics. 2011;**1**(1):1-15. DOI: 10.5296/ajfa.v4i1.810

[82] Rashid A. Board independence and firm performance: Evidence from Bangladesh. Future Business Journal. 2018;**4**(1):34-49. DOI: 10.1016/j.fbj.2017.11.003

[83] Shan YG. Managerial ownership, board independence and firm performance. Accounting Research Journal. 2019;**32.(3)**:203-220. DOI: 10.1108/arj-09-2017-0149

[84] Bhagat S, Black B. Board Independence and Long-term Firm Performance? USA: University of Colorado Boulder and Stanford Law School; 2000. pp. 1-44. Available from: https://leeds-faculty.Colorado.Edu/bhagat/bb-022300.Pdf

[85] Minton B, Taillard JPA, Williamson R. Do independence and financial expertise of the board matter for risk taking and performance? Working paper SSRN. In: Dice CA editor. Center for Research in Financial Economics. USA: The Ohio State University; 2010. Available from: https://www.eurofidai.org/Taillard_2010.pdf

[86] Adams RB. Governance and the financial crisis. International Review of Finance. 2012;**12**(1):7-38. DOI: 10.1111/j.1468-2443.2011.01147.x

[87] Busta I. Board effectiveness and the impact of the legal family in the European banking industry. Barcelona'Spain: FMA European Conference, Barcelona–Spain. 2007. Available from: https://www.researchgate.net/publication/228397225_Board_effectiveness_and_the_impact_of_the_legal_family_in_the_European_banking_industry

[88] Chen G, Firth M, Daniel NG, Rui ON. Ownership structure, corporate governance and fraud: Evidence from China. Journal of Corporate Finance. 2006;**12**(3):424-448. DOI: 10.1016/j.jcorpfin.2005.09.002

[89] Choi ON, Lai PF. Corporate governance and financial performance of bank in Asian regions and recommendations. Asian Journal of Finance &Accounting. 2014;**6**(2):377-406. DOI: 10.5296/ajfa.v6i2.6429

[90] Sánchez I. The effectiveness of corporate governance: Board structure and business technical efficiency in Spain. Central European Journal of Operations Research. 2010;**18**(3):311-339. DOI: 10.1007/S10100-009-0112-4

[91] Vafeas N. Board meeting frequency and firm performance. Journal of Financial Economics. 1999;**53**(1):113-142. Available from: Http://www.sciencedirect.com/science/article/pii/S0304-405X(99)00018-5

[92] Thu NTH, Hung PM, Anh NTL. An empirical study of corporate governance and banks' performance in Vietnamese commercial banks. SIU Journal of Management. 2016;**6**(2):1-29. Available from: https://jcwalsh.files.wordpress.com/2016/12/6-2-thu.pdf

[93] Eluyela DF, Akintimehin OO, Okere W, Ozordi E, Osuma GO, Ilogho SO, et al. Board meeting frequency and firm performance: Examining the nexus in Nigerian deposit money banks. Heliyon. 2018;**4**(10):e00850. DOI: 10.1016/j.heliyon.2018.e00850

[94] Idris AM, Ousama AA. The impact of board independence, gender diversity and nationality diversity on firm performance. Asia-Pacific Management Accounting Journal. 2021;**16**(1):323-346. DOI: 10.24191/APMAJ.V16i1-12

[95] Hanh LTM, Ting IWK, Kweh QL, Hoanh LTH. Board meeting frequency and financial performance: A case of listed firms in Vietnam. International Journal of Business & Society. 2018;**19**(2):464-472. Available from: https://hdl.handle.net/20.500.12519/134

[96] Sujan CP, Probir KB, Mohammad RI, Kaium MA, Abdullah AM. Profitability and liquidity of conventional banking and Islamic banking in Bangladesh: A comparative study. European Journal of Business & Management. 2013;**5**(24):113-123. Available from: https://www.iiste.org/Journals/index.php/EJBM/article/view/8523/8292

[97] Atyeh MH, Yasin J, Khatib A. Measuring the performance of the Kuwaiti banking sector before and after the recent financial crisis. Research

Journal of Finance & Accounting. 2015; **6**(22):76-79. Available from: https://www.iiste.org/Journals/index.php/RJFA/article/view/26920/27603

[98] Ogbeide S, Akanji B. A comparative assessment of the financial performance between religious–based and conventional banks in Nigeria. International Journal of Management Applications. 2018;**1**(1):1-7

[99] Haddad A, El Ammari A, Bouri A. Are the Islamic banks really more profitable than the conventional banks in a financial stable period? Asian Economic & Financial Review. 2019b;**9**(8):994-1018. DOI: 10.18488/journal.aefr.2019.99.994.1018

[100] Olson D, Zoubi T. Using accounting ratios to distinguish between Islamic and conventional banks in the GCC region. The International Journal of Accounting. 2008;**43**(1):45-65. DOI: 10.1016/j.intacc.2008.01.003

[101] Onakoya AB, Onakoya AO. The performance of conventional and Islamic banks in the United Kingdom: A comparative analysis. Journal of Research in Economics & International Finance. 2013;**2**(2):29-38. Available from: https://www.interesjournals.org/articles/the-performance-of-conventional-and-islamic-banks-in-the-united-kingdom-a-comparative-analysis.pdf

[102] Al-Hares OM, AbuGhazaleh NM, El-Galfy AM. Financial performance and compliance with basel III capital standards: Conventional vs Islamic banks. The Journal of Applied Business Research. 2013;**29**(4):1031-1048. DOI: 10.19030/jabr.v29i4.7914

[103] Haddad A, El Ammari A, Bouri A. Comparative and demonstrative study between the liquidity of Islamic and conventional banks in a financial stability period: Which type of banks is the most liquid? International Journal of Financial Research. 2020;**11**(1):252-273. DOI: 10.5430/ijfr.v11n1p252

[104] Ola A, Suzanna EM. Banking sector performance: Islamic and conventional banks in the UAE. International Journal of Information Technology & Business Management. 2015;**36**(1):69-81. Available from: https://ssrn.com/abstract=2748146

[105] Haddad A, El Ammari A, Bouri A. Comparative study of ambiguity resolution between the efficiency of conventional and Islamic banks in a stable financial context. International Journal of Economics & Financial Issues. 2019a;**9**(11):346-366. DOI: 10.32479/ijefi.8623

[106] Haddad A, El Ammari A, Bouri A. Are Islamic banks really more solvent than conventional banks in a financial stable period? Asian Journal of Finance & Accounting. 2019c;**11**(2):1-27. DOI: 10.5296/ajfa.v11i2.15149

[107] Cornett MM, McNutt JJ, Tehranian H. Corporate governance and earnings management at large US bank holding companies. Journal of Corporate Finance. 2009;**15**(4):412-430. DOI: 10.1016/j.jcorpfin.2009.04.003

[108] Kim PK, Rasiah D. Relationship between corporate governance and bank performance in Malaysia during the pre and post asian financial crisis. European Journal of Economics, Finance & Administrative Sciences. 2010;**21**(1):39-63

[109] Charles A, Darne O, Pop A. Risk and ethical investment: Empirical evidence from dow jones Islamic indexes. Research in International Business & Finance. 2015;**35**(C):33-56. DOI: 10.1016/j.ribaf.2015.03.003

[110] Kraft E, Tirtiroglu D. Bank efficiency in Croatia: A stochastic–frontier analysis. Journal of Comparative Economics. 1998;**26**(2):282-300. DOI: 10.1006/jcec.1998.1517

[111] Jemric I, Vujcic B. Efficiency of banks in Croatia: A DEA approach. Comparative Economic Studies. 2002;**44** (2–3):169-193. DOI: 10.1057/ces.2002.13

[112] Filip F, Vesna M, Kiril S. Corporate governance and bank performance: Evidence from Macedonia. In: Proceedings of 16th international students' conference, Faculty of Economics and Administrative Sciences. Izmir: Ege University; 2013, April. pp. 76-99. Available from: https://mpra.ub.uni-muenchen.de/id/eprint/46773

[113] Delis MD, Papanikolaou NI. Determinants of bank efficiency: Evidence from a semi–parametric methodology. Managerial Finance. 2009; **35**(3):260-275. DOI: 10.1108/03074350910931771

[114] Rashid A, Jabeen S. Analyzing performance determinants: Conventional vs Islamic banks in Pakistan. Borsa Istanbul Review. 2016; **16**(2):92-107. DOI: 10.23887/jia.v5i2.28981

[115] Gul S, Irshad F, Zaman K. Factors affecting bank profitability in Pakistan. The Romanian Economic Journal. 2011; **14**(39):61-87. Available from: Http://www.rejournal.eu/sites/rejournal.versatech.ro/files/articole/2011-02-28/2101/guletal-je39.pdf

[116] Rashwan MH, Ehab H. Comparative efficiency study between Islamic and traditional banks. Journal of Finance & Economics. 2016;**4**(3):74-87. DOI: 10.12691/jfe-4-3-2

[117] Tugba EB, David AV, Bener G. Determinants of bank efficiency in Turkey: Participation banks versus conventional banks. Borsa Istanbul Review. 2017;**17**(2):86-96. DOI: 10.1016/j.bir.2017.02.003

[118] Pathan S, Skully M, Wickramanayake J. Board size, independence and performance: An analysis of Thai banks. Asia-Pacific Financial Markets. 2007;**14**(3):211-227. DOI: 10.1007/s10690-007-9060-y

[119] Haniffa R, Hudaib M. Corporate governance structure and performance of Malaysian listed companies. Journal of Business Finance & Accounting. 2006; **33**(7):1034-1062. DOI: 10.1111/j.1468-5957.2006.00594.x

[120] Montandrau S. Activisme des investisseurs institutionnels, gouvernement d'entreprise et richesse de l'actionnaire: Le cas des alertes de l'AFG-ASFFI sur les sociétés françaises cotées. Université d'Aix-Marseille III. 2004;**1**: 467. Available from: https://www.theses.fr/2004AIX32078

[121] Kaymak T, Bektas E. East meets west? Board characteristics in an emerging market: Evidence from Turkish banks. Corporate Governance: An International Review. 2008;**16**(6): 550-561. DOI: 10.1111/j.1467-8683.2008.00713.x

[122] Hakimi A, Rachdi H, Mokni RBS, Hssini H. Do board characteristics affect bank performance? Evidence from the Bahrain Islamic banks. Journal of Islamic Accounting & Business Research. 2018; **9**(2):251-272. DOI: 10.1108/JIABR-06-2015-0029

[123] El-Chaarani H. The impact of corporate governance on the performance of Lebanese banks. The International Journal of Business &

Finance Research. 2014;**8**(5):35-46. Available from: https://www.theibfr.com/download/IJBFR/2014-ijbfr/ijbfr-v8n5-2014/IJBFR-V8N5-2014-4.pdf

[124] Tulung JE, Ramdani D. Independence, size and performance of the board: An emerging market research. Corporate Ownership & Control. 2018; **15**(2-1):201-208. DOI: 10.22495/cocv15i2c1p6

[125] Adams R, Mehran H. Corporate performance, board structure and their determinants in the banking industry. Federal Reserve Bank of New York Staff Reports. 2008;**330**:1-49. Available from: https://www.newyorkfed.org/medialibrary/media/research/staff_reports/sr330.pdf

[126] Bhagat S, Black B. The non-correlation between board independence and long-term performance. Journal of Corporation Law. 2002;**27**(2):231-243. Available from: https://www.researchgate.net/publication/312468557_The_Non-_Correlation_Between_Board_Independence_and_Long_Term_Firm_Performance

[127] Johl SK, Johl S, Cooper B. Board characteristics and firm performance: Evidence from Malaysian public listed firms. Journal of Economics Business & Management. 2015;**3**(2):239-243. DOI: 10.7763/JOEBM.2015.V3.187

Chapter 6

Causal Relationship Among Bank Capitalization, Efficiency, and Risk-Taking in ASEAN Commercial Banks

Van Anh Do

Abstract

Purpose – This chapter explores the answer to the question of whether bank capital is sufficient to absorb risk while maintaining efficiency in ASEAN countries, a new emerging part of the globalized banking system. *Design/methodology* – This chapter focuses on three objectives: first, to investigate the contemporaneous interactions of capital, risk, efficiency; second, to determine directional Granger causality of the relationship; third, to adopt a new panel vector autoregression to track the explanatory power of causation through the impulse-response functions and variance decompositions. *Results* – This chapter contributes to literature through providing evidence on the causality of bank capital on cost efficiency and bidirectional causal interactions of bank capital and risk. Better capitalization induces the improvement in efficiency in ASEAN commercial banks even with different ownership, size, and across pre- and postcrisis period. *Contribution* – This chapter is perhaps the only study so far to investigate the dynamic causality among capital, risk, and efficiency taking into account the sensitivity of the interactions to influential factors of ownership, size, and crisis in ASEAN region—an emerging player in the global banking system.

Keywords: capital, risk, efficiency, panel VAR, causality

1. Introduction

Banking sector over the world has altered significantly since the twenty-first century. As part of the globalization, the banking sector is transformed into stronger consolidation, increasing competition, stringent regulation, and innovation. The global financial crises coupled with complex financial transactions and extensive banking integration create pressure for banks in managing risks effectively but maintaining efficiency. The trade-off of bank risk, capital, and efficiency has been the interest of many studies [1–4]. Some studies show that highly cost-efficient banks experience an increase in nonperforming loans [2, 3, 5, 6], while others indicate different results. As the theoretical literature does not suggest a conclusive relation and empirical evidence does provide diverse results for the nexus between bank risk and efficiency, there is not much comprehensive evidence for the causal, dynamic relationship between risk and efficiency. It is interesting to observe whether the relationship among risk and efficiency is causal and the impact of such causation is temporary or of long-term nature. The work of [7] provides further evidence on the dynamic interactions between risk and efficiency in a more comprehensive way of identifying shock of one variable on the variability of another variable for European banks.

Despite apparent interest of researchers on the interconnectedness of bank risk and efficiency, literature on directional causation with role of bank capital in the relation among risk and efficiency remains scant. Bidirectional causality of risk and efficiency is found in US banks [8], but in European banks, causality running only from risk to efficiency [6, 9] and efficiency causes improvement in capital [10]. Few studies look at the interrelationship of capital, risk, and efficiency in emerging market [11–13], but causality is not investigated. The recent study of [14] in 2021 also evaluates the contemporaneous causal relationship in Indian banks and finds out the causality from inefficiency to bank risk as well as capital to efficiency. However, majority of studies have not addressed the components explaining the causes of changes in the variables. In addition, no prior study investigated the sensitivity of the interactions to certain influential factors of ownership structure, size, or crisis.

The aim of this study is to fill the gap in the literature and to provide a thorough assessment with regard to the causal relationship between risk, capital, and bank efficiency for commercial banks in ASEAN using the panel Vector Autoregression (VAR) analysis to allow for dynamic changes among endogenous variables. The study focuses on the two questions: How do bank capital, risk, and efficiency respond dynamically to their own and other variables' shocks? What are the primary shocks that explain the variability in each variable of capital, risk, and efficiency?

The paper contributes to literature in several ways. First, the study includes bank capital in the dynamic intertwining among risk, capital, and efficiency through a detailed assessment of a novel panel VAR techniques, which is not popularly researched in literature. Second, this is the first study to look at the causal relationship of the three variables for commercial banks in ASEAN by investigating the response of one variable upon the exogenous shock in another variable. Third, the study looks at ASEAN region, an increasingly important player in the global economy with distinctive feature. The ASEAN banking sector increases its integration into the global financial system through the formation of ASEAN banking integration framework (ABIF) to support economic growth and enhance financial inclusion. The integration process of ABIF results in more competitive banking sector, forcing banks to increase capital bases, controlling risk, and focusing on efficiency. Therefore, the region becomes an interesting place for empirical research, which can provide inference for the bank management, regulators, as well as the whole market.

The rest of the chapter is structured as follows: Section 2 presents a literature review, Section 3 covers the hypotheses and research methodology. Section 4 deals with data and data description. Analysis of result is explained in Section 5, and Section 6 concludes the paper.

2. Literature review

The theory governing the intertemporal causal relationship among bank capital, risk, and efficiency is initialized by Berger & De Young [8] with four hypotheses, namely "bad luck," "bad management," "skimping," and "moral hazard." Berger and De Young posit that the four hypotheses can occur concurrently, and they imply the different behavior of banks. Under "bad luck" hypothesis, external shock might cause non-performing loans to increase. Thereby banks react by incurring additional costs to monitor and work out with delinquent loans resulting in decrease in cost efficiency. Bad management hypothesis assumes that low cost efficiency is the result of poor management practices. Inadequate credit scoring, loan monitoring and controlling are caused by bad managers, leading to mounting problem loans. Both bad luck and bad management hypotheses predict negative association of non-performing loans and cost efficiency. Skimping hypothesis refers to the trade-off between short-term operating costs for long-term loan performance. A bank may increase cost efficiency through declining cost of credit appraisal, monitoring and controlling loans but at the expense of long-term problem loan portfolio. Skimping hypothesis predicts positive relationship between efficiency and problem loans. Moral hazard hypothesis does not imply the direct association of problem loans and efficiency. Bank managers, particularly weakly capitalized banks, can take excessive risk, given risk can be borne by creditors, thereby increasing the level of bad loans. Moral hazard can have impact on the above three hypotheses.

Berger & De Young [8] analyze US commercial bank data and find evidence that supports bad luck and bad management hypotheses. The interrelationship between efficiency and loan quality is two ways: increase in nonperforming loans followed by the decrease in cost efficiency and vice versa. Evidence for skimping hypothesis is observed for only a subset of banks, which are efficient over time. The studies from European banks of Fiordelisi et al. [6] and Williams [9] as well as the work of Prakash et al. [14] in India, support evidence of bad management behavior. Several other studies investigate the intertwinning of capital, risk, and efficiency and find mixed evidences. Kwan and Eisenbeis [3] find that less efficient US banks appear to have low risk, whereas Altunbas et al. [1] find the contrasting evidence in European banks where inefficient banks have higher capital and lower risk level. Negative association of risk and efficiency found in the studies of Bitar et al., Louati et al., Nguyen and Nghiem [11, 12, 15], and Isnurhadi in Islamic banks [16], whereas a positive relationship existed in the work of Tan and Floros [17], Tahir and Mongid [13], and Manta and Badircea [18]. Those studies do not explore in detail the direction of causation. Moral hazard behavior is found in various studies [8, 13, 19–21].

Another strand of literature pays attention on the causation in nexus between capital and efficiency. Berger and Bonaccorsi [10] examine the interactions between capital and efficiency and hypothesize that a reduction in capital ratio can improve efficiency because of the decrease in agency cost of external equity financing. This hypothesis is named "agency costs shareholders-managers" by Lešanovská and Weill [22]. Beside, another assumption is proposed that an increase in capital ratio can cause an improvement in efficiency because agency cost helps reduce the conflict between shareholders and debtholders. The assumption is called "agency cost shareholders-debtholders" hypothesis. Empirical evidences of Berger and Bonaccorsi [10], Skopljak and Luo [23], Pessarossi and Weill [24] support agency cost hypothesis where higher capital ratio is associated with improved efficiency.

Berger and Bonaccorsi [10] also look at reverse causality running from efficiency to risk. They suggest the two hypotheses that are "efficiency risk hypothesis" where more efficient banks cause lower level of capital because higher returns can substitute for financial distress risk and "franchise value hypothesis," where efficient banks maintain high capital to preserve their economic rents. The results from studies of

Berger and Bonaccorsi [10], Williams [9], and Kwan and Eisenbeis [3] show dominant substitution effect of the efficiency risk hypothesis, whereas the franchise value hypothesis is found in small banks. The result of Bagntarasian and Mamatzakis [25] finds evidence of structural breakpoint in the relationship between capital and efficiency. Evidence that supports franchise value hypothesis is found in low-efficiency banks, whereas evidence from high-efficiency banks supports the efficiency risk hypothesis.

Koutsomanoli and Filippaki [7] adopt a panel VAR framework to closely investigate the complex causal relationship of risk and efficiency. For a sample of European banks, they observe that the impact of inefficiency on risk is small and short-lived, whereas the reverse effect is negative and significant. Other study by Jouida [26] also adopts the same panel VAR framework to examine the causality of bank capital and systemic risk in French market. The study finds a negative bidirectional relationship of capital and systemic risk. Further study of Bagntarasian and Mamatzakis [25] explores the nexus of capital buffer, Zscore, and performance using dynamic panel threshold analysis. They focus on testing the efficiency risk hypothesis and franchise value hypothesis and find the evidence of efficiency's impact on capital buffer and risk.

Yet, no study so far has addressed the combined causality and directional interactions among the three factors of capital, credit risk, and efficiency and explained the different behavior among banks within this nexus. Therefore, further investigation can provide evidence on the underlying nature of the directional impact of one component on another. This chapter reveals the dynamic interactions among risk, efficiency, and capital through investigating primary shocks that cause the variability in each of the three variables. This type of comprehensive assessment of dynamic relationships can provide evidence that explains the different results in literature, particularly in ASEAN region where behavior of banks is not thoroughly studied in order to provide useful implication for management and regulators.

3. Methodology

Literature on the nexus of bank capital, risk, and efficiency has considerable growth. However, there is paucity in the studies that investigate the directional causality of triumvariate relationship [6, 8, 10, 22, 24]. Yet the focus of those studies is still on developed economies. Few studies address the dynamic intertwinning of the three variables through the use of novel vector autoregression method for panel data (PVAR) [7, 25]. However, there has not been any study looking at the comprehensive causality of the three contemporaneous factors of bank capital, risk, and efficiency using the same PVAR framework. This method combines the traditional vector autoregression with panel data technique to encounter the issue of endogeneity while allowing for inclusion of fixed effects in the model [27]. Apart from analyzing causality, the method also helps identify the response of a factor from the change in another and variance is decomposed to analyze the percentage of explanation by each component.

3.1 The hypotheses

We hypothesize the dynamic interdependencies among risk, efficiency, and capital. The relations between bank efficiency and risk can be either positive or negative and causal direction can be two-way.

Hypothesis 1a. Bank risk causes a change in bank efficiency.

Hypothesis 1b. Bank efficiency causes a change in bank risk.

Hypothesis 1a with a negative sign is the *bad luck hypothesis*. Hypothesis 1b with a negative sign is the *bad management hypothesis*. Hypothesis 1b with a positive sign is the *skimping hypothesis*. [8].

The level of capital and hence bank leverage affects efficiency because of agency costs, which arise from conflicts of interest between shareholders and managers or between shareholders and debtholders.

Hypothesis 2a. Bank capital causes a change in bank efficiency.

Hypothesis 2b. Bank efficiency causes a change in bank capital.

Hypothesis 2a with a negative sign is the *agency costs shareholders-managers hypothesis*: high equity capital and less pressure of debt give managers more cash to invest and may lead to wasteful investment, lowering efficiency. Hypothesis 2a with a positive sign is the *agency costs shareholders-debtholders hypothesis*: if shareholders are tempted to maximize their value at the expense of debtholders, a higher capital ratio will reduce agency costs and thus increase efficiency [22].

Hypothesis 2b with a negative sign is *the efficiency-risk hypothesis*: more efficient banks can generate higher returns, which can partially substitute for equity capital to protect banks in the event of financial distress. Hypothesis 2b with a positive sign is the *franchise-value hypothesis*: efficient banks will maintain a high capital ratio to protect the franchise value associated with high efficiency [10].

Bank decisions on the levels of risk and capital are interrelated, as both decisions are affected by leverage, deposit insurance, and regulation.

Hypothesis 3a. Bank capital causes a change in bank risk.

Hypothesis 3b. Bank risk causes a change in bank capital.

Negative relationship between capital and risk indicates the *moral hazard behavior* as low capitalization Granger causes high nonperforming loans, because managers have less capital to lose in the event of default, and they benefit from higher returns on risky investments [8]. Causation of bank risk on bank capital supports the *regulatory hypothesis* where regulators require banks to hold capital commensurate with their risk [28], so an increase in the risk of problem loans can force managers to replenish bank capital [9].

The baseline analysis is extended in several dimensions to study whether these hypothesized relationships are stronger for certain types of banks. “Cost skimping” is expected to occur in efficient banks [8]. Managers of efficient banks are tempted to pursue expansion through investing in risky assets or controlling cost to attain higher efficiency, thereby increasing risk. Therefore, we look at subsamples of high- and low-efficiency banks to analyze the difference in behavior of the two groups of banks.

We extend our work to assess the relationships among risk, capital, and efficiency with subsamples of different size, ownership structure, and pre- and postcrisis periods. Literature finds the impact of market structure on bank risk taking [29–31] and efficiency [4, 17, 32, 33]. Large banks span their operations in both domestic and international markets, thus having a diversified portfolio. Small banks operate in smaller geographical or regional areas, so they have limited power in the market [34]. Large banks can improve efficiency and reduce risk, as they benefit from economies of scale and portfolio diversification [15, 17, 35]. Large banks also have easier access to the capital market and thus can operate with proportionately smaller capital [19, 36, 37]. In addition, several studies have found differences in the behavior of banks with different ownership. Udell et al. [38] find that on average foreign banks perform less well than private domestic counterparts in developed countries, while reverse result is found in developing countries [39]. Finally, the 2008 global financial adversely hit the global banking sector and ASEAN banking system experiences the same effect. Banks may behave differently in response to the global crisis; therefore, subsamples of the two different periods of before and after crisis need further investigation.

3.2 The model

We model the contemporaneous relationship of capital, risk, and efficiency using panel vector autoregration (VAR), initially developed by [40] and subsequently elaborated by [41]. Panel VAR treats all variables as endogenous and can capture their dynamic interdependencies. Impulse response functions (IRFs) identify the reaction (response) of one variable to a shock (impulse/innovation) in another variable while holding all other shocks at zero [40]. This process can explain the underlying causality among endogenous variables of the model.

The system of simultaneous equations from the model is regressed using system-based GMM. Dynamic simulations are implemented involving the estimation of impulse response functions and variance decompositions [7]. There is a key identifying assumption in setting the order of variables: variables that occur earlier in the ordering affect the following variables contemporaneously, while variables that appear later in the ordering affect previous variables only with lag [40]. This sequential order is a preferred identification strategy, which is referred to as Choleski decomposition. In this study, we make an assumption that risk could be more exogenous in relation to the other variables. An economic shock, or "bad luck" [8], immediately increases nonperforming loans, which proxy for risk. Banks respond by adjusting their capital cushion. Bank capital directly affects costs by providing a source of funding other than deposits [42]. Hence, capital and cost efficiency come later in the order.

We specify the three-variable VAR model as follows:

$$CE_{i,t} = \alpha_{10} + \beta_{11}RISK_{i,t-1} + \beta_{12}CAP_{i,t-1} + \beta_{13}CE_{i,t-1} + f_{1i} + d_{1c,t} + \varepsilon_{1i,t} \quad (1)$$

$$CAP_{i,t} = \alpha_{20} + \beta_{21}RISK_{i,t-1} + \beta_{22}CAP_{i,t-1} + \beta_{23}CE_{i,t-1} + f_{2i} + d_{2c,t} + \varepsilon_{2i,t} \quad (2)$$

$$RISK_{i,t} = \alpha_{30} + \beta_{31}RISK_{i,t-1} + \beta_{32}CAP_{i,t-1} + \beta_{33}CE_{i,t-1} + f_{3i} + d_{3c,t} + \varepsilon_{3i,t}, \quad (3)$$

where $CE_{i,t}$, $CAP_{i,t}$, and $RISK_{i,t}$ represent cost efficiency, capital, and risk respectively. f_i denotes fixed effects that allow for individual heterogeneity. $d_{c,t}$ are time dummies.

Equation (1) tests the impacts of risk and capital on cost efficiency. The estimated coefficients for risk (β_{11}) and capital (β_{12}) constitute evidence for the bad luck hypothesis (H1a), agency cost, the shareholders-managers/shareholders-debtholders hypothesis (H2a).

Equation (2) examines the effects of risk and cost efficiency on capital. The estimated coefficients for cost efficiency (β_{23}) and risk (β_{21}) are used to test the efficiency-risk hypothesis/franchise value hypothesis (H2b) and the regulatory hypothesis (H3b).

Equation (3) investigates the impact of capital and cost efficiency on risk. The coefficients for cost efficiency (β_{33}) and capital (β_{32}) provide evidence of the bad management/cost skimping hypothesis (H1b) and the moral hazard/regulatory hypothesis (H3a, H3b).

We also introduce fixed effects, denoted fi in the model above, to allow for individual heterogeneity in variables [42]. The fixed effects are correlated with the regressors because the dependent variables are lagged, so in order to create unbiased coefficients, we need to eliminate fixed effects by using forward mean differencing, known as the Helmert procedure [43]. This process removes the forward mean and preserves the orthogonality between transformed variables and lagged regressors. So we can use the lagged regressors as instruments in our system GMM regression.

In addition, country-specific time dummies, $d_{c,t}$, are included to capture the country-specific macroeconomic variables. These dummies are eliminated by subtracting the means of each variable calculated for each country-year.

We analyze the impulse response functions (IRFs) to examine the reaction of one variable to a shock in another to infer the causality of the variables. Monte Carlo simulations method is used to derive a draw of coefficients. Then the matrix of variance decompositions is determined to explain the cumulative percentage of variation in a variable explained by the shock in another.

3.3 Data and variables

Our data comprise 1404 observations of 146 commercial banks in Thailand, Malaysia, the Philippines, Indonesia, and Vietnam for the period from 2005 to 2015 in an unbalanced panel data. Banks' financial statements were obtained from Bankscope. To measure bank risk, we use the ratio of loan loss provisions (LLOSS) to loans to be the proxy for credit risk. This measure is commonly used to account for bank risk [6, 9, 15] as it focuses on credit risk and derives from accounting data. The ratio of equity to total assets is used as a measure of bank capital (CAP). This widely used proxy captures the bank's financial cushion to absorb loan losses [6, 8, 9]. To measure bank efficiency, we opt to use cost efficiency (CE) determined by stochastic frontier approach, which is widely used in literature [14, 44].

4. Empirical evidence

4.1 Result of full sample

We report the parameter estimates of risk, capital, and efficiency in a system of equations that account for fixed effects and country-time effects (see **Table 1**). The relationship of risk and cost efficiency is not evidenced as the coefficient is not significant. The small but significant and positive coefficient of L.CAP indicates that higher capital ratio can improve cost efficiency as larger capital reduces the conflict between shareholders and debtholders, thereby lower agency cost [22]. In the five ASEAN countries, commercial banks that are better capitalized appear to be more efficient. This finding is consistent with results from the study of Tahir and Mongid [13] in ASEAN region and Prakash et al. [14] in Indian banks. Evidence of reverse causation from efficiency to capital is not supported. Lagged capital significantly decreases credit risk as proxied by loan loss; and vice versa, risk decreases capital significantly (at the 5% level). This bidirectional relationship supports moral hazard behavior also found by other researchers [1, 8, 45].

To confirm the effects of the three variables, we look at how one variable responds to the shock in another variable. The graphs of impulse-response functions and variance decomposition (**Figure 1**) can help explain those relationships.

Dependent variable	Independent variable	Coefficient
CE	L.LLOSS	0.000 (0.572)
	L.CAP	0.002*** (0.000)
	L.CE	0.417** (0.014)
CAP	L.LLOSS	−0.157** (0.037)
	L.CAP	0.626*** (0.000)
	L.CE	−21.66 (0.458)
LLOSS	L.LLOSS	0.797*** (0.000)
	L.CAP	−0.059*** (0.000)
	L.CE	−4.476 (0.530)

Note: CE, LLOSS, CAP stand for cost efficiency, credit risk, and capital ratio respectively. L.LLOSS, L.CAP, L.CE are lagged value of the three variables. p-value reported in parentheses.
****, **, and * indicate 1, 5, and 10% significance levels respectively.*

Table 1.
Results of full sample.

Row 2, column 1 of **Figure 1** displays the response of cost efficiency to a shock in capital, confirming the result of **Table 1** in visual form. The positive response of cost efficiency to the impulse in capital supports the agency cost shareholders-debtholders hypothesis. The response reaches the peak in year 2 and then reverts to zero after 10 years.

Row 2, column 3 of **Figure 1** shows the response of credit risk to the shock in capital. The response is negative and significant, bottoming out in year 3 and converging to equilibrium after 10 years. Large confidence interval after year 3 suggests cautious conclusion on long-term causality. The result supports moral hazard theory where capital can have impact on risk-taking. Row 3, column 2, depicts the response of capital to a shock in risk. Capital appears to decrease following an increase in credit risk. This negative influence bottoms out after 2 years and then reverts to zero. We observe a bidirectional causal relationship between capital and risk from the IRF graph, confirming evidence of moral hazard behavior.

The variance decomposition (VDC) analysis reported in **Table 2** shows the percentage of variation in one variable that is explained by the shock in another variable.

Twelve percent of variation in cost efficiency is explained by the shock in capital and only 2.69% of cost efficiency justified by risk. The variance decomposition of cost efficiency confirms again the hypothesis of agency cost shareholders-debtholders. The explanatory power of capital on variation in risk is 9%, whereas the explanation of efficiency on risk is negligible. This result suggests that banks with low capitalization take on higher credit risk due to nonperforming loans, implying the moral hazard behavior. Credit risk and cost efficiency explain only 2.78 and 4.06% of the variation in capital. The significant influence of bank capital on credit risk and cost efficiency

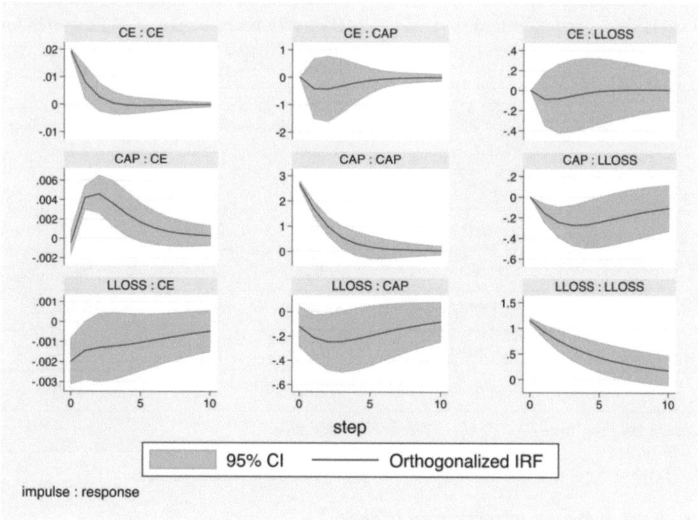

Figure 1.
Impulse-response functions for risk (LLOSS), capital (CAP), and cost efficiency (CE).

Full sample	LLOSS	CAP	CE
LLOSS	90.35%	9.26%	0.39%
CAP	2.78%	93.16%	4.06%
CE	2.69%	12.25%	85.06%

Note: Each cell indicates the percentage of variation in the row variable over a 10-year period explained by a shock to the column variable.

Table 2.
Variance decompositions for the full sample.

advocates the enhancing capital base of banks from regulatory capital requirement as enforced by international Basel standards.

4.2 Result of subsamples

In what follows, we divide our data two subsamples, one of banks with lagged cost efficiency higher than the median, and one of banks at or below median efficiency.

Table 3 presents results for subsamples of high- and low-efficiency banks. In the efficiency equation, capital causes an increase in cost efficiency, but the result is significant only for the group of low efficiency banks. The result of capital equation shows contrasting relation between efficiency and capital for the two groups. A shock in cost efficiency results in increase in capital of low-efficiency banks implying evidence of franchise value hypothesis. Low-efficiency banks tend to preserve their franchise value generated from lower returns to protect the banks from financial distress; hence, they will not assume the risk of lowering their capital base. Nevertheless, in high-efficiency banks, increase in efficiency causes a decrease in capital, supporting efficiency risk hypothesis. High efficiency banks can take on higher leverage and maintain less capital because of lower expected costs of financial distress. These findings confirm the breakpoint in the association of capital and efficiency

Dependent variable	Independent variable	High-efficiency banks		Low-efficiency banks	
		Coeff	p-value	Coeff	p-value
CE	L.CAP	0.001	0.00	0.00	0.01***
(1)	L.CE	0.64	0.00***	0.15	0.25
CAP	L.LLOSS	−0.09	0.29	−0.07	0.37
(2)	L.CAP	0.61	0.00***	0.53	0***
	L.CE	−32.8	0.04**	53.1	0.00***
LLOSS	L.LLOSS	0.86	0.00***	0.67	0.00***
(3)	L.CAP	−0.03	0.04**	−0.08	0.01***
	L.CE	−7.47	0.08*	−14.3	0.06*

****, **, and * indicate 1%, 5%, and 10% significance levels, respectively.*

Table 3.
Result for subsamples of high- and low-efficiency banks.

between high-efficiency and low-efficiency banks in the study of Bagntarasian and Mamatzakis [25] in European banks. The risk equation shows a significant negative causation of capital on risk for both subsamples. The lagged cost efficiency has negative coefficient but significant only at 10% suggesting weak evidence of bad management behavior for both high and low efficiency banks.

An impulse response function graph may help explain the impact of cost efficiency on bank capital (**Figure 2**).

The response of capital to a shock in cost efficiency is displayed in Row 1, column 2 of **Figure 2**. Contrasting responses are shown in the graphs of the two subsamples. Visual evidence in high-efficiency banks confirms the efficiency risk hypothesis where the shock in efficiency causes negative response in capital and the effect reaches the trough after 3 years and reverts to zero. High-efficiency banks expect high earnings from better efficiency to substitute for equity capital in the event of financial distress [10]. For low-efficiency banks, following the shock in cost efficiency, banks respond by an increase in capital with peak reached in 2 years and subsequently

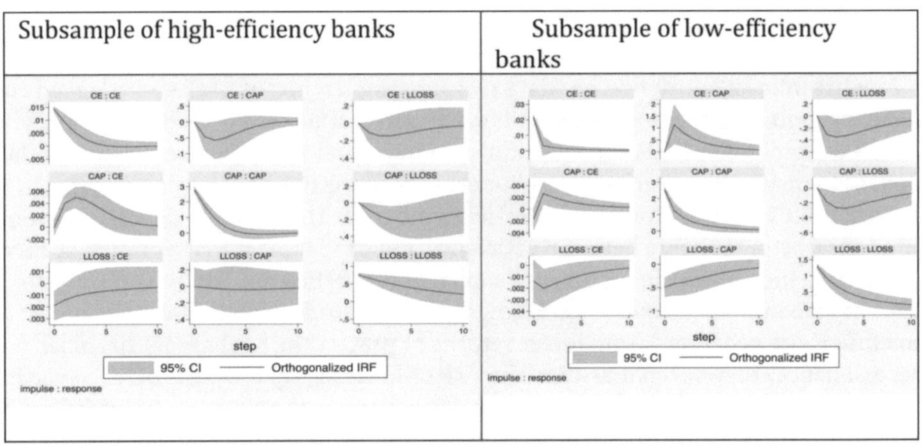

Figure 2.
Impulse response functions for subsamples. Subsample of high-efficiency banks. Subsample of low-efficiency banks.

Variable	High-efficiency banks			Low-efficiency banks		
	LLOSS	CAP	CE	LLOSS	CAP	CE
CE	2.3%	19.7%	78%	2.7%	3.7%	93.6%
CAP	0.1%	91.7%	8.3%	7.2%	72.4%	20.5%
LLOSS	85.3%	11.1%	3.6%	79.1%	8.3%	12.6%

Table 4.
VDC for subsamples of high- and low-efficiency banks.

converge to equilibrium after 10 years. This result provides visual evidence for franchise value hypothesis. Low-efficiency banks tend to protect their economic rent by increasing capital.

The result of variance decomposition of the two subsamples in **Table 4** is consistent with findings from IRFs. In the group of high-efficiency banks, capital shock can explain 19.72% of the variation in cost efficiency. The franchise value hypothesis has strongly evidenced in VDC analysis of low-efficiency banks with 20.49% explanatory power of cost efficiency on capital. On the contrary, in high-efficiency bank subsample, evidence of efficiency risk hypothesis is weaker with only 8.27% explanation. Bad management behavior is apparently evidenced in low efficiency banks with 12.59% risk variation explained by cost efficiency as compared to only 3.61% in the group of high-efficiency banks. Capital explains 11% of forecast error variance in risk for high-efficiency banks but only 8% for low-efficiency banks. The result supports the moral hazard hypothesis.

4.3 Sensitivity analysis

The empirical study is extended to how the causal relationship of capital, risk, and efficiency is sensitive to the differences in ownership type, size of banks, as well as the 2008 global crisis.

4.3.1 Results for foreign banks and domestic banks

Literature suggests that the behavior of banks can alter with different types of ownership. Therefore we divide the sample into two groups of domestic and foreign banks. **Table 5** reports parameter estimates of the model for the subsamples of foreign banks and domestic banks. There exists weak evidence of bad luck in foreign banks. The results indicate positive causation running from capital to efficiency, which supports agency cost shareholders-managers hypothesis for both foreign and domestic banks. However, the reverse causation is different among the two groups. In foreign banks, higher efficiency causes an increase in capital while efficiency in domestic banks causes a decline in capital. Bank capital negatively causes risk regardless of type of ownership, which is consistent with regulatory hypothesis.

The IRF graphs (**Figure 3**) confirm the regression results. The effect of one standard deviation shock in risk on cost efficiency is negative, bottoming out within a year and reverts to zero as shown in row 3, column 1. Row 2, column 1 indicates the shock of capital on efficiency with longer impact of more than 2 years for domestic banks as compared to 1-year influence in foreign banks. Different responses of the two groups are visualized in row 1, column of **Figure 3** as foreign banks have higher capital in a year and domestic banks reduce capital in 2 years following an efficiency shock.

Depen-dent variable	Indep- endent Variable	Foreign banks		Domestic banks		Large banks		Small banks	
		Coeff	p-value	Coeff	p-value	Coeff	p-value	Coeff	p-value
CE									
	L.LLOSS	−0.00	0.09*	0.00	0.22	0.00	0.68	0.00	0.98
	L.CAP	0.00	0.00***	0.00	0***	0.00	0.01***	0.00	0***
	L.CE	0.13	0.66	0.60	0***	0.74	0***	0.39	0.05**
CAP									
	L.LLOSS	0.11	0.61	−0.12	0.10	−0.24	0.02**	−0.07	0.61
	L.CAP	0.56	0***	0.61	0***	0.65	0***	0.56	0***
	L.CE	84.5	0.07*	−40.9	0.08*	−41.7	0.02**	8.88	0.85
LLOSS									
	L.LLOSS	0.62	0**	0.84	0***	0.75	0***	0.78	0***
	L.CAP	−0.05	0.1*	−0.07	0***	−0.17	0***	−0.05	0.01***
	L.CE	−5.05	0.77	−0.46	0.92	−8.69	0.23	−7.23	0.42

****, **, and * indicate 1, 5, and 10% significance levels, respectively.*

Table 5.
Sensitivity analysis for subsamples.

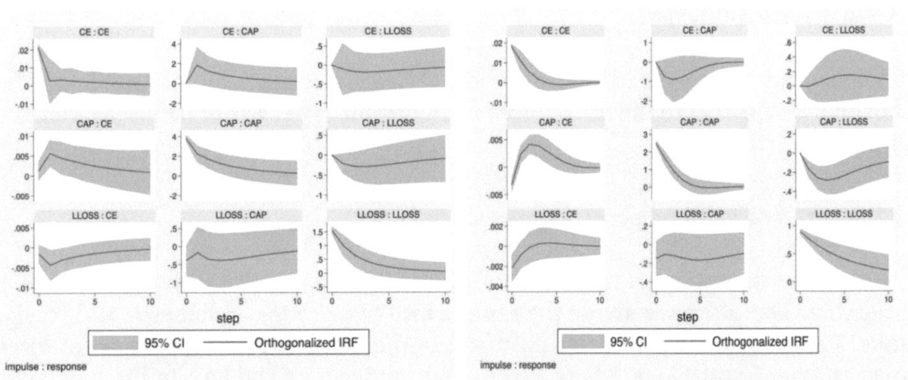

Figure 3.
Impulse response functions for foreign and domestic banks. Subsample of foreign banks. Subsample of domestic banks.

Variance decompositions for the two groups of foreign and domestic banks are displayed in **Table 6**. In total, 15 and 11% of variations in efficiency are explained by capital for foreign and domestic banks, respectively. The explanatory power of risk in efficiency variance is 7% in foreign banks but only 1% in domestic banks explains 7% of variance in efficiency for foreign banks but just 1% of efficiency variance for domestic banks. Twenty percent of capital variance can be justified by efficiency disturbance, whereas the explanation of risk is only 9% in foreign banks and 11% in domestic banks.

	Foreign banks			Domestic banks		
	LLOSS	**CAP**	**CE**	**LLOSS**	**CAP**	**CE**
CE	7.3%	14.5%	78.2%	1.0%	10.6%	88.4%
CAP	2.6%	77.2%	20.2%	1.6%	78.7%	19.7%
LLOSS	87.0%	9.0%	4.0%	84.6%	11.9%	3.6%

Table 6.
VDC for subsamples of foreign banks and domestic banks.

4.3.2 Results for large banks and small banks

Bank size does influence the relationship of capital, risk, and efficiency. The sample is divided into two groups of large and small banks. Both groups display the same impact of capital on risk and efficiency as shown in **Table 5**. However, the behavior is different in capital equation as both risk and efficiency negatively cause changes in capital of large banks while such causation is not evidenced in small banks.

Figure 4 reports the IRFs for large and small banks. Row 2 column 1 of **Figure 4** reports the capital shock on efficiency. The effect is positive for both large and small banks, but impact on large banks lasts more than 3 years as compared to 1 year in small banks. Large banks also experience a decrease in capital following the shock in efficiency, but such response is not significant in small banks. The negative and bidirectional causal relationship between risk and capital is observed in both large and small banks. Moral hazard behavior is found in ASEAN banks regardless of bank size.

VDC estimations are presented in **Table 7**. With regard to the variation of cost efficiency, capital of large banks can explain 14% and capital of small banks explains 10%. Risk can explain only negligible percentage of efficiency forecast error variance. In strong contrast, 43% of capital variation for large banks is explained by efficiency, but the explanatory power is only 1% for small banks. The influence of efficiency on capital is clearly observed in large banks only. That is, efficiency influences capitalization only in large banks. In large banks, capital and efficiency have strong explanatory power over the risk variance, but the response in small banks is opposite.

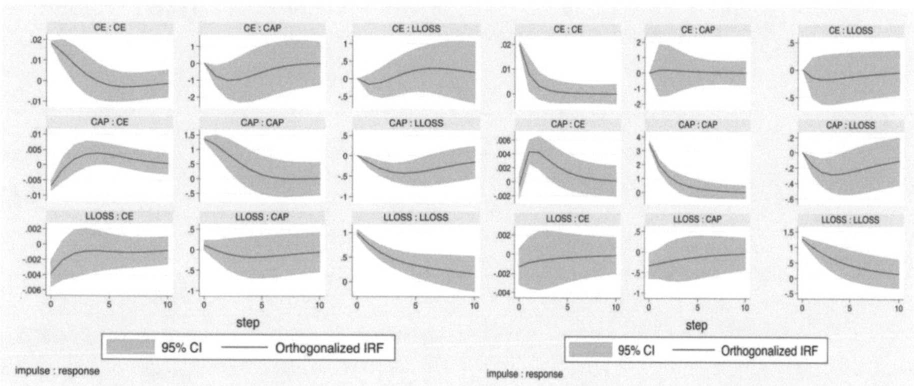

Figure 4.
Impulse response functions for large and small banks. Subsample of large banks. Subsample of small banks.

	Large banks			Small banks		
	LLOSS	CAP	CE	LLOSS	CAP	CE
CE	3.6%	14.2%	82.2%	0.7%	10.2%	89.1%
CAP	2.1%	54.4%	43.4%	1.9%	97.6%	0.6%
LLOSS	65.9%	23.6%	10.6%	88.3%	8.7%	2.9%

Table 7.
VDC for subsamples of large banks and small banks.

4.3.3 Results for the precrisis and postcrisis periods

The 2008 global crisis has adverse impact on banking and financial system around the world, and ASEAN region is not an exception. It is important to see the difference in behavior of banks before and after the crisis. To study the impact of crisis on the interactions among capital, risk, and efficiency, subsamples of pre and postcrisis are investigated. Regression results indicate that increased capital causes improvement in efficiency and reduction in risk both before and after the crisis. The impact of cost efficiency on capital displays different causation for the two periods as shown in **Table 8**. Efficiency helps improve bank capital in the precrisis period. However, such causation is not seen in postcrisis period. After the crisis, banks tend to maintain their capital in order to protect themselves against negative shocks.

Figure 5 displays the IRF graph. Before the crisis, the effect of capital shock on efficiency gradually declined, while after the crisis, the response rose over 2 years and subsequently decreased thereafter. The reverse causation, from efficiency to capital, differs between the two periods with an increase before the crisis but decrease after the crisis.

Dependent variable	Independent variable	Precrisis		Postcrisis	
		Coeff	p-value	Coeff	p-value
CE					
	L.LLOSS	−0.0001	0.865	−0.0008	0.373
	L.CAP	0.0013	0***	0.0017	0***
	L.CE	0.2346	0.259	0.4986	0.001***
CAP					
	L.LLOSS	0.2105	0.292	−0.0681	0.543
	L.CAP	0.3766	0.002***	0.6221	0***
	L.CE	178.1687	0.002***	−24.8413	0.277
LLOSS					
	L.LLOSS	0.7075	0***	0.7890	0***
	L.CAP	−0.0433	0.06*	−0.0510	0.003***
	L.CE	−9.0253	0.468	−1.3368	0.81

Table 8.
Sensitivity analysis for subsamples of precrisis and postcrisis.

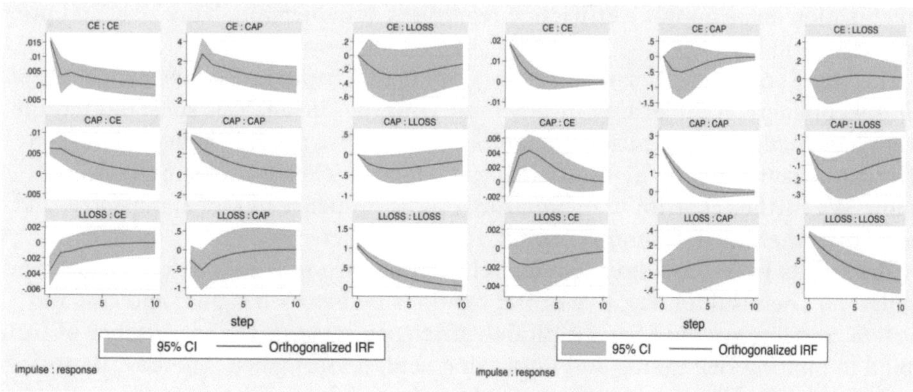

Figure 5.
Impulse response functions for pre- and postcrisis periods. Precrisis. Postcrisis.

	Precrisis			Postcrisis		
	LLOSS	**CAP**	**CE**	**LLOSS**	**CAP**	**CE**
CE	3.9%	29.0%	67.1%	2.9%	11.6%	85.5%
CAP	1.1%	65.1%	33.7%	0.6%	91.3%	8.1%
LLOSS	68.5%	18.5%	13.0%	94.9%	4.9%	0.2%

Table 9.
VDC for subsamples of precrisis and post crisis.

Table 9 reports the variance decomposition. It reveals that 29% of efficiency variance is explained by capital before crisis, but the percentage drops to 12% after the crisis. Before the crisis, efficiency disturbances explain close to 34% of the forecast error variance of capital over 10 years. The shocks in capital and efficiency explain 18 and 13% of the variation in risk in precrisis period. But after the crisis, the explanatory power of capital and efficiency is rather small. The VDC results imply a strong response of the three factors to exogenous shock in precrisis rather than post crisis period.

5. Conclusion and policy implications

This chapter empirically investigates the intertemporal and causal interdependencies among bank capital, risk, and efficiency in the five emerging countries in ASEAN region, a growing dynamic part of the global banking system. We summarize our findings as follows. Firstly, our study finds evidence supporting the bidirectional causality between capital and risk in ASEAN commercial banks. The results also confirm that banks with better capitalization are more efficient. Secondly, we observe different behavior between high-efficiency banks and low-efficiency banks. Following the shock of increasing efficiency, the high-efficiency banks tend to maintain low capital indicating evidence of efficiency risk hypothesis, whereas low-efficiency banks increase their capital ratio to protect franchise value. Lastly, sensitivity analysis of causations among the three factors of capital, risk, and efficiency reveals that stronger capitalization helps improve efficiency regardless of ownership, bank size, and pre or postcrisis period.

The study confirms prior research suggesting that capital, risk, and efficiency of ASEAN commercial banks are causally intertwinned. The analysis substantiates the positive impact of capitalization on bank efficiency. We provide new evidence on different behavior among high-efficiency and low-efficiency banks in the ASEAN region. We further contribute to literature on the influence of ownership, size, and period over the trade-off among capital, risk, and efficiency.

The results from this study provide relevant implications for bank managers and regulators. The result of negative causal relationship between capital and risk and positive causality running from capital to efficiency suggests the importance of bank capital in limiting risk-taking and improving bank performance. Thereby, imposing stronger capital requirements under Basel framework by regulators in the ASEAN region can help achieving both lower risk and higher efficiency. As globalization takes place rapidly in the region, a push to the adoption of the international standards on capital requirement from Basel Accord can help banks in ASEAN region to increase capitalization, resulting in improvement in performance and achieving greater competitiveness in the global market.

A limitation of our study is that the results are based mainly on accounting measure of risk, capital, and efficiency. The measure of risk focuses on credit risk. Other types of risks including market risk, operational risk, and liquidity risk are not captured in the model. Future studies may adopt a more comprehensive measure of risk that incorporates different types of banking risks to determine how the nexus changes in response to different risk factors.

Author details

Van Anh Do
Hanoi University, Hanoi, Vietnam

*Address all correspondence to: anhdv@hanu.edu.vn

References

[1] Altunbas Y, Carbo S, Gardener EPM, Molyneux P. Examining the relationships between capital, risk and efficiency in European banking. European Financial Management. 2007; **13**(1):49-70

[2] Berger AN, Mester LJ. Inside the black box: What explains differences in the efficiencies of financial institutions? Journal of Banking & Finance. 1997; **21**(7):895-947

[3] Kwan S, Eisenbeis R. Bank risk, capitalization, and operating efficiency. Journal of Financial Services Research. 1997;**12**(2):117-131

[4] Pruteanu-Podpiera A, Weill L, Schobert F. Banking competition and efficiency: A micro-data analysis on the Czech banking industry. Comparative Economic Studies. 2008;**50**(2):253-273

[5] Altunbas Y, Marqués-Ibáñez D, Manganelli S. Bank risk during the financial crisis: do business models matter? [Internet]. ECB Working Paper; 2011 [cited 2019 Mar 31]. Report No.: 1394. Available from: https://www.econstor.eu/handle/10419/153828

[6] Fiordelisi F, Marques-Ibanez D, Molyneux P. Efficiency and risk in European banking. Journal of Banking & Finance. 2011;**35**(5):1315-1326

[7] Koutsomanoli-Filippaki A, Margaritis D, Staikouras C. Efficiency and productivity growth in the banking industry of Central and Eastern Europe. Journal of Banking & Finance. 2009; **33**(3):557-567

[8] Berger AN, DeYoung R. Problem loans and cost efficiency in commercial banks. Journal of Banking & Finance. 1997;**21**(6):849-870

[9] Williams J. Determining management behaviour in European banking. Journal of Banking & Finance. 2004;**28**(10): 2427-2460

[10] Berger AN, Bonaccorsi di Patti E. Capital structure and firm performance: A new approach to testing agency theory and an application to the banking industry. Journal of Banking & Finance. 2006;**30**(4):1065-1102

[11] Louati S, Louhichi A, Boujelbene Y. The risk-capital-efficiency trilogy: A comparative study between Islamic and conventional banks. Managerial Finance. 2016;**42**(12):1226-1252

[12] Nguyen TPT, Nghiem SH. The interrelationships among default risk, capital ratio and efficiency: Evidence from Indian banks. Managerial Finance. 2015;**41**(5):507-525

[13] Tahir IM, Mongid A. The interrelationship between bank cost efficiency, capital and risk-taking in ASEAN banking. Journal of Economics and Management Sciences. 2013;**2**(12): 1-15

[14] Prakash N, Singh S, Sharma S. Contemporaneous or causal? Evaluating the triumvirate of insolvency risk, capitalization and efficiency in Indian commercial banking. Managerial Finance. 2021;**48**(1):136-157

[15] Bitar M, Pukthuanthong K, Walker T. The effect of capital ratios on the risk, efficiency and profitability of banks: Evidence from OECD countries. Journal of International Financial Markets Institutions and Money. 2018;**53**:227-262

[16] Isnurhadi I, Adam M, Sulastri S, Andriana I, Muizzuddin M. Bank capital, efficiency and risk: Evidence from

Islamic banks. Journal of Asian Finance, Economics and Business. 2021;**8**(1): 841-850

[17] Tan Y, Floros C. Risk, capital and efficiency in Chinese banking. Journal of International Financial Markets Institutions and Money. 2013;**26**:378-393

[18] Manta A, Badîrcea R. Empirical study on the relationship between efficiency, capital and risk into the banking system of Romania. Finante - Provocarile Viitorului Finance - Chall Future. 2015;**1**(17):58-67

[19] Rime B. Capital requirements and bank behaviour: Empirical evidence for Switzerland. Journal of Banking & Finance. 2001;**25**(4):789-805

[20] Shrieves RE, Dahl D. The relationship between risk and capital in commercial banks. Journal of Banking & Finance. 1992;**16**(2):439-457

[21] Abbas F, Masood P, Ali S, Rizwan S. How do Capital Ratios Affect Bank Risk-taking: New Evidence from the United States. SAGE Open; 2021;**11**(1):1-13

[22] Lešanovská J, Weill L. Does greater capital hamper the cost efficiency of banks? A bi-causal analysis. Comparative Economic Studies. 2016;**58**(3):409-429

[23] Skopljak V, Luo R. Capital structure and firm performance in the financial sector: Evidence from Australia. Asian Journal of Finance & Accounting. 2012; **4**(1): 278-298

[24] Pessarossi P, Weill L. Do capital requirements affect cost efficiency? Evidence from China. Journal of Financial Stability. 2015;**19**(C):119-127

[25] Bagntasarian A, Mamatzakis E. Testing for the underlying dynamics of bank capital buffer and performance nexus. Review of Quantitative Finance and Accounting. 2019;**52**(2):347-380

[26] Jouida S. Bank capital structure, capital requirements and SRISK across bank ownership types and financial crisis: Panel VAR approach. Review of Quantitative Finance and Accounting. 2019;**53**(1):295-325

[27] Shank CA, Vianna AC. Are US-Dollar-Hedged-ETF investors aggressive on exchange rates? A panel VAR approach. Research in International Business and Finance. 2016;**38**:430-438

[28] Gropp R, Heider F. The determinants of bank capital structure. Review of Finance. 2010;**14**(4):587-622

[29] Boyd JH, De Nicoló G. The theory of bank risk taking and competition revisited. The Journal of Finance. 2005; **60**(3):1329-1343

[30] Goetz M. Bank diversification, market structure and bank risk taking: theory and evidence from U.S. commercial banks [Internet]. Supervisory Research and Analysis Working Papers. Federal Reserve Bank of Boston; 2012 [cited 2020 Apr 27]. (Supervisory Research and Analysis Working Papers). Report No.: QAU12-2. Available from: https://ideas.repec.org/p/fip/fedbqu/qau12-2.html

[31] Stein JC. Information production and capital allocation: Decentralized versus hierarchical firms. The Journal of Finance. 2002;**57**(5):1891-1921

[32] Casu B, Girardone C. Testing the relationship between competition and efficiency in banking: A panel data analysis. Economics Letters. 2009; **105**(1):134-137

[33] Ferreira C. Bank market concentration and bank efficiency in the

European Union: A panel Granger causality approach. International Economics and Economic Policy. 2013; **10**(3):365-391

[34] Bikker J, Spierdijk L, Finnie P. The Impact of Bank Size on Market Power. DNB Working Paper, Netherlands Central Bank, Research Department. 2006 [cited 2020 Apr 27]. Available from: https://econpapers.repec.org/paper/dnbdnbwpp/120.htm

[35] Barth JR, Caprio G, Levine R. Bank regulation and supervision in 180 countries from 1999 to 2011. Journal of Financial Economic Policy. 2013;**5**(2): 111-219

[36] Roy PV. Capital requirements and bank behaviour in the early 1990: Cross-country evidence. International Journal of Central Banking. 2008;**4**(3): 29-60

[37] Jacques K, Nigro P. Risk-based capital, portfolio risk, and bank capital: A simultaneous equations approach. Journal of Economics and Business. 1997; **49**(6):533-547

[38] Udell G, Berger A, DeYoung R, Genay H. Globalization of financial institutions: evidence from cross-border banking performance [Internet]. Board of Governors of the Federal Reserve System (U.S.). [cited 2020 Apr 7]. Report No.: 2000–04. 2000. Available from: https://econpapers.repec.org/paper/fipfedgfe/2000-04.htm

[39] Bonin JP, Hasan I, Wachtel P. Bank performance, efficiency and ownership in transition countries. Journal of Banking & Finance. 2005; **29**(1):31-53

[40] Love I, Zicchino L. Financial development and dynamic investment behavior: Evidence from panel VAR. The Quarterly Review of Economics and Finance. 2006;**46**(2):190-210

[41] Abrigo MRM, Love I. Estimation of Panel Vector Autoregression in Stata: A Package of Programs [Internet]. University of Hawaii at Manoa, Department of Economics; Jan [cited 2019 Jun 12]. (Working Papers). Report No.: 201602. 2016. Available from: https://ideas.repec.org/p/hai/wpaper/201602.html

[42] Hughes JP, Mester LJ. Efficiency in Banking: Theory, Practice, and Evidence [Internet]. Departmental Working Papers. Rutgers University, Department of Economics; Jan [cited 2020 Apr 29]. (Departmental Working Papers). Report No.: 200801. 2008. Available from: https://ideas.repec.org/p/rut/rutres/200801.html

[43] Arellano M, Bover O. Another look at the instrumental variable estimation of error-components models. Journal of Econometrics. 1995;**68**(1):29-51

[44] Koutsomanoli-Filippaki A, Mamatzakis E. Performance and Merton-type default risk of listed banks in the EU: A panel VAR approach. Journal of Banking & Finance. 2009; **33**(11):2050-2061

[45] Deelchand T, Padgett C. The relationship between risk, capital and efficiency: Evidence from Japanese cooperative banks. Henley Business School, Reading University; Nov [cited 2019 Jun 12]. (ICMA Centre Discussion Papers in Finance). Report No.: icma–dp2009–12. 2009. Available from: https://ideas.repec.org/p/rdg/icmadp/icma-dp2009-12.html

Section 3

Technologocal Development of Emerging Markets

Chapter 7

Policies for Improving the Efficiency of Innovative Clustering in an Emerging Market

Vito Bobek, Vladislav Streltsov and Tatjana Horvat

Abstract

The main topic of this study is to define the direction of improving the state policy of Russia in achieving the maximum efficiency of clustering in the country. The chapter aims to study the interconnected influence of innovation clusters on the development of the knowledge economy in Russia and the world. Attention is focused on the improvement based on the cyclical nature of clusters using human capital, technology, policies, and management. To achieve this, a historical review of the formation and successful development of clusters in the Russian Federation is carried out to identify and assess the prominent occurrence cases, the central institutional actors, the indicators of their innovative activity, and the schematics of successful cluster management. The theory section covers current classification methods and typology of innovation-territorial economic associations. Russian innovation policy for cluster development received an up-to-date performance overview as well.

Keywords: state policy, institutions, innovation, R and D, cluster, cluster policy

1. Introduction

The strengthening of the integration effects of internationalization and globalization in the world economy characterized the last decades of the twentieth and early twenty-first centuries. Commercial expansions introduced internationalization into every sphere of production, which provoked an intensive reformation of the conditions of added value in the transnational connection of producers. Integration appeared as a systemic congregation of economic blocs supported by institutional and regulatory instruments at the mega and macro-levels.

Now at the mega level, an example of unions is the European Union, when integration at the macro-level is practiced by forming economic blocs on the state's territory. These macro-subjects are called clusters, which include firms and organizations with a strong association for finalized products. In such economic associations, it becomes necessary to consider the participants' geographical proximity and physical distance. These concentrated associations in the post-industrial period are now seen as the epicenters of colossal innovation and production potential, achieved through the effective creation and distribution of social, technological, and human capital.

In the presence of these aspects, clusters acquire the status of a stable and competitive infrastructure by realizing their production potential. It is worth noting that the system of clustering of the national economy has been adopted in 70% of the world's leading countries. Long-term practices show that innovation-territorial clusters are the basis of the most competitive developing economy. These associations have existed in Russia for 10 years, but the clustering program has a different impact on all business areas. As is customary, the programs of each innovation cluster and their associations are developed geographically. They aim to integrate research and industry to optimize the transformation of innovations integrated with the operational chain into full-fledged or experimental products.

The main topic of this study is the direction of improving the state policy of Russia to achieve the maximum efficiency of clustering in the country. Attention will be focused on the cyclical nature of this part of the economy and the perceived priorities for the optimal development of clusters through human capital, management, and technology.

The expectations set by the government and management methods deployed in the current cluster policy prove to be underwhelming. This is the problem statement for this research, which concretizes successful and effective ways to maintain innovative clusters.

The study aims to propose measures for the initial and continuous improvement of the work of innovation clusters in Russia based on the literature review, analysis of factors, and effects of successful management of economic and industrial clustering. At the same time, this research assumes that the Russian economy will become the primary environment for applying the acquired knowledge.

To achieve that, the following tasks must be specified and solved.

1. Identify the features of Russia's innovative clustering and its role in increasing global competitiveness.

2. Determine the status and explore the tools for forming high-tech industries in Russia.

3. Provide an assessment of the current political activity and strategy of cluster formation applied across the regions of Russia.

4. Define and describe the success factors for the activities of regional innovation clusters.

5. Choose practical management tools for regulating the efficiency of high-tech industries in the Russian Federation.

6. Determine the role, promising directions, and parameters of cluster progress for the future development of innovative systems.

The relevance of the research topic is characterized by the expected potential and proven effectiveness of clustering world economic entities. When extensive globalization prevails in the transition to new modes of production, it is necessary to study the appropriate management methods that will intensify scientific and technological progress to increase the competitiveness of companies and states. Many economists and writers position the cyclical nature of the ongoing changes as the main priority in studying business actors at various levels of the economy. Cluster systematization of the business environment opens new opportunities for stabilizing national innovation systems and protecting them from external economic factors. These trends in the functioning of the world economy are omnipresent and, by their existence, support the study's relevance.

Due to the relatively innovative status of the interdisciplinary study of the effects and management elements of clustering, it is observed that this topic is relatively unexplored by its contemporaries. The literature overview performed by the author confirms the presence of a research gap in this area. No academic work explores the innovative Russian economy and its development problems on this scale. In addition, current archives are dominated by publications that have lost their analytical relevance some time ago. Therefore, many factors deserve a place in updated qualitative analysis.

2. Features of Russia's innovative clustering and its role in increasing the country's global competitiveness

Expanding on the previous observations, the foreign experience of innovative development indicates that the success of implementing innovative programs strongly depends on the effectiveness of the institutional management of these programs. Therefore, developed countries are characterized by clarity, consistency, availability of infrastructure, a well-functioning management structure, and methodological, organizational, and legal documents that work as regulatory tools [1]. For these reasons, while monitoring the successes of the United States and other countries in 1999, the State Duma of the Russian Federation considered the draft law "On innovation activity and state innovation policy" [2].

After giving it some tests, the main principles of the policy of the Russian Federation in the field of scientific and technological development for 2010 were adopted with a further update until 2020. In the context of this document, the main directions, goals, objectives, implementation mechanisms, methods, and measures to stimulate the scientific, technical, and human capital activities of the policy in Russia were established. This policy was set to support the sustainable economic and innovative development of each region and the entire country. Such development of scientific and technical activities was aimed at solving the problems of socioeconomic and global progress, which were seen as the fundamental priorities for Russia after 2002 [3].

Until 2010, the second stage of the regulatory and legal delineation of innovation policy was supposed to organize a national system of innovation activity and finalize the global structure of the scientific and technological complex, but these goals were barely achieved. The effect of the successful implementation of these measures was to ensure the optimized functioning of the country in a market economy to maintain its competitive position in biological disciplines and high technologies worldwide [4].

Future redactions solidified the structure of cluster management at the regional level, which had a hierarchical direction of control over the network economy, as is shown in **Figure 1**. Over the years, this configuration of regulatory function was occasionally doubted, but it has yet to receive any substantial alteration or development.

From these normative strategies, new features were determined for the innovative work of the Russian Federation. It was assumed that at least half of the cluster

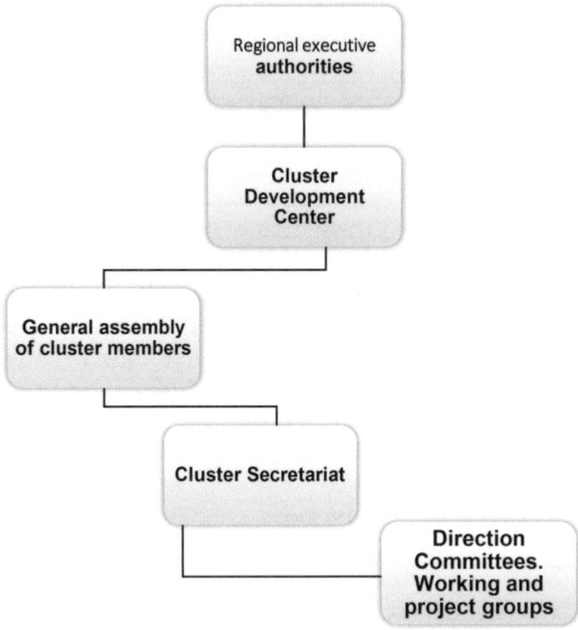

Figure 1.
Cluster management structure at the regional level of Russia. Source: [5].

participants were members of the governing body that was to establish an agreement with more of the constituent entities of the Russian Federation to act as cluster management [3].

There should have been at least 10 industrial enterprises on the territory of one or more regions in Russia, at least 1 of which was to be engaged in producing finished products. In addition, when creating and developing a cluster, special attention was paid to the space exploration strategy of the Russian Federation and the plans for overall regional development, as well as the commercial interests of companies that were located on the same territory [3].

At least 5% of industrial products, materials, and components produced by each cluster member had to be used by other members in addition to the manufacturer of the final cluster product. Also, at least 20% of the total product of a cluster member was required to be used by other cluster members, or at least 20% of the total product of a cluster member that produces the end product was used by other cluster members. In addition, at least 50% of tasks in a cluster had to show high-performance indicators [3].

The infrastructure included at least one higher professional or secondary professional education institution and two technical or industrial infrastructure subjects. Thanks to these past and present conditions, the hierarchical structure for the global management of the subjects of innovation policy was constructed. Its ambition was to effectively connect the global and regional levels of management to tighten the connection between the institutions, as shown in **Figure 2**.

In the third stage of this policy—in 2016, the Ministry of Economic Development of Russia initiated a priority project called "Development of innovative clusters – leaders in first-class investment attractiveness" [6]. Its main tasks were to create pilot epicenters of rapid economic progress, innovative development, export of high-tech

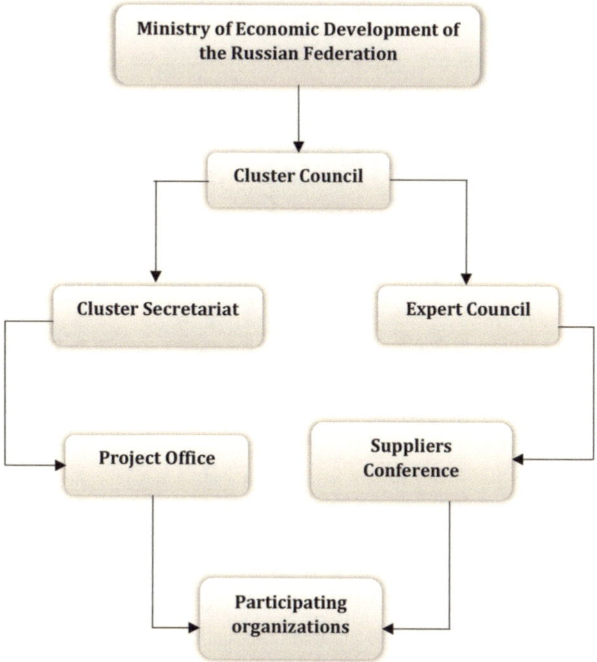

Figure 2.
Cluster management structure at the global level of Russia. Source: [5].

products and commercialization of technologies, increase in labor productivity and creation of high-performance jobs, and reflective of the past wishes, the increase of national competitiveness.

The new initiative was built on early experiments to support industrial zones and clusters. However, in the new interpretation, new priority industrial areas were emphasized [6]. The year of initiation, the status of organizational development, information on the number of participants, and characteristics of the type of functioning of these pilot innovation clusters that were actively supported by the state program are presented in **Table 1**.

However, the fundamental limitations showed themselves shortly into the implementation process when establishing these policies. One of which was the unpreparedness of local managers for innovative work in scientific, technological, and economic fields. Conclusions based on data from the Russian Cluster Observatory and colorful descriptions of the administrative cons demonstrate that the Russian economy's current level of innovative development needs to correspond to the goals and objectives of the national strategy for innovative development and its forecasts. The main reasons for this situation are the need for more effectiveness and the nonexistence of consumer orientation in the organizational mechanism of corporate innovation, the culture of which needs to be considered in the national innovation policy [7].

Accordingly, other disadvantages can be observed in the strategic concept of moderate growth of innovation in Russian policy. The lack of proper access to state statistics on the goals of managing innovative development and the delay of any statistical data should also be noted as a con. In addition, the structure of statistical indicators only partially corresponds to the tasks of the current day, which, in the absence of a detailed description of practical measures for the implementation of

Region	First-year	Specialization	Members	Organizational development	Type	Rank
Altai region	2008	Biopharmaceutical cluster	19	Medium	Vertical, state-owned, developing, sustainable, idea generator.	43
Arkhangelsk region	2012	Shipbuilding innovative territorial cluster	23	Medium	Consumer of innovations, with the state's participation, developing, sustainable, horizontal.	34
Kaluga region	2012	Pharmaceutical cluster, biotechnology, and biomedicine	54	High	Idea generator, horizontal, with the participation of the state cluster leader.	11
Kemerovo region	2012	ITK "Complex processing of coal and industrial waste."	49	Early	Consumer of innovations, horizontal, with the state's participation, developing cluster, asynchronous cluster.	35
Krasnoyarsk region	2011	The cluster of innovative technologies ZATO Zheleznogorsk	10	Early	Cluster leader, consumers of innovations, vertical, with the state's participation, developing cluster, stable cluster.	8
Moscow	2013	A cluster of microelectronics, info-communications "Zelenograd."	53	Medium	Cluster leader, with the state's participation, developing cluster, stable cluster, horizontal.	1
Moscow	2014	New materials, laser, and radiation technologies (Troitsk)	53	Early	Consumer of innovation, horizontal, state-owned, emerging clusters, sustainable.	1
Moscow region	2012	Biotechnological innovation territorial cluster, Pushchino	68	Medium	Idea generator, vertical, with the state's participation, developing cluster, sustainable.	6
Moscow region	2012	An innovative territorial cluster of nuclear physics and nanotechnologies in Dubna	80	Early	Consumers of innovation, vertical, state-owned, emerging, and sustainable.	6
Moscow region	2012	The cluster of pharmaceuticals "Phystech XXI" (Dolgoprudny)	25	Early	Idea generator, horizontal, state-owned, developing, sustainable.	6
Nizhny Novgorod Region	2015	Nizhny Novgorod industrial innovation cluster in the field of automotive and petrochemistry	33	Early	Consumer of innovations, horizontal, with the state, developing, cluster leader.	5
Nizhny Novgorod Region	—	Sarov Innovation Cluster	—	Disbanded/ integrated	—	5
Novosibirsk region	2016	The innovative cluster of information and biopharmaceutical technologies	227	High	Idea generator, horizontal, state-owned, developing, cluster leader.	7
Perm region	2012	Innovative Territorial Cluster of Rocket Engine Building "Technopolis New Zvezdniy"	44	Medium	Consumers of innovation, vertical, state-owned, developing, sustainable cluster.	16

Region	First-year	Specialization	Members	Organizational development	Type	Rank
Republic of Bashkortostan	2012	Petrochemical territorial cluster	211	High	Consumer of innovation, vertical, state-owned, developing, sustainable.	15
The Republic of Mordovia	2013	Energy-efficient lighting technology and intelligent lighting control systems	24	Medium	Consumer's innovation, vertical, state-owned, developing, sustainable.	22
Republic of Tatarstan	2012	Kama innovative territorially automotive manufacturing cluster	213	High	Cluster leader, developing, with the state, horizontal, idea generator.	3
Samara Region	2012	Aerospace cluster	13	Medium	Consumer of innovation, vertical, state-owned, developing, sustainable.	14
St. Petersburg	1999	Development of information technologies, radio electronics, instrumentation, and ITC facilities	66	High	Consumer, vertical, with the state's participation, developing, cluster leader.	2
Leningrad region	2014	The cluster of the medical, pharmaceutical industry, and radiation technologies	12	Early	Idea generator, vertical, state-owned, growing cluster, sustainable.	38
Sverdlovsk region	2012	Titanium cluster	20	Early	Consumer-generator, horizontal, without states, developing, sustainable.	9
Tomsk region	2013	Pharmaceutical, medical engineering, and information technology	52	Early	Consumer-generator, vertical, state-owned, developing, sustainable.	4
Ulyanovsk region	2009	Consortium "Scientific-educational-production cluster Ulyanovsk-Avia."	77	High	Consumer-generator, vertical, with the state, developing, sustainable.	12
Ulyanovsk region	2010	Nuclear innovation cluster of the city of Dimitrovgrad	69	High	Idea generator, vertical, horizontal, state-owned, developing, sustainable.	12
Khabarovsk region	2012	Innovative Territorial Cluster of Aircraft and Shipbuilding	62	Early	Idea generator, vertical, horizontal, state-owned, developing, sustainable.	17
Moscow	2018	Moscow Innovation Cluster, IT Center	34,645	Early	Generator-consumer of ideas, vertical-horizontal, with the state, developing, cluster leader.	1

Source: The table arranged by the authors after the qualitative research.

Table 1.
Authors' overview of the pilot and main innovation clusters in Russia.

innovation policy, provokes discoordination among the cluster members. Also, there needs to be a consolidated source of information describing the organizational functioning of innovation clusters. So, enthusiasts such as the author, who is proactive in obtaining information on local cluster management, face the limited nature of their description [8].

However, there are some positive aspects to the strategic situation of the Russian Federation. For example, there is enormous potential for editing and concretizing the strategic vision, and an extensive array of opportunities for interpreting new orientational recommendations can be introduced. With an emphasis on integrating more companies and other forms of business into clusters, small- and medium-sized businesses can be improved. In addition, the detail of procedures for subsidizing clusters is quite transparent. The current strategy extensively describes the range of sectoral and infrastructure activities for implementing the innovation program, which is a positive [6].

It is noteworthy that when discussing the actual state of Russia's innovative economy, some experts argue that a monopolistic industrial policy is necessary to accelerate economic growth, while the antitrust policy is destructive and creates unnecessary additional restrictions. However, another camp states that the conditions for the fair competition are just and that incentives for investment and the entire operation of free policy are necessary to provide market participants with advantages over competitors and deprive them of monopoly policy [9]. At the same time, the industrial policy of enterprises eliminates the interest in increasing production capacity. Without concrete guidance in this regard, the country is now open to improving the tools of state regulation, the status of legislation, and the stimulation of foreign direct investment, which have been lost due to consistent sanctions from the United States and the European Union [10]. These circumstances have outlined the multiple strengths and weaknesses of the current Russian economy, which are detailed in **Table 2**.

Many small Russian enterprises face the urgent difficulties of further innovation and survival. At the same time, the country has sufficient potential for comprehensive development: a cheap material base and empty production areas. However, the accepted superficial orientation of the economy to export actively minimized the production capacity of the manufacturing sectors and only stimulated the resource-extracting industries. Now, the competitiveness of the processing and transforming knowledge, primarily industrial and commercial products, requires the regular and tight integration of new management that embodies the best scientific results worldwide.

Now, bringing the investments to clusters should correspond with their needs and interests and the state regulations. Depending on the specific combination of companies and interests, cluster financing can be presented in various forms. Investment can be carried out based on each cluster member's self-support but according to a single agreed business plan without the involvement of third-party sources. Financing also comes from collective self-financing through creating equity in private fund institutions created by cluster members on a shared basis. Funds raised through investment loans are taken by each cluster member independently, but there is also a real possibility of financial support based on an agreed-upon business plan. Finally, according to the popular method of financing, the cluster is legally represented by a specific participant or fund, provided that some or all of the cluster participants receive government subsidies [7].

Nevertheless, the principal instruments of financial support for clusters used in Russian practice are inter-budget subsidies, targeted federal and state programs, and the activities of state companies and development agencies [7].

Strengths		Weaknesses	
Index	**Rank**	**Index**	**Rank**
Higher education	14	Regulatory quality	100
Enrollment in higher educational institutions, % of total	15	Law supremacy	109
Graduates in science and technology, %	13	Environmental sustainability	101
QS university ranking, top 3	21	GDP per unit of energy consumption	117
Trading, diversification, and market scale	17	Environmental certifications ISO 14001/bn. GDP in PPP dollars	107
The scale of the domestic market, bln PPP	6	Gross microfinance loans, % of GDP	78
Knowledge-intensive employment, %	18	Investments	116
Working women with advanced degrees, %	10	Venture capital recipients, deals/Bn PPP$ GDP	92
Payments for intellectual property, % of total trade	23	Firms offering formal training, %	94
Patents by origin/billion USD PPP GDP	15	Net FDI inflow, % of GDP	97
Utility models by origin/billion USD PPP GDP	10	ISO 9001 Quality Certifications/billion USD PPP GDP	105
Documents cited H-index	23	Printed and other media, % production	80

Source: [10].

Table 2.
Strengths and weaknesses of the Russian innovation economy.

An analysis of international and Russian experience in the formation of innovation clusters mainly shows the presence of practical problems in Russian implementation. Of course, there are many more reasons why developing an innovation policy for the Russian Federation could be more effective. However, some of the fundamental aspects can still be outlined:

- inadequacy of the system for insurance of innovative investments and leasing of high-tech products;
- active investment in the development of the raw materials industry, rather than supporting the processing industry and not making venture capital investments;
- the limited scale of development of new or promising innovative directions and innovative apathy of business;
- insufficient institutional support at the administrative and specialized levels;
- mediocre efficiency of tax incentives, tariffs, and general infrastructure;
- low commercialization of the project, as only the declarative nature of cluster activity prevails;
- inadequate relationships between large and small firms, authorized cluster members, and independent experts.

3. Status and known tools of high-tech clusters in Russia

Since 2012, two main trends in the development of clusters have been observed in the Russian Federation. The first is centralized project support from the Ministry of Economic Development of Russia, aimed at forming territorial innovation clusters in each region. Moreover, second, the Ministry of Industry and Trade of Russia provides industrial clusters with software and industrial support [9].

Nevertheless, innovative activity in innovative industries has steadily decreased: from 17.8% in 2017 to 15.1% in 2019. Other negative trends in 2017–2019 were decreased R&D activity from 46.6 to 35.6% in the pharmaceutical industry and from 29.4% to 21.5% in the production of medical devices. However, in recent years, the pandemic has substantially boosted innovation in these areas [11].

Nevertheless, at the same time, in industrial clusters, the mass form of production prevails in the current times, which is contrasted by the continuous production in innovative clusters of a limited range of products at highly specialized jobs. Therefore, mass production in Russia stayed as the long-term strategy for economic development.

As a result, automobiles, tractors, and other specialized vehicles were produced in colossal numbers; agricultural machinery reached hundreds of thousandths of sales per year. The fabrication of these products is usually carried out in unique factories or special workshops oriented toward mass production in industrial clusters. However, innovative products had different results since the population had the lowest possible demand for innovative local products and used well-established analogs from abroad.

Russia lags behind the world leaders in the development of clusters. However, this can be justified because over 75% of innovation clusters were launched after 2012. Therefore, they are still in the initial stage of formation or development, which implies the absence of progressive achievements in the context of innovative leadership or global competitiveness [11].

According to domestic experts, since 2012, when the Government of the Russian Federation announced the implementation of the clustering policy as part of its strategy for innovative development, the policy has yielded significant results only by 2020 in some regions of Russia. It is possible to note that the Republic of Tatarstan has high costs for technological innovations and product innovation activities, as well as the Kaluga region with expressive macroeconomic indicators, where clusters were formed and developed based on the existing powerful production complex. Alternatively, the Smolensk Linen Cluster was created with the participation of Vyazemsky Machine-Building Plant LLC, which reduced material and energy costs because of its innovations. The auxiliary work of this complex made it possible to create a complete production chain with the potential for further development and expansion of membership in a full-fledged cluster [9].

Moscow retains its leading position regarding the degree of innovation and development of the constituent entities of the Russian Federation in 2018/2019 when it has the 32nd position in the technological leadership table from WIPO [10]. This region continues to demonstrate the highest economic, educational, and digital development levels. IT leadership is also seen as the key to its success. There is a colossal potential for digitalization and expressive educational potential of the population in the capital. The manufacturability of the personnel ensures the high innovative activity of organizations, which brings confident costs for technological innovation and prospective confidence in the export of knowledge. The regulatory framework for innovation policy with stable organizational support assists the small innovative business of Moscow with the city's participation in the federal scientific, technical, and innovation policy [6]. The economic, technological, and innovative achievements of this policy are presented in **Table 3**.

Currently, only St. Petersburg can be perceived as the closest competitor of Moscow. However, the region lags by at least 30 percent in terms of overall digital capacity. These two clusters demonstrate the adequate development of all the advantages of innovation-territorial clusters: Holistic production chains are being created, targeted scientific developments are being conducted, and working talents are being cultivated in the masses. The final stage of the cyclical development of these regions involves the expected minimization of production costs and an increase in production profits. St. Petersburg, just like its competitor, has a confident educational potential of the population, a stable reserve of educational personnel, and a colossal innovative activity of organizations based on the active participation of the cluster in the federal scientific and technical policy [6]. However, as in Moscow, the minimum

MOSCOW			
Free innovation index	0.551		
Rank	1		
1. Socioeconomic conditions for innovative activities			
1	1.1 Main macroeconomic indicators	0.388	9
0.567	1.2 Educational potential of the population	0.646	13
	1.3 The potential of digitalization	0.864	1
2. Scientific and technical potential			
(5) 6	2.1 Funding for research and development	0.298	20
0.455	2.2 Science staff	0.560	3
	2.3 R&D performance	0.558	5
3. Innovation			
(7) 2	3.1 Innovative activity of organizations	0.886	1
0.588	3.2 Small innovative business	0.662	3
	3.3 Technological innovation costs	0.660	16
	3.4 Innovation performance	0.143	60
4. Export activity			
(2) 4	4.1 Export of goods and services	0.513	12
0.566	4.2 Knowledge export	0.637	4
5. Quality of innovation policy			
2	5.1 Normative legal framework for innovation policy	0.750	13
0.581	5.2 Organizational support of innovation policy	0.500	13
	5.3 Budget spending on science and innovation	0.331	4
	5.4 Participation in federal science, technology, and innovation policy	0.713	4

Source: Calculated by the authors based on the numbers from [10].

Table 3.
Aggregated innovation indices of Moscow.

effectiveness of innovation activity and limited costs for science and innovation from the state budget are present, as shown in **Table 4**.

Still, St. Petersburg and Moscow retain leadership in export activities. However, the northern capital has many foreign students who have achieved more impressive results in technology exports and foreign patents for inventions.

St. Petersburg, the Republic of Tatarstan, the Tomsk and Nizhny Novgorod regions, the Chuvash Republic, Moscow, and the Republic of Mordovia confidently retain leading positions in innovation. Furthermore, the ratings of the Russian Cluster Observatory demonstrate that the Republic of Tatarstan has a rich educational potential for the population and substantive costs for technological innovation. In addition, this region surprises by the absolute security of the regulatory framework and the excellent organizational support for innovation policy [6]. However, the effectiveness of innovation and scientific research is at most the levels of other leading clusters in Russia, as shown in **Table 5**.

SAINT PETERSBURG			
Free innovation index	0.530		
Rank	(3) 2		
1. SOCIOECONOMIC CONDITIONS FOR INNOVATIVE ACTIVITIES			
3	1.1 Main macroeconomic indicators	0.349	15
0.527	1.2 Educational potential of the population	0.689	5
	1.3 The potential of digitalization	0.669	2
2. SCIENTIFIC AND TECHNICAL POTENTIAL			
(3) 4	2.1 Funding for research and development	0.429	5
0.486	2.2 Science staff	0.544	4
	2.3 R&D performance	0.505	7
3. INNOVATION			
3	3.1 Innovative activity of organizations	0.829	2
0.584	3.2 Small innovative business	0.533	8
	3.3 Technological innovation costs	0.639	17
	3.4 Innovation performance	0.257	26
4. EXPORT ACTIVITY			
1	4.1 Export of goods and services	0.514	10
0.579	4.2 Knowledge export	0.666	2
5. QUALITY OF INNOVATION POLICY			
(9) 10	5.1 Normative legal framework for innovation policy	0.500	50
0.497	5.2 Organizational support of innovation policy	0.500	13
	5.3 Budget spending on science and innovation	0.126	32
	5.4 Participation in federal science, technology, and innovation policy	0.718	3

Source: Calculated by the authors based on the numbers from [10].

Table 4
Aggregated innovation indices of St. Petersburg.

Republic of Tatarstan			
Free innovation index	0.498		
Rank	(2) 3		
1. SOCIOECONOMIC CONDITIONS FOR INNOVATIVE ACTIVITIES			
(2) 4	1.1 Main macroeconomic indicators	0.427	4
0.516	1.2 Educational potential of the population	0.677	8
	1.3 The potential of digitalization	0.538	6
2. SCIENTIFIC AND TECHNICAL POTENTIAL			
(13) 17	2.1 Funding for research and development	0.220	41
0.357	2.2 Science staff	0.420	12
	2.3 R&D performance	0.476	9
3. INNOVATION			
(1) 4	3.1 Innovative activity of organizations	0.582	6
0.551	3.2 Small innovative business	0.343	28
	3.3 Technological innovation costs	0.862	5
	3.4 Innovation performance	0.475	5
4. Export activity			
(9) 11	4.1 Export of goods and services	0.457	19
0.482	4.2 Knowledge export	0.514	11
5. Quality of innovation policy			
1	5.1 Normative legal framework for innovation policy	1	1
0.581	5.2 Organizational support of innovation policy	1	1
	5.3 Budget spending on science and innovation	0.179	19
	5.4 Participation in federal science, technology, and innovation policy	0.655	7

Source: Calculated by the authors based on the numbers from [10].

Table 5.
Aggregated innovation indices of the Republic of Tatarstan.

Russian use of the cluster approach in regional development is problematic because of its necessity to constantly balance the complexity and rigidity of regional control and maximize the synergy of all the included institutions.

Before the progressive development of clusters tried to optimize domestic enterprises' position inside the production value chain, but it only contributed to an increase in the processing of extracted raw materials, import substitution, and an increase in the localization of assembly plants. It also increased the nonprice competitiveness of domestic goods and services and strengthened partnerships between government agencies and private entrepreneurs in various regions of the Russian Federation. Only now, after achieving limited results, the government focused more on the original and locally produced innovative outputs.

Under growth conditions, it is possible to form miniature clusters of progress or areas of lesser decline even within the limitations of a spontaneous economic decline. This is another positive aspect of cluster policy—structural resistance to the decline in the quality of the world economy caused by disruptive political events. Because of that, for many years, raw material enterprises have been steadily forming the dominant clusters' role, accounting for a significant part of the Russian GDP [6].

Therefore, this localized economy is a reliable and safe source of accumulated horizontal budgets for implementing other innovative cluster policies. With the successful operation of the cluster, quantitative and qualitative aspects contribute to the effective development of organizations in other areas of scientific and industrial activity. After achieving impressive results in industrial clustering, Russia can afford to use stable capital to develop commodity-oriented and innovation-based clusters, which could serve as a driving force behind the further successful technological development of the country [6].

The possibility of obtaining the lowest unit cost of production compared to other industries in the same region confirms the objective advantage of forming development clusters, which creates a favorable situation for Russia in the domestic and foreign markets. Support for cluster development is currently a legitimate priority of the state policy for the country's socioeconomic development. The foreign practice has also proven that forming and developing innovative clusters is an effective mechanism for attracting local and foreign direct investments. This trend has contributed to the foreign economic integration of Russia with China and the accumulation of infrastructure and human resources in the state. Such and other activities allow the construction of a network of competitive suppliers and service organizations to ensure that business needs are adequately considered within the framework of regional and global planning mechanisms. Thus, the increase in labor productivity, the formation of new companies, and the creation of new jobs should now be heavily encouraged.

Presently, most of the constituent entities of the Russian Federation are strengthening their positions in the world market and participating in the international exchange of information. As a result, more than 80% of regions increased their export activity, including the export of noncommodity goods, and more than 60% noted an improvement in the export of services and innovative products at the time of 2021. At the same time, more than 90% of the subjects of the Russian Federation increased the export of technologies, three-quarters of the subjects began to export educational services actively, and two-thirds of the subjects began to apply for patents abroad [6]. However, their absolute numbers could be higher for a country of its scale.

As world practice shows, one of the platforms for innovation clusters is the system that encourages operational interaction with jurisdictions and state-owned enterprises. Since Russia already has created some of the required government and regional bodies, it could be developed even further, albeit with specific significant changes. With synergies from all institutions, the development of clusters could gradually open opportunities to achieve continuous optimization of domestic enterprises in the production value chain and increase the localization of assembly lines. In addition to these benefits, improvements in domestic goods and nonprice competitive service levels and strengthening public-private partnerships can be obtained.

Based on the Russian innovation policy by 2022, the fundamental problems are the overall low demand for innovation and the structural inefficiency of the Russian economy—a tendency to purchase finished equipment abroad, which does not contribute to introducing new developments. On average, for pilot innovation clusters, increasing the level of the leading macroeconomic indicators is critical. Neither the private nor the public sector paid due attention to innovation spending because the level of corporate innovation activity is significantly lower than the indicators of the leading countries in the same field. And the costs of technological innovation do not shine with high performance [10].

However, the potential of digitalization, the staff of science, and the effectiveness of scientific research are at a moderate level. When reviewing averages, the previously described problem with insufficient funding for R&D and a general deficit in budget spending on science and innovation, which provokes lower results in innovative activity, is once again apparent. The export of goods and services and knowledge export have good indicators, but the share of innovative products in these batches needs to meet expectations.

The described trends dictate the need to streamline the current innovation policy, shifting the focus from increasing the total amount of support to using flexible and experimental approaches to solving critical issues of innovation development. The current regulatory framework for innovation policy must provide the means by the organizational state strategy [6].

The taken averages of the leading indicators for the most pivotal and successful clusters included in **Table 6** suggest that the state government's goals, missions, and strategies could be more realistic.

AVERAGE PERFORMANCE OF PILOT INNOVATION CLUSTERS IN RUSSIA		
Free innovation index	0.4235	
1. SOCIOECONOMIC CONDITIONS FOR INNOVATIVE ACTIVITIES		
0.445733	1.1 Main macroeconomic indicators	0.36305
	1.2 Educational potential of the population	0.56385
	1.3 The potential of digitalization	0.4103
2. SCIENTIFIC AND TECHNICAL POTENTIAL		
0.391067	2.1 Funding for research and development	0.34285
	2.2 Science staff	0.41965
	2.3 R&D performance	0.4107
3. INNOVATION		
0.437513	3.1 Innovative activity of organizations	0.43035
	3.2 Small innovative business	0.4081
	3.3 Technological innovation costs	0.583
	3.4 Innovation performance	0.3286
4. EXPORT ACTIVITY		
0.448425	4.1 Export of goods and services	0.4276
	4.2 Knowledge export	0.46925
5. QUALITY OF INNOVATION POLICY		
0.51695	5.1 Normative legal framework for innovation policy	0.8
	5.2 Organizational support of innovation policy	0.50515
	5.3 Budget spending on science and innovation	0.192
	5.4 Participation in federal science, technology, and innovation policy	0.57065

Source: Calculated by the authors based on the numbers from [12].

Table 6.
Average values of innovative and other work of pilot clusters.

According to the Global Innovation Index 2020, Russia ranks 47th out of 131 countries in innovative development, only two percentage points higher than in 2015. Russia's cluster development indicators are low compared to the leading countries: 95th in the world, the concentration of clusters barely matters—0.3, and the overall GII score is 3.4 out of 7.

However, in the last GII-2021 reports, Russia has risen by two more positions over the years, taking 45th place out of 132 countries. Over the 5 years, the scoring practices were changed in the country composition analysis; ranking methodologies were adjusted, multiple indicator scores were changed, missing values in the data were calculated, and so on. In contrast to these alterations, Russia's position was stable [12].

A positive observation here is that increasing the efficiency in all areas of scientific, innovative, and creative activity has narrowed the gap between the leading countries in innovation [12]. In a table of 132 countries, Russia ranked 45th in the report (between Vietnam and India). At the same time, Russia occupies high positions in various GII indicators, specifically, higher education development (14th), trade, competition, and market size (17th), knowledge production (26th), research and development (33rd), information and communication technology (36th), and Internet ideas (47th) [12].

At the same time, the indicators of the Russian Federation are significantly lower in some respects. These include environmental sustainability (101st), regulatory environment (92nd), innovative communications (88th), and creative goods and services (81st) [12]. All of the rankings that are mentioned can be found in **Table 7**.

Thus, it is necessary to note the negative factors in the practice of the current innovation strategy, which are actively associated with the immaturity of the framework conditions for innovation. Weak institutional infrastructure, underdevelopment, the backwardness of the legislative framework in this area, and a low institutional investment activity illustrate the limited state for innovations [12].

In the current situation, only direct financing and tax incentives are considered state support, which, according to critics, reduces the incentive for firms to innovate and improve. The proof of this position is the inefficiency of the Skolkovo project. Due to the lack of a commercial impulse for independent survival, the experimental potential of the company is reduced, which minimizes the innovative activity of the entire region [7].

Global Innovation Index Russia 2021						
45th rank						
Institutes	**Human capital and research**	**Infrastructure**	**Market sophistication**	**Business sophistication**	**Results of knowledge and technologies**	**Creative results**
71	30	60	55	42	50	60
Corruption Perceptions Index 2021						
29 points out of 100						
Global Competitiveness Index 2021						
43rd rank						

Source: Table compiled by the author based on the information from [12, 13].

Table 7.
Main ratings and indicators of economic and innovation in Russia, 2021.

These shortcomings are manifested in the formation of uneven clusters, which exacerbates the fragmentation of the socioeconomic development of the territory of the Russian Federation. Also, administrative efficiency still needs to be improved and is a fundamental shortcoming of Russia's competitiveness.

Just as there is no country in the world with a very high level of corruption and very competitive power, there is no country with a low level of corruption and low competitiveness. The main factors hindering national competitiveness are the inefficiency of the financial and banking sector and the inequality of institutions [12].

Also, one of the critical constraints to doing business successfully can be high levels of corruption, which is highly correlated with black market activity and overregulation. Of course, 2 years after the devastating COVID-19 pandemic, the Corruption Perceptions Index (CPI) still shows a flat rate worldwide. Despite promises on paper, 180 countries have yet to progress in fighting corruption over the past decade. Moreover, one of these countries is Russia, which scores 29 out of 100, where 100 is equivalent to a state administration that is clean of corruption [14].

In addition, significant shortcomings of the innovation policy of the Russian Federation are administrative barriers to doing business, insufficient protection of property rights, high tax rates, demanding access to financial resources, inflation, and shortcomings of the current tax system.

4. Empirical research

To assess the factors of influence of cluster elements and management organizations on innovative development and the level of competitiveness of national innovation systems in Russia and world countries, an experimental decision was made to implement statistical analysis using multiple linear regression models [15].

The empirical objectives of the study favored the determination of the following hypotheses, which reflect the meaning of the updated research questions:

- First null hypothesis (H_0-1)—there are no statistical effects of socioeconomic, scientific, technical, innovation, export, and regulatory factors on the innovation index of Russian cluster regions.

- The first alternative hypothesis (H_1-1) is a statistical effect of socioeconomic, scientific, technical, innovation, export, and regulatory factors on the innovation index of Russian cluster regions.

For the implementation of statistical analysis, 29 linear regression models were created with the participation of 119 variables, which were constructed from 9 databases containing 6656 values. Data on Russian innovation clusters were obtained from the Internet portals of the Russian Cluster Observatory [6], the values of innovation subindices and the Global Innovation Index (GII) were found on the World Intellectual Property Organization (WIPO) page, and the competitiveness ratings of states were found in the data from IMD World Competitiveness Center [12]. All data came out in 2021 and represented the most recent information provided by the publishers. This decision was made due to the need for alternative options found in the free Internet access.

To avoid the adverse effects of autocorrelation, multicollinearity, heteroscedasticity, and the size of outliers on the objectivity of the obtained statistical results, tests are carried out on the assumptions of the quality of the used models [16]. The Durbin-Watson test was used, the coefficients were studied by the test on variance inflation factor, and the graphical analysis was produced. For this reason, 23 models were assessed and established, which leveled out the conflicting interactions of variables in the implementation of regression analysis [17]. The workflow of the operations performed in the context of regression analysis can be seen in **Figure 3**.

The threat of unreliability of the obtained results is potentially present due to the limited number of observations, which eliminates the possibility of removing every cause of the statistical outliers when improving the quality of regression models. Another source of doubt about the validity of the obtained results is the indices from the Russian Cluster Observatory, WIPO, and IMD, on which databases the analysis was executed [13]. Also, the adequacy of using the WIPO's data regarding the countries' innovation achievements to represent the success of the countries' clusters can come under scrutiny. However, after conducting the qualitative analysis, the author believes this approach can be justified since the innovation clusters significantly impact the countries' innovation development.

In the first section of the regression analysis, 20 regions were selected to uncover the impact of variables on the innovation index of clusters in Russia. These regions were initiated according to pilot projects of the country's innovative cluster development [3].

To confirm or reject the first hypothesis, the relationship among the leading macroeconomic indicators, the educational potential of the population, the financing of research and development, the effectiveness of research and development, the export of goods and services, the regulatory and legal framework for innovation policy, the organizational support for innovation policy, budget expenditures on science, and innovations on the dependent variable—innovation index of cluster regions of Russia—is explored. This procedure is presented in **Table 8**.

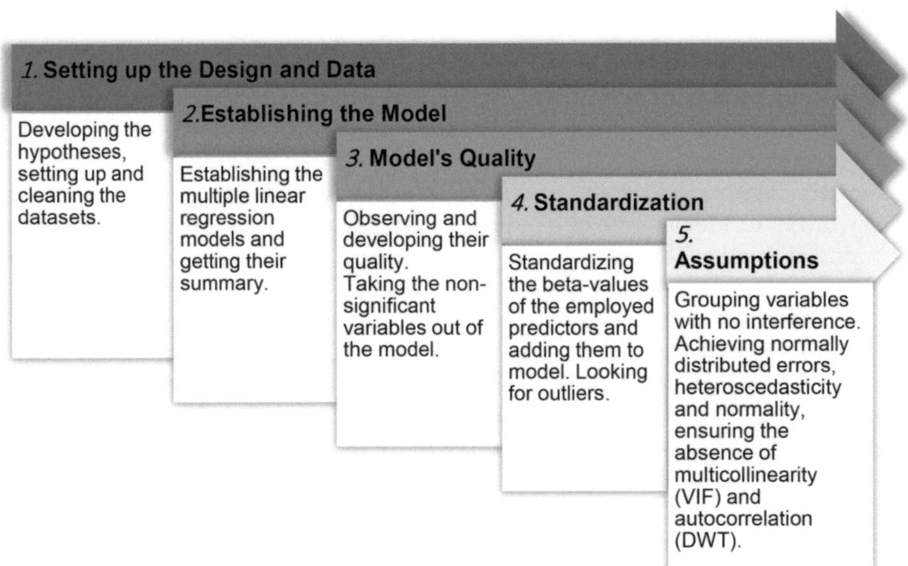

Figure 3.
Methodical thinking behind the regression analysis. Source: The figure and research were designed and carried out by the authors.

Multiple linear regression on generalized indicators of Russian clusters					
lm(formula = i_index ~ main_macro_indic_1_1 + educ_pot_pop_1_2 + fund_res_dev_2_1 + res_dev_ef_2_3 + exp_gds_srvs_4_1 + norm_lgl_frmwk_innov_pol_5_1 + org_sup_innov_pol_5_2 + bdgt_spndg_scien_innov_5_3, data = clustdata_0_1)					
Residuals:	Min	1Q	Median	3Q	Max
	−0.037898	−0.017679	−0.005385	0.017936	0.052210
Coefficients	Estimate	Standard Error	t-value	Pr (>|t|)	Significance
main_macro_indic_1_1	0.156983	0.158810	0.988	0.34416	
educ_pot_pop_1_2	0.103351	0.093309	1.108	0.29166	
fund_res_dev_2_1	0.085849	0.066333	1.294	0.22211	
res_dev_ef_2_3	0.364625	0.100133	3.641	0.00388	**
exp_gds_srvs_4_1	0.217058	0.108300	2.004	0.07029	.
norm_lgl_frmwk_innov_pol_5_1	0.034244	0.044993	0.761	0.46261	
org_sup_innov_pol_5_2	−0.011056	0.024747	−0.447	0.66372	
bdgt_spndg_scien_innov_5_3	0.155944	0.082524	1.890	0.08543	.
Significance codes	0 '***'	0.001 '**'	0.01'*'	0.05'.'	0.1
Residual standard error:		0.03394 on 11 degrees of freedom			
Multiple R-squared	0.8297		Adjusted R-squared	0.7058	
F-statistic	6.698 on 8 and 11 DF		p-Value	0.002566	

Source: Table compiled by the author based on the summary from RStudio.

Table 8.
First variables' influence on the innovation index of clusters in Russia.

According to the analysis of all variables, the effectiveness of research and development has a high statistical significance (0.00388) with the regional innovation index. On average, each change in research and development performance is accompanied by an increase in the innovation index by 0.364625, while other variables remain the same.

The export of goods and services (0.07029) and budget expenditures on science and innovations (0.08543) have the minimum significance. The first variable provides a positive effect of 0.217058, and the second is 0.155944 on the performance indicator of the statistical model.

For these variables, p-values allow us to move away from the first null hypothesis (H_0-1) to accept that the variables are related to the innovation index.

Based on the adjusted R-square value (0.7058), the fitted model explains 70.58% of the statistical relationships of the linear regression variables. Also, the model's p-value (0.002566 < 0.05) demonstrates the rejection of the null hypothesis about the absence of effects of variables on the result, which confirms the statistical reliability of this regression analysis.

Like the last time, a new group of variables was compiled to accept or refute the first hypothesis. It aims to explore the relationship between the leading macroeconomic indicators, the potential of digitalization, scientific personnel, the innovative activity of organizations, small innovative businesses, the cost of technological innovation, the effectiveness of the innovative activity, export of knowledge, and participation in federal scientific, technical, and innovation policy with the same dependent variable. This procedure is presented in **Table 9**.

According to the analysis of all predictors, the moderate statistical significance (0.0477) with the innovation index of the region is observed when looking at the cost of technological innovation. On average, each change in the cost of technological innovation is accompanied by an increase in the innovation index by 0.08538 when other variables remain unchanged. Also, the p-value allows us to move away from the first null hypothesis (H_0–1) to accept that the predictor has a relationship with the output indicator.

Based on the adjusted R-square value (0.8744), the fitted model explains 87.44% of the statistical relationships of the linear regression variables. Also, the model's p-value (0.0000884 < 0.05) demonstrates the rejection of the null hypothesis about the absence of effects of variables on the result, which confirms the statistical reliability of this regression analysis.

A review of the subindices of the new group of variables is carried out to accept or reject the first hypothesis. It is done to see if there is any impact on the dependent variable from the share of organizations implementing technological innovations, the share of organizations implementing nontechnological innovations, the share of organizations developing technological innovations on their own, the share of

Multiple linear regression on generalized indicators of Russian clusters

lm(formula = i_index ~ main_macro_indic_1_1 + pot_digit_1_3 + scien_pers_2_2 + innov_act_org_3_1 + sml_innov_bus_3_2 + tech_innov_cost_3_3 + effect_innov_3_4 + know_exp_4_2 + part_fed_scien_tech_innov_pol_5_4, data = clustdata_0_2)

Residuals:	Min	1Q	Median	3Q	Max
	−0.036253	−0.005312	0.002120	0.007110	0.033507
Coefficients	Estimate	Standard error	t-value	Pr (>|t|)	Significance
main_macro_indic_1_1	0.10712	0.10206	1.050	0.3186	
pot_digit_1_3	0.10810	0.06133	1.763	0.1084	
scien_pers_2_2	0.04794	0.12276	0.391	0.7044	
innov_act_org_3_1	0.11851	0.08768	1.352	0.2063	
sml_innov_bus_3_2	−0.04066	0.06137	−0.663	0.5226	
tech_innov_cost_3_3	0.08538	0.03785	2.256	0.0477	*
effect_innov_3_4	0.01163	0.07793	0.149	0.8843	
know_exp_4_2	0.01354	0.08315	0.163	0.8739	
part_fed_scien_tech_innov_pol_5_4	0.12489	0.08778	1.423	0.1852	
Significance codes	0 '***'	0.001 '**'	0.01 '*'	0.05 '.'	0.1
Residual standard error:	0.02217 on 10 degrees of freedom				
Multiple R-squared	0.9339		Adjusted R-squared	0.8744	
F-statistic	15.7 on 9 and 10 DF		p-Value	0.0000884	

Source: Table compiled by the author based on the summary from RStudio.

Table 9.
Second group's variables' influence on Russia's innovation index.

organizations participating in scientific cooperation, the share of small enterprises implementing technological innovations, the intensity of costs for technological innovations, the share of innovative products, the share of new innovative products, and the share of organizations that have reduced material and energy costs as a result of innovation. This procedure is presented in **Table 10**.

Looking at the analysis results of all variables, the moderate statistical significance (0.042635) and (0.023314) can be observed in the share of organizations participating in scientific cooperation and the intensity of costs for technological innovation. These variables increase the innovation index of the region by 0.119038 and 0.126316 when other variables remain unchanged. For these variables, the p-value allows us to move away from the first null hypothesis (H_0-1) to accept that the variables are related to the output variable.

The minimum significance (0.098626) with an impact (−0.092058) on the innovation index also has the share of small enterprises that carried out technological innovations.

Based on the adjusted R-square value (0.8306), the fitted model explains 83.06% of the statistical relationships of the linear regression variables. Also, the model's p-value (0.0003683 < 0.05) demonstrates the rejection of the null hypothesis about the

Multiple linear regression on detailed indicators of Russian clusters					
lm(formula = i_index ~ shre_org_tech_innov_3_1_1 + shr_org_impl_nontech_innov_3_1_2 + shr_org_dev_tech_innov_own_3_1_3 + shr_org_part_sci_coop_3_1_4 + shr_sml_entrp_tech_innov_3_2_1 + cst_int_tech_innov_3_3_1 + shr_innov_prod_3_4_1 + shr_innov_prod_new_markt_3_4_2 + shr_org_rduc_mat_enrg_csts_bcs_innov_3_4_3, data = clustdata_1)					
Residuals:	Min	1Q	Median	3Q	Max
	−0.052539	−0.008196	0.000218	0.008474	0.030817
Coefficients	Estimate	Standard error	t-value	Pr (>|t|)	Significance
shre_org_tech_innov_3_1_1	0.135564	0.075956	1.785	0.104614	
shr_org_impl_nontech_innov_3_1_2	−0.050623	0.097501	−0.519	0.614910	
shr_org_dev_tech_innov_own_3_1_3	0.042541	0.075620	0.563	0.586119	
shr_org_part_sci_coop_3_1_4	0.119038	0.051268	2.322	0.042635	*
shr_sml_entrp_tech_innov_3_2_1	−0.092058	0.050555	−1.821	0.098626	.
cst_int_tech_innov_3_3_1	0.126316	0.047231	2.674	0.023314	*
shr_innov_prod_3_4_1	−0.005347	0.031848	−0.168	0.870012	
shr_innov_prod_new_markt_3_4_2	−0.032560	0.030977	−1.051	0.317939	
shr_org_rduc_mat_enrg_csts_bcs_innov_3_4_3	0.046774	0.051330	0.911	0.383605	
Significance codes	0 '***'	0.001 '**'	0.01 '*'	0.05 '.'	0.1 "
Residual standard error:	0.02576 on 10 degrees of freedom				
Multiple R-squared	0.9108		Adjusted R-squared	0.8306	
F-statistic	11.35 on 9 and 10 DF		p-value	0.0003683	
Source: Table compiled by the author based on the summary from RStudio.					

Table 10.
Third group's variables' influence on Russia's innovation index.

absence of effects of variables on the result, which confirms the statistical reliability of this regression analysis.

Going forward, the detailed group of variables is reviewed to see if they influence the innovation index of Russian cluster regions. The group includes the export of goods, nonresource exports of goods, exports of services, the share of exports in the volume of innovative products, patent activity abroad, the export of technologies, and the share of foreign students of higher education programs. This procedure is visualized in **Table 11**.

There is visible a moderate statistical significance (0.04952) of the export of services. This variable increases the dependent variable by 0.12507 when other variables remain unchanged. Also, patent activity abroad has a minimum significance (0.08445) and influence (0.10925) on the output variable.

For these variables, the p-value allows us to accept that the variables are related to the innovation index.

The fitted model explains 50.46% of the statistical relationships of the linear regression variables. Also, the model's p-value ($0.02154 < 0.05$) demonstrates the rejection of the null hypothesis about the absence of predictor effects on the final result, confirming the moderate statistical reliability of this regression analysis.

Further, the review of the variables from the new group of subindices is carried out. The model tests if there is an impact on the innovation index of clusters in Russia

Multiple linear regression on detailed indicators of Russian clusters					
lm(formula = i_index ~ exp_gds_4_1_1 + non_commty_exp_gds_4_1_2 + exp_srvs_4_1_3 + shr_exp_vol_innov_prod_4_1_4 + pat_act_abrd_4_2_1 +exp_tech_4_2_2 + shr_int_stud_hi_ed_prog_4_2_3, data = clustdata_1)					
Residuals:	Min	1Q	Median	3Q	Max
	−0.078164	−0.015184	−0.000364	0.018768	0.065586
Coefficients	Estimate	Standard error	t-value	Pr (>|t|)	Significance
exp_gds_4_1_1	0.06137	0.06471	0.948	0.36162	
non_commty_exp_gds_4_1_2	−0.20444	0.16858	−1.213	0.24857	
exp_srvs_4_1_3	0.12507	0.05726	2.184	0.04952	*
shr_exp_vol_innov_prod_4_1_4	0.07178	0.06463	1.111	0.28852	
pat_act_abrd_4_2_1	0.10925	0.05808	1.881	0.08445	.
exp_tech_4_2_2	0.03801	0.04454	0.853	0.41021	
shr_int_stud_hi_ed_prog_4_2_3	0.03211	0.08702	0.369	0.71857	
Significance codes	0 '***'	0.001 '**'	0.01 '*'	0.05 '.'	0.1 "
Residual standard error:		0.04404 on 12 degrees of freedom			
Multiple R-squared	0.6871		Adjusted R-squared	0.5046	
F-statistic	3.765 on 7 and 12 DF		p-value	0.02154	

Source: Table compiled by the author based on the summary from RStudio.

Table 11.
Fourth group's variables' influence on Russia's innovation index.

coming from the innovation development strategy, allocated territories for innovation development, the regional law on innovation, the innovation support program, the coordinating body for innovation policy, the regional institute for innovation development, the share of allocations for science in the regional budget, the share of the federal budget in the costs of technological innovation, the share of the regional budget in the cost of technological innovation, the number of innovative projects that received federal support, the number of federal development institutions that support innovative projects, the federal funding of innovative projects, the number of territories for innovative development with federal status, and the number of objects of innovative infrastructure to support SMEs. The results of the analysis are shown in **Table 12**.

Multiple linear regression on detailed indicators of Russian clusters					
lm(formula = i_index ~ innov_strtg_dev_5_1_1 + ded_ars_innov_dev_5_1_2 + reg_innov_law_5_1_3 + sup_prog_innov_5_1_4 + coord_bdy_innov_pol_5_2_1 + reg_instit_innov_dev_5_2_2 + apprp_shr_sci_reg_budg_5_3_1 + shr_fed_budg_tech_innov_csts_5_3_2 + shr_reg_bdg_rech_innov_csts_5_3_3 + num_innov_proj_recid_fed_sup_5_4_1 + num_fed_instit_dev_sup_innov_proj_5_4_2 + fed_fund_innov_proj_5_4_3 + num_innov_terris_dev_fed_stats_5_4_4 + num_obj_innov_infra_sme_sup_5_4_5, data = clustdata_1)					
Residuals:	Min	1Q	Median	3Q	Max
	−0.061067	−0.008884	−0.002866	0.010845	0.037298
Coefficients	Estimate	Standard error	t-value	Pr (>|t|)	Significance
innov_strtg_dev_5_1_1	0.004517	0.027741	0.163	0.8760	
ded_ars_innov_dev_5_1_2	−0.016090	0.028542	−0.564	0.5934	
reg_innov_law_5_1_3	0.046156	0.053114	0.869	0.4182	
sup_prog_innov_5_1_4	0	0	0	0	
coord_bdy_innov_pol_5_2_1	0.031588	0.026327	1.200	0.2754	
reg_instit_innov_dev_5_2_2	0.017134	0.028138	0.609	0.5649	
apprp_shr_sci_reg_budg_5_3_1	−0.033758	0.057385	−0.588	0.5778	
shr_fed_budg_tech_innov_csts_5_3_2	−0.015759	0.046658	−0.338	0.7471	
shr_reg_bdg_rech_innov_csts_5_3_3	0.832111	0.815242	1.021	0.3468	
num_innov_proj_recid_fed_sup_5_4_1	0.277054	0.131118	2.113	0.0790	.
num_fed_instit_dev_sup_innov_proj_5_4_2	0.095848	0.092846	1.032	0.3417	
fed_fund_innov_proj_5_4_3	−0.092737	0.118653	−0.782	0.4642	
num_innov_terris_dev_fed_stats_5_4_4	0.054240	0.095728	0.567	0.5915	
num_obj_innov_infra_sme_sup_5_4_5	−0.047130	0.057579	−0.819	0.4443	
Significance codes	0 '***'	0.001 '**'	0.01 '*'	0.05 '.'	0.1 ''
Residual standard error:	0.03635 on 6 degrees of freedom				
Multiple R-squared	0.8934		Adjusted R-squared	0.6624	
F-statistic	3.868 on 13 and 6 DF		p-Value	0.05324	

Source: Table compiled by the author based on the summary from RStudio.

Table 12.
Fifth group's variables' influence on Russia's innovation index.

Of all the predictors of this group, the potential minimum statistical significance of 0.0790 has the number of federal development institutions that support innovative projects. This variable raises the variable used as the output by 0.277054 when other factors remain unchanged. It is also decided to accept that the predictors are associated with the dependent variable based on the p-value.

When looking at the adjusted R-squared value (0.6624), it can be observed that the fitted model explains 66.24% of the statistical relationships of the grouped variables of the linear regression. However, the model's p-value ($0.05324 > 0.05$) does not demonstrate confidence in rejecting the null hypothesis about the absence of predictor effects on the final result, which casts doubt on the statistical reliability of the model.

5. Conclusion

The authors revealed the features of the transformation of the innovation policy of developed countries under the influence of multiple predictors in the economy and developed directions for improvement of the cluster policy in Russia. This work also concretizes the fundamental theoretical and methodological provisions that reveal the essence of clusters and their advantages and identify factors for transforming industry clusters into global clusters. Also, the innovative development of high-tech industries in the international economy was assessed through statistical and qualitative analysis methods.

A qualitative analysis made it possible to identify the features of Russia's innovative clustering and its role in increasing the country's global competitiveness. After that, the status was determined, and the tools for forming high-tech industries in Russia were investigated. Despite the growth of clusters in certain regions of the country, it was shown that the high-tech cluster policy in Russia has assertive imperfections. The difficulty of launching individual cluster initiatives is ever-present with the limited globalization of innovative products by management bodies and business organizations. In addition, technological cooperation between Russian and foreign enterprises is even more critical.

The authors assessed the influence of cluster elements and management organizations on the innovative development of national innovation systems in Russia and the world countries. The sources of a positive impact on the productivity of the Russian innovation policy were identified: a high level of education of the population and a high fundamental scientific potential. The interdisciplinary research system of the institutions could be excellent with the improvement of the policies and proper equipment for the innovation projects.

Appendix

Group	Variable	Explanation
Group 1. Generalized variables' influence on the innovation index of clusters in	main_macro_indic_1_1	GRP per employee; the coefficient of renewal of fixed assets; Share of employed in high-tech industries; share of people

Group	Variable	Explanation
Russia. Variables represent the following fields: Macroeconomics, educational potential of the population, financing of scientific research and development, efficiency of scientific research and development, export of goods and services, regulatory legal framework for innovation policy, organizational support for innovation policy, and budget costs for science and innovation.		employed in knowledge-intensive service industries.
	educ_pot_pop_1_2	The proportion of the adult population with higher education; The number of students in higher education programs per 10 thousand people; the number of students in higher education programs per 10 thousand people; coverage of the employed population with continuing education; number of students in secondary vocational education programs per 10,000 people; share of students in mid-career STEM programs.
	fund_res_dev_2_1	Share of research and development costs in GRP; share of research and development costs in GRP; business share in research and development funding; salary in science as a percentage of the average in the region.
	res_dev_ef_2_3	Publication activity of researchers; patent activity; development of advanced manufacturing technologies.
	exp_gds_srvs_4_1	Export of goods; noncommodity export of goods; export of services; share of exports in the volume of innovative products.
	norm_lgl_frmwk_innov_pol_5_1	Innovative development strategy; allocated territories for innovative development; regional law on innovation; innovation support program;
	org_sup_innov_pol_5_2	Coordinating body for innovation policy; regional institutes of innovative development.
	bdgt_spndg_scien_innov_5_3	The share of allocations for science in the budget of the region; The share of the federal budget in the cost of technological innovation; the share of the federal budget in the cost of technological innovation.
Group 2. Variables' influence on Russia's innovation index. Variables represent the following fields:	main_macro_indic_1_1	GRP per employee; GRP per employee; share of employed in high-tech industries; The share of people employed in knowledge-intensive service industries.

Group	Variable	Explanation
Macroeconomics, digitalization potential, science personnel, activity in the field of technological and nontechnological innovations, small innovative business, costs for technological innovations, innovation performance, export of knowledge, participation in federal scientific, technical, and innovation policy.	pot_digit_1_3	The share of organizations using broadband access with speeds above 100 Mbps; percentage of organizations providing digital skills training to staff; percentage of organizations providing digital skills training to staff.
	scien_pers_2_2	Share of employed in research and development; share of young researchers; percentage of researchers with advanced degrees
	innov_act_org_3_1	Share of organizations that carried out technological innovations; percentage of organizations implementing nontechnological innovations; Percentage of organizations that developed technological innovations on their own; share of organizations participating in scientific cooperation
	sml_innov_bus_3_2	Share of small enterprises implementing technological innovations
	tech_innov_cost_3_3	Technological innovation spending intensity
	effect_innov_3_4	Share of innovative products; share of innovative products new to the market; percentage of organizations that have reduced material and energy costs due to innovation.
	know_exp_4_2	Patent activity abroad; export of technologies; percentage of foreign students in higher education programs.
	part_fed_scien_tech_innov_pol_5_4	A number of innovative projects that received federal support; number of federal development institutions supporting innovative projects; federal financing of innovative projects; number of territories for innovative development with federal status; number of innovative infrastructure facilities to support SMEs.
Group 3. Variables' influence on Russia's innovation index. Variables represent the following fields	shre_org_tech_innov_3_1_1	Percentage of organizations implementing technological innovations
	shr_org_impl_nontech_innov_3_1_2	Percentage of organizations implementing nontechnological innovations

Group	Variable	Explanation
Technological and nontechnological innovation activity, small innovative business, technological innovation spending, and innovation performance.	shr_org_dev_tech_innov_own_3_1_3	Percentage of organizations developing technological innovations in-house
	shr_org_part_sci_coop_3_1_4	Share of organizations participating in scientific cooperation
	shr_sml_entrp_tech_innov_3_2_1	Share of small enterprises implementing technological innovations
	cst_int_tech_innov_3_3_1	Cost intensity for technological innovation
	shr_innov_prod_3_4_1	Share of innovative products
	shr_innov_prod_new_markt_3_4 _2	Share of innovative products new to the market
	shr_org_rduc_mat_enrg_csts_bcs_innov_3_4_3	The share of organizations that reduced material and energy costs as a result of innovation
Group 4. Variables' influence on Russia's innovation index. Variables represent the following fields: Export of goods and services and export of knowledge.	exp_gds_4_1_1	Export of goods
	non_commty_exp_gds_4_1_2	Noncommodity export of goods
	exp_srvs_4_1_3	Export of services
	shr_exp_vol_innov_prod_4_1_4	Share of exports in the volume of innovative products
	pat_act_abrd_4_2_1	Patent activity abroad
	exp_tech_4_2_2	Technology export
	shr_int_stud_hi_ed_prog_4_2_3	Share of foreign students in higher education programs
Group 5. Variables' influence on Russia's innovation index. Variables represent the following fields: regulatory legal framework for innovation policy, organizational support for innovation policy, budget expenditures on science and innovation, and participation in federal science, technology, and innovation policy.	innov_strtg_dev_5_1_1	Innovative development strategy
	ded_ars_innov_dev_5_1_2	Allocated territories for innovative development
	reg_innov_law_5_1_3	Regional innovation law
	sup_prog_innov_5_1_4	Innovation support program
	coord_bdy_innov_pol_5_2_1	Coordinating body for innovation policy
	reg_instit_innov_dev_5_2_2	Regional institutes of innovative development
	apprp_shr_sci_reg_budg_5_3_1	The share of allocations for science in the budget of the region
	shr_fed_budg_tech_innov_csts_5_3_2	The share of the federal budget in the cost of technological innovation
	shr_reg_bdg_rech_innov_csts_5_3_3	The share of the regional budget in the cost of technological innovation
	num_innov_proj_recid_fed_sup_5_4_1	Number of innovative projects that received federal support

Group	Variable	Explanation
	num_fed_instit_dev_sup_innov_proj_5_4_2	Number of federal development institutions supporting innovative projects
	fed_fund_innov_proj_5_4_3	Federal financing of innovative projects
	num_innov_terris_dev_fed_stats_5_4_4	Number of territories for innovative development with federal status
	num_obj_innov_infra_sme_sup_5_4_5	Number of innovative infrastructure facilities to support SMEs

Table A1.
Indices used from Russian ranking innovation scoreboard [18].

Author details

Vito Bobek[1*], Vladislav Streltsov[2] and Tatjana Horvat[3]

1 Faculty of Social Sciences, University of Ljubljana, Slovenia

2 Univeristy of Applied Sciences FH Joanneum, Graz, Austria

3 Faculty of Management, University of Primorska, Koper, Slovenia

*Address all correspondence to: vito.bobek@guest.arnes.si

References

[1] Islankina EA. Internationalization Of Regional Clusters: Theoretical And Empirical Issues. HSE Working papers WP BRP 41/STI/ Belgorod. Russia: National Research University, Higher School of Economics; 2015

[2] NRUHSE - National Research University Higher School of Economics. Innovation clusters are leaders. 2017. Available from: https://cluster.hse.ru/leaders [Accessed: February 20, 2022]

[3] Russian government. On the approval of the Strategy for Innovative Development of the Russian Federation for the period up to 2020: Decree of the Government of the Russian Federation of December 8, 2011, N 2227-r. Electronic Fund of Legal and Regulatory Technical Documents. 2011. Available from: https://docs.cntd.ru/document/902317973 [Accessed: May 20, 2022].

[4] Akopyan AR. Evolution of scientific approaches to clustering of subjects of the world economy. 2017. Available from: https://cyberleninka.ru/article/n/evolyutsiya-nauchnyh-podhodov-k-klasterizatsii-subektov-mirovogo-hozyaystva (Accessed: November 25, 2020].

[5] Skvortsov EN, Guskov ND. Analysis of organizational structures of management systems for innovative industrial clusters in Russia. Scientific and technical statements of SPbSPU. Economic Sciences No. 1. 2016. Available from: https://cyberleninka.ru/article/n/analiz-organizatsionnyh-struktur-sistem-upravleniya-innovatsionnymi-promyshlennymi-klasterami-v-rossii/viewer [Accessed: May 20, 2022]

[6] NRUHSE - National Research University Higher School of Economics. Innovation clusters. 2017. Available from: https://cluster.hse.ru/innovative_clusters [Accessed: March 14, 2021].

[7] Pogodina TV, Kuznetsov NV, Abdikeev NM. Financial and Economic Mechanisms for Creating Innovative Territorial Clusters. Moscow, Russia: Bulletin of the Financial University; 2016

[8] Brykov SS, Maslennikov MI. Management Component of Innovation-Technological Clustering of Single-Industry Towns in Russia. Vol. 2. Warsaw, Poland: Management Issues. 2017. pp. 89-100

[9] Invest Foresight. Clusters: new fashion or investment driver? 2019. Available from: https://www.if24.ru/klastery-novaya-moda-ili-driver-investitsij/ [Accessed: March 5, 2021].

[10] WIPO. Global Innovation Index 2021 Report. Russian Federation. 2021. Available from: https://www.wipo.int/edocs/pubdocs/en/wipo_pub_gii_2021/ru.pdf [Accessed: March 10, 2022]

[11] Bazhenov SI, Makarova IV, Petrov AA. Management of the Implementation of the Investment Policy of the Entrepreneurial Cluster. Perm, Russia: Ars Administrandi (The Art of Management); 2016

[12] WIPO World Intellectual Property Organization. Global Innovation Index (GII). 2022. Available from: https://www.wipo.int/global_innovation_index/en/ (Accessed: March 15, 2022].

[13] IMD. World Competitiveness Ranking. 2021 results. 2021. Available from: https://www.imd.org/centers/world-competitiveness-center/rankings/world-competitiveness/ [Accessed: June 3, 2022].

[14] Transparency International. Corruption Perceptions Index 2021. 2021. Available from: https://images.transparencycdn.org/images/CPI2021_Report_EN-web.pdf (Accessed: May 18, 2022)

[15] Statology.org. Introduction to Multiple Linear Regression. 2020. Available from: https://www.statology.org/multiple-linear-regression/ [Accessed: November 6, 2022].

[16] Statology.org. How to Calculate Variance Inflation Factor (VIF) in R. 2019. Retrieved from: https://www.statology.org/variance-inflation-factor-r/ [Accessed: April 6, 2022].

[17] Statology.org. Standardization vs. Normalization: What's the Difference? 2021. Available from: https://www.statology.org/standardization-vs-normalization/ [Accessed: May 6, 2022].

[18] Rospatent. Quantitative data on Russian innovative clusters. 2021. Available from: https://rospatent.gov.ru/ru [Accessed: December 5, 2022].

Chapter 8

Exploiting Technology during the Pandemic: Early Lessons from Sub-Saharan Africa

James Alic Garang

Abstract

The paper adopts mixed methods to examine how countries deployed technology to provide services during the COVID-19 pandemic. It reviews the literature, analyzes secondary data to discern patterns, and uses deductive reasoning to inform findings and draw policy implications. The paper finds that the pandemic exposed weaknesses in firm services, government operations, and revenues with revealed financing gaps; it motivated innovations which fostered a shift to digital platforms; and the internet-enabled social connections and became a lifeline for many businesses, households, and governments, thereby enhancing services, and reducing vulnerabilities to corruption. The technology, therefore, galvanized material improvements during the pandemic but also disseminated fake news, which undermined confidence in vaccinations, leading to vaccine hesitancy. Finally, the chapter documents the use of technology during the pandemic citing the case of Kenya, Nigeria, and South Sudan in SSA, while highlighting benefits and challenges, and drawing policy implications, including for critical investments.

Keywords: technology, innovative digital financial systems, financial inclusion, pandemic, sub-Saharan Africa

1. Introduction

The COVID-19 pandemic altered society and accelerated innovative applications in several channels of service provision and decelerated others. It affected every aspect of life, both private and public, on a scale never seen before. Closures of restaurants, shopping malls, convenient stores, gyms, schools, hospitals, sports, and public places speak volumes [1]. Consequently, governments undertook swift and synchronized measures to contain the virus by declaring curfews, enacting social distancing, and enforcing facemasks, with individuals ending up interacting with their handheld devices to stay abreast of virus developments and getting informed while at home. According to Kuboye [1], zoom, Huawei Cloud, WeLink, and WebEx, for instance, became commonplace. The pandemic led institutions to set up facilities to support work from home (see IMF and World Bank, [2]), while airports closed or downsized or canceled flights; shops ran out of essential products; and families scrambled to purchase food, water, toilet papers [3, 4], hand sensitizers, and many more necessities amidst excessive demand–supply constraints. The fears that toilet paper would run out led to excessive demand, and with supply chain disruptions in place, stores ran out of tissues, resulting in the great toilet paper crisis [5].

Following the negative repercussions of the pandemic, though at different paces and phases across the regions, many lives were also transmuted in a downward direction. Notably, the aftermaths of massive job losses and a rise in poverty amidst a lack of social safety nets in some low-income countries (LICs), especially in Sub-Saharan Africa. It was unclear when the pandemic restrictions would be lifted and whether the new normal would be established sooner than later.

The pandemic's impact and strategies varied across regions. The US authorities immediately imposed social restrictions, and social distancing gained wide acceptance starting in March 2020. Public offices and institutions began to accommodate online platforms, to reach targeted audiences [6]. Where internet connection was strong, everyone had access, and the government moved to provide digital services, including cash transfers, with digital technologies offering opportunities to support the COVID-19 responses. According to Reagan and Bulume ([7], p. 10), "As the pandemic intensified with lockdowns, millions of people turned to internet-enabled digital platforms to transact payments, access credit, connect with friends and family, and access education and health information."

While different definitions of technology exist out there, Kumar, Gupta, and Srivastava ([8], p. 570) offered the following:

> *Technology refers to techniques, frameworks and devices which are the aftereffect of scientific information being utilized for practical purposes. Artificial intelligence can be characterized as Machine Learning (ML), Natural Language Processing (NLP), and Computer Vision applications. These abilities instruct computers to use huge information-based models to design, depict, and predict.*

The pandemic constrained mobility, compelling governments, businesses, and households to devise ways to overcome it. In medicine, the search to stop the spread of the virus and find a cure for the disease fostered digitalization. This helped track disease and predict its evolution. Marketing departments disseminated information and enticed customers to purchase products via technology. Some sports training moved online. While physical distance remained vital, many services moved to virtual platforms without sparing any field of human inquiry.

Going digital was not like a walk in the park. No matter the warnings, contact-intensive jobs demanded physical presence, exposing healthcare professionals to infections at hospitals and clinics. Among contact-intensive jobs, the impact was more acute among lower-income docile, women, and poor [9, 10]. Second, some households lacked access to the internet, and basic handheld devices, which limited their ability to work from home. Third, notwithstanding the best intentions to circumvent the pandemic and reduce costs, technology has become vulnerable to abuse, including by spreading fake news. The Board of Directors of Facebook, for example, suspended the account of former President Donald J. Trump from using his account to spread fake news, to millions around the globe, especially following the riot on January 6, 2021, at the U. S Capitol. Considering such susceptibilities, critics advanced conspiracy theories against vaccines [11].

Despite global improvements in big data, privacy laws, consumer protection, and regulatory architecture following the post-global financial crisis, technological benefits remained inequitable and constrained by illiteracy, lack of internet, limited access to energy, and extreme poverty. According to Signe [12], the pandemic changed how the global economy works, exposing many limitations of existing systems and demonstrating the need to reimagine the role of information technology as a critical tool for economic growth and development.

Three case studies covering Kenya, Nigeria, and South Sudan supported the central thesis, illustrating the extent to which the governments deployed technology to provide services during the pandemic, despite lack of widespread internet connection [13]. In Kenya, the government used mobile money to transfer financial support to the vulnerable. Kenya Revenue Authority (KRA) also digitized revenues and provided related information. In Nigeria, the government used digital platforms to do several tasks, including improving tax collections, providing services to the vulnerable, and announcing containment measures against the pandemic. In South Sudan, where digital platforms remain limited, the government relied on national television, mobile networks, and call centers [14] to pass important messages to its citizens. The authorities also used other social media outlets, including personal phones, WhatsApp groups, Facebook, and other outlets, to pass vital information, including on infections, and vaccinations. Therefore, even in South Sudan, where digital uptake remains the lowest, the government managed to rely on some digital platforms to support the COVID response.

The paper's objectives are to (i) identify how digital platforms have been exploited; (ii) highlight the benefits of technology; and prevailing impediments; and (iii) offer proposals to enhance technological services to provide efficient services in future pandemics.

The study contributes to the literature by documenting how the pandemic fostered the use of technology to provide services to household and ensure minimal disruption of firm operations. The countries analyzed exhibit disparities in access to the internet, electronic devices, literacy levels, and propensity to adopt new ways of life. However, digitization of services excludes some segments of society from critical government services, which is insupportable in progressive societies. Even if all supply-side constraints are addressed, some segments of society will not use digital services. The paper thus discusses incentives that discourage nondigital channels, to enable a reader to draw insights into how services can be improved, going forward.

The chapter proceeds in sections. Section 2 reviews the literature and examines how the pandemic has compelled society to exploit technology to provide basic services; Section 3 outlines a conceptual framework linking technology to select theories; Section 4 discusses case studies; and Section 5 draws policy implications. Finally, Section 6 concludes the paper.

2. The literature on technological channels and digital services during the pandemic

In citing a global system for mobile communications association (GSMA) paper [15], Kuboye [1] reported that close to half of the world population "use mobile internet and those living outside those covered areas of mobile broadband network continue to reduce as a result of the upgrade of 2G sites to 3G and 4G especially in Sub-Saharan Africa." **Table 1** shows a marked global use of technology during the pandemic.

A recent World Bank study finds that about 58 governments in developing countries had used digital payments to deliver pandemic assistance, including by depositing benefits into existing and opening new accounts. It found that most regulatory measures rolled out in response to COVID-19 were in the digital space, including digital savings,

Area	Service provider	Area of usage percent increase (% in bracket)	Source
	AT&T (US)	Core Network traffic (22)	AT& AT
Telecommunication traffic	British telecom (UK)	Fixed network traffic (60 on weekdays)	British telecom
	Telecom Italy	Internet traffic (70)	Telecom Italia
	Vodafone	Mobile data traffic in Italy and Spain	Vodafone
Over the top	Facebook	Facebook messenger (50)	Facebook
		WhatsApp (overall: 50; Spain: 76)	WhatsApp
		Video calling (100)	Facebook
	Netflix	Subscriber base (9.6)	Netflix
	E-commerce (Mexico)	Numbers of users	Competitive intelligence
Video conference	Zoom	Daily usage (300)	JP Morgan
	Cisco WebEx	Subscribers (33)	Cisco
	Teams (Italy)	Monthly users (775)	

Source: Kuboye [1].

Table 1.
Internet usage increase triggered by the COVID-19 pandemic.

banking, and capital raising. While the pandemic has originated a greater disposition toward digital finance, some consumers did not rapidly jolt toward those. According to Klapper and Miller [13, 16], "Consumers needed connectivity, including ownership of a mobile phone, access to internet and digital skills to manage mobile apps and online applications to use digital financial services." Hence digital uptake presupposes access to technology, capacity building, and consciousness, to leverage existing digital ecosystem, such as Government-to-Person (G2P) payments, to accelerate their use.

The chapter reveals six instances where the public relied on digital platforms to reduce costs and provide services during the pandemic. We discuss them below.

2.1 Education services going digital

While educational institutions were on the path to increasing online presence in the years before the pandemic, the onset of the scourge accelerated online migration. There were more than 1.2 billion children in 186 countries affected by school closures due to the pandemic in March 2020.

2.2 Health services going digital

The pandemic altered how services were accessed. Text messages and group chats became instant sources of information about the virus. The internet-enabled platforms allowed various actors to provide innovative solutions in health through telehealth, contact tracing, retailing, and addressing supply disruptions, expanding information sharing, starting smart manufacturing and factory automation, supporting e-tourism, and modernizing entertainment. Despite challenges, these proved useful in the fight against the pandemic [17].

Sierra Leone, like other developing countries, faces numerous challenges, including slow uptake of digital technology. Nonetheless, the trend toward digital platforms started with the official launch of the financial inclusion agenda in 2009 upon joining the Alliance for Financial Inclusion (AFI), announcing its commitment to the Maya Declaration in 2012, and developing an innovative program that supported digitalized cash payments during Ebola from 2014 to 2016. Therefore, when the country experienced the Ebola outbreak in 2014, the authorities used mobile technology to pay salaries of health workers; monitor, track, manage, and provide cash to infected communities and households. They also relied on two emergency hotlines, 117 and 711.

2.3 Businesses increased online presence during the pandemic

Some firms advertised through and shifted to operations online, increasing sales and changing the mode of services. Mugume and Bulime [7] and Mburu [18] reached similar conclusions on sales during the lockdowns. Mburu [18] found that the lockdown in Kenya was associated with a 35 percent growth in online purchases of food, an 18 percent growth in pharmaceuticals, and a 54 percent growth in agribusinesses.

Similarly, Brazil paid low-income workers via the state-owned bank Caixa Economica Federal (CEF) into their digital accounts. Available evidence indicates that men and wealthy people were more likely to use merchant payments than women and the poor. Further, person-to-person remittance transfers remained the most common type of digital transaction and proved resilient [13]. While digitization made headways, cash still dominates merchant payments globally, and there are instances in which merchants reverted to cash payments. Examples from Sierra Leone showed that firms formed partnerships with Mobile Network Operators (MNOs) and signed MoUs with banks, to use digital platforms. This led MNOs to introduce products such as Orange Money and Lajor Loan by Orange Mobile Company, as well as Afrimoney and Africredit, enabling mobile customers to pay electricity bills, transfer money to and from their bank accounts and access digital credits. Firms also advertised through WhatsApp, Facebook, and other social media platforms.

2.4 Governments services going digital

Before the pandemic, the idea of e-government was in vogue. When the pandemic struck, governments moved to collect taxes online and achieved economies of scale. Some also moved services online, including applications for food, medicines, and conditional cash transfers. Collecting taxes online, including by filing returns, grew, and some NGOs (nongovernmental organizations) in LICs, including in South Sudan, appreciated this approach as efficient. Sierra Leone also transferred cash through digital platforms. Since 2014, the National Commission for Social Action (NaCSA) has been running a cash transfer program, "Ep Fet Po," to fight poverty. The NaCSA, with World Bank support, provided emergency cash to four provincial headquarters to 29,000 vulnerable informal households, which is about US$135.

2.5 Work from home (WFH) arrangements expanded

The pandemic altered the future of work. On March 13, 2022, for example, the IMF advised its staff to work from home for the first time since the virus broke out.

The staff heeded the advice and explored WFH options. In terms of technology, staff used WebEx, Zoom, Polycom platform, and Microsoft Teams. The transition proved challenging and compelled investments on the part of employees in terms of time, resources, and institutional change. The technical glitches were noted, but over time, staff adapted, and today, WFH has become a new normal. In the case of SSA, these arrangements differ greatly. For the countries with the means, staff worked from home and those without means such as South Sudan, staff reduced hours and days but still had to come to offices.

2.6 The pandemic accelerated digital payments

Kosse and Szemere [19] reported that cash in circulation reached a record high due to an increase in demand for high-value banknotes, indicating that the public steadily held cash as a store of value rather than for mere transaction demand. It also indicated that the pandemic motivated a move toward Central Bank Digital Currencies (CBDCs) and an increased in contactless payments. The Ernst & Young publication [20] indicated what FinTech can and cannot do. It showed that the use of FinTech applications increased following the pandemic, rising by 72 percent. The Findex 2021 report shows that the pandemic catalyzed growth in the use of digital payments, namely:

> *In developing economies in 2021, 18 percent of adults paid utility bills directly from an account. About one-third of these adults did so for the first time after the beginning of the COVID-19 pandemic. The share of adults making a digital merchant payment also increased after COVID-19. For example, in India about 80 million adults made their first digital merchant payment during the pandemic. In China, 82 percent of adults made a digital merchant payment in 2021, including over 100 million adults (11 percent) who did so for the first time after the start of the pandemic. In developing economies, excluding China, 20 percent of adults made a digital merchant payment in 2021. Contained within that 20 percent are the 8 percent of adults, on average, who did so for the first time after the start of the pandemic, or about 40 percent of those who made a digital merchant payment. These data point to the role of the pandemic and social distancing restrictions in accelerating the adoption of digital payments.*

The pandemic forced many things to move online instantly, including shopping for food, and advent of useful services such as DoorDash, which went public in December 2020, focusing on delivering at customers' doorsteps. The shift was disruptive, but countries and people adapted. "Further, the International Monetary Fund [38] indicates that massive data generation, advances in computer algorithms and increases in processing power explain the recent development of FinTech" ([7], p. 163).

The move toward digital life is not without perils. In countries that lacked developed digital ecosystems, people relied on cash even during the lockdowns. Nigeria provides one of the examples relating to a firm FarmCrowdy. It was compelled to switch from digital payments to cash for its operations in rural areas, given that the local agent networks ceased to function. Ethiopia also provides another example. Given its low penetration of mobile money prior to the pandemic, its online shopping platform, Helloomarket, had to authorize cash on delivery and provide other forms of cash deposits, post offices, or with agents outside the capital [13].

3. The conceptual framework

The pandemic touched on many economic theories, from the Keynesian to human capital theory to access to finance, among others. Keynesianism posits that fluctuations in components of the aggregate demand such as household consumption, government spending, firm investment, or net exports, have a bearing on growth, while theories on access to finance point to constraints induced by long distance, affordability, prohibitive borrowing cost, illiteracy, lack of credit histories and firm viability. Human capital is conceived to rely on critical investments, while productivity and efficiency gains can be augmented through greater training and educational improvements.

The pandemic touched on several theoretical frameworks and the application of technology underlies them. To minimize disruption to education, kids moved to online courses; to enhance access to finance, firms exploited digital platforms to extend services; and to stimulate aggregate demand, taxation, and spending moved online. Therefore, technology played a moderating role during the pandemic and underpinned major theoretical arguments and different channels (see **Table 2**).

The paper uses a specific platform (**Table 2**) to assess the use of technology to provide services.

4. Three case studies in Sub-Saharan Africa

The three countries differ in several ways. Growth has been uneven across them, while inflation has broadly remained low in Kenya but very elevated in Nigeria and South Sudan since 2012. Given its past conflict, South Sudan's inflation has been among the highest before the pandemic relative to SSA averages. The countries also differ in poverty rates, access to finance, public health, and more. These countries are, therefore, different in terms of resources, political dispensations, and policies, with these differences expected as seen in **Table 3**.

Previous studies underscore the centrality of financial inclusion to foster economic growth, with implication to reduce poverty, and enhance equality (see [7, 23–27]). While access to finance remains a major constraint to firms [28–29], access to mobile technology has helped in recent years and picked up steeply during the pandemic. This reality has led many researchers over the years to examine the determinants of financial inclusion in Africa. It continues with the advent of the pandemic, which fostered digitalization relative to the previous years [30, 31].

Country	Uninform indicators for comparison across the three countries				
	Digital financial services	Digital health services	Digital learning services	Digital government services	Digital business products
Kenya	Substantial	Substantial	Substantial	Substantial	Substantial
Nigeria	Substantial	Substantial	Substantial	Substantial	Substantial
South Sudan	Insignificant	Limited	None	None	Limited

Source: Author's Construct, [21].

Table 2.
The platform to assess the three countries.

		Year									
Country	Series	2012	2013	2014	2015	2016	2017	2018	2019	2020	2021
Kenya	GDP (%)	4.6	3.8	5.0	5.0	4.2	3.8	5.6	5.1	−0.3	7.5
	CAB (%)	−7.5	−7.9	−9.3	−6.3	−5.4	−7.0	−5.4	−5.2	−4.8	−5.2
	Inf (%)	9.4	5.7	6.9	6.6	6.3	8.0	4.7	5.2	5.4	6.1
Nigeria	GDP (%)	4.2	6.7	6.3	2.7	−1.6	0.8	1.9	2.2	−1.8	3.6
	CAB (%)	3.7	3.7	0.2	−3.1	1.3	3.6	1.7	−3.1	−3.7	−0.4
	Inf (%)	12.2	8.5	8.1	9.0	15.7	16.5	12.1	11.4	13.2	17.0
South Sudan	GDP (%)	46.1	13.1	3.4	−10.8	..	..	..	..	..	..
	CAB (%)	..	..	−5.7	−4.2	−5.8	8.3	−9.0	−4.2	−35.0	−0.1
	Inf (%)	45.5	−0.1	1.7	52.8	380.0	187.9	83.5	87.2	29.7	10.5
SSA	GDP %)	2.7	5.1	4.9	2.8	1.4	2.5	2.8	2.6	−2.1	4.2
	CAB (% of GDP)	..	..	..	..	..	..	..	..	..	..
	Inf (%)	6.6	4.9	4.4	3.6	5.4	5.2	4.1	2.8	3.3	4.6

Source: World Development Indicators, [22].
Key: CAB = current account balance as % of GDP; inf = inflation, consumer prices, as annual growth.

Table 3.
Select indicators for Kenya, Nigeria, South Sudan, and SSA average, 2012–2021.

The pandemic accelerated the use of digital technology. In Sierra Leone, for example, value of transactions grew by 73.8 percent in September 2021 to Le 9.6 trillion from Le 5.5 trillion in 2019 (**Figure 1**). The volume of transactions also rose from 1.4 m to 2.2 m during the same period [32]. Transactions conducted through digital accounts increased by 32 percent to 14.3 m in December 2020 [33]. The value of digital transactions in December 2020 reached Le 1.7b, an increase of 69 percent from December 2019.

The increased use of mobile technology comes with downside risks, including associated fraud and abuse of confidential data. This led to a loss of trust in big data for public entities, bankruptcies of mobile money operators, insufficient user protection, and over-indebtedness [34–37].

The next subsection illustrates the increasing use of technology in the three case studies to provide services during the pandemic.

4.1 Kenya's use of technology to provide services during the pandemic

4.1.1 Access to finance and digital payments

Payment systems have evolved over millennia from barter to gold or silver to cash payment to mobile money (MM) to other forms of money, including central bank digital currencies (CBDCs), crypto assets, stableCoins, and suchlike (see [38]). Distinct reasons have been cited for using CDBCs, which include the need to reduce cash. Traditionally, payment systems in Kenya have focused either on largest-value transactions or retailed or low-value transactions, with the latter including card payments, mobile money, account clearing house (ACH), and real-time gross settlements (RTGS). That said, CBDCs carry some risks, including financial exclusion, technology risks, privacy breaches, and competition with deposit banks.

Kenya launched in 2007 the m-PESA is mobile money in Kenya, which increased digital money and cemented the position of Kenya in the continent as a global leader in the industry. As Mugume and Bulime [7] show, recent estimates indicate that Africa accounts for half of the global 1.2 billion mobile money accounts [31, 35, 36, 39]. The digital platforms boosted the circulation of mobile phone inflows, again driving appreciable growth in the mobile money industry. In Kenya, one study found that the adoption of mobile money by businesses reduced the incidence of theft, boosted

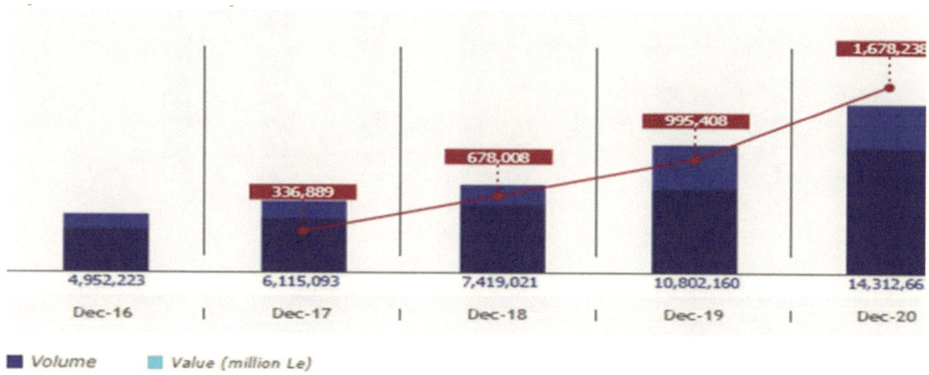

Figure 1.
Toward digital financial transactions in Sierra Leone, 2016–2020. Source: UNCDP [21].

productivity, and sped up transactions between businesses and suppliers [40, 41]. In addition, Kenya's main E-commerce platform—Jumia Kenya—partnered with the agricultural value-chain platform Twiga Foods to sell baskets of fruits and vegetables to consumers.

The Government of Kenya, businesses, and individuals turned to mobile financial services (DFS) to reduce costs and mitigate the spread of the virus. Government formed partnerships, and some international financial institutions (IFIs) transferred cash through the DFS. Kenya, like other countries, used digital platforms to advance financial inclusion. In a study focusing on 52 countries from emerging markets and developing economies (EMDEs), Kenya was ranked third in financial inclusion after Mongolia and China. Digital financial inclusion has come to overtake traditional bank financial inclusion in Kenya. According to the recent FinAccess data, the financial inclusion index rose to 83 percent in 2021 from 26 percent in 2006. There were 67.8 million registered mobile money accounts by May 2021. It is noted that 79 percent of adults have a mobile money account relative to 40 percent of adults with a bank account in 2021.

The use of digital technology can be observed both from volume and value for transactions in Kenya during the pandemic (see **Figure 2**). First, mobile penetration[2] went up to 129 percent in 2021 from 31 percent in 2007 [38]. The value of transactions saw a whopping 24, 440 percent, rising from \$0.2 billion in 2007 to \$49 billion (about \$150 per person in the US) in 2022. Mobile transactions, as a share of total transactions, rose about 56 percent to 80 percent during the pandemic in Kenya. Volume and value of digital transactions grew by about 82 percent and 39 percent, respectively, by March 2021. In addition, the mobile money mitigation measures outlined to shield the public against the shocks of the COVID-19 pandemic also contributed to this growth.

In a study using micro-level data in Kenya, and Uganda, Mugume, and Bulime [7] examine the factors that drive DFS to boost gender equality, enhance financial inclusion, and support growth [43]. They find that individuals with at least one registered

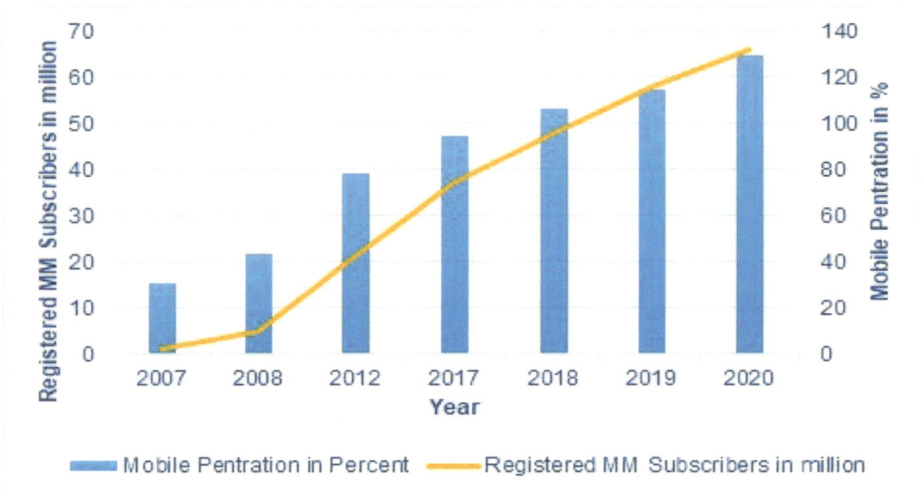

Figure 2.
Appreciable growth in mobile money during the pandemic. Source: CBK Supervision Department, [42].

SIM card; those who trusted mobile money agents; middle-aged males; and the employed are highly likely to adopt DFS. They found that women tended to use DFS less than men in the study and that while gaps exist, Kenya is far ahead of Uganda. The observed difference in gender inequalities in DFS is primarily underpinned by several socioeconomic factors such as limited affordability and financial literacy skills, which hamper women's digitalization [43, 44]. Low trust in mobile money agents also affected DFS in Uganda than in Kenya.

Even from the Findex 2021 report, we see an appreciable growth in registered mobile money accounts during the pandemic in Kenya (see **Figure 3**).

4.1.2 Cash transfers through digital platforms

To support vulnerable members of the community, the Government of Kenya established in 2015 the Inua Jamii program, a cash transfer program, to support the beneficiaries with limited payments to help mitigate poverty and extreme hunger. It is usually paid through their bank accounts. The Government also launched a complementary nutrition program called Nutrition Improvement through Cash and Health Education (NICHE), which targets vulnerable households with cash, nutrition counseling, and child protection services to tackle undernutrition and vulnerability. They received funds in 2023, with the government releasing Sh8.6 billion to 1.1 million to Inua Jamii beneficiaries and another Sh11.2 million for NICHE. To protect beneficiaries' data and enhance efficiency, Inua Jamii has resolved to digitize payments starting in 2023.

In countries where governments set up benefit programs for the elderly and pay through bank accounts, providing support during the pandemic became swift and safe. The authorities used cash transfers to support the vulnerable, according to the World Bank study. These were one-off payments, and at times complementing existing support payments to households. Kenya, for instance, illustrates a potency that comes from leveraging digital platforms during a crisis:

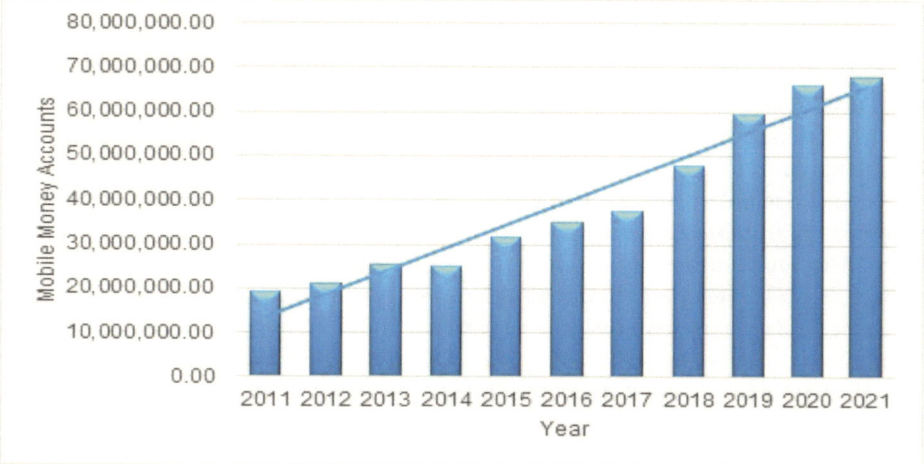

Figure 3.
Number of registered mobile money accounts. Source: IMF Financial Access Survey, [34].

Private sector firms and non-profit organizations created Shikilia to raise money and advocate for monthly cash transfers for low-income households in Kenya to offset the impact of COVID-19. Working in collaboration with GiveDirectly, a nonprofit organization that links online donors (including individual donors) with people in need, Shikilia sends monthly benefits to low-income households, many of which have lost income during COVID-19, using mobile money. One of the noteworthy aspects of the Shikilia initiative is the analysis of geospatial, demographic and telecommunications data to identify communities at greatest risk and target them for support.

Several factors support the shift to digital platforms in Kenya. First, the government encouraged and invested in digital platforms before the pandemic. Second, commercial banks increased the lending limits, to allow more cash or digital money in the hands of the customers (see Mburu, [18]). Third, the government encouraged competitive entry for the MNOs, which promoted DFS. Fourth, the pandemic induced shifts in digital transactions by firms, including marketing; and springing up of social and religious events. Maina [45] reported that all banks in Kenya had put in place digital strategies long before the pandemic, with the latter enhancing implementation. He found that international tier 1 banks implemented diverse digital strategies during the pandemic, including digitization of more banking processes and services, creating partnerships with Fintechs and Telecoms, and introducing digital signatures and workflow automation. That said, challenges included cyber security risks, wastage of resources and time in remote working, regulatory challenges, internet access, increase in emergency investments, and resistance to change.

Maina [45] urged banks to be agile in their culture, and strategies; the policymakers to address challenges of executing digital strategies; ensure adequate policies and resources to cope with the challenges; and Central Bank of Kenya (CBK) to expedite the review and approval of new digital products and services during the pandemic and in future. Following the pandemic, CBK [46, 47] puts in place relief measures such as flexibility in the repayment of loans, extension of payment periods, and loan restructuring. To facilitate the use of digital platforms, CBK requested banks to waive all charges for balance inquiry and eliminate charges for transfers between mobile wallets and bank accounts.

The business community innovated and offered unique products to their customers beyond Kenya. This saved time and served customers' needs, as **Table 4** illustrates, across SSA and yonder.

The pandemic exposed digital divide in Kenya, like in other LICs. Lack of internet in some counties and limited cell phone uptake in some areas speak volume. Cybercrime also became an issue in Kenya, rising in 2020 during the pandemic by 30 percent. It amplified the vulnerability of connections, providing an advantage for fraudsters to maneuver [48]. Therefore, early lessons from Kenya are distinctively clear. Mobile technology was already ascending in Kenya and rose during the pandemic, and on a positive note, Kenya already has an ID system linked to the KRA PIN number. Anyone above 18 must get an ID in Kenya to transact. Nonetheless, the government still needs to act, including by addressing cyber threats, tackling supply-side gaps in the delivery of quality financial services, and improving connectivity.

4.1.3 Delivery of education during the pandemic

Following the abrupt closure of schools, the Ministry of Education provided little or no clarity regarding the fate of the end-year examinations. As confusion reigned,

Country	Platform	Focus	Payment methods	Credit	COVID-19 response
Kenya	Twiga foods	Agriculture (B2B)	Mobile money	Digital credit (piloted with IBM Research)	Launched business-to-consumer solution in partnership with Jumia
Kenya	Sendy	Transport, deliveries, logistics (B2B)	Mobile money	-	Launched grocery deliveries in partnership with stores and supermarkets
Nigeria	FarmCrowdy	agriculture	Cash on delivery, mobile money	Linked to the crowdfunded platform, CrowdInvest	Increased demand to participate in the platform. Had to discontinue mobile payments due to disruption in agency network
Kenya/Nigeria	Flutterwave	Payments	Online payments	-	Launched Flutterwave market to help MSMEs digitize their business
Uganda	SafeBoda	Motorbike taxis	Prepaid e-wallet, cash on delivery	Loans for motorbike purchases in partnership with Finca Uganda	Launched grocery and restaurant deliveries via motorbike
Ethiopia	Helloomarket	General merchandise	Mobile money, cash on delivery, deposits at agents or bank branches	Plans to partner with banks for credit products	Increased interest from vendors and sales of essential items
Brazil	Compre Local	Local grocery stores and restaurants	Payment link via SMS and WhatsApp	-	Started to support local businesses affected by the lockdown

Source: Buboye [1].

Table 4.
Examples of new and NICHE platforms employing innovative business models and focusing on traditionally underserved market segments.

schools worried about whether they would be able to complete the syllabus in time once they reopened, as the closure was seen as a temporary measure. As the reopening was delayed, private schools became innovative and began to embrace online learning. As a result, and for fear of failing to complete the syllabus in time, they started to experiment with online learning. The need to complete the syllabus in time and the urge to protect their incomes motivated them as they were unused to unexpected interruptions. After the experimentation, public schools and universities quickly went digital. Although they faced poor internet and mobile telephone access in those areas, the rest of the other places continued with the approach until schools reopened. The notable platforms used included WebEx and Microsoft Teams. To better deliver education to the students, educational institutions in Kenya created and distributed digital learning materials, video lectures, and online assessments.

4.1.4 Health services delivery

For fear of infections, patients and doctors avoided contact, embracing the concept of telemedicine and allowing doctors and patients to interact via video calls or phone. In addition, there arose an upsurge in digital health apps such as Byon8 in Kenya to provide health information, COVID-19 updates, and self-assessment tools. On its part, the government used digital technology to support contact tracing, resulting in reduced growth of the COVID-19 virus.

4.1.5 E-commerce and work from home

For the fear of contracting the virus, individuals changed how they did business. Those who used to frequent the fast-food places and hang out resorted to the use of food delivery services such as Glovo, Uber Eats, Jumia Food Kenya, and Jikoni Eats through increased delivery apps and services. Online shopping grew as the E-commerce platforms saw a rapid growth in demand for these services as customers resorted to online purchases for essential and nonessential goods.

Public and private sector workers were forced to stay home until the pandemic ended. However, they embraced and continue to provide services through digital tools such as video conferencing apps such as Zoom, WebEx, and Microsoft Teams. In addition, cloud-based productivity suites and project management software have become important for working remotely and virtual meetings.

4.2 Nigeria's uptake of technology during the pandemic

Nigeria is the largest economy and the most populated nation in Africa, with major strides in access to technology, even before the pandemic hit. Just like other countries in the region, the use of technology in Nigeria faces some constraints. Nigerian mobile money provider Paga reported, at the outset of the pandemic, that it had doubled the number of merchants in its network, witnessing a 200 percent increase in quarterly users. "In the autumn of 2020, Innovations for Poverty Action (IPA) conducted phone surveys with 793 digital finance users in Nigeria. They found that 51 percent of respondents reported being exposed to attempted fraud or swindles during the pandemic, while the share of the same was 57 percent in Kenya." Buboye ([1], p. 36) also noted that "In the course of the outbreak of COVID-19, the Nigerian society adopted digital life as an alternative to physical interaction so as to keep afloat in the period of the lockdown."

4.2.1 Digital platform supporting tax revenues

From the perspective of digital revolution, Nigeria moved in 2021 to tax foreign tech firms, thereby increasing its tax proceeds (see Nigeria's Finance Act 2021 and the Digital Tax Framework). It is noted that Nigeria had modified its corporate tax legislation to enable the taxation of nonresident digital businesses between 2019 and 2020. Notwithstanding gains made thus far, existing literature points to the need for the authorities in Nigeria to improve digital networks, and enhance taxpayers' knowledge and usage of digital finance instruments to comply with their tax responsibilities, including those that are transnational [49, 50].

4.2.2 Financial services going digital

The use of mobile money platforms also rose during the pandemic. Examples include Moniepoint, a mobile money platform created during the pandemic to provide financial services to households that wanted to minimize exposure to the pandemic and save time.

4.2.3 Telemedicine shored up in Nigeria during the pandemic

Telemedicine also became a reality in Nigeria. Companies including Helium Health, which specializes in digitizing medical records, debuted their online consultation platform to meet patient demand resulting from the pandemic in late 2020. If the customer has access to the internet, a mobile device, and a link to a meeting, they become clicks away from medical services. This platform allows the patient and health care professionals to interact, while diagnosing and recommending applicable treatment or drugs.

4.2.4 E-learning

Although e-learning took off in Nigeria in 2006 with the National Open University of Nigeria (NOUN) at the apex tertiary level, many in the form of primary and post-primary education driven by the private sector embraced e-learning during the COVID-19 pandemic. With the pandemic becoming intense, the use of e-learning platforms increased in the public sector, including at the subnational levels, while it almost became a norm in the private sector.

4.2.5 Social media became a source of information and marketing tools

Available evidence also indicates that digital platforms, including WhatsApp groups and Facebook motivated the online sales of firms owned by low-income women during the lockdown in Nigeria [7, 51]. Their use includes passing information, mobilizing support, and achieving causes such as encouraging remittances for family support. In the end, the federal government, and multilateral organizations noticeably espoused digital platforms to advance cash and social transfers to vulnerable populations during this crisis.

4.3 South Sudan's use of technology during the pandemic

South Sudan is a fragile, LIC, and its use of technology remains negligible. It is also among the least affected by the pandemic, at least from the public data and partly due to underreporting of cases. The lack of advances in mobile technology did not stop the public and the government from finding ways to circumvent the effects of the pandemic. Two examples bolster this point: limited use of m-Gurush (local mobile money) and national call center through a public hotline 6666.

4.3.1 The pandemic and public health in South Sudan

The Ministry of Health established the South Sudan National Public Health Call Center on May 12, 2020, to respond to the COVID-19 pandemic and advise the public on other epidemic-prone diseases. Individuals would call the center, providing both verified and unverified information [14]. The receiving team would send these calls to the Ministry of Health (MoH) to provide proper management.

This initiative proved successful. It allowed officers to address inbound and outbound calls; with most inquiries and issues triaged; referrals made on time; health education and psychological support rendered; communication among officers improved; critical records maintained; MoH/PHEOC/Partners received monthly reports; and they efficiently deployed funds. Notwithstanding, MoH, and officials from the call center identified serious challenges, including poor network, unreliable internet, weaknesses in the call forwarding system or poor call distribution, weak coordination, and delays in responding to the referred alerts. Some mobile phones or toll-free lines also became spoiled and proved inefficient in receiving incoming calls. Lack of auto security locks for the center rooms; lack of computer's anti-virus services; inadequate number of call agents to manage calls; and delay of incentives payments became challenging as well.

Broadly, the officers, for example, received calls such as those depicted in **Figure 4**.

4.3.2 Minimal use of technology to provide services during the pandemic

Despite the surmountable constraints, South Sudan minimally used the technology during the pandemic. First, individuals resorted to using WhatsApp groups to pass information. Through the MoH, national health officials used radio and national TV to pass critical message to the masses, concerning infections rate, quarantines, and vaccines. WhatsApp groups that became sources of information, for both credible and false alarms, include the Sunrise Forum, Republic, Social Net, Jieng Nation Forum, Pentagon, Red Army Foundation, diverse South Sudanese Community

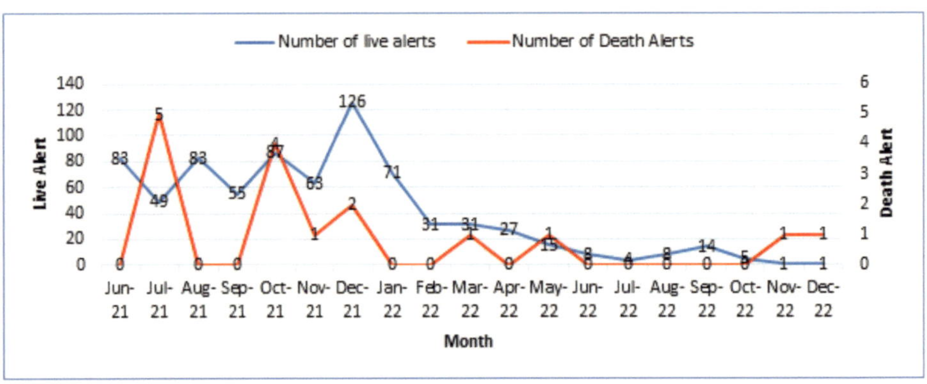

Figure 4.
Increased calls to National Hotline during the pandemic in South Sudan. Source: MoH, [52].

Associations, and many more. Second, the National Revenue Authority (NRA) moved toward greater digitalization of tax revenue and other electronic measures to remain effective. Some NGOs and large taxpayers welcome this approach owing to related efficiency gains and convenience. Finally, international partners that provided cash transfers to qualifying vulnerable populations relied on both cash delivery and digital platforms to provide the needed services.

Despite these benefits, South Sudan was clearly constrained in using technology to contain the pandemic and provide basic services. This subsection highlights a few constraints.

First, the lack of reliable power constrained hospitals and impeded essential operations. At times, generators ran out of power during operations, and patients unfortunately lost lives at hospitals, including Juba Teaching Hospital.

Second, unlike in Kenya or Nigeria, kids in South Sudan remained at home and did not attend online classes because families lacked facilities deployed in other countries. This led to kids losing out, affecting the achievement of key Sustainable Development Goals. Examples documented in other countries indicate that those that lack resources to avail of online learning opportunities resulted in huge setbacks, with students losing months or years of schoolwork [53].

Finally, shallow mobile penetration limited access to DFS in South Sudan. A few mobile money operators remain constrained by a host of challenges, including illiteracy, lack of supportive regulatory and supervisory framework, poor power supply, and poverty. Many households could not afford handheld devices or access expensive internet services. Modem costs more and the fee is unaffordable to many households. Those with jobs worked in face-to-face contexts and became exposed due to underreporting in South Sudan. Broadly, South Sudan lacks social safety nets, complicating compliance with pandemic measures. Garang [54] had this to say:

> *Without facilities to work from home, and lacking social safety nets, households have been caught between a rock and a hard surface. Some found themselves facing tough decisions: either they stay home and starve or come out and risk infection. Many chose the latter; some suffered a fatal ending from Covid-19, but went uncounted, partly due to the lack of contact tracing and limited testing.*

5. Preliminary lessons from the pandemic and implications over the use of technology

While different economic actors faced digital challenges, the use of technology, nonetheless, enabled firms, households, and governments to provide critical services, including facilitating access to finance, offering medicine, transporting goods, fostering online learning, and enabling communication over distance and e-tourism [55]. The paper draws four preliminary lessons, including building trust in public institutions; investing in technology; considering mobile technology as a two-edged sword; and leveraging technology for all sectors.

5.1 Building public trust counts

In a survey conducted in Thailand in March 2020 following the declaration of the pandemic, teachers showed a cheerful outlook on using technology to teach online. Nonetheless, they face many online teaching problems [56–60]. In places where public health authorities were deemed credible by the public, the message and advice on prevention and treatment were well received. Thus, building trust and a positive attitude toward technology are key.

5.2 Technology as public goods

The importance of disseminating knowledge across borders, companies, and the entire society became clear. If online learning technology can play a role here, it is incumbent upon all of us to explore its full potential. As Mburu [18] showed, those that have invested in digital platforms benefited a lot during the pandemic. The public sector and private sectors do matter. Hence, the public has a role in fostering healthy and effective digitalization. Accelerating post-pandemic recovery rests in attracting private investment into mobile money operators, offering different financial products beyond loans to include savings and insurance products, and enhancing employment opportunities, especially for women and youth, with implications on reducing poverty.

5.3 Technology cuts both ways

The authorities must also know that technology remains a two-edged sword. It can advance public goods (see policy tracker) when properly exploited and public bads, if misused, as the examples of fake news, indicate in the foregoing paragraphs, aggravating vaccine hesitancy.

5.4 Public policy remains indispensable in serving different demographics

In a panel discussion during the 2023 IMF/WB Spring Meetings, discussants emphasized that technology is not the issue per se but what the authorities are trying to address. In this context, public policy on the use of a particular technology should revolve around three problems:

a. How to identify the vulnerable households to receive public support

b. How to get the support needed to those identified, verified, and paid

c. How to deploy a particular technology to achieve the identified objectives

The foregone literature review clearly unveils the vital role demography plays in the uptake of mobile technology across the three countries. Owning more than one SIM card increases the chance of using digital platforms; women are less likely to use DFS than men, indicating a need to resolve gender inequalities, and that lack of trust in DFS could account for exclusion. In addition, increased competition among MNOs improves the quality and diversity of DFS services. These developments call for appropriate technology along with efficient regulations and supervision to better serve various segments of society. Therefore, interventions should aim to address infrastructural limitations, promote public–private partnerships, and the digital divide in all its dimensions, including from a gender and rural/urban perspective.

Private and public investments in information and communications technology and infrastructure development should be central; enhancing the capacity of research institutions to participate in research and development activities as well as protecting intellectual property, with positive impact on growth. Creating institutions to manage technological disruption, supporting innovation, and ensuring security remain key. As Signe [61] notes, "Policies to support innovation and protect citizens are only as good as the institutions that enforce them," and in this context, leaders are advised to set up agile institutions empowered to work across ministries.

6. Conclusion

This chapter has set out to answer the two related research questions on the uptake and use of technology in Africa during the pandemic. From the foregoing discussions, public institutions, including schools, universities, industries, hospitals, and clinics, became altered in some fundamental ways during the pandemic. The local and national authorities began to explore new ways and leverage related technologies to continue their daily operations in a seamless fashion. They used technology to provide education, public health, finance, and basic services. However, as the three case studies show, countries differ in their approach to technology deployments. In large part, this is due to existing challenges such as illiteracy, poverty, low mobile penetration, unreliable power supply, and public attitude toward disease, which invariably constrain the uptake of mobile technology. These resulted in differential outcomes across regions and countries.

In particular, the chapter analyzed the question on how countries have deployed technology to provide services during the COVID-19 pandemic and arrived at key findings. First, the paper finds that SSA countries have embraced technology to address challenges such as reducing costs and providing services in the areas of education, health, financial sector, and education. Second, existing gaps in access to technology exist across and within countries and in other dimensions, including gender, income classes, age, and education. Third, the paper finds that the technology has been two-edged swords, supporting the authorities in mitigating the impact and enhancing disinformation in some circles. Finally, the paper finds that role of trust in public institutions is key for addressing the pandemic or related challenges.

Going forward, the paper recommends public investments in financial literacy, digital platforms, and knowledge creation, which remain central to tackling future pandemics and crises. Therefore, interventions should aim to address infrastructural limitations, promote public–private partnerships, and tackle digital divide in all its dimensions, including from a gender and rural-urban perspective.

This study has some limitations. The research has been constrained by a small sample size of three studies, a short time frame, and the qualitative nature of the methodology. Future research could focus on examining longer time dimensions and increasing the regional coverage in the future to include broad categories such as east, north, south, and west Africa.

Author details

James Alic Garang[1,2,3,4,5]

1 IMF Board, Washington DC

2 Africa Center for Financial Inclusion, South Sudan

3 Faculty of Economic and Social Studies, Upper Nile University, South Sudan

4 Ebony Center for Strategic Studies, South Sudan

5 The Sudd Institute, South Sudan

*Address all correspondence to: aliabugalu@gmail.com

References

[1] Kuboye BM. Impact of COVID-19 on internet traffic in Nigeria. Communications and Network. 2021;**14**(1):36-44

[2] IMF. Country Reports: Sierra Leone Selected Issues; 2022

[3] Abe T, Higashi D, Nishiyama D, Toriumi F, Galam S, Ishii A. The toilet paper issue during the COVID-19 crisis. In: IEEE/WIC/ACM International Joint Conference on Web Intelligence and Intelligent Agent Technology (WI-IAT); 14 December 2020. Melbourne, Australia: IEEE; 2020. pp. 655-659

[4] Boone T, Ganeshan R. The great toilet paper buy: Lessons for the supply chain. Foresight: The International Journal of Applied Forecasting. 2021;**61**

[5] Berube DM. A story about toilet paper: Pandemic panic-buying and public resilience. In: Pandemic Communication and Resilience; 8 August 2021. Cham: Springer International Publishing; 2021. pp. 143-165

[6] Bakibinga-Gaswaga E, Bakibinga S, Bakibinga DB, Bakibinga P. Digital technologies in the COVID-19 responses in sub-Saharan Africa: Policies, problems, and promises. The Pan African Medical Journal. 2020;**35**(Suppl 2)

[7] Mugume R, Bulime EW. Post-COVID-19 recovery for African economies: Lessons for digital financial inclusion from Kenya and Uganda. African Development Review. 2022;**34**:S161-S176

[8] Kumar A, Gupta PK, Srivastava A. A review of modern technologies for tackling COVID-19 pandemic. Diabetes & Metabolic Syndrome: Clinical Research & Reviews. 2020;**14**(4):569-573

[9] Avdiu B, Nayyar G. When face-to-face interactions become an occupational hazard: Jobs in the time of COVID-19. Economics Letters. 2020;**197**:109648

[10] Guntin R. Working from Home and Contact-Intensive Jobs in Uruguay [Working Paper]. Rochester, New York, United States of America: University of Rochester; 2020

[11] Stein RA, Ometa O, Shetty SP, Katz A, Popitiu MI, Brotherton R. Conspiracy theories in the era of COVID-19: A tale of two pandemics. International Journal of Clinical Practice. 2021;**75**(2)

[12] Signe L. Harnessing Technology and Innovation for a better Future in Africa: Policy Priorities for Enabling the 'Africa we Want,' Brookings Institution Working Paper. 2022

[13] Klapper L, Miller M. The Impact of COVID-19 on Digital Financial Inclusion. World Bank. 2021. Available from: https://openknowledge.worldbank.org/handle/10986/35870 [Accessed: November 23, 2022]

[14] Ministry of Health [MoH]. South Sudan Annual Report for 2022 under the Public Health Emergency Operation Centre (PHEOC): Primary Health Care Health Education & Promotion. 2022

[15] Global System for Mobile Communications [GSMA]. The State of Mobile Internet Connectivity Report2020. p. 2020

[16] Klapper L, Miller M. The impact of COVID-19 on digital financial inclusion. World Bank Report. 2021;**2021**

[17] Siriwardhana Y, De Alwis C, Gür G, Ylianttila M, Liyanage M. The fight

against the COVID-19 pandemic with 5G technologies. IEEE Engineering Management Review. 2020;**48**(3):72-84

[18] Mburu J. How COVID-19 has affected digital payments to merchants in Kenya. Financial Sector Deepening Kenya. 2020

[19] Kosse A, Szemere R. Covid-19 accelerated the digitalisation of payments. In: Commentary on the BIS Committee on Payments and Market Infrastructures (CPMI). 2021

[20] Ernst & Young publication. Stocktake of External Debt of the Government of South Sudan. Draft Report, December 2022. Retrieved from: South-Sudan-External-Stock-Debt-Draft-report.pdf (mofp.gov.ss). 2022

[21] Author's construct and IMF Fin Access Survey data are what they are. UNCDF. The State of Digital Financial Services in Sierra Leone. 2020

[22] World Bank. World Development Report 2022: Finance for an equitable recovery. The World Bank; 2022

[23] Banerjee AV, Newman AF. Occupational choice and the process of development. Journal of Political Economy. 1993;**101**(2):274-298

[24] Clarke GR, Xu LC, Zou HF. Finance, and income inequality: What do the data tell us? Southern Economic Journal. 2006;**72**(3):578-596

[25] Cull R, Ehrbeck T, Holle N. Financial Inclusion, and Development: Recent Impact Evidence. Vol. 92. Washington, DC: World Bank Group, nota de enfoque CGAP; 2014

[26] King RG, Levine R. Finance, and growth: Schumpeter might be right. The Quarterly Journal of Economics. 1993;**108**(3):717-737

[27] Levine R. Finance and growth: Theory and evidence. Handbook of Economic Growth. 2005;**1**:865-934

[28] Garang JA. How to leverage oil resources to enhance SME financing in South Sudan. International Journal of Economic Policy in Emerging Economies. 2015;**8**(2):119-137

[29] Demirgüç-Kunt A, Klapper LF. Measuring financial inclusion: The global findex database. World bank policy research working paper. 2012;**6025**

[30] Songwe V. The Role of Digitalization in the Decade of Action for Africa. Addis Abab, Ethiopia: United Nations Conference on Trade and Development; 2020

[31] United Nations Economic Commission for Africa. COVID-19 in Africa: Protecting Lives and Economies. Addis Ababa, Ethiopia: Economic Commission for Africa; 2020

[32] International Monetary Fund. Country Reports: Sierra Leone Selected Issues. 2022.

[33] UNCDF. The State of Digital Financial Services in Sierra Leone. 2020

[34] International Monetary Fund. The promise of Fintech: Financial inclusion in the post COVID-19 era. IMF; 2020a

[35] Machasio IN. COVID-19 and digital financial inclusion in Africa. 2020

[36] Global System for Mobile Communications. The causes and consequences of mobile money taxation: An examination of mobile money transaction taxes in sub-Saharan Africa. 2020b

[37] Global System for Mobile Communications. The State of Mobile

Internet Connectivity Report 2021. Retrieved from GSMA | The State of Mobile Internet Connectivity Report 2021 - Mobile for Development. 2021

[38] Central Bank of Kenya. Discussion Paper on Central Bank Digital Currency. Nairobi, Kenya: Central Bank of Kenya; 2022

[39] Machasio IM. COVID-19 and Digital Financial Inclusion in Africa: How to leverage digital technologies during the pandemic. Office of the Chief Economist, Africa Region, World Bank. 2020;**4**:1

[40] Beck T, Pamuk H, Ramrattan R, Uras B. Mobile money, trade credit and economic development: theory and evidence. 2015

[41] Benni N. Digital finance and inclusion in the time of the COVID-19 pandemic. In: Lessons, experiences and proposals. The Food Agricultural: Organization of the United Nations; 2021

[42] CBK. Emergency Measures to Mitigate the Adverse Economic Effects on Bank Borrowers from the Coronavirus Pandemic. Press Release; 2020

[43] Hedricks S. The role of financial inclusion in driving women's economic empowerment. Development in Practice. 2019;**29**(8):1029-1038

[44] Muhura E. Accelerating digital inclusion for women in Kenya. Global System for Mobile Communications. 2019

[45] Maina FW. Implementing Digital Strategy for Attaining Competitive Advantage During Covid–19 Pandemic by International Tier 1 Banks in Kenya (Doctoral dissertation,. University of Nairobi); 2021

[46] Central Bank of Kenya. Emergency Measures to Mitigate the Adverse Economic Effects on Bank Borrowers from the Coronavirus Pandemic. Press Release. [Accessed: March 16, 2020]. Available from: https://www.centralbank.go.ke/uploads/press_releases/1908080057_Press%20Release%20-%20Emergency%20Measures%20to%20Mitigate%20the%20Adverse%20Economic%20Effects%20on%20Bank%20Borrowers%20from%20the%20Coronavirus%20Pandemic.pdf

[47] Central Bank of Kenya. 2022. Nairobi Kenya: Discussion Paper on Central Bank Digital Currency; 2022

[48] Serianu. Africa cybersecurity report, Kenya 2019/20. Ltd: Serianu Co.; 2020

[49] Okanga O. The Political Economy of Nigeria's Digital Tax Experiment. Available at SSRN 3640318. Rochester, New York: SSRN (Social Science Research Network)- Elsevier; 2020

[50] Omodero CO, Okafor MC. Digital financing and taxation in the 4th industrial revolution: Evidence from Nigeria. Universal Journal of Accounting and Finance. 2021;**9**(6):1594-1601

[51] Iwueze J. COVID-19 unlocks e-commerce and digital finance among low-income women in Nigeria. Research blog. New York, USA: Women's World Banking; 2021

[52] MoH- Ministry of Health. South Sudan. 2021

[53] Morgan H. Best practices for implementing remote learning during a pandemic. The Clearing House: A JOURNAl of Educational Strategies, Issues, and Ideas. 2020;**93**(3):135-141

[54] Garang JA. Will the impact of the pandemic on the expected National Output Persist? Living in an Era of Emerging Pandemics. 2021;**182**

[55] Ndou V, Mele G, Hysa E, Manta O. Exploiting technology to deal with the covid-19 challenges in travel & tourism: A bibliometric analysis. Sustainability. 2022;**14**(10):5917

[56] Rahayu RP, Wirza Y. Teachers' perception of online learning during pandemic covid-19. Jurnal Penelitian Pendidikan. 2020;**20**(3):392-406

[57] Eziakonwa A. Africa's Digital Solutions to Tackle COVID-19. Brookings Institution; 2020

[58] Li C, Lalani F. The COVID-19 Pandemic Has Changed Education Forever. This Is How. World Economic Forum; 2020. Available from: https://www.weforum.org/agenda/2020/04/coronavirus-education-global-covid19-online-digital-learning [Accessed: February 14, 2021]

[59] Muma B, Micheni E, Mundia C. Covid-19 as a driver towards technology shift: A focus on Kenya. Appropriate Technology. 2020;**12**(30)

[60] Sahay MR, von Allmen MU, Lahreche MA, Khera P, Ogawa MS, Bazarbash M, et al. The Promise of Fintech: Financial Inclusion in the Post COVID-19 Era. International Monetary Fund; 2020

[61] Signe L. Harnessing technology and innovation for a better future in Africa: Policy priorities for enabling the 'Africa we want,' Brookings Institution working paper. 2022

Chapter 9

Technological Adoption in Emerging Economies: Insights from Latin America and the Caribbean with a Focus on Low-Income Consumers

Silvana Dakduk, David Van der Woude and Camilo Alarcon Nieto

Abstract

This chapter delves into the dynamics of technological adoption in emerging economies, specifically focusing on Latin America and the Caribbean region. Understanding technical adoption patterns and drivers is crucial for researchers and practitioners promoting inclusive development. While previous studies have explored technological adoption in these regions, there is a need for a deeper examination of low-income consumers, who represent a significant segment of the population. Uncovering insights into their behavior and decision-making processes can illuminate the challenges and opportunities for bridging the digital divide. Drawing on a rich body of empirical evidence, this chapter investigates the factors influencing the adoption of technologies, such as mobile phones, internet access, and digital services, among low-income consumers in Latin America and the Caribbean. In addition, it explores the role of affordability, infrastructure, digital literacy, social networks, and cultural factors in shaping adoption patterns. The findings provide valuable insights for policymakers, businesses, and organizations seeking to enhance technological adoption and digital inclusion in emerging economies, ultimately fostering sustainable economic growth and social development.

Keywords: technological adoption, emerging economies, low-income consumers, the bottom of the pyramid, e-learning, telemedicine

1. Introduction

In recent years, the rapid advancement of technology has emerged as a crucial factor in shaping the economies of various regions, particularly in emerging markets. This chapter delves into the realm of technological adoption in emerging economies, specifically focusing on Latin America and the Caribbean, shedding light on the experiences of low-income consumers. While technology undeniably holds immense potential as a catalyst for poverty alleviation and overall development in these nations, it still needs concerted public and private efforts. Moreover, digital transformation should include the most marginalized sectors of society in digital transformation, particularly in the areas that bear the most significant vulnerabilities: education and healthcare, and access. Only by fostering collaboration and targeted initiatives can we ensure that technology becomes an empowering force, uplifting the lives of those who need it the most.

While technology can potentially drive economic and social development, the lack of resources and limited adoption among its intended beneficiaries can perpetuate underdevelopment and exacerbate these countries' crises. In the present era, where technological advancements are reshaping industries and cities worldwide, the absence of access to and utilization of technology further deepens the existing disparities. The divide between those who can harness the power of technology to enhance their lives and those who are left behind widens, intensifying the cycle of poverty and exclusion. This chapter delves into the intricate dynamics of technological adoption in emerging economies, shedding light on the challenges faced by low-income consumers in Latin America and the Caribbean. By understanding the complex interplay between technology, socio-economic factors, and adoption rates, we can unravel the complexities and pave the way for inclusive and sustainable technological development in these regions.

2. Technological development in emerging economies

Digital transformation has substantially changed the dynamics of modern life [1]. The impact of the arrival and expansion of technology is currently evident in all industrial sectors and, consequently, in people's lives. According to Internet World Stats (2022), the growth of the Internet between 2000 and 2023 globally has been 1392% of new users, implying that more people and organizations have used the different resources developed on various platforms to carry out a large part of their daily activities [2]. This growth is the product of the increase in Internet penetration, which currently stands at 70% of the world's population. Despite this surprising figure, this growth trend has not been symmetrical for all countries because when analyzing this information by region, there are evident inequalities between the availability and use of the service. Developed economies, such as North America and Europe, dominate penetration, while Asia and Africa have the lowest Internet service availability and use (see **Figure 1**).

In the case of emerging economies, these inequalities are also evident within each region, specifically in the Americas. America has 80.5% penetration with a share of 10% of total global users. However, this share presents apparent inequalities at the sub-regional level. North (94%), South (85%), and Central (78%) America are above-average penetration, while the Caribbean (67%) has significant differences concerning the other regions of the Americas.

The pandemic made a notable contribution to promoting the use of technology in the face of the mobility restrictions imposed by the countries. According to the available data, this digital transformation is occurring asymmetrically or unevenly in emergent economies. Adoption of advanced digital technologies, such as 5G mobile networks, the Internet of Things, artificial intelligence, and robotics, among others, is transforming consumption, business, and production models, ushering in a new era

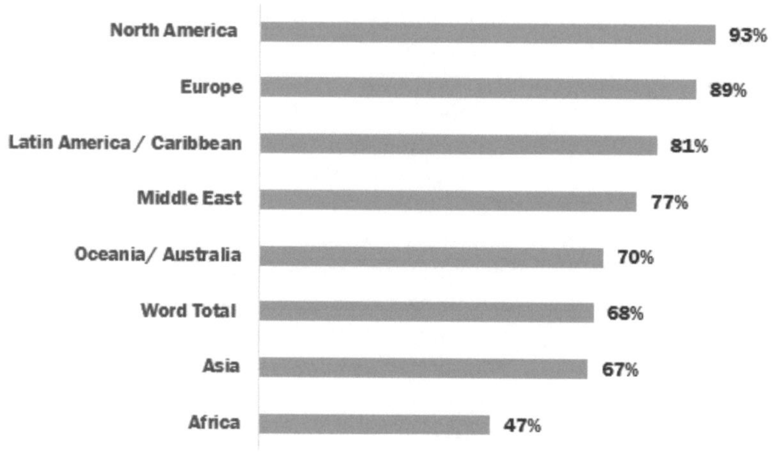

Figure 1.
Global Internet penetration rate based on percentage of total population 2023 [2].

in which we are transitioning from a hyperconnected society to a digitized world on the economic and social levels. According to Report, this new paradigm implies the coexistence of the traditional economy's organizational, productive, and governance modalities with the latest models emerging from digital transformation [3].

Finally, the Economic Commission for Latin America and the Caribbean (ECLAC) [3] assures that technological transformation presents challenges. That can help industrial development, especially in small and medium-sized enterprises in emerging economies and Latin America. This impact of technology extends to all industrial sectors and affects people's daily lives. Despite this, Latin America still faces challenges in investing in digital infrastructure to ensure universal coverage and access to high-speed broadband. Digital transformation has also enabled the generation of new business models and has been fundamental in defining new growth and social and economic development paradigms. Increasing digital accessibility is due to network infrastructure deployment, the widespread use of smartphones, and access to information, social networks, and audiovisual entertainment.

2.1 Digital inequality in emerging economies

Emerging economies often experience digital divides due to several factors: lack of technological infrastructure, digital skills shortages, lack of technological investment, corruption, conflicts, and poverty. These factors can negatively affect access to and adoption of digital technologies, resulting in a digital divide between developed and emerging countries. According to the World Economic Forum's 2021(FEM), [4], less developed countries face a significant digital deficit compared to more advanced countries regarding Internet access and ICT use. The report also notes that the digital divide had widened due to the COVID-19 pandemic even before the problem existed, which was helpful. However, as a result, many emerging countries have experienced disruptions in education, trade, and the economy due to a lack of access to the Internet and digital technologies. For example, a study of the digital divide in Latin America and the Caribbean conducted by the IDB in 2021 found that 32% of the population did not have access to the Internet in the region and that there was a large gap between connectivity in urban and rural areas. In addition, the study found that the need for Internet access limits opportunities for education, employment, and citizen participation in the region [5]. The availability and accessibility of the Internet are closely linked to infrastructure, which has facilitated industrial development driven by technological advancements such as big data, artificial intelligence, and the Internet, transforming economic growth's speed and method.

The digital economy has emerged as a critical component of modern economies; however, its uneven development across the globe has led to a digital divide that further exacerbates economic disparities. According to Cai et al. [6], digital infrastructure is crucial to the digital economy and trade. Studies show that the diffusion of Internet technology significantly impacts the growth of e-commerce in several European countries. The quality and quantity of telecommunications infrastructure are also essential factors; when lands are affected, it can impact the trade of goods. The role of government and the importance of ICT infrastructure is crucial in the growth of the digital economy in different countries, as Di et al. [7] emphasized, also underscore the significance of innovation capacity and population in economic development. Due to their late embrace of digital technologies, low-income countries have seen rapid dispersion of Internet technology and broadband connectivity. On the other hand, technology spreads slowly in high-income countries because of their more advanced Internet infrastructure.

Digital data is taking on a strategic role as a source of economic, social, and environmental value creation in this ecosystem. The process of consolidating a new interconnected digital system is in full swing, combining models from both worlds to create complex ecosystems in organizational, institutional, and regulatory adaptation, constantly advancing along with technological advancements, and potentially enhancing well-being, productivity, and ecological sustainability in a variety of areas including society, production, and government. It comprises three dimensions: the connected economy, the digital economy, and the digitized economy. The connected economy involves expanding digital infrastructure, massifying access devices, and increasing people's connection to machines through the Internet of Things.

On the other hand, the digital economy refers to economic production based on business models enabled by digital technologies, which promote the generation and collection of data to offer new value propositions in the supply of goods and services in various economic sectors. In summary, the digital divide in emerging economies is due to multiple factors. Its solution involves investment in technological infrastructure, education, and digital skills, as well as public policies encouraging the adoption of digital technologies and poverty reduction [8].

2.2 Why focus on emerging economies?

Accelerated economic growth and government policies favoring economic liberalization and adopting a free-market system are the hallmarks of a rising economy. In contrast, there has yet to be a consensus on defining an emerging economy, although widespread agreement should identify its member nations for their rapid economic development. Nevertheless, detailed criteria for identifying an emerging economy's economic growth rate and other economic factors remain to be determined [9].

One of the significant challenges facing the region is the adoption of digital technologies in the production process. Although there are no significant gaps in fundamental indicators, such as Internet access and use of electronic banking by companies, compared with OECD member countries, these differences are more evident in hands, such as Internet use in the supply chain and sales through digital channels.

According to Digital 2023 [10], in January 2023, there were 353.3 million internet users in Latin America, representing a decrease over the previous year. There were also 312.4 million social network users, representing 71% of the region's population. Regarding de- vice usage, the report shows that smartphones are the most widely used device in the area, with a penetration rate of 68%; according to recent data, laptops take second place in usage. Interestingly, smartwatches and bracelets have experienced a significant increase in usage. Additionally, the majority of users use mobile links to access the Internet. However, there is a substantial difference in connectivity between the urban and rural populations, with 71% and 37%, respectively, having access to connectivity options, according to the report [5]. It is essential to remember that these are only some general indicators and that the situation in each country may vary.

Adopting digital technologies in production poses a significant challenge for the region. While there are no major gaps in fundamental indicators like Internet access and electronic banking usage in companies, there are noticeable differences in areas such as Internet use in the supply chain and sales through digital channels compared to OECD member countries. Smartphones are the most used device in the region, with a 64% penetration rate, followed by laptops at 34%. There has also been a 39% increase in the use of intelligent devices like smartwatches and bracelets. The report also reveals that mobile devices are the most popular means of accessing the Internet, with 66% of users doing so through their mobile devices. However, there is a significant disparity in connectivity between urban and rural populations, with 71% and 37%, respectively, having access to connectivity options, according to a report titled "Bridging the digital divide in Latin America and the Caribbean" by IICA, the IDB, and Microsoft in 2021. It is important to note that these indicators are general and that individual countries' situations may vary.

2.3 Accelerating development: Unlocking the potential of emerging economies

The advent of digitalization can enhance people's well-being by improving their quality of life, income, and working conditions. This shift has opened access to information and digital goods, which can minimize travel times, reduce costs, and promote social inclusion. Furthermore, it can create job opportunities, encourage entrepreneurship, and enable individuals to maintain a healthy work-life balance. Entertainment and social networking can also contribute positively to one's well-being. Moreover, the digitized economy provides the opportunity to consume intelligent and personalized products that cater to individual preferences, encourage sustainable consumption practices, and reward environmentally friendly choices based on data related to the product's environmental footprint.

Current economic and social conditions, including the fourth industrial era driven by the digital revolution, climate change, the pandemic, and geopolitical tensions, have led to the implementation of renewed and ambitious, productive development policies. These policies are essential to improve competitiveness, increase participation in technological activities and improve the quality of employment and wages. However, these policies must consider the need for environmental sustainability and social cohesion rather than replicating traditional industrial development strategies. Effective development policies in the digital era must address data flows and consider cybersecurity and international data governance. In addition, it is essential to foster the creation of integrated and focused digital ecosystems in strategic sectors, especially those that are innovation-intensive and export-oriented, that play a crucial role in supply chains and creating value networks while contributing to employment, productivity, and sustainability. The establishment of such digital ecosystems requires the backing of technological endeavors.

3. Low-income consumers

The category of low-income consumers is vast. It defines the members of the socioeconomic group with limited incomes [11]. Most of the population in emerging economies consists of this group. Despite the magnitude of this group, there has yet to be a consensus regarding who constitutes low-income consumers. Moreover, the definition of low-income consumers is frequently contingent on the official definition of poverty, which varies by country and political criterion. In addition to these differences, low-income refers to those with insufficient financial resources to meet their basic requirements and limited access to essential public services [12].

Consumers in these emerging markets have significantly less money to spend on goods and services than consumers in developed countries [13, 14]. Further, these emerging markets are characterized by corruption, illiteracy, inflation, poor infrastructure, and red tape [15, 16]. These phenomena, unfortunately, worsened during the pandemic.

Accordingly, Correa et al. [11]state that low-income consumers are vulnerable and highly susceptible to adverse conditions. This vulnerability results from demographic, economic, psychological, and social factors [17, 18]. Consumers at the bottom of the pyramid tend to have fewer payment methods, and a smaller fraction of them own a bank account relative to high-income consumers. Therefore, low-income consumers are constrained by spending and the type and variety of payment methods available [19].

However, according to [20], despite the limited purchasing power of the Bottom of Pyramid (BoP), this group's overall spending has a significant impact on the global economy, with an estimated 5 billion USD in purchasing power parity [21]. Given this impact, the BoP market represents a tremendous business opportunity in developing nations since it has been underserved for many years, even though this market segment contains many consumers who aspire to spend in the same product categories as higher-income consumers [22].

Furthermore, Blocker et al. [23] state that, similar to affluent market contexts, education, age, and gender affect product adoption in disadvantaged environments [24]. Even within a limited income range, income can affect consumption experiences for new products. Some shoppers can explore, while others focus on survival [25]. Malnourishment and other biophysical factors can dramatically affect vulnerability [26]. Illiteracy and numeracy also have drawbacks [27]. In particular, the inability to digest package information, deconstruct persuasive messages, or tally up cash at the register can reduce consumption [28]. Impoverished living increases cognitive load and buffer [23], reducing contextual sensitivity and impairing decision-making [29–31].

These five aspects frame low-income customers' consumption and openness to new products. These deficits show how low-income customers are constantly stressed and anxious in the marketplace [23, 28, 32], suggesting that businesses should focus on building trust and relationships with low-income consumers, providing them with value-added services, and using social media and mobile technology to reach them [23].

According to Roy et al. [33], understanding the purchase behavior of low-income consumers is crucial for developing effective marketing strategies to increase sales and profits. The study finds that low-income consumers prioritize price, quality, and convenience when purchasing. Therefore, businesses should focus on building trust and relationships with low-income consumers, providing value-added services, and using social media and mobile technology to reach them. The study also highlights the importance of understanding low-income consumers' cultural and social context and tailoring marketing strategies accordingly.

Moreover, Pels and Sheth [34] conclude that serving low-income consumers in emerging markets requires a different approach to business models than serving high-income consumers. The paper proposes a conceptual framework, a 2x2 matrix, to help businesses understand the needs and preferences of low-income consumers and design appropriate business models. The report also highlights the importance of understanding the social context dynamics and marketing environment approaches that moderate or counter some of the limits of poverty, making adopting new products possible. In addition, the paper emphasizes the need for innovation and strategic responses to enter low-income markets successfully. Finally, the report provides guidelines for future exploration of the business-to-business research domain and highlights the importance of global branding management in a rapidly changing environment.

Building on the market orientation literature, [22] identify a distinct firm capability, i.e., their base of the pyramid orientation (BOPO), that allows firms to create and capture opportunities in emerging markets. Moreover, they argue that BOPO enables firms to serve consumers' needs better and mitigate the risks and costs associated with emerging markets, consequently enhancing firm performance. All in all, this literature suggests that firms operating in emerging markets are more likely to succeed when they understand the consumers' needs and the challenges associated with these markets and take appropriate actions to address them.

However, despite BOP's theorized and observed importance in improving firms' success [22, 35], we need a more comprehensive understanding of how BOP affects firm outcomes. Moreover, research has yet to adequately address the assumed tensions between the firms' strategies to meet consumer needs in emerging markets and their environmental implications. Indeed, Arnold and Williams [36] state that firms may inadvertently harm themselves by degrading the natural environment in their desire to serve consumers in emerging markets.

Furthermore, more recent trends in literature have focused on new models to address the needs of low-income consumers. Tesfaye and Fougere [37] conclude that frugal innovation, which focuses on co-creation with the informal economy to create low-cost, quality goods and services for the poor, has been hijacked and co-opted in a hegemonic project that leverages powerful ambiguous signifiers, with co-creation acting as an empty signifier. The paper argues that frugal innovation has been transformed into a tool for corporate interests rather than empowering low-income people. The authors call for a critical examination of frugal innovation and its co-option power and for a reclamation of the concept for its original purpose of creating more inclusive markets and contributing to socio-economic development.

Finally, Blocker et al. [23] studied consumer self-confidence among low-income consumers. The study finds that self-confidence affects consumers' information search and share intention and significantly affects product expertise. The paper also highlights the importance of self-awareness and self-efficacy in acceptance of disability, better health, and an active lifestyle. Additionally, the article discusses the moderating role of self-confidence and risk acceptance on the relationship between perceived risk and intention to use Internet banking, concluding that research must look beyond the effects of low income on price sensitivity to provide sustainable business models and educational strategies for emerging markets.

In conclusion, the current literature presents the challenges and opportunities of serving low-income consumers in emerging markets. The definition of low-income consumers varies by country and political criterion. However, it generally refers to those with limited financial resources to meet their basic requirements and limited access to essential public services. Consumers in emerging markets have significantly less money to spend on goods and services than consumers in developed countries and are vulnerable and highly susceptible to adverse conditions. However, despite the limited purchasing power of the Bottom of Pyramid (BOP), this group's overall spending significantly impacts the global economy. Therefore, inclusive businesses targeting low-income consumers face the challenge of designing business models that provide genuinely beneficial products and services at affordable prices.

Finally, the evidence suggests that firms operating in emerging markets are more likely to succeed when they understand the consumers' needs and the challenges associated with these markets and take appropriate actions to address them, highlighting the importance of consumer self-confidence in product acceptance among low-income consumers, which affects the information search and share intention of consumers, and significantly affects product expertise.

4. Technology adoption

The emergence of novel technologies promotes the development of human social civilization [38]. Therefore, the impact of technological transformation has been prominent and multi-dimensional. From a business perspective, the opportunities for innovation are endless in developing products and services adapting to customers' needs, given that technology can optimize any point in the value chain in any industry. Changes in the offerings, more market-like forms of production and distribution, delivery service, payment methods, and communication channels are just some possible transformations [39, 40]. From the customer's perspective, technology can also contribute at any stage of their purchasing decision process, offering the possibility of having everything in an accessible, fast, and adaptable manner to any segment profile. Based on this background, the benefits in terms of productivity, efficiency, competitiveness, and growth for private and public organizations globally by technological evolution are unquestionable [41].

However, as pointed out, the scenario is quite different in emerging markets, especially for these countries' most vulnerable sectors. Moreover, new technologies have demonstrated that more than they are needed to generate well-being in the lives of individuals and organizations because many innovations are not widely available and used as expected. This suggests that, despite digital innovations being a global phenomenon, their impact must still be globally equitable. The reasons for explaining these inequalities in terms of development are diverse; however, from the end-user outlook, adoption has become a hot issue in understanding how to promote a symmetrical impact [38]. Technology adoption refers to the stage in which technology is selected for use by individuals and organizations [42]. The study of this process has a long-standing research tradition. Still, it was not until the introduction of Rogers' Diffusion of Innovations Theory (DOI) that it gained widespread use and recognition in the academic field [43].

According to Rogers, diffusion can be defined as the process by which an innovation is communicated through various channels over time among individuals in a social system. Invention, on the other hand, refers to an idea, practice, or object perceived as new by an individual or other unit of adoption. Rogers developed DOI based on five elements - innovation, communication channels, time, and social system - that can be identified in all research on diffusion, and a process of Innovation Decision divided into several stages, which individuals or organizations must overcome to achieve the final degree of adoption of an innovation [44].

Since its introduction, this model has been embraced by various fields and disciplines to understand how individuals and organizations adopt innovations. Due to its prominence and versatility, the application of this model in understanding technological innovations has been extensive, leading to the emergence of specific models and theories that attempt to address the technology use and acceptance process.

4.1 Models of technology adoption

The Technology Acceptance Model (TAM) by [45] was the first theoretical approach for understanding technology acceptance, focusing on predicting user disposition and use of new technology. TAM is an adaptation of the Theory of Reasoned Action (TRA), which is part of the assumption that a person's reaction and perception of something will determine that person's attitude and behavior. TAM was grounded in the proposition that the acceptance and use of technology can be explained by an individual's internal cognitive constructs, including beliefs, attitudes, and intentions.

Five primary constructs form the basis of the Technology Acceptance Model: (a) Perceived Usefulness (PU), (b) Perceived Ease of Use (PEOU), (c) Attitude (Att), (d) Behavioral Intention to Use (BI), and (e) Actual Usage (AU) (see **Figure 2**). PU refers to a user's perception of the subjective probability that the use of technology will help improve their performance when using an information system. Alternatively, PEOU refers to the individual's appreciation that mastering a particular technology involves the least possible effort.

Following TAM, PEOU, and PU are beliefs that directly and indirectly affect attitude or disposition, while PU also directly affects PEOU. Yoon [46] proposed a direct causal relationship between Attitudes, Perceived Usefulness, and Intention, where Intention is the primary determinant of behavior. Many researchers' empirical studies have replicated and tested the model under different conditions for TAM's extended

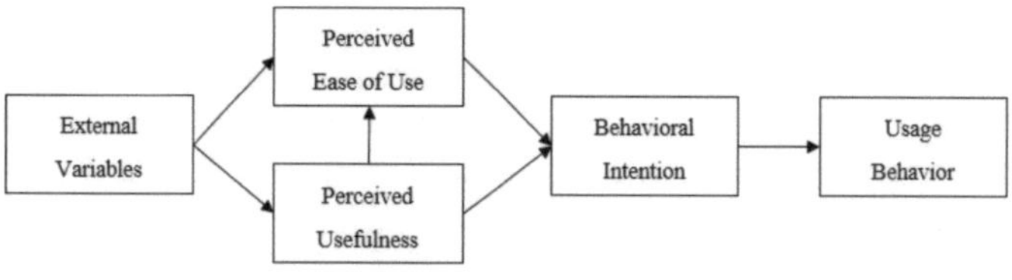

Figure 2.
Technology acceptance model [45].

variables as general measures by explicitly including IT acceptance variables, such as extrinsic and intrinsic motivators.

A significant number of researches have confirmed that perceived usefulness (PU) and perceived ease of use (PEOU) may be influenced by user-related external variables, such as user experience [47], customer satisfaction [48], motivation [49], self-efficacy [50], and demographic factors [51]. Similarly, technology-related variables, such as system quality [52], interface design [53], and compatibility [54], among other factors, may also influence the prediction of behavioral intention. Venkatesh and Davis [55] subsequently introduced a revised version of the Technology Acceptance Model (TAM), known as TAM2, which omitted the construct of attitude towards use and incorporated additional variables such as experience and subjective norm in which recognizes the role of social influence and intrinsic variables in the process. However, the fundamental principles of the model remained intact. TAM2 was tested using longitudinal data collected regarding four different systems at four organizations considering voluntary usage and involving mandatory usage. The findings of this model extension have generated significant practical implications. Mandatory, compliance-based strategies for introducing new systems demonstrate diminishing effectiveness over time compared to harnessing social influence to facilitate positive shifts in perceived usefulness. Therefore, exploring feasible alternatives to usage mandates that capitalize on social information is recommended. For instance, they are developing and evaluating methods that enhance the credibility of social data to encourage internalization or the creation of communication campaigns that elevate the perceived prestige linked to system utilization to foster identification.

Over a decade, the proliferation of research on TAM and TAM2 has led to confusion among researchers, as they often found themselves compelled to pick and choose features from a wide array of competing models. In response to this confusion and to integrate the literature on technology acceptance, [56] developed a unified model that proposes an alternative approach to user and innovation acceptance: The Unified Theory of Acceptance and Use of Technology (UTAUT) [57].

UTAUT consists of four core constructs: (a) performance expectancy (PE), (b) effort expectancy (EE), (c) social influence (SI), and (d) facilitating conditions (FC), applied to determine behavioral intention (BI), which in turn, predicts usage behavior (UB) [58]. PE refers to the level consumers perceive technology to provide benefits in performing specific activities. EE is defined as the degree of ease associated with consumers' utilization of technology. SI (Social Influence) represents the extent to which consumers perceive those influential individuals (e.g., family and friends) to believe they should adopt a particular technology. Finally, FC refers to "consumers' perceptions of the resources and support available to perform a behavior.

The UTAUT proposes that these fundamental constructs (PE, EE, SI, and FC) directly influence behavioral intention and behavior. Furthermore, these constructs are moderated by gender, age, experience, and voluntariness of use [56, 58]. In 2012 [58] proposed and tested UTAUT-2, new constructs, specifically Hedonic motivation (HM), Price Value (PV), and Habit (HB). HM refers to the positive emotion of individual immediate satisfaction, PV refers to the return on investment that the consumer is aware of, and Habit refers to "the degree to which the consumer automatically performs actions with technology (see **Figure 3**).

Since their inception, UTAUT and UTAT-2 have emerged as widely utilized theoretical frameworks in technology adoption and diffusion research. However, despite its prominence, the scientific literature on this concept also reveals disparities in study contexts and samples.

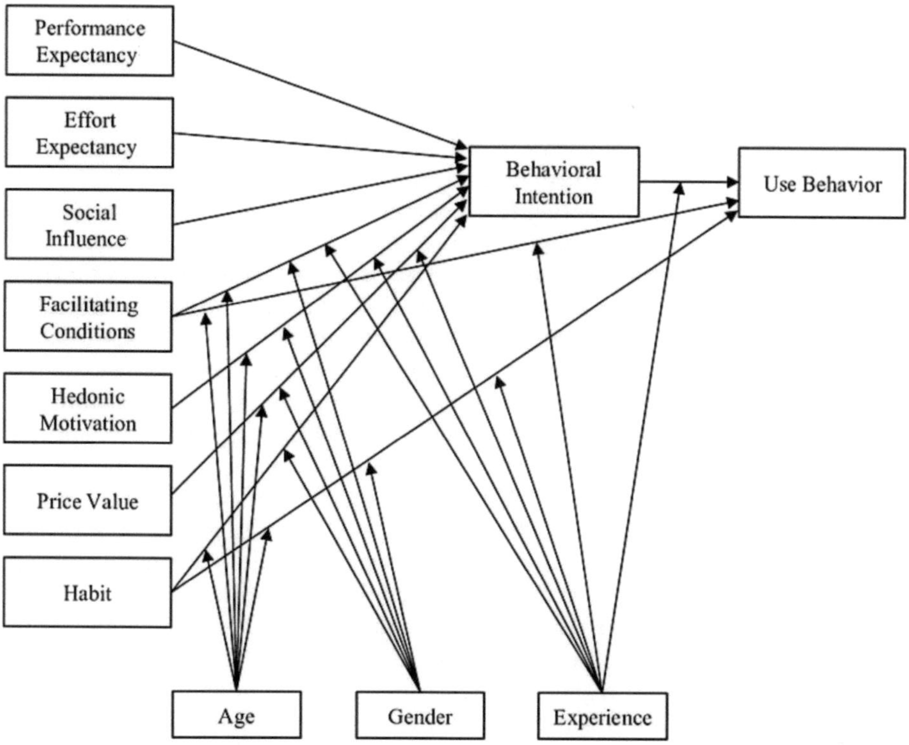

Figure 3.
A unified extended theory of acceptance and use of technology (UTAUT2) [56].

In a literature review conducted by [57], 10 years after the initial development of the UTAUT model, an examination of UTAUT research conducted from 2004 to June 2011 was performed. This review was based on a search in ISI Web of Knowledge and Google Scholar, yielding 174 usable research papers. The analysis revealed that the model had been applied to address various purposes and in diverse contexts, incorporating additional constructs. However, despite the model's popularity, the analysis indicated that the scientific production surrounding the model was concentrated in the United States (25%) and Asia (26%) for primary data collection. Approximately 47% of the research was dispersed among developed economies, predominantly in Europe. Additionally, the study found that only around 20% of the studies were conducted in emerging economies. Regarding the systems used in UTAUT studies, the review established 52%.

Lastly, the review revealed that performance expectancy and social influence emerged as the strongest predictors of behavioral intention in the literature examined. A subsequent study by [59] also confirmed the predictive power of PE and SI and the central role of individuals' attitudes or dispositions. However, although the contribution of these constructs may vary according to the context, user profile, or platform under study, the evidence generally supports their contribution to the acceptance of a new system. Regarding the weight of the variables, a post-review study established that UTAUT explains approximately 70% of the variation in behavioral intention, surpassing previous models [60]. The result is that essential variables in adopting a new system are the expectation of potential users to benefit from the technology and the influence of those surrounding the user who urges its adoption.

4.2 Adoption of new technologies in emerging economies?

The extensive use of DOI, TAM, and UTAUT models in the literature on technology adoption is widely accepted [61]. In addition, these investigations have allowed us to ascertain that cultural variability can influence individual behavior, explaining the gaps in technology usage and acceptance across different cultures [62, 63].

However, one factor contributing to deepening this disparity is the asymmetry of scientific contribution in emerging economies, as most research, except India, has been conducted in developed or developing economies. A clear example of this is the meta-analysis conducted by [64] on the drivers of digital transformation adoption, which revealed that out of 88 evaluated articles representing a total of 34,485 samples studied in 33 countries, 51% of the samples came from India (22%), United States (13%), Germany (8%), and China (8%). The remaining samples were distributed across 29 countries, predominantly in Europe. The reduced participation of specific research from emerging economies is a common factor in studies reviewing the topic.

This situation is even more acute in the case of Latin America and the Caribbean (LAC), despite representing 64% of the Americas and 9% of the world population [2]. Only some studies have dealt with these contexts. Considering that over 60 million people could benefit from fostering digital adoption initiatives in this region [65], several authors who have found evidence supporting cultural differences have emphasized the importance of focusing on understanding this area [20, 63, 66]. Additionally, not only is the regional evidence for Latin America and the Caribbean scarce, but also studies focusing on the most representative sector in emerging economies, low-income consumers. Although the figures may vary by nation, approximately 32% of the population lives in poverty or extreme poverty, while 39% has medium income levels [67].

On the other hand, the proliferation of digital transformation in diverse industries and sectors has resulted in a growing body of research on technological adoption. However, instead of emphasizing the profile of potential users, these studies predominantly concentrate on platform usage to generalize model findings. This trend is evident in research endeavors that assess various areas such as digital payment [68, 69], mobile apps [70, 71]; e-commerce [72, 73], free and open-source software [74], on-demand service platforms [75, 76], artificial intelligence [77, 78], social media [79, 80] virtual reality [81, 82], Business Intelligence and Analytics [83], among others.

Despite the diversity of sectors in which a wide range of technologies can intervene to contribute to the development of emerging economies, health and education constitute key pillars due to their direct impact on a country's economic growth. Research in these sectors was significantly boosted by the COVID-19 crisis enabling substantial progress in utilizing technology-mediated services in various formats and platforms.

Given the high occurrence of chronic diseases in Latin America and the Caribbean, implementing telemedicine and technology-based educational pro- grams for health prevention could have significant positive impacts. The latest data from the Global Burden of Disease study (2019) reveals that conditions such as diabetes, hypertension, obesity, respiratory diseases, and mental health disorders, which account for eight out of 10 premature deaths worldwide, are more prevalent in low- and middle-income countries, including those in Latin America [84, 85].

The evidence in the case of the healthcare sector in emerging economies in Latin America indicates that, although mobile telemedicine options have significantly expanded, allowing these services to reach rural areas and vulnerable populations, they remain a privilege adopted by a minority group of people. In Latin America, mainly due to vast distances, telemedical consultations could improve access to healthcare for populations residing in remote areas far from major medical centers. The Pan American Health Organization/World Health Organization (PAHO/WHO) supports with over 900 virtual rooms remote communication through its Virtual Collaboration program, which provides training on various virtual communication methods and collaborates with those in need of utilizing these tools to disseminate health knowledge where it is most needed. The increasing digitization and availability of telemedicine services in countries like Chile and Argentina present a significant opportunity for Latin America and the Caribbean to export these services across borders, including to neighboring countries. However, there are several challenges that the region must address to seize this opportunity. To deepen the knowledge of these barriers, the Integration and Trade Sector of the Inter-American Development Bank [86] has led a study on International Telemedicine in Latin America, which explores the motivations, uses, results, strategies, and policies that lead to a diagnosis of the sector in the region. This report includes an extensive literature review, an online survey with 1443 healthcare professionals from 19 countries, and in-depth interviews with 29 telemedicine experts.

The report's findings demonstrate a positive correlation between the utilization of international telemedicine and the productivity and efficiency of healthcare professionals. For instance, statistical analysis corroborates that 49% of survey participants reported enhancing their professional skills linked directly to cross-border telemedicine services. Moreover, international telemedicine is associated with improved outcomes for national health systems. Statistical analysis confirms that 43% of respondents connect it to a reduction in social health inequalities, 42% perceive an enhancement in the provision of national health services, and 40% recognize improvements in their countries' overall health status. Nevertheless, the survey reveals that despite these benefits, only 17% of healthcare professionals utilize international telemedicine systems. However, a slightly higher proportion (20%) intend to start using them.

Additionally, there are slight variations in these percentages across different countries in the region. Nevertheless, the potential in terms of volume and impact is enormous. It is projected that by the year 2025, the estimated value of the telemedicine market in Latin America will grow 120%, increasing its value from US$ 1570 million in 2020 to US$ 3480 million in 5 years [87]. As more services and products shift towards digital platforms, telemedicine has emerged as a continuously growing trend, closely linked to the increasing internet penetration rates. However, the fundamental challenge lies in the adoption and acceptance of these services by the healthcare system for their delivery and by users for their utilization.

The education landscape bears many similarities to the healthcare sector in emerging economies. LAC has approximately 193 million children and adolescents of school age, encompassing early childhood, primary, and lower secondary education. However, 14 million are not enrolled, and 15.6 million attend school while facing failures and signs of inequality, manifesting in two or more years of lag in grade-age alignment or educational delay [88]. Children in Latin America and the Caribbean experienced some of the most prolonged and consistent school closures due to COVID-19 worldwide. On average, since the pandemic's beginning, students in the region have lost, either partially or entirely, two-thirds of in-person school days, resulting in an estimated loss of 1.5 years of learning [89]. The pandemic and economic needs have excluded over 3 million school-aged children from education in the past 3 years [90]. Exclusively considering primary and secondary education, according to data from the World Bank and the United Nations Children's Fund (UNICEF), 15 million children and adolescents are out of school, equivalent to a country's population in a country like Ecuador.

In addition to the conditions of poverty that impede access to education, it is estimated that there are 8 million children with disabilities, of which approximately 30% do not attend school due to a lack of physical and technological infrastructure that can accommodate them. This situation exposes them to a high risk of complete dropout from the education system [88]. The primary factors driving online learning are enhancing access to education, training, and the quality of learning, reducing costs, and improving education's cost-effectiveness [91]. Implementing e-learning tools could play a pivotal role in closing these gaps by promoting inclusion and expanding the reach of the education system, particularly for those residing in rural areas. However, beyond the technical requirements, the adoption of e-learning by children and members of the education system remains the next barrier to overcome in harnessing the power of online education. As illustrated, substantial improvements in the education system could be achieved with the widespread availability of Internet access.

Regarding previous research in a literature review on the acceptance of online learning conducted by [92] and an analysis of 14 research studies published between 2005 and 2021 that utilized integration of the TAM model allowed for the conclusion that Course Information, Perceived Usefulness, Attitude, System Quality, User Satisfaction, Perceived Ease of Use, and Academic Performance are the crucial drivers for the acceptance and continued usage of online learning systems. However, the study highlights limitations in the included research, particularly the generalizability of the results, as the studies were conducted on samples from specific countries, none of which encompassed the more vulnerable sectors of Latin America or the Caribbean.

The review emphasizes limitations and suggestions derived from the examined research, highlighting the need for future studies to be conducted in diverse contexts and with varied populations. Additionally, it underscores the importance of undertaking longitudinal studies that account for individual factors to comprehensively understand how this process unfolds. Such research endeavors will provide a broader perspective and shed light on the dynamic nature of technology adoption and its implications. By exploring different contexts and incorporating longitudinal approaches, researchers can delve deeper into the complexities of technology acceptance and uncover valuable insights that contribute to advancing knowledge in this field. Furthermore, a limitation of this review is that it needs to specify how the reported findings may vary according to the level of education. Considering that individual factors influence adoption, it is reasonable to expect differences across various educational levels. Exploring these variations can provide valuable insights into the nuances of technology adoption and its relationship with educational attainment. Future research should consider incorporating analyses examining individual factors' differential impact on adoption within different educational contexts. Addressing this aspect, a more comprehensive understanding of technology adoption's complexities concerning academic levels can be achieved.

The analysis of over 100 articles on eLearning Acceptance and Adoption Challenges in Higher Education, retrieved from significant databases between 2012 and 2022, reveals similar findings. The predominant use of TAM and ITAU models, integrated with other variables and models, highlights the impact of perceived usefulness and perceived efficacy on adopting new technologies. However, more literature must specifically address vulnerable sectors in emerging economies [1]. The authors suggest undertaking studies aimed at identifying potential resolutions to these challenges.

5. Digital challenges in emerging economies: How to benefit the low-income consumers?

Thus far, scientific literature aligns with the theoretical frameworks employed to study technological adoption. Although the impact of these model variables may vary depending on the study context, user profiles, and platform under investigation, there is ample evidence to infer the relevance of the factors influencing the acceptance and usage of new technologies. However, the disparities in the digital transformation's impact between emerging and developed economies prompt crucial reflections on the future research agenda to generate a more significant effect on the most disadvantaged sectors within emerging economies.

Bringing well-being to the poorest sectors of Latin America and the Caribbean through technology is not a solitary endeavor; it requires the collaborative efforts of both the public and private sectors. The success of such initiatives largely depends on building an ecosystem that provides the necessary infrastructure and accessible services to meet the needs of this population. Work collaboratively to establish complementary commitments and investments for the most precarious sectors, such as health and education, especially to promote inclusive digital learning, prioritizing marginalized groups.

Universities and their researchers play a crucial role in achieving the synergies necessary to take technology adoption to another level in underserved populations. Historically, they have fostered dialog between the government and the private sector. The new digital economy has shown that geographical borders are no longer an obstacle, and the main benefit of new technologies lies in generating cross-border solutions. In this regard, Latin America has an advantage since Spanish is the predominant language in almost all countries, unlike Europe and other regions. However, the disadvantages in health and education and the limitations in human, economic, and technical resources are a shared challenge in the area.

It is imperative that academic research, as highlighted by existing literature reviews, transitions towards a more collaborative model that focuses on cross-cultural, longitudinal investigations, mainly targeting groups whose findings can translate into significant social impact. By adopting this approach, researchers can better understand the complexities and dynamics of technological adoption in diverse contexts, identify patterns and trends over time, and uncover insights that contribute to developing effective strategies for promoting and maximizing the social benefits of technology adoption in emerging economies.

Moreover, future research opportunities and implications must transcend the limitations section of publications and serve as a foundation for practical actions that contribute to the region's progress. This requires aligning the research agenda on technological adoption with regional strategic plans for digital development, aiming to generate knowledge with practical implications. Significantly, emphasizing the synergy and collaboration between academia and strategic plans also enhances the sustainability of research by facilitating re-source mobilization for universities. By forging these connections, universities can secure the necessary funding and support to sustain their research endeavors, ultimately fostering long-term progress and positive societal impact in technological use in the low-income sector.

Finally, based on the recommendations of [1, 3, 5, 88, 90, 93] the following proposals are put forth to contribute to a more digital and inclusive region. These proposals draw from the collective knowledge and expertise of these organizations and scholarly sources, aiming to address the challenges and opportunities in technological adoption in Low- income consumers within emerging economies. In addition, these proposals aim to foster a comprehensive approach encompassing policy frameworks, infrastructure development, capacity-building initiatives, and inclusive digital literacy programs by synthesizing insights from diverse stakeholders. Through these concerted efforts, the vision of a digitally empowered and inclusive region can be realized, fostering sustainable development and equitable access to the benefits of technology for all.

6. Conclusions

This chapter has highlighted several key aspects of promoting technological adoption in emerging economies. First, by fostering collaborative mechanisms and strengthening existing alliances, it is crucial to facilitate the development of public policies, research, and implementation of digitalization projects across countries. Second, establishing governance structures that integrate various stakeholders and stages of the digital strategy development journey is essential. Third, delegating responsibilities to exist entities or creating new instances that coordinate the required processes and actions for regional digitalization in different sectors is necessary.

Moreover, establishing a clear framework for the training, management, and compensation of healthcare and education professionals is vital. Finally, standardizing practices for those responsible for bridging the gap in medical care and educational services in underserved sectors is crucial, ensuring a consistent approach and guidelines.

Coordinated regulation, registration, and monitoring of education and healthcare services across different countries are also crucial. This requires establishing legal clarity and compatible rules across borders. Additionally, facilitating the international standardization of professional licenses can overcome licensing barriers when professionals and beneficiaries are in different countries. Finally, creating a global registry that enables a recognition of healthcare and education professionals from a specific country at a regional level can be a solution.

Furthermore, incentive measures to ensure security and privacy when dealing with international patient and student data are imperative. Countries should reach agreements to regulate privacy administration, confidentiality, and data protection. These actions are crucial for promoting the interoperability of information technology systems among nations, enabling data sharing and exchange of essential knowledge required for international healthcare and education services.

The involvement of academic communities in these initiatives is essential to increase knowledge and enhance the adoption and satisfaction with technology-mediated healthcare and education services. In addition, engaging the private sector through fiscal policies and financing mechanisms that incentivize investment in healthcare and education is vital for advancing proposals in these areas. Emerging economies can realize the full potential of technological adoption and generate positive social impact by embracing these recommendations and working collaboratively. However, doing so requires a comprehensive strategy integrating research efforts, policy agendas, and practical implications, resulting in a digitally empowered and more inclusive region.

Acknowledgements

The authors are deeply thankful for the collaborative efforts and support received from both the Finance and Marketing Laboratory at Universidad de los Andes School of Management and the colleagues involved, as their contributions have played a vital role in the successful completion of this book chapter.

Conflict of interest

The authors declare no conflict of interest.

Notes/thanks/other declarations

All information is private for this chapter.

Author details

Silvana Dakduk[1], David Van der Woude[2]* and Camilo Alarcon Nieto[1]

1 Universidad de los Andes School of Management, Bogotá, Colombia

2 CESA School of Business, Bogotá, Colombia

*Address all correspondence to: davidv@cesa.edu.co

References

[1] Ahmad S, Mohd Noor AS, Alwan AA, Gulzar Y, Khan WZ, Reegu FA. eLearning acceptance and adoption challenges in higher education. Sustainability. 2023;**15**:6190. DOI: 10.3390/SU15076190

[2] Internet World Stats. Americas – Internet Usage Statistics, Population and Telecom Reports. 2022. Available from: https://www.internetworldstats.com/stats2.htm [Accessed: May 04, 2023]

[3] ECLAC, "Un camino digital para el desarrollo sostenible de América Latina y el Caribe," Santiago, 2022. Available from: www.issuu.com/publicacionescepal/stacks . [Accessed: May 04, 2023]

[4] World Economic Forum. Accelerating Digital Inclusion in the New Normal. 2021

[5] CAF. Desigualdad 4.0: A cerrar la brecha digital. 2021. Available from: https://www.caf.com/es/actualidad/noticias/2021/05/desigualdad-40-a-cerrar-la-brecha-digital/ [Accessed: April 30, 2023]

[6] Cai B, Du H, Cong Y, Xie F, Zhang J. Research on angle steel tower climbing robot system based on digital twin. In: 2020 7th International Conference on Information, Cybernetics, and Computational Social Systems (ICCSS), Guangzhou, China. 2020. pp. 749-754. DOI: 10.1109/ICCSS52145.2020.9336893. Available from: https://ieeexplore.ieee.org/abstract/document/9336893

[7] Di Y, Zhi R, Song H, Zhang L. Development and influencing factors of international trade in digitally deliverable services. Frontiers in Psychology. 2022;**13**:2740. DOI: 10.3389/FPSYG.2022.908420/BIBTEX

[8] Kshetri NK. Blockchain's roles in meeting key supply chain management objectives. International Journal of Information Management. 2018;**39**:80-89. DOI: 10.1016/j.ijinfomgt.2017.12.005

[9] Arnold DJ, Quelch JA. New strategies in emerging markets. MIT Sloan Management Review. 1998;**40**:1. Available from: https://sloanreview.mit.edu/article/new-strategies-in-emerging-markets/ [Accessed: May 11, 2023]

[10] S. Kemp and We Are Social. Digital 2023: Global Overview Report. 2023. Available from: https://datareportal.com/reports/digital-2023-global-overview-report [Accessed: May 23, 2023]

[11] Correa JC, Dakduk S, Van Der Woude D, Sandoval-Escobar M, Lopez-Llamas R. Low-income consumers' disposition to use automated banking services under a Creative Commons Attribution (CC-BY) 4.0 license. View supplementary material Low-income consumers' disposition to use automated banking services PUBLIC INTEREST STATEMENT. 2022. 10.1080/23311975.2022.2071099

[12] Tarafdar M, Anekal P, Singh R. Market development at the bottom of the pyramid: Examining the role of information and communication technologies. Information Technology for Development. 2012;**18**(4):311-331. DOI: 10.1080/02681102.2012.690172

[13] Cavusgil ST, Ghauri PN, Akcal AA. Doing Business in Emerging Markets. London, United Kingdom: Sage; 2012

[14] Cuervo-Cazurra A, Ramamurti R. Home country underdevelopment and internationalization: Innovation-based and escape-based internationalization.

Competitiveness Review: An International Business Journal. 2017;**27**(3):217-230

[15] Adomako S, Ahsan M, Amankwah-Amoah J, Danso A, Kesse K, Frimpong K. Corruption and SME growth: the roles of institutional networking and financial slack. Journal of Institutional Economics. Cambridge, England: Cambridge University Press; 2021;**17**(4):607-624. DOI: 10.1017/S1744137421000011

[16] Kistruck GM, Webb JW, Sutter CJ, Ireland RD. Microfranchising in base–of–the–pyramid markets: Institutional challenges and adaptations to the franchise model. Entrepreneurship Theory and Practice. 2011;**35**(3):503-531

[17] Coppack M, Raza Y, Sarkar S, Scribbins K. Consumer vulnerability. Financial Conduct Authority [FCA] Occasional Paper No. 8. London: FCA; 2015:1-103. Available from: https://www.fca.org.uk/publication/occasional-papers/occasional-paper-8.pdf

[18] Ka AA, Subramanian R. Current status of research on mobile banking: An analysis of literature. Vision. 2022;**2022**:09722629211073268

[19] Shy O. Low-income consumers and payment choice. Research in Economics. 2020;**74**(4):292-300

[20] Dakduk S, Santalla-Banderali Z, Siqueira JR. Acceptance of Mobile Commerce in Low-Income Consumers: Evidence from an Emerging Economy. Amsterdam, Netherlands. 2020. DOI: 10.1016/j.heliyon.2020.e05451. Available from: https://www.sciencedirect.com/science/article/pii/S2405844020322945

[21] Rahman MS, Mannan M, Amir R. The rise of mobile Internet: The adoption process at the bottom of the pyramid. Digital Policy, Regulation and Governance. 2018;**20**(6):582-589. Available from: https://www.emerald.com/insight/content/doi/10.1108/DPRG-05-2018-0024/full/html

[22] Zhu F, Wei Z, Bao Y, Zou S. "Base-of-the-pyramid (BOP) orientation and firm performance: A strategy tripod view and evidence from China," International Business Review. Dec 2019;**28**(6):101594. DOI: 10.1016/J.IBUSREV.209.101594

[23] Phillips Blocker C. Beyond Radical Affordability in the Base of the Pyramid: The Role of Consumer Self-Confidence in Product Acceptance Time Perspective and Decision Making View Project. United State. 2023. DOI: 10.1111/joca.12514

[24] Burgess S, Steenkamp J-B, Burgess SM, Steenkamp J-BEM. Marketing renaissance: How research in emerging markets advances marketing. International Journal of Research in Marketing. 2006;**23**:337-356. DOI: 10.1016/j.ijresmar.2006.08.001. Available from: https://www.sciencedirect.com/science/article/abs/pii/S0167811606000607

[25] D'Andrea G, Ring LJ, Aleman BL, Stengel A. Breaking the myths on emerging consumers in retailing. International Journal of Retail and Distribution Management. 2006;**34**(9):674-687. DOI: 10.1108/09590550610683193/FULL/XML

[26] Baker SM, Gentry JW, Rittenburg TL. Building understanding of the domain of consumer vulnerability. Journal of Macromarketing. 2005;**25**(2):128-139. DOI: 10.1177/0276146705280622

[27] Viswanathan M, Rosa JA, Harris JE. Decision making and coping of functionally illiterate consumers and some implications for marketing management. 2005;**69**(1):15-31. DOI: 10.1509/JMKG.69.1.15.55507

[28] Chakravarti D. Voices unheard: The psychology of consumption in poverty and development. Journal of Consumer Psychology. 2006;**16**(4):363-376. DOI: 10.1207/S15327663JCP1604_8

[29] Mani A, Mullainathan S, Shafir E, Zhao J. Poverty impedes cognitive function. Science. 2013;**341**(6149):976-980. DOI: 10.1126/SCIENCE.1238041/SUPPL_FILE/MANI-SM.PDF

[30] Shah AK, Shafir E, Mullainathan S. Scarcity frames value. Psychological sciencc. 2015;**26**(4):402-412. DOI: 10.1177/0956797614563958. Available from: https://www.acrwebsite.org/volumes/v42/acr_v42_17568.pdf

[31] Shah AK, Zhao J, Mullainathan S, Shafir E. Money in the mental lives of the poor. 2018;**36**(1):4-19. DOI: 10.1521/SOCO.2018.36.1.4

[32] Blocker CP et al. Understanding poverty and promoting poverty alleviation through transformative consumer research. Journal of Business Research. 2013;**66**(8):1195-1202

[33] Roy G, Debnath R, Mitra PS, Shrivastava AK. Analytical study of low-income consumers' purchase behaviour for developing marketing strategy. International Journal of System Assurance Engineering and Management. 2021;**12**(5):895-909. DOI: 10.1007/S13198-021-01143-6/METRICS

[34] Pels J, Sheth JN. Business Models to Serve Low-income Consumers in Emerging Markets. London, United Kingdom. DOI: 10.1177/1470593117704262

[35] Phong Nguyen N, Adomako S, Ahsan M. The base-of- the-pyramid orientation and export performance of Vietnamese small and medium enterprises. Journal of Business Research. 2023;**154**:113314. DOI: 10.1016/J.JBUSRES.2022.113314

[36] Arnold DG, Williams LHD. The paradox at the base of the pyramid: Environmental sustainability and market-based poverty alleviation. International Journal of Technology Management. 2012;**60**(1-2):44-59. DOI: 10.1504/IJTM.2012.049105

[37] Tesfaye LA, Fougère M. Frugal innovation hijacked: The co-optive power of co-creation. Journal of Business Ethics. 2021;**2021**:1-16

[38] Xu Z, Ge Z, Wang X, Skare M. Bibliometric analysis of technology adoption literature published from 1997 to 2020. Technological Forecasting and Social Change. 2021;**170**:120896. DOI: 10.1016/j.techfore.2021.120896. Available from: https://www.sciencedirect.com/science/article/abs/pii/S0040162521003280

[39] Abbad M, Magboul IHM, AlQeisi K. Determinants and outcomes of e-business adoption among manufacturing SMEs: Insights from a developing country. Journal of Science and Technology Policy Management. 2022;**13**(2):456-484. DOI: 10.1108/JSTPM-03-2021-0049/FULL/XML

[40] Lee KR. Impacts of Information Technology on Society in the new Century. Business and management. Lausanne-Vidy – Switzerland. 2002;**5**(6):46-55. Available from: https://www.zurich.ibm.com/pdf/news/Konsbruck.pdf

[41] Fatima ST. Globalization and technology adoption: Evidence from emerging economies. Aug. 2017;**26**(6):724-758. DOI: 10.1080/09638199.2017.1303080

[42] Cyprian Eneh O. Technology transfer, adoption and integration: A review overcoming difficult people view

project. Journal of Applied Sciences. 2010;**10**(16):1814-1819. DOI: 10.3923/jas.2010.1814.1819

[43] Lundblad JP. A review and critique of Rogers' diffusion of innovation theory as it applies to organizations. Organization Development Journal. 2003;**21**(4):50-64. Available from: https://www.proquest.com/docview/197971687

[44] Rogers EM. Diffusion of Innovations. 5th ed. New York: Free Press; 2003

[45] Davis FD, Bagozzi RP, Warshaw PR. User acceptance of computer technology: A comparison of two theoretical models. Management Science. 1989;**35**(8):982-1003. DOI: 10.1287/mnsc.35.8.982

[46] Tong DYK. A study of e-recruitment technology adoption in Malaysia. Industrial Management & Data Systems. 2009;**109**(2):281-300

[47] Al-Shamaileh O, Sutcliffe A. Why people choose Apps: An evaluation of the ecology and user experience of mobile applications. International Journal of Human-Computer Studies. 2023;**170**:102965. DOI: 10.1016/j.ijhcs.2022.102965

[48] Tang YM, Lau Y, Ho UL. Empowering digital marketing with interactive virtual reality (IVR) in interior design: Effects on customer satisfaction and behaviour intention. Journal of Theoretical and Applied Electronic Commerce Research. 2023;**18**(2):889-907. DOI: 10.3390/JTAER18020046

[49] Salimon MG, Bin Yusoff RZ, Mohd Mokhtar SS. The mediating role of hedonic motivation on the relationship between adoption of e-banking and its determinants. International Journal of Bank Marketing. 2017;**35**(4):558-582. DOI: 10.1108/IJBM-05-2016-0060/FULL/XML

[50] Park SY. An analysis of the technology acceptance model in understanding university students' Behavioral intention to use e-learning. Journal of Educational Technology Society. 2009;**12**(3):150-162. Available from: http://www.jstor.org/stable/jeductechsoci.12.3.150

[51] Tarhini A, Elyas T, Akour MA, Al-Salti Z. Technology, demographic characteristics and E-learning acceptance: A conceptual model based on extended technology acceptance model. Higher Education Studies. 2016;**6**(3):72-89. DOI: 10.5539/hes.v6n3p72

[52] Fathema N, Shannon DM. Expanding The Technology Acceptance Model (TAM) to Examine Faculty Use of Learning Management Systems (LMSs) in Higher Education Institutions. 2015. Available from: https://www.researchgate.net/publication/281842180 [Accessed: May 25, 2023]

[53] Liu IF, Chen MC, Sun YS, Wible D, Kuo CH. Extending the TAM model to explore the factors that affect intention to use an online learning community. Computers in Education. 2010;**54**(2):600-610. DOI: 10.1016/J.COMPEDU.2009.09.009

[54] Chan FKY, Thong JYL, Venkatesh V, Yan Tam K. Modeling citizen satisfaction with mandatory adoption of an E-Government technology. Journal of the Association for Information Systems. 2010;**11**(10):519-549. DOI: 10.17705/1jais.00239. Available from: https://aisel.aisnet.org/jais/vol11/iss10/2/

[55] Venkatesh V, Davis FD. A theoretical extension of the technology acceptance model: Four longitudinal field studies. Management Science. 2000;**46**(2):186-204

[56] Venkatesh V, Morris MG, Davis GB, Davis FD. User acceptance of information

technology: Toward a unified view. MIS Quarterly. 2003;**27**(3):425-478. DOI: 10.2307/30036540

[57] Williams MD, Rana NP, Dwivedi YK. The unified theory of acceptance and use of technology (UTAUT): A literature review. Journal of Enterprise Information Management. 2015;**28**(3):443-488

[58] Venkatesh V, Thong JYL, Xu X. Consumer acceptance and use of information technology: Extending the unified theory of acceptance and use of technology. MIS Quarterly. 2012;**2012**:157-178

[59] Dwivedi YK, Rana NP, Jeyaraj A, Clement M, Williams MD. Re-examining the unified theory of acceptance and use of technology (UTAUT): Towards a revised theoretical model. Information Systems Frontiers. 2019;**21**:719-734

[60] Aytekin A, Özköse H, Ayaz A. Unified theory of acceptance and use of technology (UTAUT) in mobile learning adoption: Systematic literature review and bibliometric analysis. COLLNET Journal of Scientometrics and Information Management. 2022;**16**(1):75-116

[61] Salahshour Rad M, Nilashi M, Mohamed Dahlan H. Information technology adoption: A review of the literature and classification. Universe Access Information Society. 2018;**17**:361-390

[62] Srite M, Karahanna E. The role of espoused national cultural values in technology acceptance. MIS Quarterly. 2006;**2006**:679-704

[63] Peña-García N, Gil-Saura I, Rodríguez-Orejuela A, Siqueira-Junior JR. Purchase intention and purchase behavior online: A cross-cultural approach. Heliyon. 2020;**6**(6):e04284

[64] Cavalcanti DR, Oliveira T, de Oliveira Santini F. Drivers of digital transformation adoption: A weight and meta-analysis. Heliyon. 2022;**8**(2):e08911

[65] Worldometer. Latin America and the Caribbean Population. 2023. https://www.worldometers.info/ [Accessed: May 25, 2023]

[66] Aithal RK, Choudhary V, Maurya H, Pradhan D, Sarkar DN. Factors influencing technology adoption amongst small retailers: Insights from thematic analysis. International Journal of Retail & Distribution Management. 2023;**51**(1):81-102

[67] Statista. Percentage distribution of the population of Latin America in 2021, by income stratum. 2023. Available from: https://es.statista.com/estadisticas/1289588/america-latina-distribucion-de-la-poblacion-segun-estrato-de-ingresos/ [Accessed: May 25, 2023]

[68] Kanojia P, Lal M. Moderation effect of demographic factors in adoption of electronic payments. International Journal of Management Practice. 2023;**16**(1):18-37

[69] Ravichandran R, Sathyanarayana N. Impact of Covid-19 on Digital Payments and Transformation Happening in the Payment System: An Empirical Study. Delhi, India. 2023. Available from: https://www.allmultidisciplinaryjournal.com/uploads/archives/20230103103140_F-22-139.1.pdf

[70] Kamau CG, Asser JH, Ibua MP, Otiende IO. Adoption of accounting mobile apps in Kenya: The effect of user reviews and user ratings. United Kingdom. Apr 2023;**16**(1):36-43. Available from: http://scipg.com/index.php/102/article/view/632

[71] Swaminathan V, Pattanayak SK. A critical analysis on the factors impacting the consumers adoption of fitness applications on smartphones. IJFMR-International Journal for Multidisciplinary Research. 2023;**5**(1):1-20. Available from: https://www.ijfmr.com/papers/2023/1/1316.pdf

[72] Junejo I, Kumar D, Khan MA, Rahoo LA, Ahmed J. Use of E-commerce during Covid-19 and purchase intention: The mediating role of social norms. Journal of Positive School Psychology. 2023;**2023**:959-974

[73] Subagja AD. Analysis of factors leading to E-commerce adoption. Apollo: Journal of Tourism and Business. 2023;**1**(1):1-5

[74] Silva JE. Franquicias. Una alternativa Para emprendedores. Revista Escuela de Administración de Negocios. 2003;**47**:116-121. Available from: https://www.redalyc.org/pdf/206/20604709.pdf

[75] Lim T, Lim BC, Leong C, Phang IG, Foong WH. Consumer adoption of on-demand digital platforms: An integrated model. Global Business and Organizational Excellence. 2023;**00**:1-14. DOI: 10.1002/joe.22210

[76] Delgosha MS, Hajiheydari N. On-demand service platforms pro/anti adoption cognition: Examining the context-specific reasons. Journal of Business Research. 2020;**121**:180-194

[77] Upadhyay N, Upadhyay S, Al-Debei MM, Baabdullah AM, Dwivedi YK. The influence of digital entrepreneurship and entrepreneurial orientation on intention of family businesses to adopt artificial intelligence: Examining the mediating role of business innovativeness. International Journal of Entrepreneurial Behavior & Research. 2023;**29**(1):80-115

[78] Alhumaid K, Naqbi S, Elsori D, Mansoori M. The adoption of artificial intelligence applications in education. International Journal of Data and Network Science. 2023;**7**(1):457-466

[79] Kamboj S, Sharma M. Social media adoption behaviour: Consumer innovativeness and participation intention. International Journal of Consumer Studies. 2023;**47**(2):523-544

[80] Yadav J, Yadav A, Misra M, Rana NP, Zhou J. Role of social media in technology adoption for sustainable agriculture practices: Evidence from twitter analytics. Communications of the Association for Information Systems. 2023;**52**(1):35

[81] Gupta KP, Bhaskar P. Teachers' intention to adopt virtual reality technology in management education. International Journal of Learning and Change. 2023;**15**(1):28-50

[82] Huang Y-C, Li L-N, Lee H-Y, Browning MHEM, Yu C-P. Surfing in virtual reality: An application of extended technology acceptance model with flow theory. Computers in Human Behavior Reports. 2023;**9**:100252

[83] Wu Q, Yan D, Umair M. Assessing the role of competitive intelligence and practices of dynamic capabilities in business accommodation of SMEs. Economic Analytical Policy. 2023;**77**:1103-1114

[84] IMARC. Latin America Telehealth Market: Industry trends, share, size, growth, opportunity and forecast 2023-2028. Market Research Report. 2023. Available from: https://www.imarcgroup.com/latin-america-telehealth-market [Accessed: May 25, 2023]

[85] IDB – Inter-American Development Bank. Health Sector Framework

Document. 2021. https://www.iadb.org/en/sector/health/sector-framework [Accessed: May 25, 2023]

[86] IDB – Inter-American Development Bank. Promoting international telemedicine in Latin America. 2021. Available from: https://blogs.iadb.org/integration-%20trade/en/promoting-international-telemedicine-in-latin-america/ [Accessed: May 25, 2023]

[87] Statista. Telemedicine market value in Latin America from 2020 to 2025. 2023. Available from: https://www.statista.com/statistics/800293/telemedicine-market-value-latin-america/ [Accessed: May 25, 2023]

[88] UNICEF. Children in Latin America and the Caribbean: Overview 2020. 2020

[89] The World Bank. Four in Five Children in Latin America and the Caribbean Will Not Be Able to Understand a Simple Text. 2023. Available from: https://www.worldbank.org/404_response.htm [Accessed: May 25, 2023]

[90] UNICEF. Reimagining Education in Latin America and the Caribbean. 2021. Available from: https://www.unicef.org/lac/reimaginar-la-educacion-en-america-%20latina-y-el-caribe [Accessed: May 25, 2023]

[91] Panigrahi R, Srivastava PR, Sharma D. Online learning: Adoption, continuance, and learning outcome—A review of literature. International Journal of Information Management. 2018;**43**:1-14

[92] Mustafa AS, Garcia MB. Theories integrated with technology acceptance model (TAM) in online learning acceptance and continuance intention: A systematic review. In: 2021 1st Conference on Online Teaching for Mobile Education (OT4ME), Alcalá de Henares, Spain. Alcalá de Henares, Spain: IEEE; 2021. pp. 68-72. Available from: https://ieeexplore.ieee.org/abstract/document/9638934

[93] Aguirre-Sosa J, Vargas-Merino JA. Telemedicine management: Approaches and perspectives—A review of the scientific literature of the last 10 years. Behavioral Sciences. 2023;**13**(3):255

Chapter 10

Dynamics of Innovation Ecosystems: Orchestrating Actors and Interactions in Emerging Economies

Stefan Bernat

Abstract

Innovation ecosystem (IE) literature explores the interdependencies between partners that jointly innovate and create value. IEs comprise various actors such as focal firms, suppliers, complementary innovators, and customers. This study elaborates on actors' interactions that promote the emergence and evolution of IEs in emerging economies. System of Systems (SoS) literature—which classifies the types of authority between the system and its components into virtual, collaborative, acknowledged, and directed—is applied to propose a conceptual framework for analyzing IEs. Following a multiple case study, three ecosystems were selected from the Brazilian armored vehicle sector and analyzed according to the proposed framework. The results revealed that the organizational environment impacts IEs by promoting their emergence and evolution or even leading to their death. The interaction between ecosystem actors can also contribute to the success or failure of IEs. Managing to reach the optimal type of authority can be a valuable tool for orchestrating actors and their interactions in IEs.

Keywords: Brazil, defense industry, emerging economies, geopolitical factors, innovation ecosystems, military vehicles, organizational environment, platforms, system of systems, windows of opportunity

1. Introduction

Many disruptive innovations require complementary innovations to attract customers and succeed [1]. As a result, innovative firms have become increasingly dependent on the efforts of other innovative actors within their environments [2]. Managing such dependency and complementary innovations outside firms poses significant challenges for many organizations [3], especially in emerging economies, where the number of innovative firms remains low [4].

Several models, such as supplier innovation, strategic R&D [5, 6], and the innovation ecosystem (IE), have been proposed to explain how innovative firms work with other creative partners. Among them, IE literature moves beyond the challenges within firms by encompassing the development of complementary products and services in addition to the main ones. Furthermore, it explores the interdependencies and coordination between partner organizations that jointly create value [2]. IEs comprise focal firms, suppliers, complementary innovators, customers, and other actors [7]. However, recent studies have raised several questions about how actors' interactions impact the emergence and evolution of IEs [8–11]. These questions indicate that the IE concept has not yet been consolidated [7], especially in emerging economies [12], where firms face an environment of resource scarcity, structural gaps, and institutional voids [13].

To strengthen empirical research and manage the theoretical flaws of ecosystems, scholars have recommended applying a hybrid view of biological systems and industrial engineering systems [14]. A similar approach has also been proposed to study supply chain management by merging the literature on business operation and System of Systems (SoS) engineering [15]. SoS can provide a complementary perspective based on actors' interactions. SoS is an assemblage of individual systems with operational and managerial independence that work together as collaborative systems [16]. SoS focuses on integrating multiple complex systems supported by different managers, sponsors, funding, and goals [17].

Accordingly, by combining IE and SoS literature and exploring multiple cases of armored vehicles within the Brazilian defense industry, this study aims to elaborate on the following research question: considering the typical organizational environment of emerging economies, how do actors and their interactions impact the emergence and evolution of IEs?

This chapter is organized into six sections. The following section outlines the literature on IE, presents the types of authority in SoS, and introduces a tentative framework for analyzing ecosystems. The research method, case selection, and data collection are then described. Later, the cases are presented in detail and followed by a discussion that scrutinizes the impact of the organizational environment, the actors' roles, and their interactions in IEs. The last section summarizes the study's main contributions and limitations and offers suggestions for further research.

2. Theoretical background

This section provides background information on IE and SoS literature. Lastly, a tentative framework based on both literature is proposed to analyze actors' ecosystem interactions.

2.1 Innovation ecosystem

The term "ecosystem" implies an analogy with complex biological systems. The comparison is intended to bring attention to features of business networks and unveil drivers of business success and failure [18]. Concepts in biological ecosystems such as predation, parasitism, and symbiosis may shed light on innovation and technology management [14]. When dealing with innovation challenges, some parallels with biological ecosystems can help infer which ecosystem will survive [19]. The ecosystem construct also makes the interdependencies between actors more explicit [2].

An IE is a network of interconnected and interdependent actors who cooperate and compete for value co-creation [7]. It includes the focal firm, suppliers, complementary innovators, regulatory authorities, standard-setting bodies, the judiciary, research institutions, distributors, outsourcing firms, technology providers, and other actors [18, 20]. Among ecosystem actors, complementors deserve special attention. The more innovative complementors are, the more value they deliver to the ecosystem [21].

Ecosystems are supposed to have a life cycle and follow a co-evolutionary process [7]. According to Moore [19], ecosystems develop in birth, expansion, leadership, self-renewal, and death stages. Dedehayir et al. [8] suggested the phases of preparation, formation, and operation across the genesis of IEs. However, despite the existence of coordination and governance mechanisms that guide the ecosystem life cycle, relationships between actors are always unstable, as partners can change independently of formal contracts or informal agreements [7]. Further, each actor has different attributes, decision principles, and beliefs and thus makes decisions according to them [14]. Changes in the organizational environment, such as government regulations, customer buying patterns, and macroeconomic conditions, may also threaten the ecosystem and its evolution [19].

It is also argued that IEs are built on platforms. Gawer et al. [21] defined platforms as products, services, or technologies used as a basis for other firms to create complementary innovations. Platforms can be clearly observed in the information technology industry because of their high modularity [14]. However, they can be noted in other sectors, such as automotive, aircraft, and consumer electronics [21]. Keystone organizations usually create platforms. The goal is to allow third parties to develop new products more efficiently, thus increasing productivity and improving the ecosystem's overall health [18]. Platforms can also be understood as a standard structure composed of subsystems and interfaces from which a firm can design and develop a family of products [21].

Matching a firm's strategy to ecosystem activities and innovations is one of the crucial aspects of the firm's success [1]. For example, high-definition television was expected to succeed in the early 1990s. However, other critical components, such as signal compression technology and broadcasting standards, were unavailable. Michelin's run-flat tire was introduced in 1997, but its complements of alert lights and automobile repair shops were ready only 9 years later. The online music-retailing category started in the mid-1990s but had to wait a couple of years until digital-rights-management solutions and the emergence of broadband connectivity had been settled. In short, getting to the market is of value only if ecosystem partners can get there simultaneously [1]. As these examples show, while focal firms innovated cutting-edge technology, they could not capture the value for many years since they did not synchronize their innovation strategy with complementary products and services.

2.2 System of systems

SoS research became a new focus for engineering in the 1980s when the US military aimed to integrate an independent weapon system into a large-scale system [22]. It differs from the traditional field of systems engineering. Whereas systems engineering is focused on single-complex systems, SoS engineering focuses on integrating multiple complex systems [23]. Today, various examples of SoS can be observed, such as in energy supply, water supply, air transportation, and the Internet [24].

There are many definitions of SoS. This study adopted the description provided by Krygiel [[25], p. 33]: "A system of systems is a set of different systems so connected or related as to produce results unachievable by the individual systems alone."

Maier [16] postulated five key characteristics that help understand the field of SoS:

1. Operational independence of constituent systems: Usually, the component systems exist before the formation of the SoS and can also be required to support other SoS.

2. Managerial independence of constituent systems: Owners and managers may evolve their systems to meet other particular needs.

3. Geographical distribution: Systems can be geographically distributed.

4. Evolutionary development process: SoS development depends on the development of the constituent systems, which may happen asynchronously and incrementally.

5. Emergent behavior: It emerges from the interactions between the constituent systems.

Similar to ecosystems, SoS can also be built on platforms. Platforms are applied to integrate different systems, usually developed independently and asynchronously. For example, a military platform, such as a ship, an aircraft, or a ground vehicle, is equipped with sensors, weapons, and communications systems, which are independent systems integrated into a common platform to support user needs [24].

A practical framework applied to conceptualize and categorize SoS is based on the degree of authority between the SoS and its constituent systems. According to the Office of the Deputy Under Secretary of Defense for Acquisition and Technology [17], in the United States, the authority in SoS can be classified into four types:

1. Virtual: There is a lack of central authority to manage the SoS and no overall goal. The organizing mechanisms are relatively invisible, and interoperation is achieved through recognized protocols and not by individual agreements between the constituent systems.

2. Collaborative: The component systems interact voluntarily to meet agreed purposes and realize shared benefits. Relationships are based on agreements between the systems.

3. Acknowledged: There is a designated manager and recognized objectives for the SoS. The constituent systems have a contractual relationship with the SoS manager but retain their independent ownership and goals.

4. Directed: The SoS is centrally managed to fulfill specific purposes. Consequently, the component systems are typically subordinated to those purposes.

Dahmann [24] suggests that most SoS are a combination of different types of authority. In fact, an SoS is often comprised of constituent systems that exhibit characteristics of various kinds. For example, in some cases, an SoS owner may have subordinated systems while maintaining independence from other collaborative ones.

2.3 A conceptual framework

Scholars of the IE and SoS literature have proposed further studies beyond their specific fields. For example, Tsujimoto et al. [14] suggested simultaneously applying a hybrid view of biological and industrial engineering systems to strengthen ecosystem research. In turn, Zhang et al. [26] recommended that engineered systems realize living organism abilities, such as perception, adaptation, and self-recovery, to maintain and improve system vitality.

Following these suggestions to merge the literature, the author combined the generic schema of ecosystems from Adner et al. [2] with the types of SoS from the Office of the Deputy Under Secretary of Defense for Acquisition and Technology [17]. As a result, the study developed a conceptual framework to analyze the emergence and evolution of ecosystems. The emphasis is on actors and their interactions. **Figure 1** presents the conceptual framework. The model characterizes a simplification of reality and highlights the various types of authority between actors in ecosystems. The actors and interactions outlined in the figure are just one possible example and vary for each ecosystem.

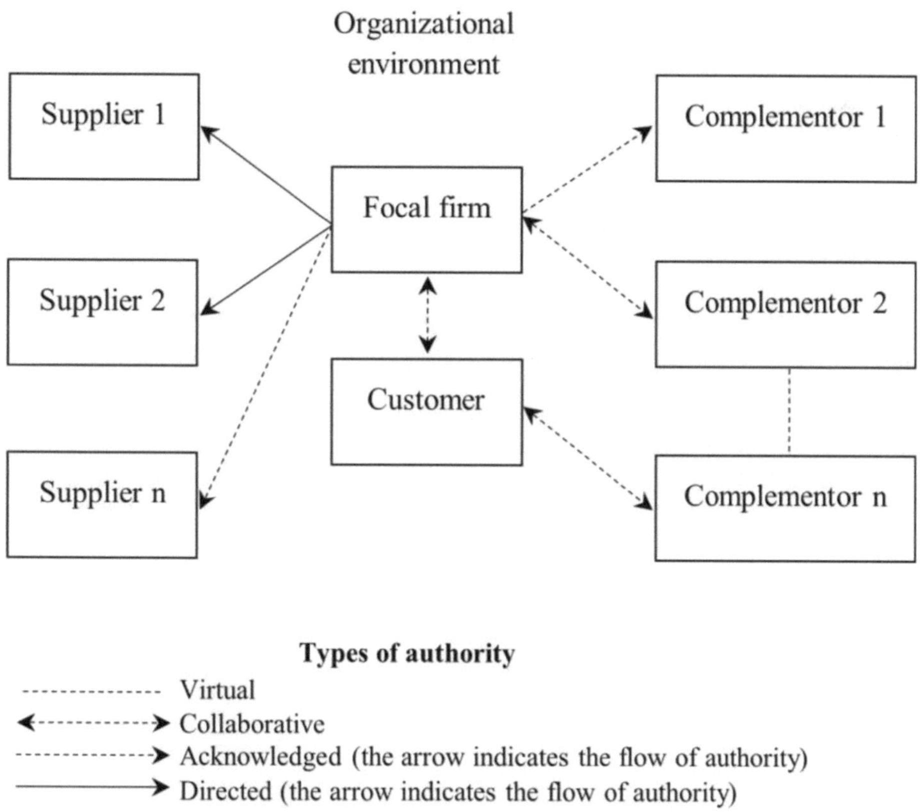

Figure 1.
A conceptual framework to analyze interactions between ecosystem actors. Source: The author, based on [2, 17].

3. Research method

3.1 Design

This study investigated contemporary events involving actors and interactions in emerging economy ecosystems. As the author was interested in understanding the dynamics within the phenomenon [27] and exploring the emergence and evolution of IEs, a "how" question was posed to guide the research. Data were accessed from diverse sources, such as project reports, requirement lists, public documents, and interviews. Based on these conditions, the author adopted the case study methodology [28] to identify the fundamental entities, their relationships, the main events, and what causes them to happen [29]. In addition, the study investigated multiple cases to provide compelling evidence and more robust conclusions [28]. Multiple cases increase external validity and help avoid observer bias [30].

3.2 Case selection

Elaborating on the tentative framework, the author adopted a theoretical sampling strategy [31, 32] and selected cases according to the following criteria:

1. Ecosystems from emerging economies—to identify the main features of ecosystems in emerging economies, as literature is absent [13].

2. Ecosystems composed of several actors—to explore different types of interaction between the ecosystem's participants.

3. Ecosystems within the same industry—to predict similar results for literal replication [28].

For the first criterion, the author selected Brazil, a notable emerging market suggested for further investigation [33, 34]. In Brazil, large ecosystems and SoS were found in the defense industry [35], as military systems usually have hundreds of suppliers and several innovative complementors. Furthermore, cases in the defense domain are also worthy of study as they pose particular challenges not seen in other sectors [36, 37]. Accordingly, the author selected three ecosystems from the Brazilian armored vehicle sector to support the multiple case study. First, during the 1970s, Engesa built the Cascavel ecosystem to develop and produce wheeled armored vehicles for the Brazilian armed forces. Second, Engesa also initiated the Osorio ecosystem in 1982 by designing main battle tanks. Finally, Iveco Defense Vehicles became part of the Guarani ecosystem in 2007 to develop a new family of wheeled armored vehicles. The goal was to substitute Engesa's armored vehicles, which are still in use by some Brazilian military units after more than 40 years.

3.3 Data collection

As Engesa went bankrupt in 1993, primary sources were not found available. Therefore, data supporting the Cascavel and Osorio ecosystems were collected only from secondary sources such as articles, theses, books, and magazines. For the Guarani ecosystem, in addition to secondary sources, which included official documents

Interviewee background and experience	Date	Type	Length
Electronics Eng., 1.5 years in the project	29 March 2016	Written	5 pages
Electronics Eng., 2 years in the project	29 March 2016	Written	5 pages
Project manager, 3 years in the project	29 March 2016	Written	5 pages
Quality Eng., 5 years in the project	29 March 2016	Written	7 pages
Manufacturing manager, 8 years in the project	29 March 2016	Written	5 pages
Product development Eng., 5 years in the project	29 March 2016	Written	5 pages
Communications Eng., 10 years in the project	7 March 2019	Face-to-face	90 min
Mechanical Eng., 5 years in the project	14 March 2019	Face-to-face	90 min
Communications Eng., an expert in the defense industry	11 April 2019	Face-to-face	90 min
Mechanical Eng., 2 years in the project	21 Jan. 2020	Face-to-face	60 min
Signal corps officer, 3 years in the project	2 Feb. 2020	Video call	60 min
Mechanical Eng., 1 year in the project	3 Feb. 2020	Video call	50 min
Bachelor of computer science, 4 years in the project	6 Feb. 2020	Video call	50 min
Signal corps officer, 6 years in the project	17 Feb. 2020	Video call	180 min
Mechanical Eng., 10 years in the project	4 May 2020	Video call	110 min
Expert in armored vehicles	12 May 2020	Video call	105 min
Mechanical Eng., 7 years in the project	19 Oct. 2020	Video call	50 min
Communications Eng., 5 years in the project	26 Nov. 2020	Video call	70 min

Source: Compiled by the author.

Table 1.
Summary of interviews and questionnaires.

and project reports from the Brazilian Army, the study administered six questionnaires and conducted 12 interviews. **Table 1** summarizes the interviews and questionnaires for the Guarani case.

3.4 Data analysis

Based on the literature review and the research question, relevant topics were selected to code the collected data. Suppliers, complementors, focal firms, emergence, evolution, innovation, managerial issues, and technical issues are examples of codes applied during the study. Based on the cross-case synthesis for data analysis of multiple cases [28], the author organized the coded data according to the proposed framework and searched for cross-case patterns to interpret the data and elaborate on the research question.

4. Results

The design of armored vehicles requires complex innovation, since it aims to integrate and balance firepower, mobility, and armored protection in the same vehicular platform [38]. By focusing on the interactions between the involved actors, this section describes the Cascavel and Osorio ecosystems developed by Engesa and the Guarani ecosystem built by Iveco.

4.1 The Cascavel ecosystem

In 1952, after the Second World War (WWII), Brazil and the United States signed a military agreement aiming at a common defense for both countries [39]. The negotiation allowed the provision of military vehicles from the United States to Brazil, such as tanks, wheeled armored vehicles, trucks, jeeps, and tractors. However, during the 1960s, the United States began to restrict sales of military equipment to Latin American countries [40]. As a result, at the end of the 1960s, the Brazilian auto industry started substituting, adapting, and refurbishing many of those vehicles. For example, working on adapting gearboxes and suspensions, Engesa developed a new suspension system called Boomerang, which was used to adapt more than a hundred military trucks used by the Brazilian Army and Marines [41].

In 1970, the Brazilian Army and Engesa also completed the prototype for Brazil's first wheeled armored vehicle. It was a 4 × 4 vehicle named VBB-1. Ladeira Jr. [42] listed Engesa among the leading suppliers for the gearbox and traction, Mercedes-Benz for the diesel engine, and Trivellaco for the armor. Although the prototype was approved in tests, the Brazilian Army was willing to use a 6 × 6 vehicle [43]. Then, a new model was designed and developed. It was a 6 × 6 wheeled armored vehicle for reconnaissance named EE-9 Cascavel. Another vehicle was also developed by Engesa using the Cascavel platform: a 6 × 6 wheeled amphibious armored personnel carrier. It was named EE-11 Urutu. Later, using 4 × 4 traction, Engesa developed a lighter vehicle for reconnaissance, the EE-3 Jararaca [40].

In 1970, Engesa delivered the Cascavel prototypes to the Brazilian Army and Urutu to the Marines. Serial production started in 1974. However, Engesa realized the internal market was insufficient to promote the company's business expansion [41]. Thus, Engesa's salespeople went abroad and offered their vehicles, including two newly developed trucks, to recently independent African countries looking for new business options apart from their former colonizers. At the same time, the oil crisis in 1973 made oil-producing countries in Africa and the Middle East rich overnight, thus increasing their need for defense equipment. As a result, Engesa found a favorable environment for its military vehicles in the international market [42].

Over time, Engesa improved Cascavel to deliver a better product to the external market. The US 37-mm cannon was substituted by a French 90-mm cannon, improving the range and aim. However, after selling the first lot of 200 cannons, the French company raised prices and made the business unfeasible. To get around this situation, Engesa acquired licenses from the Belgium company Cockerill and started producing the 90-mm cannon and its ammunition in Brazil. In addition, Engesa increased the vehicle dimensions and adapted a Mercedes-Benz engine. As a result, Cascavel became a more suitable product for the external market [42].

Several countries ordered Engesa's vehicles in the following years. Qatar is regarded as one of Engesa's first international contracts [41]. Libya ordered 200 Cascavels initially, and even before receiving them, it ordered another lot of 200 vehicles. At the same time, Engesa sold about a hundred Cascavels to Chile. New sales were also made to other African and South American countries. Regarding the Iran-Iraq War in 1980, Iraq emerged as another relevant importer of Engesa's armored vehicles [42]. **Table 2** summarizes Engesa's international orders from 1970 to 1990. Comparing these purchases with the Brazilian internal market, the Brazilian armed forces ordered 409 Cascavels and 223 Urutus [44].

Recipient	Quantity	Vehicle	Year of order	Year of delivery
Bolivia	(24)	EE-11 Urutu	(1977)	1979–1980
	(24)	EE-9 Cascavel	(1977)	1979–1980
Chile	83	EE-9 Cascavel	(1974)	1974–1976
	(37)	EE-11 Urutu	(1975)	1976
Colombia	(76)	EE-11 Urutu	1981	1983–1984
	120	EE-9 Cascavel	1981	1983–1984
Cyprus	(10)	EE-11 Urutu	(1982)	1984
	(36)	EE-3 Jararaca	(1982)	1984–1985
	(126)	EE-9 Cascavel	1982	1984–1988
Ecuador	(18)	EE-11 Urutu	(1983)	1984
	10	EE-3 Jararaca	1983	1984
	(28)	EE-9 Cascavel	1983	1984
Gabon	12	EE-11 Urutu	(1981)	1984
	12	EE-3 Jararaca	1981	1984
	14	EE-9 Cascavel	1981	1983
Iraq	(100)	EE-11 Urutu	1979	1980
	(200)	EE-9 Cascavel	(1979)	1979–1981
	(100)	EE-11 Urutu	1981	1982–1984
	(280)	EE-3 Jararaca	1981	1984–1985
	(200)	EE-9 Cascavel	1981	1982–1985
Libya	(500)	EE-9 Cascavel	1973	1975–1978
	(180)	EE-11 Urutu	(1981)	1981–1982
Nigeria	(75)	EE-9 Cascavel	(1992)	1994
Paraguay	12	EE-11 Urutu	(1984)	1985
	28	EE-9 Cascavel	(1984)	1985
Qatar	(20)	EE-9 Cascavel	1978	1979
Tunisia	(18)	EE-11 Urutu	1982	1983
	(24)	EE-9 Cascavel	1982	1983
Venezuela	(38)	EE-11 Urutu	1983	1984
Zimbabwe	90	EE-9 Cascavel	1983	1984–1987

Source: The author, according to the Stockholm International Peace Research Institute (SIPRI) Arms Transfers Database. Information in brackets indicates that the accuracy of the data is uncertain.

Table 2.
Engesa's international orders for wheeled armored vehicles (1970–1990).

4.2 The Osorio ecosystem

At the beginning of the 1980s, Engesa realized that the market niche of main battle tanks might be another opportunity to diversify its armored vehicle portfolio [41].

Therefore, the company started developing the tank EE-T1 Osorio in 1982, intended to reach both internal and external markets. Due to the need for a more sophisticated embarked technology, Engesa adopted a different approach to suppliers and complementors. While the previous wheeled vehicles relied mainly on the Brazilian auto industry, the Osorio tank became widely dependent on European companies [42]. Engesa also faced retaliation from international competitors. They warned European suppliers and complementors about the inconvenience of cooperating in Engesa's new development [42]. **Table 3** presents Osorio's leading suppliers and complementors according to Conca [45].

During the 1980s, Saudi Arabia negotiated with Germany to substitute the German tank Leopard-1 with the new version, Leopard-2. However, the German government refused to sell the tanks to countries outside the North Atlantic Treaty Organization (NATO). Aiming to occupy this new market, Engesa sent a prototype of Osorio to Saudi Arabia in 1987 to compete in international bidding against tanks from the United Kingdom, France, and the United States. Although Osorio was declared feasible in the bidding, Saudi Arabia decided on the US M-1 Abrams in 1990 [40]. At that time, Engesa's exports had also deeply declined, and some customers could not pay for their orders [46]. For example, Iraq stopped paying the contracts in 1987 as the oil price had decreased and the Iran-Iraq War (1980–1988) had depleted its financial resources [42]. These facts led Engesa to declare bankruptcy in 1993 [40].

4.3 The Guarani ecosystem

The Guarani program was initiated to modernize mechanized cavalry and transform motorized infantry into mechanized infantry. The program comprises a family of armored vehicles for the personnel carrier, mortar carrier, reconnaissance, engineering, communications, command post, radar, ambulance, demining, bridge launcher, and rescue. In 1999, the Brazilian Army issued Basic Operational Requirements for the light and medium versions of the Guarani-Reconnaissance (Guarani-R) and Guarani-Personnel Carrier (Guarani-PC) [47]. **Table 4** presents a sample of the Guarani-PC Basic Operational Requirements.

Country	European suppliers and complementors	Component
The UK	Dunlop	Hydropneumatic suspension
	Vickers	Turret
	RBO/Vickers	105-mm cannon
	Marconi	Shooting control system
	Airscrew Howden	Cooling system
Germany	Zahnradfabrik Friedrich	Gear
	MWM	Diesel engine
	Diehl	Track system
France	GIAT	120-mm cannon
Netherlands	Philips	Shooting control system

Source: Adapted from Conca [45].

Table 3.
Osorio's leading suppliers and complementors.

Type of requirement	Requirement number	Requirement description
Absolute	04	Maximum height of 2.70 m, excluding the turret and weaponry
Absolute	11	Minimum running gear of 6 × 6
Absolute	20	Autonomy greater than 600 km on a class 2 highway
Absolute	67	Allow the installation of communication systems used by the Brazilian Army
Absolute	76	Carry one commander, one shooter, one driver, and seven marines in safety and comfort, regardless of the type of weapon or tower
Absolute	80	Allow the installation of armored turrets with 360° of horizontal movement driven by electrical or hydraulic systems
Desirable	05	Low radar signature
Complementary	01	Multi-fuel engine

Source: Compiled by the author based on [47].

Table 4.
Sample of Guarani-PC basic operational requirements.

Based on the Brazilian Army's methodology for the life cycle management of defense products, Army Staff convened interested parties and stakeholders in 2006 for the first decision-making meeting about the Guarani program. As a result, Army Staff started the program with the 6 × 6 amphibious armored vehicle for personnel carrier—Guarani-PC, intended to be the base platform for other types of wheeled armored vehicles. The prioritization for the personnel carrier was based on the need to substitute the Urutu vehicles developed by Engesa in the 1970s, still in use by the Brazilian Army. Army Staff also decided to obtain Guarani-PC by autonomous development through the Department of Science and Technology in partnership with a national company or consortium. In 2007, after public bidding, the Brazilian Army selected Iveco Defense Vehicles, a Brazilian subsidiary of the Fiat Group and later the CNH Industrial Group, to develop and produce 1 prototype and 16 vehicles for the pilot lot. In addition, several other companies and organizations joined the Guarani program, ranging from public institutions to military organizations and private companies. **Table 5** summarizes the main involved organizations.

Iveco took 6 years, from January 2008 to December 2013, to design, develop, and deliver the first prototype. Iveco based the Guarani-PC platform on technologies and components used by commercial trucks. The goal was to take advantage of commercial off-the-shelf components provided by the existing Brazilian auto industry and make development and production costs cheaper.

> *"The great advantage of the Guarani-PC design was not only the use of shelf components but also shelf ideas. Guarani-PC was designed with a V-frame on top of two bars, which is the chassis concept used in commercial trucks. It is the same concept, placing all parts on top of a chassis. So, it is an idea that came from commercial vehicles and made the development cost cheaper." (Army project member)*

Despite the use of commercial off-the-shelf components, many parts still had to be developed by suppliers. To ensure the quality of parts, Iveco runs a Supplier

Organization	Type of organization	Role in the Guarani program
Army Staff	Military	Client
Army Project Office	Military	Program management
Department of Science and Technology	Military	Main contractor for the design and development phase
Logistic Command	Military	Main contractor for the serial production phase
Army Technology Center	Military	Design and development
Manufacturing Directorate	Military	Design, development, and project management
Army Evaluation Center	Military	Operational and technical evaluation
4th Mechanized Cavalry Brigade, 3rd Motorized Infantry Brigade, 9th Motorized Infantry Brigade, 15th Mechanized Infantry Brigade	Military	User
Iveco Defense Vehicles	Private	Vehicle assembler
More than a hundred suppliers: Fiat Powertrain Technologies, ZF do Brasil Ltda, Bosch Rexroth Ltda, Euroar Sistemas Automotivos Ltda, Dana Industriais Ltda, Iveco Brasil, etc.	Private	Supplier of vehicular components, for example, engine, transmission, water propeller, air conditioner, drive axles, gearbox, and suspension
Several complementors: Harris Corporation, Geocontrol, AEL Sistemas S. A., Ares Aeroespacial e Defesa, Army Technology Center, Pearson Engineering Ltd., Systems Development Center	Private and military	Provider of complementary systems, for example, communications system, tactical computer, turret, remote-controlled weapon station, construction engineering tools, and battlefield management system
Federal Legal Consulting	Public	Provider of legal advice regarding the legal feasibility of bids and contracts
Federal Court of Accounts	Public	Accounting, financial, budgetary, operational, and patrimonial inspection regarding the legality, legitimacy, and economy

Source: Compiled by the author.

Table 5.
Main organizations involved in the Guarani program.

Quality Engineering process. The process includes several activities, such as meeting suppliers to review materials, documents, drawings, recordings, packing, storage, and product identification. As a result, Guarani-PC has already reached 91% nationalization regarding the number of parts produced by the Brazilian industry. However, suppliers were not always interested in producing just a few parts per month for Guarani-PC as they were used to supplying hundreds of components per month for commercial trucks and thousands of components per month for passenger vehicles. In this context, the negotiation with the Guarani-PC suppliers for fair prices was based on the purchasing power of the CNH Industrial Group, to which Iveco belongs.

"Developing suppliers in Brazil with low production volumes is a challenge. As a result, the purchasing group relies on the unified strength of the CNH Industrial Group to impose certain conditions on suppliers." (Iveco supplier quality analyst)

In addition to the prototype and the pilot lot, the Brazilian Army acquired some Guarani-PCs for doctrine experimentation by infantry and cavalry troops. Furthermore, these lots allowed user feedback to the project management team, thus improving vehicle development. After approving the vehicle in 2016, the Brazilian Army officially adopted Guarani-PC and hired Iveco to produce 1580 vehicles. The 400th Guarani-PC was delivered in July 2019. **Table 6** summarizes the contracts through which Iveco has been hired to produce Guarani-PCs, including the internal market of Brazil and the external markets of Lebanon and the Philippines.

Based on the requirements, Guarani-PC was designed to allow the installation of complementary systems such as communication equipment (requirement number 67) and armored turrets (requirement number 80). The integration of these complementary systems has provided additional capabilities and contributed to the Guarani-PC's evolution. For example, command and control (C2) systems and a remote-controlled weapon station (RCWS) have already been developed and integrated into Guarani-PC.

C2 systems aim to provide situational awareness for vehicles and troops on the field. The system comprises one radio for voice communication, one radio for data exchange, one tactical computer, and a battlefield management system (BMS) software. The system allows the troops to exchange relevant information in real time, such as maneuver coordination, vehicle positions, and messages, thus supporting the command and control of military operations. In 2013, the Systems Development Center developed the first BMS prototype. Army Staff issued the C2 Basic Operational Requirements for Guarani-PC in 2015. Lately, due to subject complexity and the need to organize the C2 suppliers involved, Army Staff created the C2 Management Committee in 2017 to advise on decisions about C2 systems.

Recipient	Quantity	Vehicle	Year of order	Selling price
Brazil	17	Guarani-PC (1 prototype and 16 vehicles for the pilot lot)	2007	US$ 18,213,420.34
Brazil	86	Guarani-PC (infantry doctrine experimentation lot)	2012	US$ 118,638,010.04
Brazil	26	Guarani-PC (infantry doctrine experimentation lot)	2013	US$ 31,211,317.46
Brazil	75	Guarani-PC (cavalry doctrine experimentation lot)	2014	US$ 86,548,082.80
Brazil	1580	Guarani-PC (serial production)	2016	US$ 1,774,309,852.72
Lebanon	(20)	Guarani-PC	2014	Not available
The Philippines	28	Guarani-PC	(2020)	Not available

Source: Compiled by the author according to the Brazilian Federal Government Transparency Portal and the SIPRI Arms Transfers Database. Information in brackets indicates that the accuracy of the data is uncertain. The selling price was converted into US dollars based on the contract completion date.

Table 6.
Summary of Guarani-PC contracts.

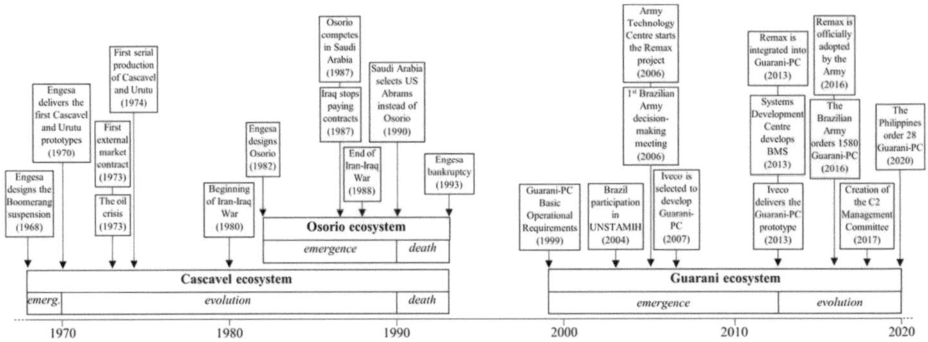

Figure 2.
The studied ecosystems' timeline. Source: The author.

The need for an RCWS system was observed in 2004 during the United Nations Stabilization Mission in Haiti (UNSTAMIH). Brazilian troops were deployed in Haiti for military operations in urban terrain and used 16 Urutu vehicles to support police operations. In this scenario, the driver and the machine gunner were vulnerable to short-range shots, and the turrets had to be adapted to protect the crew. Consequently, in partnership with Ares Aeroespacial e Defesa, the Army Technology Center initiated a project in 2006 to design and develop an RCWS prototype named Remax. It was the first RCWS to be developed in the Southern Hemisphere. After being tested and approved in other vehicular platforms, Remax was finally integrated into the prototype of Guarani-PC in 2013 and was officially adopted by the Brazilian Army in 2016.

Summarizing the section, **Figure 2** shows the three studied ecosystems in a timeline view of their main events within the stages of emergence, evolution, and death.

5. Findings

This study investigated how actors and their interactions impact the emergence and evolution of IEs in emerging economies. To elaborate on this topic, the author integrated IE and SoS models and studied three ecosystems from the Brazilian defense industry: Cascavel, Osorio, and Guarany. The cases were compared and analyzed by applying the framework proposed in the theoretical background section. **Table 7** helps highlight the interdependencies between the main actors and the organizational environment for each ecosystem.

5.1 The impact of the organizational environment on IEs

The organizational environment plays a significant role in the emergence, evolution, and death of IEs. For example, during the 1960s, most military vehicles in Brazil were at the end of their life cycle. These vehicles were made during WWII. International suppliers were no longer providing logistical support for the vehicles. The United States also restricted the sale of defense products to Latin American countries. To overcome this situation, the Brazilian government promoted the production of defense products in Brazil. In this favorable scenario for Brazilian companies, Engesa found a window of opportunity to initiate the Cascavel ecosystem.

Ecosystem	Organizational environment	Suppliers	Complementors
Cascavel (Engesa)	• Need for replacement of WWII vehicles in Brazil • The oil crisis in 1973 • Need for defense equipment in Africa and the Middle East • Iran-Iraq War (1980–1988)	• Mostly from the existing Brazilian auto industry	• A French supplier raised the price of the 90-mm cannon and made the business unfeasible • Engesa acquired licenses to produce the 90-mm cannon and ammunition in Brazil
Osorio (Engesa)	• The German government refused to sell Leopard-2 to countries outside NATO	• Widely dependent on European companies • Engesa's international competitors warned European suppliers and complementors about the inconvenience of cooperating with Osorio's development	• Widely dependent on European companies • Engesa's international competitors warned European suppliers and complementors about the inconvenience of cooperating with Osorio's development
Guarani (Iveco)	• Need for replacement of Cascavel and Urutu vehicles in Brazil, produced by Engesa in the 1970s and 1980s • Need for an RCWS system in Haiti during UNSTAMIH	• The platform is based on technologies and components used by commercial trucks • 91% of Guarani-PC parts are produced by Brazilian industry • Iveco imposed certain conditions on suppliers to guarantee delivery of Guarani-PC parts	• The C2 system comprises other systems such as radio equipment, tactical computer, and BMS software • The Brazilian Army created the C2 Management Committee to organize suppliers • CTEx and Ares designed and developed the RCWS system in Brazil

Source: The author.

Table 7.
Summary of the studied ecosystems.

In the following decades, other factors supported the evolution of the Cascavel ecosystem. The oil crisis in 1973 left oil-producing countries in the Middle East rich overnight, increasing their demands for defense products [48]. Newly independent African countries started looking for military equipment suppliers other than their former European colonizers. The Iran-Iraq War that began in 1980 also boosted the need for defense products. Such geopolitical factors pushed Engesa to improve the performance of its vehicles to conquer the external market, thus contributing to the evolution of the entire ecosystem. Engesa also started developing the Osorio tank to enter the Saudi Arabian defense market, as the German government had refused to sell tanks to countries outside NATO. Lee et al. [49] have studied such critical factors related to changes in technology, changes in demand, and changes in institutions and public policy that may open windows of opportunity for latecomer firms to emerge as international leaders.

However, these supportive conditions changed when oil prices fell in the late 1980s, and the Middle East countries sharply decreased purchasing. Iraq stopped paying contracts in 1987 as the Iran-Iraq War had consumed its financial resources. The end of the Cold War also reduced the need for defense products worldwide.

At that time, Brazil faced several economic difficulties, such as a fall in GDP, increased unemployment, and economic recession [42]. These adverse conditions contributed to Engesa's bankruptcy in 1993 and the death of the Cascavel and Osorio ecosystems [cf. [50]].

In addition, emerging economies face other intrinsic conditions in their innovation environments. Emerging economies have a limited number of innovative companies [4], directly impacting the supply of parts and complements to IEs. Brazil, for example, despite moving up a few positions in the Global Innovation Index, going from 69th in 2016 [51] to 57th in 2021 [52], still has a long journey ahead in supporting innovative companies. As noted by Letaba et al. [53], the dynamics of IEs in developing countries are quite different from those in the developed countries.

Advanced economies generally deny critical technologies, making the catch-up process harder [50]. This situation is even worse concerning defense products, as seen in Osorio's development. The Brazilian Army also took considerable time without projects for armored vehicles after Engesa's bankruptcy. Fourteen years passed before the Army started a new project of armored vehicles. During this period, companies that might have developed sophisticated technologies could not keep their production lines running and had to leave the sector as the government did not promote new projects. This context is also typical in emerging economies, as investments in defense compete with other pressing and urgent problems, such as unemployment, education, and public health [54].

In short, during the 1970s, geopolitical and economic factors provided windows of opportunity for the emergence and evolution of the Cascavel ecosystem and, lately, for the emergence of the Osorio ecosystem. However, in the 1990s, new geopolitical circumstances and the typical scenario of developing countries were unfavorable, leading the Cascavel and Osorio ecosystems to death. Therefore, in line with Pankov et al. [55], this study emphasizes that the organizational environment can either promote or restrict the emergence and evolution of ecosystems.

5.2 The impact of actors and interactions on IEs

Several actors are involved in IEs. Focal firms are generally responsible for assembling components from suppliers and integrating complementary systems from complementors. Any innovation, whether by the focal firm, supplier, or complementor, contributes to innovating and evolving the ecosystem. For this study, Engesa was the focal firm of the Cascavel and Osorio ecosystems, whereas Iveco was the focal firm of the Guarani ecosystem.

Both focal firms created platforms for their ecosystems. For example, Engesa designed a wheeled armored vehicular platform upon which several armored vehicles were assembled, such as Cascavel and Urutu. Engesa also developed the Osorio platform, a main battle tank platform. In turn, Iveco developed the Guarani platform as a basis for several armored vehicles, such as personnel carriers, reconnaissance, and engineering vehicles. By creating a standardized platform and allowing access to other ecosystem members, focal firms provide a mechanism that facilitates interaction with suppliers and complementors, thus promoting the development of innovative components and delivering value to the ecosystem [18, 21].

Engesa based the vehicular platform of Cascavel on components from the Brazilian auto industry. The company also acquired factories in Brazil to supply critical parts, such as suspension, traction, transmission, and gearboxes, thus improving control over suppliers. Regarding complementors, similar management approaches had to be used. As mentioned, the French provider of 90-mm cannons raised prices after selling the first lot of weapons. To address this situation, Engesa acquired licenses from the Belgium company Cockerill and started producing the cannons in Brazil. According to SoS literature, Engesa adopted directed authority on most suppliers and complementors of the Cascavel ecosystem. This approach helped Engesa guide the emergence and evolution of the Cascavel ecosystem.

However, for the Osorio ecosystem, Engesa had to adopt a different approach to suppliers and complementors. As the Brazilian defense industry was very limited in developing more sophisticated technologies for main battle tanks, Engesa became heavily dependent on European suppliers and complementors. Quinn et al. [56] have already investigated the relative costs and risks of strategic outsourcing, especially those related to losing control over suppliers. Accordingly, Engesa had reduced control over other ecosystem actors, as most of its relationships were based on contracts. To make Engesa's situation more challenging, international competitors warned European companies about the inconvenience of cooperating in Osorio's development. Following the SoS literature, the interactions in the Osorio ecosystem can be primarily classified as acknowledged. This approach hampered the birth of the Osorio ecosystem, as European suppliers denied the provision of critical technologies and avoided cooperating with Engesa in its new development.

In turn, Iveco adopted different types of authority in the Guarani ecosystem related to suppliers and complementors. Because suppliers were unwilling to provide a small number of parts per month to the Guarani platform, Iveco used the CNH Industrial Group name to impose conditions during negotiations. Therefore, despite being based on formal contracts, which would classify the authority as acknowledged, Iveco's authority with suppliers must be primarily understood as the directed type [17]. Regarding the complementors, interactions were looser. For example, after selecting the weapon and communications systems, the Brazilian Army hired Iveco to integrate them into the Guarani platform. Accordingly, the interaction between Iveco and complementors can be classified as acknowledged. This tighter approach with suppliers and greater flexibility with complementors has proven successful [21]. Iveco has been provided with parts and components to produce the armored vehicle while allowing complementary innovations to the platform, such as the RCWS and C2 systems. Promoting such relevant innovations help emerging economies grow globally [57].

In addition, it is worth highlighting that a C2 system can also be framed as a minor ecosystem. For example, several actors supply radio equipment, tactical computers, and software to integrate a C2 system. Initially, the relationship between these actors was closer to the collaborative type. Later, the Army realized the need to increase its authority and created the C2 Commission to organize and manage the actors and their systems. Therefore, approaching interconnected or related systems as an ecosystem may help managers deal with challenges in integrating and orchestrating the actors involved.

In summary, applying the proposed framework helped the author identify the type of authority between actors in the studied ecosystems. Based on this relationship and the role played by each actor, whether supplier or complementor, it was possible to conjecture the success or failure of the ecosystems. As illustrated, the Cascavel ecosystem presented a direct relationship between Engesa, suppliers, and complementors, facilitating the conduction of the ecosystem. On the other hand, for the Osorio ecosystem, Engesa's relationship with suppliers and complementors was of the acknowledged type with less authority and reduced control, as interactions were based only on contracts, thus hampering the guidance of the ecosystem. In turn, Iveco adopted two types of relationship: direct authority with suppliers, which ensured the development of the vehicle, and acknowledged authority with complementors, which allowed the integration of innovative complements into the vehicle. Therefore, it can be inferred that identifying the interaction between actors and managing to establish the optimal type of authority can be considered a helpful tool to orchestrate the emergence and evolution of IEs.

6. Conclusions

This study explored the emergence and evolution of IEs in emerging economies. Following the suggestions of recent studies [14, 15], SoS literature was combined with ecosystem literature to strengthen the research. More specifically, the study adopted the types of authority proposed in the SoS literature (virtual, collaborative, acknowledged, and directed) to analyze actor interactions in IEs. Three ecosystems from the Brazilian armored vehicle sector were studied to elaborate on the topic.

The study found that the organizational environment can antagonistically impact innovation ecosystems. For example, geopolitical and economic factors can either open windows of opportunity and promote the emergence and evolution of ecosystems or even lead to their deaths. In addition, the research identified that the type of authority between ecosystem members might also contribute to the success or failure of these ecosystems. Therefore, this study suggests that knowing the current type of authority between ecosystems' actors and managing to reach the optimal one can be a valuable tool to orchestrate the ecosystem evolution.

Finally, as this research is limited to the Brazilian defense industry, further studies on other sectors and countries may help clarify its tentative contribution to the IE literature.

Acknowledgements

The author would like to thank Gen. Tales Eduardo Areco Villela for supporting the Guarani Ecosystem interviews and Gen. Juraci Ferreira Galdino for his insightful thoughts on the Brazilian defense industry. This work was supported by the National Council for Scientific and Technological Development (CNPq), Brazil (reference number: 203048/2015-6), and Sweden's Innovation Agency (Vinnova), Sweden (research grant numbers: 2018-02930 and 2021-03523).

Author details

Stefan Bernat
Department of Management and Engineering, Linköping University, Linköping, Sweden

*Address all correspondence to: stefan.bernat@liu.se

References

[1] Adner R. Match your innovation strategy to your innovation ecosystem. Harvard Business Review. 2006;**84**(4): 98-107

[2] Adner R, Kapoor R. Value creation in innovation ecosystems: How the structure of technological interdependence affects firm performance in new technology generations. Strategic Management Journal. 2010;**31**(3):306-333. DOI: 10.1002/smj.821

[3] Ollila S, Yström A. Exploring design principles of organizing for collaborative innovation: The case of an open innovation initiative. Creativity and Innovation Management. 2016;**25**(3): 363-377. DOI: 10.1111/caim.12177

[4] Fleury A, Fleury MTL, Borini FM. The Brazilian Multinationals' approaches to innovation. Journal of International Management. 2013;**19**(3): 260-275. DOI: 10.1016/j.intman.2013.03.003

[5] Eng T-Y, Ozdemir S. International R&D partnerships and intrafirm R&D–marketing–production integration of manufacturing firms in emerging economies. Industrial Marketing Management. 2014;**43**(1):32-44. DOI: 10.1016/j.indmarman.2013.07.013

[6] Karabag SF, Tuncay-Celikel A, Berggren C. The limits of R&D internationalization and the importance of local initiatives: Turkey as a critical case. World Development. 2011;**39**(8): 1347-1357. DOI: 10.1016/j.worlddev.2010.12.012

[7] Gomes LAV, Facin ALF, Salerno MS, Ikenami RK. Unpacking the innovation ecosystem construct: Evolution, gaps and trends. Technological Forecasting and Social Change. 2018;**136**:30-48. DOI: 10.1016/j.techfore.2016.11.009

[8] Dedehayir O, Mäkinen SJ, Ortt JR. Roles during innovation ecosystem genesis: A literature review. Technological Forecasting and Social Change. 2018;**136**:18-29. DOI: 10.1016/j.techfore.2016.11.028

[9] Hayashi T, Ishimura G, Ohsawa Y. Structural characteristics of stakeholder relationships and value chain network in data exchange ecosystem. IEEE Access. 2021;**9**:52266-52276. DOI: 10.1109/ACCESS.2021.3070017

[10] Tejero A, Pau I, León G. Analysis of the dynamism in university-driven innovation ecosystems through the assessment of entrepreneurship role. IEEE Access. 2019;**7**:89869-89885. DOI: 10.1109/ACCESS.2019.2926988

[11] Yung KL, Jiang Z-Z, He N, Ip WH, Huang M. System dynamics Modeling of innovation ecosystem with two cases of space instruments. IEEE Transactions on Engineering Management. 2020. DOI: 10.1109/TEM.2020.3018782

[12] Sun Y, Li L, Chen Y, Kataev MY. An empirical study on innovation ecosystem, technological trajectory transition, and innovation performance. Journal of Global Information Management. 2021;**29**(4):148-171. DOI: 10.4018/JGIM.20210701.oa7

[13] Cao Z, Shi X. A systematic literature review of entrepreneurial ecosystems in advanced and emerging economies. Small Business Economics. 2021;**57**:75-110. DOI: 10.1007/s11187-020-00326-y

[14] Tsujimoto M, Kajikawa Y, Tomita J, Matsumoto Y. A review of the ecosystem

concept — Towards coherent ecosystem design. Technological Forecasting and Social Change. 2018;**136**:49-58. DOI: 10.1016/j.techfore.2017.06.032

[15] Choi T-M, Cai Y-J, Shen B. Sustainable fashion supply chain management: A system of systems analysis. IEEE Transactions on Engineering Management. 2018;**66**(4): 730-745. DOI: 10.1109/ TEM.2018.2857831

[16] Maier MW. Architecting principles for systems-of-systems. Systems Engineering: The Journal of the International Council on Systems Engineering. 1999;**1**(4):267-284. DOI: 10.1002/(SICI)1520-6858(1998)1:4 <267::AID-SYS3>3.0.CO;2-D

[17] Office of the Deputy Under Secretary of Defense for Acquisition and Technology, Systems and Software Engineering. Systems Engineering Guide for Systems of Systems, Version 1.0. Washington, DC: ODUSD(A&T)SSE; 2008

[18] Iansiti M, Levien R. Strategy as ecology. Harvard Business Review. 2004;**82**(3):68-78

[19] Moore JF. Predators and prey: A new ecology of competition. Harvard Business Review. 1993;**71**(3):75-86

[20] Teece D. Explicating dynamic capabilities: The nature and microfoundations of (sustainable) enterprise performance. Strategic Management Journal. 2007;**28**(13): 1319-1350. DOI: 10.1002/smj.640

[21] Gawer A, Cusumano MA. Industry platforms and ecosystem innovation. Journal of Product Innovation Management. 2014;**31**(3):417-433. DOI: 10.1111/jpim.12105

[22] Zhang H, Huang B, Ju H. An improved SoSE model – The 'V+' model. In: 15th International Conference of System of Systems Engineering; June 2–4. Budapest, Hungary: IEEE; 2020. pp. 403-409. DOI: 10.1109/SoSE50414. 2020.9130496

[23] Keating C, Rogers R, Unal R, Dryer D, Sousa-Poza A, Safford R, et al. System of systems engineering. Engineering Management Journal. 2003; **15**(3):36-45. DOI: 10.1080/10429247. 2003.11415214

[24] Dahmann J. Systems of systems Characterization and Types. Systems of Systems Engineering for NATO Defence Applications (STO-EN-SCI-276). 2015. pp. 1-14

[25] Krygiel AJ. Behind the Wizard's curtain. An integration environment for a system of systems: Office of the Assistant Secretary of Defense (OASD), Command & Control Research Program (CCRP). 1999

[26] Zhang H, Huang B, Zhang P, Ju H. A new SoS engineering philosophy-vitality theory. In: 14th Annual Conference System of Systems Engineering (SoSE); May 19–22. Anchorage, AK, USA: IEEE; 2019. pp. 19-24. DOI: 10.1109/ SYSOSE.2019.8753870

[27] Eisenhardt KM. Building theories from case study research. Academy of Management Review. 1989;**14**(4): 532-550. DOI: 10.5465/AMR.1989. 4308385

[28] Yin RK. Case Study Research Design and Methods. 3rd ed. Thousand Oaks, CA, USA: SAGE Publications; 2003

[29] Easton G. Critical realism in case study research. Ind Market Manag. 2010;

39(1):118-128. DOI: 10.1016/j.indmarman.2008.06.004

[30] Voss C, Tsikriktsis N, Frohlich M. Case research in operations management. International Journal of Operations & Production Management. 2002;**22**(2):195-219. DOI: 10.1108/01443570210414329

[31] Patton MQ. Qualitative Evaluation and Research Methods. Thousand Oaks, CA, USA: SAGE Publications; 1990

[32] Shakir M. The selection of case studies: Strategies and their applications to IS implementation case studies. Research Letters in the Information and Mathematical Sciences. 2002;**3**:191-198

[33] Frank AG, Cortimiglia MN, Ribeiro JLD, Oliveira LS. The effect of innovation activities on innovation outputs in the Brazilian industry: Market-orientation vs. technology-acquisition strategies. Research Policy. 2016;**45**(3):577-592. DOI: 10.1016/j.respol.2015.11.011

[34] Kearney C. Emerging markets research: Trends, issues and future directions. Emerging Markets Review. 2012;**13**(2):159-183. DOI: 10.1016/j.ememar.2012.01.003

[35] de Barros Paes CE, Neto VVG, Moreira T, Nakagawa EY. Conceptualization of a system-of-systems in the defense domain: An experience report in the Brazilian scenario. IEEE Systems Journal. 2018;**13**(3):2098-2107. DOI: 10.1109/JSYST.2018.2876836

[36] Harrison KR, Elsayed S, Garanovich I, Weir T, Galister M, Boswell S, et al. Portfolio optimization for defence applications. IEEE Access. 2020;**8**:60152-60178. DOI: 10.1109/ACCESS.2020.2983141

[37] Komani L, Bobek V, Horvat T. What can the EU learn from the USA in the field of innovation? Journal of Economics and Management Sciences. 2021;**4**(1):29-49. DOI: 10.30560/jems.v4n1p29

[38] Hobday M. The project-based organisation: An ideal form for managing complex products and systems? Research Policy. 2000;**29**(7–8):871-893. DOI: 10.1016/S0048-7333(00)00110-4

[39] Civil House of Brazil. Acordo de Assistência Militar entre os Estados Unidos do Brasil e os Estados Unidos da América. 1953

[40] Strachman E, Degl'Iesposti EHB. A indústria de defesa brasileira: o setor de carros de combate e a Engesa. Ensaios FEE. 2010;**31**(1):31-58

[41] Dagnino RP. A indústria de armamentos brasileira: uma tentativa de avaliação [thesis]. Campinas, SP, Brazil: Unicamp. 1989

[42] Ladeira Jr. PC. A Ascensão e Queda, e os Desafios ao Crescimento das Empresas de Defesa Avibrás e Engesa [thesis]. Rio de Janeiro, RJ, Brazil: Universidade Federal do Rio de Janeiro; 2013

[43] Rocha CM. O Carro de Combate Nacional. A Defesa Nacional. 1966;**52**(606):119-122

[44] Bastos ECS. Uma realidade brasileira: as exportações dos veículos militares Engesa. Revista Da Cultura, Rio de Janeiro, ano VI. 2006;**10**:36-41

[45] Conca K. Manufacturing Insecurity: The Rise and Fall of Brazil's Military-Industrial Complex. London: Lynne Rienner Publishers; 1997

[46] Gouvea R, Kassicieh S. Shifting the technology paradigm: Moving towards commercialization. Latin American Business Review. 2004;**4**(3):91-109. DOI: 10.1300/J140v04n03_05

[47] General Secretariat of the Brazilian Army. Army Bulletin 21/99. Brasilia-DF: SGEX; 1999

[48] Campbell JC. Oil power in the Middle East. Foreign Affairs. 1977;**56**: 89-110

[49] Lee K, Malerba F. Catch-up cycles and changes in industrial leadership: Windows of opportunity and responses of firms and countries in the evolution of sectoral systems. Research Policy. 2017; **46**(2):338-351. DOI: 10.1016/j.respol. 2016.09.006

[50] Karabag SF. Factors impacting firm failure and technological development: A study of three emerging-economy firms. Journal of Business Research. 2019;**98**: 462-474. DOI: 10.1016/j.jbusres.2018. 03.008

[51] Dutta S, Lanvin B, Wunsch-Vincent S. The Global Innovation Index 2016: Winning with Global Innovation. Geneva, Switzerland: Cornell University, INSEAD, and the World Intellectual Property Organization (WIPO); 2016. DOI: 10.34667/tind.28216

[52] Dutta S, Lanvin B, Wunsch-Vincent S, León LR. Global Innovation Index 2021: Tracking Innovation through the COVID-19 Crisis. Geneva, Switzerland: World Intellectual Property Organization (WIPO); 2021. DOI: 10.34667/tind.44315

[53] Letaba PT, Pretorius MW. Toward sociotechnical transition technology roadmaps: A proposed framework for large-scale projects in developing countries. IEEE Transactions on Engineering Management. 2021;**69**(1): 195-208. DOI: 10.1109/TEM.2021.3050812

[54] Bernat S, Karabag SF. Accumulating technological capabilities through R&D projects: Studies on the Brazilian defence industry. International Journal of Technological Learning, Innovation and Development. 2018;**10**(3–4):203-230. DOI: 10.1504/IJTLID.2018.093721

[55] Pankov S, Velamuri VK, Schneckenberg D. Towards sustainable entrepreneurial ecosystems: Examining the effect of contextual factors on sustainable entrepreneurial activities in the sharing economy. Small Business Economics. 2021;**56**:1073-1095. DOI: 10.1007/s11187-019-00255-5

[56] Quinn JB, Hilmer FG. Strategic outsourcing. MIT Sloan Management Review. 1994;**35**:4

[57] Hintringer TM, Bobek V, Milost F, Horvat T. Innovation as a determinant of growth in outperforming emerging markets: An analysis of South Korea. Sustainability. 2021;**13**(18):10241

Section 4

Sectors and Consumers

Chapter 11

Perspective Chapter: eCommerce in the Web3 Era

Sudeep Krishnan

Abstract

eCommerce merchants anticipate adoption of cryptocurrencies in a vast scale in the coming years. While the concepts of Web3 are being adopted, business leaders and decision makers need to understand key the elements of Web3 and technological constructs behind the evolution of Web3. This study focuses on defining these constructs of Web3 and explain technological differences as compared to Web 2.0. Using extensive academic, industry, and online information, the study defines major characteristics of Web3, show cases early adopters, use cases, and opportunities in the area. Web3 is still evolving and there are many challenges which needs to be addressed. eCommerce businesses who are going to sustainably change the business models or disrupt with a new Web3 business is likely to succeed in the coming years. The findings of this study are also validated with an expert interview.

Keywords: Web3, web 3.0, Blockchain, NFT, eCommerce, Metaverse, decentralized applications, cryptocurrency

1. Introduction

85% of American merchants believe cryptocurrency will be a well-accepted payment method in the next 5 years [1]. While enabling an alternate method of payment and accepting cryptocurrency payment as a norm by 2026, these retailers also need to understand the underlying technology changes and impact to the businesses in their respective industries. The terminologies and concepts such as cryptocurrencies, metaverse, blockchain etc. are widely used by individuals and enterprises currently. However, most of them are using it without understanding the relevance in the Web3 world or misrepresenting the concepts.

The World Wide Web or simply known as 'the web' is the foundation of what we know and use as internet providing infrastructural support such as the website itself and enable application services such as an email or an eCommerce website, The web has evolved over the years from Web 1.0 to Web 2.0 and now to Web3. Web 1.0 had mainly unidirectional information flow such as the MSN news services provided to users, Web 2.0 involved more user generated content, centralized databases to manage these contents, and like Web 1.0 infrastructural support to these application services. While Web 3.0 was initially envisioned as an internet capable of acting autonomously without human intervention (semantic web), and the machines being capable to acting on a knowledge-centric model by which a better user experience was created [2], Web3 as being used currently is as technological form of advancement to Web 2.0. This chapter focuses on the architecture, application and uses cases of Web3, a concept that is still evolving and focusing on decentralization. However, generally accepted in current industry is Web3 as a natural evolution of Web 2.0 and as synonymously used with Web 3.0 as a terminology. All usage of Web3 (and Web 3.0) in this chapter relates to the decentralized web and not the sematic definition of Web 3.0.

Web3 is a seismic shift compared to Web 2.0 is terms of its nature of decentralized control. Web3 uses de-centralized control and 'trustless' security. The de-centralization is commonly known as the blockchain technologies and instead of a central authority to provide trust and security to the services, these technologies rely on distributed consensus. All interactions or transactions are available in the public and can be verified by any of the users. While Web 2.0 relied on providing users with relevant and dynamic content such as the social networks, the focus of Web3 is on applications which have relevance in peer-to-peer networks and programmatic approach to digital ownerships. Even by the usage of peer-to-peer interactions Web3 concept of decentralization is entirely different from distributed computing. The concept of distributed computing is well-researched, and highlighted benefits such as speed of operations, ease of execution, and similar efficiency gains using multiple nodes (or peers) [2]. The major differentiating factor is the centralized control in some manner for the distributed systems while decentralization avoids this central authority. Some of the most relevant applications of Web3 include Decentralized Finance (DeFi), cryptocurrencies, Non-Fungible Tokens (NFTs), and applications or services that fall under the universe of Metaverse.

Businesses and key decision makers need a focused and simple training on Web3 and related technologies. This chapter will look at evolution of eCommerce in Web3 focusing on the elements of blockchain, NFTs, and other arenas opened with a completely decentralized commercial space. While the concepts of Metaverse is gaining momentum, the chapter will focus on the infrastructure, economical elements, and market places these concepts bring in. The evolution of businesses to meet the changing environment, opportunities decentralized eCommerce brings, the challenges, and requirement of an ecosystem will be discussed. Use-cases such as NFT marketplaces, examples of successful businesses, and upcoming areas in the metaverse/Web3 area will be discussed in depth. The chapter focuses on clearly defining what Web3 is and how it is different in terms of what it has to offer, technological aspects, its relevance to eCommerce and how business leaders and executives should think about evolving the current way of operating. Industry publications, literature review and web publications on leading and relevant websites are main sources for this research. An interview with an industry leader (CEO of a Web3 platform company) is also conducted to validate the findings.

The chapter is structured in the following format. Research methodology is briefly discussed in the next section. Web3 is defined and along with the details of most used Web3 terminologies, a basic comparison with Web 2.0 technological elements is provided in the first section of the findings. Details of early adopters and select use cases are provided in the next section. The chapter then looks at the relevance of Web3 and changes it brings to eCommerce business ecosystem. Current known challenges are detailed in the next part. The findings from this study are validated with an interview with an industry expert. The next section covers the details of this interview. Conclusion and limitations of this study are provided in the last section.

2. Research methodology

This chapter explores the concept of Web3, which is relatively a new domain and still evolving in its nature and adoption across digital businesses. Since the nature of the study is perspective on an emerging area, a mix of exploratory research methodologies are used to reveal major structural constructs, which require proper definition and clarification for business and academic readers to understand the concept of Web3. Exploratory research is generally qualitative in nature and explores topics which are not generally researched in-depth. The topic of Web3 also falls under such category of topics due to its inherent nature and recent advancements. Since there are no preexisting knowledge and limited academic research, this study resorts to review of available academic research materials, published online articles, analysis of ongoing projects and eCommerce businesses, and knowledge of the author by participating in actual Web3 projects. Interview with an expert is used to validate the findings (provided in Section 8) and explore areas that require further research.

3. Findings

Based on the literature review, it shows there is no single accepted definition of Web3 and several constructs of Web3 is still perplexing to researchers and business adopters. This would generate challenges in the form of business adoption and developing eCommerce propositions around Web3. Moreover, the technological elements are still evolving, and a clear differentiation as compared to current Web 2.0 technologies need to be laid out. There are available published materials showing areas of adoption and several use cases. Based on the review of materials and available project discussion a basic methodology by which Web3 can be well discussed is as follows.

- Provide a proper definition and clarification on what Web3 stands for
- Clarify from a technological and usability standpoint how Web3 is different from Web 2.0
- Explore relevance for eCommerce, provide details of current domains of adoption and select use cases
- Define areas and users to further investigate the relevance to eCommerce businesses
- Explore current known challenges in adoption of Web3

The subsequent sections of this chapter detail the findings in this particular order.

4. What is Web3 and how it is different?

Web3 can be broadly defined as the digital infrastructure whereby the protocols and underlying technology elements (mainly blockchain) facilitates direct interaction between users and removes the need of any centralized agencies (or trusted intermediaries) to verify users or transactions [3]. Currently there are not many academic works that has studied Web3 in detail or provided a well-accepted definition. Liu et al. defines Web3 as an *"era of computing where the critical computing of applications is verifiable"* [4]. The three critical infrastructure elements as outlined for Web3 by these experts [4] include:

1. Smart-contract capable blockchains

2. Platforms that facilitate operations that are unable to be executed on the chains

3. Decentralized client applications with inter-operable features.

While using this definition, this chapter attempts to provide an easy-to-understand comparison with Web 2.0 infrastructure so that readers can understand how the concept of decentralization will impact technology elements that will drive the eCommerce business models. **Table 1** provided below identifies some of the most used Web3 related terms and their definitions.

4.1 Architecture and technological difference: Web3 and Web 2.0

Users may only find a small difference while interacting with Web3 applications as compared to Web 2.0 applications. The notable difference will be on the sign-on service. Web 2.0 relies on the centralized platform to verify the user (such as using an

Terminology	Definition
Blockchain	A record book or public ledger that records all transactions and contracts in a secure decentralized manner. These records are public and can never be tampered with.
Ethereum and Bitcoin	Two popular blockchain technology networks. While Bitcoin processes transactions Ethereum can also support smart contracts. There are also coins that are used on these networks which are widely used cryptocurrencies
Fiat currency	Regular currencies we use – such as US Dollars, Sterling Pound, or Indian Rupee.
Cryptocurrency	A digital version of the currency in which all transactions are maintained in a blockchain.
NFT	Non-Fungible Tokens (NFTs) are digital assets that can be transacted (created, sold, or purchased). Transactions happen on marketplaces that are built on public blockchain networks.
Metaverse	A virtual reality space in which users can interact with other users (mostly in decentralized manner). Metaverse is a use case of Web3 concept providing realistic eCommerce marketplaces and 3D immersive spaces.
Marketplace	Decentralized networks that connect buyers and sellers directly and do not use a central authority. The marketplace is supported by smart contracts on a blockchain.
Minting	Process of turning a digital file into an NFT on a blockchain and stored in the decentralized database making it impossible to tamper with.
Smart Contract	A programmatic approach to creating rules or contracts that gets executed on the blockchain when called by a user or program.
Gas fee	Cost of completing a transaction on a blockchain. The operators (or nodes) who complete the execution of a smart contract on a blockchain gets paid this gas fee.
Wallet	An application that can access digital assets such as cryptocurrency, NFTs and allows storage, purchase, lending and borrowing on decentralized exchanges

Table 1.
Web3 common terminologies and definitions.

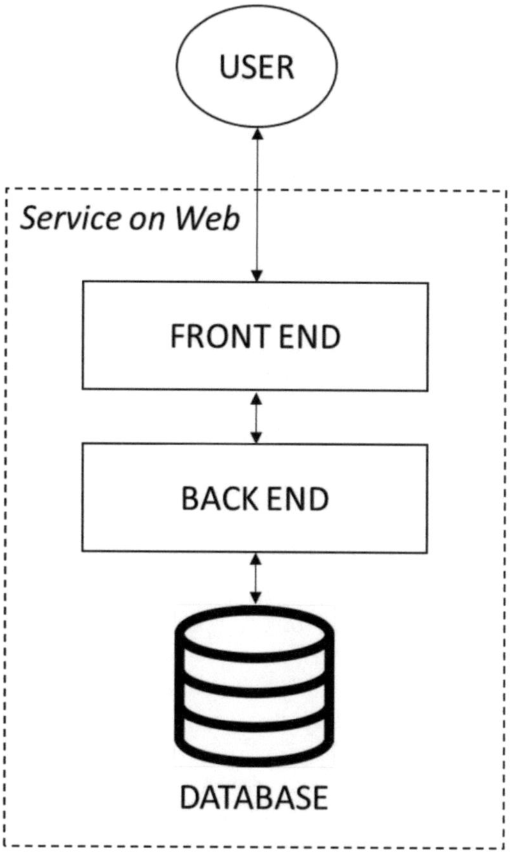

Figure 1.
Web 2.0 basic architecture.

email and password), whereas the decentralized applications use primarily a wallet or signer service which connects the unique address of the user (to verify all transactions) on blockchain. **Figure 1** below shows the basic architecture of a Web 2.0 application.

The database or the data storage captures all essential data for the application such as consumer information, details of transactions, or any activities of relevance to the business. For an application like a social network, it would include all user details and posts by the users, comments, likes, and so on. The database constantly interacts with the back-end business logic and updates the information. The back end of the application runs the core business services or logic. All actions corresponding to the expected behavior – such as what happens when a new user signup, makes a purchase, or writes a new post is managed by this engine. The front end of the business interacts with its users (normally called the User Interface (UI)) and defines the look and feel along with expected changes to the application interfaces. Users normally interact with the front end using a web-based browser, mobile application interface etc. This architecture helped Web 2.0 applications to evolve as Service Oriented Architecture (SOA), which basically improved the accessibility and providing the basic set of applications (common functionalities) using the inherent technological backbone [5].

Unlike centralized databases and control, Web3 relies on blockchains to build the applications [6]. Each of the blocks defines all the transactions and states and has strict rules on how it is transitioned in the next state. No central entity controls these blocks, and it is always maintained by multiple anonymous nodes on the internet. Like the backend logic of the application, developers create smart contracts – the logic that would run on the blockchain defining the state changes such as a transaction logic for transfer of a cryptocurrency from buyer to seller (wallets). **Figure 2** describes the high-level architecture for a Web3 application based on the author's understanding of how Web3 applications currently work. The users interact very similar to a regular Web 2.0 application, however there are no central entities to verify the users and users generally use a signer service like MetaMask or Coinbase wallet service that connects users to the applications front end.

Since the blockchain is public and state machines, anyone can deploy their smart contracts and hence it all works on the same shared public blockchains. The virtual machine executes the code on the blockchain to execute the code. The virtual machines are normally termed Ethereum Virtual Machine (EVM) as Ethereum is the blockchain that supports transactions and smart contracts. All related blockchains such as Binance or Polygon uses the same Ethereum blockchain as the architectural backbone. Hence, unlike the Web 2.0 application backend program, the method by which the logic is executed on Web3 applications is entirely different. However, the front end or UI remains almost the same. But the way in which the front end communicates with the blockchain is different. The services are provided by nodes that help front end interact with the blockchain and they are called the providers. Once the provider helps the front end connect to the blockchain, the application can read the current state of the blockchain and gives permission to write (make any changes) to the blockchain. These changes are signed in public by the application. By this process it ensures these transactions are captured and later cannot be refuted by the signing entity and this process runs without

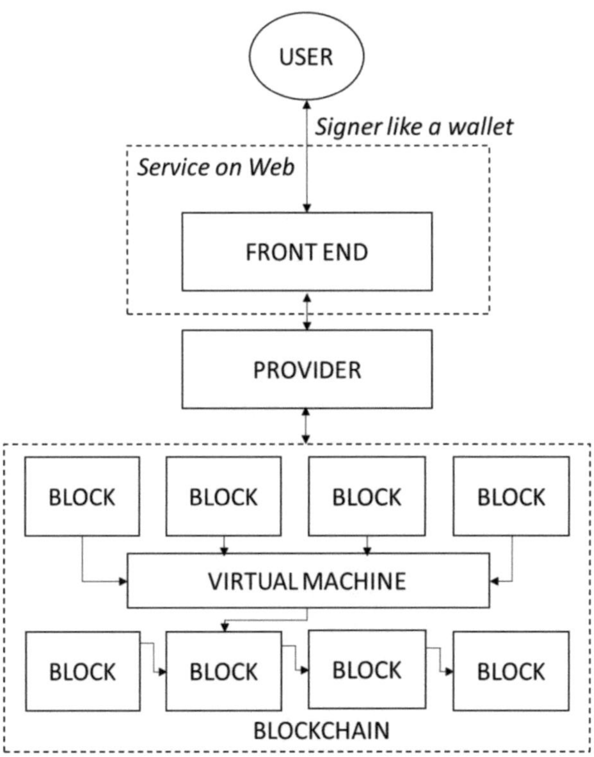

Figure 2.
Web3 basic architecture.

the requirement of a central entity to verify these transactions. As a summary, Web3 application will include an access layer (like a wallet or Web3 enabled browser), a use case layer (the front end or application such as a marketplace of decentralized financial service), an infrastructure layer (provider, virtual machine to run the logic, communication enablers etc.) and finally the backbone protocol layer (underlying blockchain).

There are other details specific to blockchain on how the signature process happens, how nodes accept each of the transactions, file storage within the blockchain etc. which are more technical in nature. Business leaders and Web3 users need to understand only the basic difference in technological infrastructure to identify new business opportunities, requirements to modify existing business operations, and understand the need to develop an ecosystem for users to directly interact with each other.

5. Early adopters and select use cases

Since the central entity does not own end-user information or does not even require the end-users to provide more information than necessary (like connecting their smart wallets) businesses does not require special methods for data privacy. The inherent nature of blockchains safeguards applications and users from hacking and other fraudulent activities. The wide-spread adoption of cryptocurrencies has augmented the swift progress of Web3. Some industries because of its inherent nature and acceptability of peer-to-peer transactions have become early adopters of Web3 applications. At the same time, Web3 has resulted in emerging concepts such as the creator economy and Decentralized Autonomous Organizations (DAOs). This section covers some of the notable use cases and industries of adoption. The examples also bring clarity to some of the terminologies currently being used synonymously with Web3 which are use cases, for example metaverse.

5.1 Decentralized finance

One of the industries with wide adoption of Web3 and having application of peer-to-peer transaction is financial services. The decentralized application in this sector is called Decentralized Finance of DeFi. DeFi is an alternate economy making use of public blockchain for financial transactions [7]. DeFi in conjunction with cryptocurrencies has led to more transparency, reduction in transaction fees, and more importantly can avoid intermediaries such as banks and clearing houses. Use-cases of DeFi itself varies across asset management, lending, derivatives etc. across the financial services. However, peer-to-peer lending and cryptocurrency-based transactions (across borders) are the widely used ones. All cryptocurrency projects broadly fall under the DeFi category and some of the new projects include POLYGON, SOLANA, CARDANO, CHAINLINK, AVALANCHE etc.

5.2 Decentralized autonomous organizations

An interesting aspect of Web3 adoption as compared to Web 2.0 adoption in early stages is not due to the characteristics of User Experience (UX) or ease of use from a front-end perspective, rather it is because of the blockchain features. The decentralized feature of blockchain initiated the idea of collective governance without a centralized authority and one of the best use-cases of Web3 is the DAO. Any governance parameter is dependent on the consensus of DAO members and smart contracts are used to replicate votes of DAO members this form of on-chain governance has gained relevance with Web3 adoption. Few of the notable examples include Uniswap, Decentraland, American CryptoFed DAO etc. [8].

5.3 Metaverse

Metaverse is one of the broadly used terminology in conjuncture with Web3 and is sometimes referred synonymously with Web3. However, metaverse is a boundless virtual world or a three-dimensional internet representing the real world as close as possible. Metaverse and the experience of the virtual world can be provided using Web 2.0 or Web3 features. Metaverse focuses on user experience and uses many of the Web3 feature applications. Creator economy (NFTs), peer-to-peer transactions, decentralized control, and multiple other features are applied to enable realism in the metaverse. Retailers providing virtual experience of the shopping, virtual real-estate experience, and projects such as the one from Meta (Facebook) to enable real life experiences on the web all fall under the category of Metaverse. Relevance to Metaverse in Web3 comes from the digital content it has to offer creating a marketplace for NFTs and smart contracts which are deployed on the Metaverse for peer-to-peer transactions. The virtual or augmented reality projects apply the concepts of Web3 in its transactions it is likely to be considered as the most accepted use case of Web3.

5.4 Creator economy

The creative industry including creators such as developers, artists, musicians, photographers, etc. uses Web3 for monetization opportunities. The creators can directly sell their artwork to interested buyers without any intermediaries. Web3 based businesses for creators focus on the artists and by enabling payments, licensing, intellectual property, storage, ownership, and digital asset management on the blockchain develop a value-based economy for the artists [9]. The digital assets are called the NFTs, and smart contracts are used on blockchains to track ownership of the NFTs. Any secondary sale of NFTs also result in monetary benefits to the creators. NFTs can also be used to incentivize community members, provide special access to events, offer exclusivity, and even provide business services. Marketplaces such as opensea (opensea.io) and foundation (foundation.app) are well used NFT marketplaces directly aligning buyers and sellers. NFT collections are also released by big corporations such as Coca-Cola, Adidas etc. for their branding, business activities and charity.

5.5 Blockchain gaming

Gaming on blockchain develops a new level of experience for the gamers. The next generation games provide play to earn opportunities, ownership of NFTs (such as for gaming avatars, skins etc.) and allow players to earn, lend, and trade financial assets such as cryptocurrencies or game specific tokens. This also develops monetization opportunities for the creators. The applications of Artification Intelligence (AI), Augmented Reality (AR) and Virtual Reality (VR) is extended by blockchains to create an economical environment in addition to the leisure benefits gaming provides [10]. Axie Infinity, Mobox, Upland etc. are blockchain based gaming platforms gaining attention.

5.6 Other areas

Multiple other areas of adoption of Web3 include real estate, remote workspaces, social media, digital infrastructure, privacy management, asset management and so on as explored by practitioners in the current Web3 space [11]. Other novel areas of application ranges from net zero (carbon emissions) tracking, automotive sales through immersive web experience, actual contracts being replaced by smart contracts, healthcare treatment, and treatment planning on metaverse and so on. The common features that make the use cases relevant are the decentralized governance, public record of transactions, and ability for any application to access, verify, and record transactions to the blockchain.

6. Relevance of Web3 in eCommerce

Any new advancement in technology creates two paths for existing businesses, a sustaining path, and a disruptive path [12]. The sustaining path include adoption of the new technology but maintaining the core business model while the disruptive path leads to an entirely new business model – either a new solution being provided to the user or disruption in the manner products or services are being delivered. The adoption of Web3 can also be analyzed using a similar framework. Value creating economies, removal of the need for central authority, and improved security and trust opens multiple opportunities and challenges to the existing business models. Like the Web 1.0 to Web 2.0 transition where most of the heavily used platforms and services suddenly lost significance, it is likely to see a similar transition with current eCommerce platforms.

Technology-enabled live shopping improves customer satisfaction and engagement in virtual and augmented reality as compared to regular online environment [13], which is a good case of how eCommerce business adopts a new technology to provide better experience. For example, a retail fashion store does not stop selling clothes, but the way consumers can try out the products without being at a physical store is an entirely new way of selling. NFT marketplaces, such as opensea (opensea.io) or foundation (foundation.app) has created an entirely new artist-centric business model dismantling the regular agency-centered art business models [9] – including art galleries who generally takes a large part of the proceeds. This is an example of disruptive change. NFT itself created a market size of over $20 billion in 2022 and is expected to reach over $211 billion by 2030 with a growth rate of 33.9% year or year [14].

Even though not a Web3 example, let us take the example of YouTube and Patreon. In YouTube, content creator must wait for the audience to watch the content and monetization is a function of elements such as watch time, physical location of viewers, ads being run etc. The monetary aspects are not known while something is being created. However, Patreon as a platform guarantees a revenue based on already subscribed users who are willing pay for the content from a particular creator. What eCommerce focused businesses need to understand is that the consumer base and the solution they find accessible are evolving. With Web3, solution providers gain advantage in multiple forms – such as avoidance of transaction fees, cost of implementing trust, lesser requirement of intermediaries to solve problems, accessibility to a global market, and lower risk of fraud.

Major retailers have applied the concepts of the virtual and augmented reality currently in their online businesses. However, most of these advancements in user experience does not currently use Web3 features. The retailers can easily implement options such as all virtual buying experiences including smart contracts and crypto payments etc. Similarly, Web3 has opened avenues for marketplaces (such as the ones for NFTs) for buyers and sellers to interact directly. Even though these marketplaces are centrally controlled (marketplace itself being owned by a single commercial entity), they avoid multiple other intermediaries and charge only limited transaction fees as compared to the legacy markets for these industries, like the art galleries. Similar opportunities exist for multiple industries ranging from agriculture, healthcare, oil & gas, travel & transportation and so on for the stakeholders to interact directly.

Another use case to apply new business would be to provide differential experiences. Ranging from concerts and sports events to application of Metaverse in complex healthcare procedures are some of the areas where these concepts have relevance. Overall, business which rely on their online presence must focus on either sustainable change as well as the new technologies opens up a wide variety on opportunities to eCommerce businesses.

7. Challenges in Web3 adoption

Analysis of currently available details of development and deployment of Web3 based applications highlights few major challenges that may impact adoption of these technologies. Even though not exhaustive some of the known challenges are listed below based on the author's experience working on Web3 projects and available online/expert sources.

7.1 Evolving standards

Smart contracts are the backbone of Web3 based applications. There are multiple standards for representing ownership of fungible and non-fungible tokens on blockchains. There are multiple organizations and individuals working to improve, optimize, and reduce transaction fees (gas fees). We can evaluate changes to a few of the standards over the past few years. Ethereum Request for Comment 20 (ERC 20) refers to a scripting standard within Ethereum blockchain for fungible tokens (like currencies) and ERC 721 is a standard for non-fungible tokens. ERC 721A is an extension which allows multiple minting at the same time (an extension of ERC 721) to reduce gas fees. There are multiple other processes and standards evolving to optimize this space, such as lazy minting where the creator pays the gas fees and makes the artwork an NFT only when there is agreed seller and so on. The uncertainties and changing technological infrastructure would impact eCommerce platforms and users would expect the latest standards to be implemented and there are multiple studies calling for standardization of standards for the ease of use [15]. Web3 programming and standard adoption would be an ongoing requirement for all eCommerce initiatives in this space.

7.2 Centralization in the decentralized world

Even though the governing principle of all Web3 platforms is decentralization, the eCommerce platforms tend to still act as a centralized platform. For example, NFT marketplaces such as opensea (opensea.io) or foundation (foundation.app) stores all user details, NFTs and any associated transactions on their platform. Other platforms like wallet providers and exchanges also have 'centralized' control on users. The inefficiencies in the current Web3 architecture is causing the inevitable centralization in the decentralized Web3 world [16]. This can create any of the Web 2.0 related issues such as fraud, ownership issues, and centralized control of users. Moreover, most of the DeFi platforms allow users for decentralized transactions and apply a platform fee and perform their centralized control. While the underlying principles are strongly decentralized, each of these eCommerce initiatives still show a varying degree of centralized control and can be resolved only with platforms with total decentralized user networks being created (that can identify users without the requirement of a centralized agency).

7.3 Institutional adoption

A significant challenge posed for the blockchain is its energy inefficiency. Multiple miners (nodes) are running and consuming energy in a non-optimal fashion. There are studies showing negative impact on energy consumption and carbon emissions from increase adoption of blockchains [17]. This will continue a major challenge in adoption majorly for large corporations and individuals with environmental conscience. However, technological advances such as Proof-of-Concept (PoC) to Proof-of-Stake (PoS) (PoS being a consensus method allowing users not to spend as much energy as needed in the PoC stage) will improve the energy consumption [18]. Ethereum blockchain is moving to PoS stage in September 2022 which is expected to reduce energy consumption and hence significant gas fees reduction. If there are positive technological advancements, agreed standards, and governance mechanisms, we will see an improved adoption from an institutional perspective.

7.4 Public acceptance

Technological acceptance is a well-researched topic in the overall internet and overall Information Technology and Information Services (IT/IS) areas. There are recent studies [19] that have adopted this area research in the advanced technological areas such as augmented reality which may be very relevant in the metaverse and overall Web3 context. Perceived positive impact, novelty, ease of use, informativeness, usefulness, and enjoyment are some of the highlighted determinants of acceptance in the context of this study. The determinants might be a good start point for eCommerce businesses to analyze their service and check user acceptance.

7.5 Lack of an ecosystem

A business ecosystem (from a solution creator perspective) requires partners or providers of technology, ready to use applications or Software as a Service (SaaS), platform providers, legal and governing methods and so on. However, none of these areas have achieved significance maturity in the Web3 space mainly due to unavailability of talent, specialized tools, and even agreed standards as mentioned above. There are studies which highlight the importance of a business ecosystem with complex business environments and helps organizations with self-organization, emerge, co-evolve and adapt [20].

Question	Response	Analysis
What is your role in the Web3 space?	*An engineer turned media explorer and been building products for creative entrepreneurs for some time now. With the current startup, Canvas (Canvas. Space), building a micro monetization platform for creators where they can build interactions on any part of their content in crypto, fiat currencies or as NFTs*	The respondent has experience in Web3 space as an eCommerce provider and has relevant technical knowledge to respond to the research objectives of this study.
What opportunities do you see currently in the Web3 space?	*Creating a safe space for the creative entrepreneurs of today. A space where they are not pulled down by a centralized discovery system, which allows them a fair chance of building a sustainable lifestyle.*	Respondent has highlighted one of the areas this study demonstrated as an early adopter in the Web3 eCommerce space.
What is your favorite blockchain or Web3 project?	*The overall space of DAO is exciting along with the scope of game theories and personally love the current scope of a project like Polygon or what Meta is trying to accomplish.*	DAOs was highlighted as an application area that emerged with blockchains. However, the study did not highlight relevance in this magnitude. Even a creative entrepreneur is emphasizing the importance of governance on blockchain.
Since Web3 is a seismic shift compared to Web 2.0, what is your suggestion to businesses using Web 2.0 as their current solution platform?	*Do not force your way into Web3 due to peer pressure. If your current business line or some aspect of your existing plans or a new area which could enhance your overall brand by integrating with Web3, go ahead. Do not rush. You have a lot of time. This space is just getting started.*	As highlighted in this study multiple times, the concept of Web3 is still in its nascent stage and evolving. The respondent highlights the importance of proper planning and adoption in the Web 3 space.
Which all domains are likely to be early adopters of Web3 technologies?	Real estate, social media, creator economy, art domain, memberships across domains.	The application areas except membership was discussed in detail. Respondent highlights this key application area of Web3.
With the de-centralized construct and closer touchpoints to consumers –do you think businesses will know about consumers better and improve the overall business models?	At this juncture, it's too early. There are a lot of pieces of this Web3 puzzle which needs to be solved before we deep dive on this point. But, yes, it has a clear possibility and probability.	The study focused on elements of Web3 in relation with the application in eCommerce. The response from the expert clearly shows aligned in terms of what eCommerce business may achieve by Web3 adoption.
How will business broadly use Web3 technologies?	Enhancing security layers, interactions and in fact credibility	Enhanced trust provided by public ledgers in the blockchain is a critical element highlighted in this study.
How do you think a business ecosystem will evolve in the web 3.0 space – deciding on the technology, partners, regions of operations and especially end-user acceptance?	It's going to take a while for the business ecosystem to evolve in this Web3 space. As we all know, the partner ecosystems, including technology, SaaS and other capabilities are getting developed as we speak.	This response is also inline with the challenges highlighted in this study.

Question	Response	Analysis
Will the technical aspects of different public blockchains impact adoption of one of the other and if so, which public blockchain/s is/are probably going to drive Web3 business for the future?	Yes, it will. It has a higher probability of creating confusion to people who would adopt to one of them. Now, the way a blockchain like Ethereum has driven the creative business with NFTs, I am sure, there will be multiple projects which could coexist and set the road ahead globally. More like front runners, but with enough scope for everyone entering the space.	Acceptance of a particular public blockchain or a project was not well discussed in this study. A possible extension of this study can be analysis of specific blockchains, projects or technological elements.
What role does standards play for smart contracts and how having different standards will impact businesses? Do you see consolidation happening?	The rule of business is standardization. Any domain, for ease of governance, it will be good to have some skeleton. Personally, I do not have enough data points to converge on the consolidation now.	The standardization as mentioned is highlighted by the respondent as well. However, it does not seem there will be consolidation yet on the evolving standards.
What do you think are the major challenges impacting Web 3.0 based technology adoption?	1. Newness & complexity of the technology 2. Sea of companies, terms getting thrown around, which creates confusion for people who are genuinely interested in being a part of this.	This study has attempted to clarify some of these challenges and provided inputs to business owners and key decision makers to better understand Web3 space and the applicable terminologies.
How do you think known issues as such energy efficiency, scalability, and efficient de-centralization of blockchains are going to be addressed?	I truly believe that we as humans always will figure solutions to anything through innovative ways. The challenges around energy efficiency, scalability is indeed critical, but a lot of us in this space are already aware about the challenge and are trying to come up with solutions. I am confident about some pathbreaking innovations which shall happen soon.	The response on energy efficiencies of blockchain and the related processes are inline with the expected efforts in the Web3 space and energy conservation.

Table 2.
Interview based validation.

8. Validation of the findings

Most of the findings in the research are based on project experience, academic research, published online materials, and research reports. To validate the findings, identify any possible misrepresentations, and explore additional research areas, an in-depth interview was conducted with Vignesh Ramaswamy, CEO of Canvas, a Web3 startup with focus on creator economy and has personally gone through the entire journey from inception to launch of the company including securing of a good investment. The summary of the interview along with a comparison with the details explored in this study is provided below (**Table 2**).

Overall, the interview helps in understanding the focused findings of this study are inline with the thought process of experts in the area. However, the responses also show there are many areas unexplored in this study and provides scope for future research. Moreover, availability of more experts in this area may have helped to converge the findings of this study. It is suggested as a future research opportunity to explore the subject of Web3 from the perspective of industry experts from multiple industries and geographies adopting Web3/blockchain elements in their respective businesses.

9. Conclusion and limitations

Web3 adoption is expected to shape eCommerce business future and findings from this research shows a clear path and the application areas of Web3 concepts. While certain industries may have an inherent advantage due to the peer-to-peer nature of the business and have resulted in early adoption, the technological advancement through blockchains and smart contracts have resulted in entirely new business areas such as creator economy covering NFTs, DeFi using cryptocurrencies, new decentralized governance such as DAOs, and so on. It is important for eCommerce businesses and stakeholders to learn and apply these technologies in the backend as most successful businesses would evolve to adopt to Web3 from the current Web 2.0 technology stack. As the research finds, there are still evolving standards and similar adoption challenges in the industry which are actively been worked upon and researched. From large corporations to new startups will keep bringing changes in the overall outlook of Web3, but the benefits and overall defining features of Web3 such as decentralized control, public verifiable information, and ability to operate on transactions on the chains are going to stay and the benefits are going to improve (such as speed and cost of executing the transactions). It is hence imperative as a business leader and decision maker to understand these technological advancements and apply to their respective businesses.

Limited empirical research in Web3 is a major drawback while performing a detailed analysis on trends and opportunities Web3 bring in. This study used available academic research, industry reports, online published information from credible sources, and discussions with experts to derive the findings. Unavailability of multiple respondents to this study as expert respondents is another limitation of this study. Author acknowledges these limitations and there might be areas uncovered within each of the sections. However, the intention of this study is to provide business leaders and decision makers with an easy-to-use guide on Web3 technologies. The use-cases highlighted, and areas of research are all possible new research areas by its own which can be explored by other Web3 researchers.

Acknowledgements

Author would like to thank Vignesh Ramaswamy, CEO of Canvas.Space a Web3 platform supporting creator economy for the in-depth interview provided on his perspectives on eCommerce adoption in the Web3 space. Author would also like to thank his employer EXL Service (NASDAQ: EXLS) for supporting his initiatives in the Web3 space.

Author details

Sudeep Krishnan
EXL Service, Houston, USA

*Address all correspondence to: sudeepkrish@gmail.com

References

[1] Tanco CC. Merchants Getting Ready for Crypto. USA: Deliotte; 2022. Available from: https://www2.deloitte.com/content/dam/Deloitte/us/Documents/technology/us-cons-merchant-getting-ready-for-crypto.pdf. [Accessed: August 15, 2022]

[2] Almeida F, Santos JD, Monteiro JA. E-commerce business models in the context of web3. 0 paradigm. International Journal of Advanced Information Technology (IJAIT). 2014;**3**(6):1-12. DOI: 10.48550/arXiv.1401.6102

[3] Krishnan S, Pal D. Designing a distributed microfinance credit bureau system. In: Ashta A, Barnett B, Dayson K, Supka G, editors. Management Information Systems for Microfinance: Catalyzing Social Innovation for Competitive Advantage. Newcastle upon Tyne, UK: Cambridge Scholarship Publishing; 2015. pp. 300-319

[4] Liu Z, Xiang Y, Shi J, Gao P, Wang H, Xiao X, et al. Make Web3. 0 connected. IEEE Transactions on Dependable and Secure Computing. 2021;**19**(5):2965-2981. DOI: 10.1109/TDSC.2021.3079315

[5] Howerton JT. Service-oriented architecture and web 2.0. IT Professional. 2007;**9**(3):62-64. DOI: 10.1109/MITP.2007.54

[6] Wang Q, Li R, Wang Q, Chen S, Ryan M, Hardjono T. Exploring web3 from the view of blockchain. arXiv preprint. 2022. DOI: 10.48550/arXiv.2206.08821 [Preprint]

[7] Kumar P. Top 10 Decentralized Finance (DeFi) Use Cases. Chennai: Finextra; 2022. Available from: https://www.finextra.com/blogposting/21958/top-10-decentralized-finance-defi-use-cases. [Accessed: August 27, 2022]

[8] The Best Examples of DAOs Everyone Should Know About. 2022 Available from: https://www.forbes.com/sites/bernardmarr/2022/05/25/the-best-examples-of-daos-everyone-should-know-about/?sh=572cb77b40c3. [Accessed: August 27, 2022]

[9] Potts J, Rennie E. Web3 and the creative industries: How blockchains are reshaping business models. In: Cunningham S, Flew T, editors. A Research Agenda for Creative Industries. Northampton, MA, USA: Edward Elgar Publishing; 2019. pp. 93-111. DOI: 10.4337/9781788118583.00013

[10] Attaran M, Gunasekaran A. Blockchain for gaming. In: Sethi S, editor. Applications of Blockchain Technology in Business. New York, NY, USA: Springer; 2019. pp. 85-88. DOI: 10.1007/978-3-030-27798-7_12

[11] Takyar A. Web3 Use Cases and Applications. LeewayHertz; 2022. Available from: https://www.leewayhertz.com/web3-use-cases-and-applications/. [Accessed: October 22, 2022]

[12] Krotov V. The internet of things and new business opportunities. Business Horizons. 2017;**60**(6):831-841. DOI: 10.1016/j.bushor.2017.07.009

[13] Kovacova M, Horak J, Higgins M. Behavioral analytics, immersive technologies, and machine vision algorithms in the Web3-powered Metaverse world. Linguistic and Philosophical Investigations. 2022;**21**: 57-72. DOI: 10.22381/lpi2120224

[14] Non-fungible Token Market Size, Share & Trends Analysis Report by Type (Physical Asset, Digital Asset),

by Application (Collectibles, Art, Gaming), by End Use, by Region, and Segment Forecasts, 2022-2030. San Francisco, USA: Grand View Research; 2022. Available from: https://www.grandviewresearch.com/industry-analysis/non-fungible-token-market-report. [Accessed: August 27, 2022]

[15] Norvill R, Fiz B, State R, Cullen A. Standardising smart contracts: Automatically inferring ERC standards. In: Proceedings of IEEE International Conference on Blockchain and Cryptocurrency (ICBC). Seoul, Korea (South): IEEE; 2019. pp. 192-195

[16] The Web3 Decentralization Debate Is Focused on the Wrong Question. 2022 Available from: https://www.wired.com/story/web3-blockchain-decentralization-governance/. [Accessed: October 22, 2022]

[17] Li J, Li N, Peng J, Cui H, Wu Z. Energy consumption of cryptocurrency mining: A study of electricity consumption in mining cryptocurrencies. Energy. 2019;**168**:160-168. DOI: 10.1016/j.energy.2018.11.046

[18] Monrat AA, Schelén O, Andersson K. A survey of blockchain from the perspectives of applications, challenges, and opportunities. IEEE Access. 2019;**7**:117134-117151. DOI: 10.1109/ACCESS.2019.2936094

[19] Oyman M, Bal D, Ozer S. Extending the technology acceptance model to explain how perceived augmented reality affects consumers' perceptions. Computers in Human Behavior. 2022;**128**:107127. DOI: 10.1016/j.chb.2021.107127

[20] Peltoniemi M, Vuori E. Business ecosystem as the new approach to complex adaptive business environments. In: Proceedings of eBusiness Research Forum Sep 22, 2004. Tampere, Finland: Frontiers of e-Business Research; 2004. pp. 267-281

Chapter 12

Fashion-Strategizing Leadership in Sports

Anna Sergeevna Khvorostyanaya

Abstract

Technology today plays a pivotal role in shaping societies, economies, and personal lives. The intersection of fashion and technology in the sports industry has led to innovations that enhance performance, safety, and style. The fashion industry as a vivid representation of the creative economy has limitless potential for meeting the major challenges of technological superiority in different industries. The sports industry has long been a championship of more than just a person's talent, but also the right strategy application to ensure victory. Technology transfer can be an effective tool for cooperation between the fashion and sports industries. This article proposes a strategic model for the creation of a technology transfer center adapted to the needs of sports. The basis of strategic conceptualization has become the strategy theory and methodology of strategizing developed by Foreign Member of the Russian Academy of Sciences (Life-time), Dr. Sc. (Econ.) Vladimir L. Kvint and fashion-strategizing process methodology. The methods of induction and deduction, synthesis and analysis were used in the study. Further research could be devoted to assessing the effectiveness of such center. The practical significance of the study is related to the solution's implementation possibility proposed by the author in science and technology policy.

Keywords: strategy, fashion-strategizing process, sports industry, fashion industry, technology transfer

1. Introduction

The creative economy development is now a major global trend. In essence, the worlds of sport and fashion constantly influence each other, with trends from one often migrating to the other, creating a dynamic and ever-evolving relationship. Sport and fashion have a long intertwined history. Brands often create exclusive clothing lines or accessories for major sporting events. Sports celebrities as fashion icons launch clothing lines or become the face of major fashion campaigns. Sportswear as a fashionable style is on the rise. The materials used in sportswear have influenced mainstream fashion due to their comfort and utility. Also, many sports brands collaborate with high-end designers or celebrities.

In an era of technological superiority, the issue of utilizing the industrial potential of the fashion industry to address the sports industry issues comes to the forefront.

2. The fashion industry complex

The fashion industry is a collection of enterprises engaged in the development, production, and sale of clothing, shoes, and various accessories. Unlike other production segments of the market, fashion industry enterprises have a close connection with the sociocultural aspect of the development of modern society, since the products of such enterprises emphasize the social status of consumers, their esthetic tastes and preferences, cultural differences, and many other social aspects of life. The fashion industry is one of the few branches of the modern economy that relies on the socio-value aspect of consumption, which should be understood as a set of ways and methods of self-expression (representation) of a person through the acquisition and use of specific categories of goods.

The fashion industry is a vivid example of creative economy development that is imbued with the individual talent imagination, design vision, as well as strict strategy development and implementation and strong economic concept. Through the years, various forms and methods of strategic and brand management have been created. This branch of economy is specific; it differs from the traditional ones by its peculiarities of functioning and attracting investments. Today, economic activity in this segment of the market is characterized by massiveness. It has all the properties of economic objects: product and regional diversification, mergers and acquisitions, large volumes of investment, complex production and technological process, and active participation in the stock market [1]. Fashion economy is a set of economic tools used in conjunction with creativity to create new forms and works, as well as to translate creative images and ideas into real products, form public opinion and demand for them, and organize advertising campaigns that promote their further purchase. In the modern world, fashion has become an object of commercial activity; it is involved in the market economy mechanism: a special economic mechanism of creation and implementation of new fashion concepts is developed, including the system of protection of creative ideas, pricing principles, organization of work of creative teams and their interaction, and sales commercial structures. There is no doubt that today, the place and role of this industry is increasing, overtaking other sectors of the economy. It is the industry that has a significant impact on the global textile and apparel industry. The largest national markets are in America, France, UK, and Germany. Entire faculties of such famous educational institutions such as The Central Saint Martins College, The London College of Fashion, The University for the Creative Arts, and The Sotheby's Institute of Art are dedicated to this industry [1].

All of the aforementioned is a solid testament of the increasing role and importance of the fashion industry in the global economy. That is why the fashion industry has long been the research object of many scholars around the world.

The scientific discourse about the fashion industry is quite extensive. Thus, there is a lot of research on the etymological and philosophical side of the fashion industry [2, 3], about the cultural phenomenon [4] and social interactions of people through style [5, 6]. With the increasing complexity of economic processes, the emerging markets phenomenon occurrence [7], the business consolidation, the development of a marketing communications system [8], and approaches to long-term consumer attention retention, the scientific discourse about the fashion industry has moved into the plane of analyzing long-term competitive advantages. The issues of brand management [9] and other intangible assets began to play a vital role. The transformation of the economy toward the development of the ability to use the economic potential of a person's creativity has led to the rapid creative economy establishment. The fashion industry has a wide range of influence on different levels—state policy in the field of solving national security, sectoral issues, or companies competitiveness due to the relevant and fashionable things provision.

Today, the fashion industry is inextricably responding to environmental challenges, which makes the ESG-agenda extremely relevant for further strategic development. Transformations also concern modern consumers—the ethical side comes to the prime focus. In this regard, many corporate players are revising their strategic documents in the direction of greening business processes. High-quality innovations as a source of solving the issues of reducing the external environment negative impact as well as industry superiority are becoming key success factors in highly competitive market.

The sports industry plays a significant role in society as it is a multibillion dollar industry, providing jobs, forming country image and reputation, driving tourism, and generating revenue for host cities. Sports has the ability to unite people from diverse backgrounds despite its excessive politicization in recent times. Global sporting events have an impact on the fashion industry companies' strategy development. For example, the Olympic Games stimulate the marketing of a healthy lifestyle as well as the sale of sportswear, accessoriess and related products. The Olympic Games helps to build long-term relationships with customers of global brands through sponsorship relationships and thoughtful advertising campaigns that influence consumer loyalty, increasing brand awareness. The economic efficiency of sporting events plays an important role—it is important to make the right strategic decisions, because most sports organizations do not have the time or budget for a long search for solutions to problems and concentration of resources.

However, there is a lack of systematic research in the field of technology cooperation between fashion industry and the sport industry. This determined the purpose of this study.

3. Materials and methods

The rapid pace of globalization of the world economy has led in recent years to a sharp increase in competition in almost all industries and spheres of activity. Companies are constantly searching for new approaches to the formation of competitive advantages that can ensure stable socioeconomic development, taking into account the influencing factors of the external and internal environment and current and promising threats and opportunities.

Sectoral strategies are the potential for economic development. Business strategy allows you to respond in a timely manner to ongoing or expected changes, to identify the most successful combinations of resources to achieve strategic goals. The development and achievement of high results in sports and obtaining financial profit become impossible without the use of a strategic approach.

In the modern world, strategy is the basic tool for the stable and effective development of any economic system. The development of organizations in the sports and fashion industries should be based on a strategic approach, which is the result of a systematic analysis of the external and internal environment of the facility, the correct determination of competitive advantages and strategic priorities, and setting strategic goals.

The development of an effective strategy is impossible without the presence of a specific methodological apparatus, the use of which will minimize many types of risks, to choose the correct tactics taking into account the impact of external and internal factors and apply effective tools to adapt to changing market conditions.

This article applies the strategy theory and methodology of strategizing [10, 11] developed by Dr. Vladimir Kvint and fashion-strategizing process methodology [12]. Dr. Vladimir Kvint in his works offers a unique methodological model of strategizing, the main advantage of which is adaptation to any external conditions. Dr. Vladimir Kvint emphasizes that there is a certain relationship between forecasting, strategizing, and planning. Strategy development is impossible without an analysis of global, regional, and industry development trends, on the basis of which a long-term forecast is made, which later acts as a basic strategic document for defining the mission, vision, strategic goals, and objectives and their corresponding strategic priorities.

Despite the fact that the model includes a large number of individual stages, it allows to form all the necessary strategic documents of a fashion industry enterprise and determine key strategic priorities for the development of the enterprise, based on existing resource constraints and taking into account current opportunities and threats of the external environment.

At the first stage of the fashion-strategizing process methodology [1], fashion industry enterprises should conduct a thorough analysis of global and regional trends in the environmental field. Special attention at this stage should be paid to the study of industry reports, materials of industry experts, and up-to-date statistics of leading companies in the industry. This will allow to determine which areas of development in the medium and long-term will be the highest priority for the entire industry. Then, it will allow the company to correctly place emphasis points in the strategic priorities in the future. For the fashion industry, special attention should be paid to updating the used and promising sales channels, communication methods with the consumer audience, the possibility of organizing new supply chains of raw materials, and the development and implementation of innovative technologies that can positively affect both the optimization of production capacities and create the opportunity to reduce production costs, which ultimately will optimize the policy-selling prices and create a competitive price advantage.

Based on the analysis and the forecast, the fashion industry company can begin to develop the main strategic documents—the mission and strategic vision. The mission in accordance with the strategy theory of Dr. Vladimir Kvint is the general message of the company's functioning in the market and, most importantly, what benefits the company brings to society. The mission is based on the individual and social values of a particular organization and emphasizes how the subject achieves a qualitative improvement in life.

Strategic vision is philosophy and ideology. It is a system of strategic priorities and ensuring their implementation of the competitive advantages of a particular organization operating in a competitive environment. Examples of such competitive advantages in the industry can be the following:

- Access to unique technologies for processing raw materials and materials;
- High level of brand awareness;
- Financial stability;

- Flexible organizational structure;

- Competitive creative potential of human resources, and so forth.

The effective use of these advantages through the prism of formulated strategic priorities allows successful fashion industry enterprises to achieve success both in a stable market condition and in emergency periods. Over the past few years, the fashion industry has become one of the most dynamically developing industries, which is based on a combination of elements of the creative economy, technological, and digital achievements.

Leadership as one of the management system main elements plays a crucial role in long-term development. According to Dr. Vladimir Kvint, the methodology identifies five main elements necessary for the strategic management system formation: strategic leadership; organizational structure senior management, managers and administrative staff; strategic decision-making process; management tools, infrastructure and strategic information technology. Strategic leaders with strategic thinking question old views and established paradigms, encourage the creation of new perspectives and ways of action, and are always in a new ideas search and strategic opportunities monitoring. This kind of leaders who are able to develop and implement a strategy of fundamentally new forefront opportunities that will increase the commercial efficiency of services and investment projects. Modern leaders nowadays are focused on the technological sovereignty establishment.

4. Technological leadership

The new era is characterized by a significant acceleration of goods, services, and new emerging markets life cycles. At the same time, in essence, the only way for businesses to "keep up" with the market is to accelerate the new markets development and the new products and services launch. Technology transfer allows long-term development of intellectual potential and scientific reserve of subjects of economic activity [13]. That is why in the fashion industry, technology transfer is playing an increasingly prominent role in terms of competitiveness strengthening. In the context of changing geopolitical reality as well as new challenges the role of new technological solutions, innovative projects and ideas are increasing. All subjects of economic activity are interested in innovations as they are long-term competitive advantages that open unlimited strategic opportunities. Large industrial companies build their strategic leadership on the advanced technological base, while small and medium-sized businesses automate production and increase the maturity of their business processes.

For example, many companies adapt technological solutions based on the use of AR/VR technologies, which create the opportunity to introduce digital fitting rooms with augmented reality, where the consumer, by combining their own photos and digital clothing models, can try on. Other manufacturers are introducing innovative digital tools for self-designing clothes, which creates a personalized approach to customer service. The issues of using advanced technologies in the fashion industry have been discussed in the scientific community for many years. So, for example, the work of Chinese researchers notes that technological innovations, including in the field of technologies for creating new materials, can be used to create clothes and shoes in demand by consumers [14]. The most important opportunity for the production and marketing enterprises of the fashion industry in emerging markets is currently the active introduction of various digital technologies that reduce production costs and provide additional coverage to the consumer buyer audience.

The modern sport is an absolute high-achievement industry, where the natural athletes' talents, the infrastructure maturity, the pharmaceutical industry benefits, the management approaches combination, and long-run motivation tools come together. Tailored suit with specific characteristics can provide better sliding performance and better air permeability—it all affects the end result in sport. For example, for companies producing apparel and related equipment, the Olympics Games are often a technological challenge. SPEEDO's LZR Racer swimsuits are believed to have had a positive impact on athletic performance—98% of the medals at the Olympics were won by athletes wearing the LZR suit, including renowned swimmer Michael Phelps. The swimsuit, developed in conjunction with NASA, consists of extremely lightweight LZR Pulse fabric that is ultrasonically welded together. NASA estimates that the ultrasonic seam welding process helped reduce drag by 6% [15].

5. Strategizing process of a fashion technology center for sports industries necessity

Stimulating industrial prosperity requires remodeling and implementing new cooperative chains to grow a new national market and satisfy consumer preferences.

The specialized center may be created to solve technological problems for creating excellence in athlete outfitting by light industry and fashion industry enterprises. The domestic light industry and fashion industry can create such a fashion technology center (FTC).

The FTC mission is to commercialize and promote light industry and fashion industry developments for the sports field as well as to create a unified environment for technology transfer and cooperation facilitation.

The strategic key functions of such a FTC could be:

- Formation of a consortium of organizations holding technologies or research innovation projects for sports industry;
- Building a standardized project management system for all members of the consortium focused on technology transfer for sports industry;
- Creation of high-quality and accessible services to facilitate the entry of domestic technologies into the market;
- Development of a system of interaction between the stakeholders to meet the interests.

According to the aforementioned methodology, hereinafter strategic priorities are presented linked with relevant strategic goals system (**Table 1**).

Given the strategic trend of digitalization and its impact on management decision support tools, an industry-specific digital platform is required. Digital platform as a decision support system can establish continuous knowledge transfer.

Strategic priority 1	Creation of a fashion technology center	Goal 1 Formation of the FTC structure Goal 2 Formation of a strategic brand
Strategic priority 2	Creation of a digital platform for sectoral knowledge and experience transfer	Goal 1 Creation of a digital platform Goal 2 Formation of the platform's strategic brand Goal 3 Control and monitoring of the digital platform development
Strategic priority 3	Creating a pool of strategic labor resources	Goal 1 Organization of a talent recruitment system Goal 2 Organization of long-run motivation system

Table 1.
The FTC strategic priorities system.

A new type of employees should be formed; basic skills and competencies should be revised. An industry professional in the fashion industry, engaged in fashion and light industry strategizing, fashion strategist, should understand the mechanisms of technology and innovation transfer in sports.

6. Conclusion

Fashion strategy as a basis for long-term development of light industry and fashion enterprises opens new horizons of activity, enhances the synergetic effect of all factors of production, and emphasizes the DNA of cultural and creative industries—unique intangible assets expressed in creativity. Successful entrepreneurship in this sphere requires the ability to adapt commercial products to the interests and values of the target audience, to identify strategic trends and patterns, and to increase or create your competitive advantages. The results of intellectual activity as intangible assets play a significant role in the formation of additional sources of income for companies.

The fashion industry can help address the challenges of athlete excellence by creating unique technological apparel items. One of the key solutions for the fashion and sports industries to cooperate could be the creation of a unique technology transfer center.

Author details

Anna Sergeevna Khvorostyanaya[1,2]

1 Center for Strategic Studies at Lomonosov Moscow State University' Institute of Mathematical Research of Complex Systems, Moscow, Russia

2 Economic and Financial Strategy Department at Lomonosov Moscow State University' Moscow School of Economics, Moscow, Russia

*Address all correspondence to: khvorostyanayaas@gmail.com

References

[1] Khvorostyanaya A. Strategizing the Fashion Industry: Theory and Practice. Saint Petersburg: North-Western Institute of Management. Branch of RANEPA; 2021. p. 272. (Strategist Library). (In Russ.)

[2] Baudrillard J. The Consumer Society, Trans. JP Mayer. London: Sage Publication; 1970

[3] Baudrillard J. Simulations, Trans. Paul Foss, Paul Patton and Philip Beitchman. New York: Semiotext[e]; 1983

[4] Veblen T. The Theory of the Leisure Class: An Economic Study of Institutions. New York: MacMillan; 1899

[5] Simmel G. The metropolis and mental life. In: Wolff KH, editor. The Sociology of Georg Simmel. New York: The Free Press; 1950. pp. 409-424

[6] Blumer H. Fashion: From class differentiation to collective selection. The Sociological Quarterly. 1969;**10**(3):275-291. DOI: 10.1111/j.1533-8525.1969.tb01292.x

[7] Kvint V. Strategy for The Global Market: Theory and Practical Applications. New York: Routledge Taylor and Francis Group; 2015. p. 548. DOI: 10.4324/9781315709314

[8] Kapferer J-N. The New Strategic Brand Management: Advanced Insights and Strategic Thinking. 5th ed. London: Kogan Page; 2012. p. 492. Available from: http://www.123library.org/book_details/?id=94330 [Retrieved: October 2, 2023]

[9] Kotler P. Kotler on...... In: Management Decision. 1991;**29**:2. DOI: 10.1108/00251749110004961

[10] Kvint V. The Concept of Strategizing. Kemerovo: Kemerovo State University; 2020. p. 170. DOI: 10.21603/978-5-8353-2562-7

[11] Kvint V. Strategizing: Theory and Practice. Tashkent: TASVIR; 2021. p. 160

[12] Khvorostyanaya A. Using the methodology of financial strategy in asset management of the creative economy. Economics and Management. 2017;**8**:142

[13] Pyataeva O, Ustinova L, Evdokimova M, Khvorostyanaya A, Gavrilyuk A. Digitalization of technology transfer for high-technology products. In: Gibadullin A, editors. Digital and Information Technologies in Economics and Management. DITEM 2021. Lecture Notes in Networks and Systems. Vol. 432. Cham: Springer; 2022. DOI: 10.1007/978-3-030-97730-6_2

[14] Qiu C, Hu Y. The research and development of the future fashion design. American International Journal of Contemporary Research. 2014;**4**(12):126-130

[15] Record Breaking Benefits [Internet]. 2012. Available from: https://www.nasa.gov/offices/oct/home/tech_record_breaking.html [Accessed: September 08, 2023]

Chapter 13

The Future of Education: Writing Exams in the Metaverse at South African Universities

Bonginkosi A. Thango

Abstract

The advent of the Metaverse has revolutionized education, particularly in the realm of assessment. This chapter explores the future of education and the impact of the Metaverse on assessment, with a specific focus on writing exams in South African universities. It begins by defining the Metaverse and its role in education. The advantages of utilizing the Metaverse for exam writing, such as creating immersive environments that foster active learning, are examined. Additionally, the potential for reducing costs associated with traditional exam administration is explored. The chapter also delves into the challenges of writing exams in the Metaverse. Issues of accessibility and equity, including the need for reliable and affordable internet access for all students, are discussed. Privacy and data security concerns are examined, highlighting the importance of implementing safeguards to protect student information. Furthermore, the chapter discusses the skills and competencies required for writing exams in the Metaverse. It emphasizes the significance of digital literacy, proficiency, and the adaptability of educators to new technologies and teaching methodologies. Universities play a crucial role in preparing students for the Metaverse, promoting digital citizenship skills and ethical behaviour online.

Keywords: metaverse, education, assessment, writing exams, South African universities

1. Introduction

The concept of the Metaverse has been gaining increasing attention in recent years, particularly in the fields of gaming and virtual reality [1, 2]. However, the potential of the Metaverse extends far beyond entertainment, and it has the potential to transform the way education and assessment is approached. In this section, the definition of the Metaverse, its role in education, and the potential benefits it can bring to the learning experience is discussed.

1.1 Defining the metaverse

The Metaverse is a term that describes a collective virtual shared space where users can interact with a computer-generated environment and other users in real-time [3].

The Metaverse is not limited to any specific platform, but it includes a wide range of technologies, such as virtual and augmented reality, 3D modeling, artificial intelligence, and blockchain [1]. The term was first introduced in Neal Stephenson's 1992 novel "Snow Crash" and has since been used to describe the idea of a shared online universe. The Metaverse represents a significant evolution in the concept of the internet, moving from a collection of static web pages to an interactive, immersive, and dynamic shared space. In the Metaverse, users can create and customize avatars, explore virtual environments, and interact with other users in real-time. The Metaverse has already begun to impact various industries, including gaming, entertainment, social media, and e-commerce. However, the Metaverse has also shown potential in the field of education.

1.2 The role of the metaverse in education

The Metaverse can have a significant impact on education, particularly in the realm of assessment. The traditional model of assessment, which typically involves written exams or essays, can be limiting in terms of accurately assessing a student's understanding and mastery of a subject. The Metaverse provides an opportunity to create immersive and interactive environments that promote active learning and encourage students to demonstrate their knowledge in real-time. The Metaverse can also help to reduce the costs associated with traditional assessment practices. Physical exam venues and paper-based exams can be expensive to administer, and the Metaverse provides a potential solution to this problem. Additionally, the Metaverse can help to level the playing field for students by providing equal access to assessments, regardless of their location or economic background [4]. An example of a class held in metaverse by a school in Tokyo is illustrated (**Figure 1**).

1.3 Benefits of using the metaverse in education

There are several benefits to using the Metaverse in education, including the following:

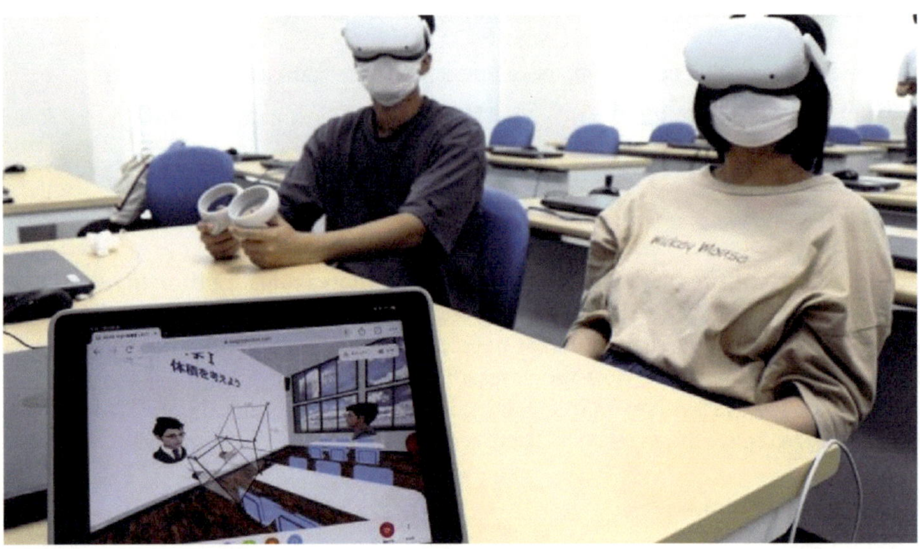

Figure 1.
Class in Metaverse [5].

1. *Increased engagement and motivation:* The Metaverse can create an immersive and engaging environment that motivates students to learn and actively participate in the learning process [6].

2. *Real-time feedback:* The Metaverse provides an opportunity for real-time feedback, which can help students to identify areas where they need to improve and adjust their learning strategies accordingly [1].

3. *Customizable learning environments:* The Metaverse allows for the creation of customizable learning environments that cater to different learning styles and preferences [4].

4. *Access to a wider range of resources:* The Metaverse provides access to a wider range of resources, including virtual libraries, museums, and galleries, which can enhance the learning experience [2].

5. *Opportunity for collaboration:* The Metaverse provides an opportunity for students to collaborate with each other, regardless of their physical location, which can enhance the learning experience and promote social interaction [3].

As with any emerging technology, there are challenges to be addressed when implementing the Metaverse in education. These challenges include ensuring the security and privacy of student data, ensuring that assessments are valid and reliable, and addressing issues related to access and connectivity. However, with proper planning and implementation, the Metaverse has the potential to revolutionize the way education and assessment is approached.

In the following sections, how the Metaverse can be used in education, including its potential applications in assessment, teaching, and learning will explored in more detail. Some of the challenges associated with implementing the Metaverse in education and provide strategies for addressing these challenges will also be examined. Finally, the implications of the Metaverse for the future of education and what steps need to be taken to ensure that this technology is used in an ethical and equitable manner will be discuss.

2. The advantages of writing exams in the metaverse at South African Universities

The Metaverse is an emerging technology that has the potential to transform the way South African universities approach exam writing and assessment. By creating immersive and interactive environments, the Metaverse can provide students with a more engaging and personalized learning experience. Additionally, the Metaverse can help to reduce the costs and inequalities associated with traditional assessment practices by providing equal access to assessments regardless of location or economic background. This section will explore the advantages of writing exams in the Metaverse at South African universities.

2.1 Advantages of writing exams in the metaverse

1. *Improved accessibility and flexibility:* One of the key advantages of writing exams in the Metaverse is the increased accessibility and flexibility it provides. Students

can take exams from anywhere with an internet connection, eliminating the need to travel to physical exam centers. This is particularly beneficial for students in rural areas or those with disabilities who may struggle to travel to exam centers. Additionally, the Metaverse can provide flexibility in terms of exam scheduling, allowing students to take exams at a time that suits them best.

2. *Enhanced security and authenticity:* The Metaverse can provide enhanced security and authenticity in exam writing by incorporating biometric identification and real-time monitoring. This can help to prevent cheating and ensure that exam results are accurate and reliable.

3. *Personalized learning experience:* The Metaverse can provide a personalized learning experience by allowing students to engage with content in a more interactive and immersive way. This can help to improve understanding and retention of course material, leading to better exam results.

4. *Reduced costs and environmental impact:* Writing exams in the Metaverse can help to reduce the costs and environmental impact associated with traditional exam writing practices (see **Table 1**). It eliminates the need for physical exam centres, reduces the use of paper and printing, and can help to reduce the costs of exam administration.

2.2 Case study examples

1. *University of Cape Town:* The University of Cape Town has implemented the use of the Metaverse in exam writing for their law students. By using a virtual reality platform, students are able to simulate real-life legal scenarios and apply their knowledge to solve problems. This has led to improved engagement and understanding of course material, resulting in better exam results [7].

2. *University of Pretoria:* The University of Pretoria has incorporated the use of biometric identification in their Metaverse exam writing process. This ensures that students are accurately identified and prevents cheating, leading to more reliable exam results.

Table 1 shows the estimated costs of traditional exam writing practices compared to the estimated costs of using the Metaverse for exam writing for a class of 100 electrical engineering students at a South African university. The traditional exam

Exam writing costs	Traditional	Metaverse
Staff salaries	R20,000	R10,000
Ink and paper	R2,000	R1,000
Biometric scanning	R0	R5,000
Total cost	R22,000	R16,000

Table 1.
Costs example for a class of 100 electrical engineering students writing an exam at a South African University.

writing costs include staff salaries and ink and paper costs, while the Metaverse exam writing costs include biometric scanning in addition to staff salaries. The total cost for traditional exam writing is estimated to be R22,000, while the total cost for Metaverse exam writing is estimated to be R16,000. This represents a cost savings of R6,000 by using the Metaverse for exam writing.

The Metaverse provides numerous advantages for writing exams at South African universities. These advantages include improved accessibility and flexibility, enhanced security and authenticity, personalized learning experience, and reduced costs and environmental impact. By incorporating the use of the Metaverse in exam writing, South African universities can provide students with a more engaging and efficient learning experience, leading to improved exam results and ultimately, better career prospects.

3. Reducing costs and enhancing engagement through immersive environments

As the world becomes more connected and technology advances, educational institutions are seeking ways to improve their offerings and create more engaging experiences for students. One way to do this is through the use of immersive environments, such as virtual reality and augmented reality. These environments allow students to learn in a more interactive and engaging way, while also reducing costs for institutions. In this section, the advantages of immersive environments for education and provide case study examples of their successful implementation will be explored. The cost savings associated with immersive environments and how they can benefit educational institutions will also be examined.

3.1 Advantages of immersive environments for education

Immersive environments offer many advantages for education. They provide a way for students to learn in a more interactive and engaging way, which can improve their understanding and retention of information. For example, virtual reality environments can simulate real-world scenarios and allow students to practice skills in a safe and controlled environment. This is particularly useful for fields such as medicine and engineering, where hands-on experience is essential.

Immersive environments can also enhance collaboration and communication among students. In virtual reality environments, students can interact with each other as avatars, which can break down barriers and increase participation. This is particularly useful for students who may be hesitant to speak up in traditional classroom settings.

Finally, immersive environments can provide cost savings for educational institutions. By reducing the need for physical materials and resources, such as textbooks and laboratory equipment, institutions can save money while still providing high-quality education. Additionally, immersive environments can reduce the costs associated with travel and accommodation for students attending remote campuses or taking distance learning courses.

3.2 Case study examples

1. Several educational institutions have successfully implemented immersive environments to enhance their offerings and reduce costs. One example is the

University of Central Florida, which has implemented a virtual reality simulation for nursing students. The simulation allows students to practice clinical skills, such as administering medication, in a virtual hospital environment. This has reduced the need for expensive medical equipment and improved student outcomes [8].

2. Another example is the University of Melbourne, which has implemented a virtual reality classroom for language learning. The classroom simulates real-world environments, such as a restaurant or a market, allowing students to practice language skills in context. This has improved engagement and retention among language learners [9].

3.3 Cost savings associated with immersive environments

Immersive environments can provide cost savings for educational institutions in several ways. By reducing the need for physical materials and resources, such as textbooks and laboratory equipment, institutions can save money while still providing high-quality education. Additionally, immersive environments can reduce the costs associated with travel and accommodation for students attending remote campuses or taking distance learning courses.

For example, the University of Phoenix has implemented a virtual reality classroom for its business courses. This has reduced the need for physical classroom space and has allowed the institution to reach a wider audience of students. The University estimates that it has saved $2.5 million in classroom costs alone [10].

Immersive environments offer many advantages for education, including improved engagement and retention, enhanced collaboration and communication, and cost savings for institutions. Educational institutions can implement immersive environments in a variety of ways, from virtual reality simulations to augmented reality classrooms. By embracing these technologies, institutions can provide high-quality education to more students while reducing costs and enhancing the overall learning experience.

4. Challenges and considerations for writing exams in the metaverse

The Metaverse has revolutionized the way students learn and interact with each other, but it is not without its challenges. This section explores the challenges and considerations that universities in South Africa must consider when implementing the use of Metaverse technology for exam writing. The section examines issues such as student readiness, the need for appropriate hardware and software, security and privacy, and the role of faculty in ensuring a successful transition. The section concludes by offering solutions to these challenges and making recommendations for a smooth transition to the Metaverse exam writing environment.

Student readiness: One of the primary challenges in implementing Metaverse technology for exam writing is ensuring that students are ready for the transition. While many students are tech-savvy and comfortable with virtual environments, some may struggle to adapt to the new format. It is essential to provide students with training and support to help them navigate the Metaverse exam writing environment. Universities must provide students with access to the necessary hardware and software, as well as offer orientation sessions, tutorials, and technical support.

Hardware and software: Another critical consideration is the hardware and software required to run Metaverse exams. The Metaverse requires high-end graphics and processing power, which may not be available on all devices. Universities must ensure that students have access to appropriate hardware and software, which can be a significant expense. The cost of hardware and software must be weighed against the benefits of using the Metaverse for exam writing.

Security and privacy: Security and privacy are critical considerations when implementing the Metaverse for exam writing. The Metaverse is vulnerable to hacking, data breaches, and other security threats. Universities must ensure that appropriate security measures are in place to protect student data and prevent cheating. Universities must also comply with data protection regulations and ensure that student privacy is protected.

Role of faculty: The faculty plays a crucial role in ensuring a successful transition to the Metaverse exam writing environment. Faculty members must be trained to use the Metaverse and provide support to students during the exam writing process. The faculty must also ensure that the exam content is appropriate for the Metaverse environment and that the exams are fair and accurately reflect the course material.

The Metaverse represents a significant advancement in the way students learn and interact with each other. However, implementing the use of the Metaverse for exam writing is not without its challenges. Universities must consider issues such as student readiness, hardware and software requirements, security and privacy, and the role of faculty in ensuring a smooth transition. By addressing these challenges and providing appropriate support, universities can successfully implement the use of the Metaverse for exam writing and enhance the learning experience for their students.

5. Ensuring accessibility and equity for all students

Accessibility and equity in education are fundamental values that ensure that every student has an equal opportunity to succeed regardless of their background or disability. With the emergence of new technologies, including the Metaverse, universities have a unique opportunity to address accessibility and equity issues. However, there are several challenges that universities need to overcome to ensure that all students have equal access to education. This section will explore the challenges and considerations for ensuring accessibility and equity for all students in the Metaverse.

Accessibility challenges: Accessibility challenges in the Metaverse arise due to the differences in hardware and software requirements for accessing the platform. The Metaverse requires a high-speed internet connection and powerful computing devices, which may not be accessible to all students, especially those from low-income backgrounds. Additionally, students with disabilities may require specialized equipment or software to access the platform, which can further widen the accessibility gap. To address these challenges, universities can provide equipment loan programs, offer virtual desktop infrastructure, and ensure that their Metaverse platform is accessible to students with disabilities.

Equity challenges: Equity challenges in the Metaverse arise due to the potential for bias in the design of virtual environments. For example, virtual environments may not accurately represent the cultural, ethnic, or racial diversity of the student population, leading to feelings of exclusion and disengagement. Additionally, students from marginalized groups may not have the same access to technological resources as their peers, leading to further disparities in educational outcomes. Universities can address these challenges by involving diverse students in the design and development of virtual environments, ensuring that the platform is culturally responsive and inclusive, and providing targeted support to students from marginalized backgrounds.

The Metaverse has the potential to transform education by improving accessibility and equity for all students. However, to ensure that this potential is realized, universities need to address the accessibility and equity challenges that arise in virtual environments. By providing equipment loan programs, involving diverse students in the design of virtual environments, and providing targeted support services, universities can ensure that all students have equal access to education in the Metaverse.

6. Protecting student privacy and security: safeguards for metaverse exams

With the increasing use of the Metaverse for conducting exams in universities, it is essential to ensure the privacy and security of students' information. Metaverse exams pose unique challenges to protecting student privacy and security, as students' personal data is stored in the cloud and accessed by multiple parties. This section will explore the challenges and considerations for protecting student privacy and security in the Metaverse.

Challenges: The challenges in protecting student privacy and security in the Metaverse arise from the collection, storage, and sharing of student data. Students' personal data, including their names, identification numbers, and exam answers, are stored in the cloud, accessible to multiple parties involved in the exam process, including the university, the Metaverse platform provider, and the exam proctors. Additionally, as the Metaverse is a new technology, there are no established guidelines or regulations to govern the use of student data in virtual environments.

Considerations: To address the challenges of protecting student privacy and security, universities must take several considerations. These considerations include:

1. *Data protection:* Universities must ensure that student data is encrypted and stored securely to prevent unauthorized access.

2. *Data access:* Universities must limit access to student data to authorized personnel only, such as exam proctors and administrators.

3. *User authentication:* Universities must implement user authentication measures, such as two-factor authentication, to ensure that only authorized users can access student data.

4. *Privacy policies:* Universities must have clear and concise privacy policies that outline how student data is collected, used, and shared.

Case study examples: The University of Oxford in the United Kingdom implemented a Metaverse platform for their final exams to protect student privacy and security. To address the privacy and security concerns, the university implemented a data protection policy that required all student data to be encrypted and stored securely. The university also limited access to student data to authorized personnel only and implemented user authentication measures, such as two-factor authentication, to prevent unauthorized access [11–14].

Protecting student privacy and security is crucial when conducting exams in the Metaverse. Universities must take several considerations to address the challenges posed by the collection, storage, and sharing of student data. By implementing data protection policies, limiting access to student data, implementing user authentication measures, and having clear and concise privacy policies, universities can ensure that student data is protected and secure in the Metaverse.

7. Developing the skills and competencies for writing exams in the metaverse

As universities increasingly adopt the Metaverse for conducting exams, students must develop the skills and competencies needed to navigate and succeed in this virtual environment. Writing exams in the Metaverse requires a range of skills and competencies, including digital literacy, adaptability, critical thinking, and problem-solving. This section will explore the skills and competencies needed for writing exams in the Metaverse and how universities can develop and enhance these skills in their students. Skills and Competencies:

1. *Digital literacy:* Writing exams in the Metaverse requires students to have a strong foundation in digital literacy. Students must be proficient in using various software and platforms, including the Metaverse platform, to navigate the virtual environment and complete their exams.

2. *Adaptability:* The Metaverse is a dynamic and constantly evolving environment, and students must be adaptable to changes in the platform and exam processes. Students must be able to adapt quickly to new challenges and environments to succeed in the Metaverse.

3. *Critical thinking:* Writing exams in the Metaverse requires students to think critically and apply their knowledge in novel situations. Students must be able to analyze and evaluate complex information, make informed decisions, and solve problems in real-time.

4. *Time management:* Writing exams in the Metaverse requires students to manage their time effectively. Students must be able to balance their exam-taking responsibilities with other academic and personal commitments.

Developing and enhancing skills: To develop and enhance the skills and competencies needed for writing exams in the Metaverse, universities must take several measures. These measures include:

1. *Training and education:* Universities must provide training and education on digital literacy, adaptability, critical thinking, and time management skills. Training can take the form of workshops, tutorials, and online resources.

2. *Practice and simulation:* Universities can provide students with opportunities to practice writing exams in the Metaverse through simulations and mock exams.

This practice can help students develop and enhance their skills and competencies.

3. *Feedback and support:* Universities must provide students with feedback and support to help them identify areas for improvement and develop strategies to enhance their skills and competencies.

Writing exams in the Metaverse requires a range of skills and competencies, including digital literacy, adaptability, critical thinking, and time management. Universities must take several measures, such as training and education, practice and simulation, and feedback and support, to develop and enhance these skills in their students. By providing students with the necessary skills and competencies, universities can ensure that students are prepared to succeed in the virtual environment of the Metaverse.

8. The role of universities in preparing students for the metaverse

The Metaverse, a virtual world where individuals interact with each other in a three-dimensional environment, is transforming the way of learning and working. With advancements in technology, the Metaverse is becoming increasingly popular, and it is crucial for universities to prepare students for this new digital frontier. This section will discuss the role of universities in preparing students for the Metaverse, including the skills and competencies necessary for success in this environment.

The importance of Metaverse skills: As more industries begin to embrace the Metaverse, students with skills in this area will have a significant advantage in the job market. The skills needed for the Metaverse go beyond technical knowledge and include skills such as creativity, collaboration, communication, and critical thinking. Universities must provide students with opportunities to develop these skills and prepare them for a future where Metaverse skills are in high demand.

Examples of university Metaverse preparation: Many universities are already taking steps to prepare students for the Metaverse. For instance, the University of Michigan has launched a Metaverse Roadmap initiative, which aims to identify the skills and competencies students need to succeed in the Metaverse. Another example is the University of Washington, which has integrated virtual reality experiences into its curriculum, giving students a chance to explore and experiment in a virtual environment.

Opportunities for skills development: There are several opportunities for universities to provide students with the skills needed for the Metaverse. One such opportunity is through experiential learning programs that offer students hands-on experience with Metaverse technologies. Another opportunity is through collaborations with industry partners who can provide students with internships and work experience in Metaverse-related fields.

Challenges and considerations: While preparing students for the Metaverse is important, there are several challenges and considerations that universities must consider. For example, there is a lack of standardization in Metaverse technologies, making it difficult for universities to develop a uniform curriculum. Additionally, the cost of Metaverse technologies can be prohibitive, limiting access to these resources for students from lower socioeconomic backgrounds.

Preparing students for the Metaverse is essential for universities, and it requires a multidisciplinary approach that includes both technical and soft skills. Universities must take a proactive role in developing students' Metaverse competencies and skills by providing them with experiential learning opportunities, collaborating with industry partners, and addressing challenges related to access and standardization. By doing so, universities can ensure that their students are well-prepared for the challenges and opportunities of the Metaverse.

9. Conclusion: opportunities and challenges for writing exams in the metaverse at South African Universities

The Metaverse is a rapidly evolving technology that has the potential to revolutionize various aspects of education, including exam writing. This chapter has examined the opportunities and challenges of writing exams in the Metaverse at South African universities. How this technology can reduce costs, enhance engagement, and promote accessibility, while also highlighting the challenges of ensuring privacy and security, developing necessary skills and competencies, and preparing students for this new environment has been explored. This concluding section will summarize the main findings and offer some recommendations for future research and implementation.

The analysis of the literature suggests that the use of the Metaverse for exam writing has significant potential benefits. One of the most prominent advantages is the reduction of costs associated with traditional exam writing methods. In addition, the Metaverse provides a more immersive and engaging environment for students, which can lead to better learning outcomes. Moreover, it promotes accessibility and equity by allowing students to take exams from anywhere and at any time. However, there are also significant challenges to be addressed, such as ensuring privacy and security, developing the necessary skills and competencies for using the Metaverse, and preparing students for this new environment.

Based on the analysis, several areas for future research are recommended. Firstly, there is a need to explore the effectiveness of the Metaverse in promoting learning outcomes and student engagement. Secondly, further research is needed to identify and address privacy and security concerns associated with Metaverse exam writing. Thirdly, there is a need to develop strategies for promoting digital literacy and Metaverse-related skills among students and faculty. Lastly, future research should also explore the potential of the Metaverse for promoting equity and accessibility in education.

Recommendations for implementation: In addition to research, there are several steps that universities can take to implement Metaverse exam writing successfully. Firstly, universities need to invest in the necessary infrastructure and technology to support Metaverse exam writing. Secondly, they need to develop policies and guidelines that address privacy and security concerns while ensuring that the technology is accessible to all students. Thirdly, universities should provide training and support for faculty and students to develop the necessary skills and competencies for using the Metaverse. Lastly, universities should engage in outreach and advocacy to promote the use of the Metaverse for exam writing and to raise awareness of its potential benefits.

Conclusion: The Metaverse represents a significant shift in the way we think about education and the way exams are delivered. While there are challenges that need to be addressed, such as privacy and security concerns, the potential benefits of the Metaverse for reducing costs, enhancing engagement, and promoting accessibility are substantial. It is therefore essential that universities invest in the necessary infrastructure and technology to support Metaverse exam writing, while also providing training and support for faculty and students to develop the necessary skills and competencies. The successful implementation of Metaverse exam writing has the potential to transform the status quo about exams and education, ultimately leading to better learning outcomes and a more equitable and accessible educational system for all.

Author details

Bonginkosi A. Thango
University of Johannesburg, Johannesburg, South Africa

*Address all correspondence to: bonginksit@uj.ac.za

References

[1] Chen C-M, Lai C-L, Chang C-Y. The potential of virtual reality technology in the assessment of spatial learning ability: A scoping review. Journal of Educational Technology & Society. 2019;**22**(2):1-16

[2] Le Dinh T, Chen C-M, Lai C-L. The use of virtual reality technology in education: A scoping review. Educational Research Review. 2021;**34**:100374

[3] Kivikangas JM, Järvelä S, Kallinen K, Ravaja N. Digital games as a context for developing students' science learning skills. Journal of Educational Computing Research. 2019;**57**(1):95-115

[4] Cochrane T, Antonczak L, Keegan H. Designing for mobile virtual reality in education. TechTrends. 2020;**64**(3):351-361

[5] Ogawa A. Distance-learning high school holds classes in the metaverse. The Japan News. 2022. Available from: https://asianews.network

[6] Lu X, Qin J, Wang X. Virtual reality in education: A systematic review of literature. Educational Technology & Society. 2021;**24**(1):73-86

[7] University of Cape Town. UCT Computer Science Students Take First Exam in a Virtual World. 2018. Available from: https://www.news.uct.ac.za/article/-2018-

[8] Manches A, O'Malley C, Benford S. The role of virtual and augmented reality in the future of education and training. British Journal of Educational Technology. 2017;**48**(2):623-625

[9] Papadakis S, Kalogiannakis M, Zaranis N, Grammatikopoulos V. Virtual and augmented reality educational tools in remote areas: A systematic literature review. Interactive Learning Environments. 2019;**27**(3):295-309

[10] Pilgrim M, Bouchard S. Virtual reality and education: Reflections on pedagogical applications. Journal of Educational Technology & Society. 2019;**22**(2):1-15

[11] Salmon ED, Al-Azawi R. Virtual reality in higher education: A review of the literature from 2012 to 2017. Journal of Education for Teaching. 2019;**45**(3):373-387

[12] Bekele TA, Menzies RW. A framework for preparing students for the fourth industrial revolution: A Case Study of a Canadian University. International Journal of Higher Education. 2019;**8**(5):35-46

[13] Michigan News. U-M Launches Metaverse Roadmap Initiative to Prepare Students for Virtual Future. 2022. Available from: https://news.umich.edu/u-m-launches-metaverse-roadmap-initiative-to-prepare-students-for-virtual-future/

[14] University of Washington. Virtual Reality in the Classroom. 2022. Available from: https://www.washington.edu/teaching/topics/technology-in-teaching/virtual-reality-in-the-classroom/

Chapter 14

MNC Strategy in Contested Environments: Stay Put or Stay Foot?

Ulf Bosch

Abstract

The chapter *'MNC Strategy in Contested Environments: Stay Put or Stay Foot?'* provides a contemporary view on the key questions relating to the strategic orientation of multinational corporations (MNCs) in emerging markets with a particular focus on China. Until recently, possible heterogeneity in business strategy and firm performance was concealed by the seemingly endless growth story in the emerging market arena. In view of increasingly harsh conditions, both in terms of host-country markets and institutions, foreign-invested firms may either choose to concede, conform, contest, compete, collaborate or co-create, to name a few conspicuous configurations. More than four decades have passed in which emerging markets have burgeoned as the preeminent growth drivers propelling the efficiency- and market-seeking MNCs to the forefront of cross-border economic activity. This development has been supported by global integration, multilateralism as well as institutional transition and reform. Hence, institutional factors, alongside external industry structures as well as internal firm resources, have been credited with having superior explanatory power in emerging economies. Moreover, high-level dynamism and discontinuities have always been the hallmarks of emerging markets. However, a new level of turbulence has emerged triggered by exogenous shocks such as Covid-19 as well as geopolitical conflicts and power shifts. MNCs face unprecedented challenges; and their commitment in terms of foreign direct investment (FDI) have been put to the test like never before. Decision makers in MNC subsidiaries and their headquarters ask themselves the question: *'Stay Put or Stay Foot?'*.

Keywords: international business strategy, strategic choice, typology-driven theorising, institutional theory, multinational corporation, China

1. Introduction

The chapter starts out by encapsulating the conceptual underpinnings of international business (IB) strategy, the theory of the MNC and motives to go abroad. In order to (re-)strategize possible strategic avenues of MNCs under increasingly challenging conditions, this text draws on typology-driven theorising and reflects on the convergence of the IB strategy literature and institutionalism. The chapter also discusses the impact of environmental discontinuities, current research trajectories and questions for future research.

IntechOpen

2. The reshaped anatomy of the MNC

The starting point for answering the question whether foreign-invested firms should stay invested or pull out of emerging markets is a discourse of their major reasons to go abroad [1]. The fundamental questions of why MNCs exist and which strategies they pursue lie in the heart of IB strategy and the theory of the MNC [2–4]. An exploration of these motives is crucial for any remain/exit decision.

2.1 The changing contour of IB strategy

The MNC traditionally refers to any corporation that is registered, owns and manages entities in more than one country [5]. These organisations undertake FDI and possess or, to a certain degree, control value-added activities in several countries. The ACRONYM MNC is often synonymously applied for multinational enterprise or multinational company. Recently, foreign-invested firms have sought to become more socially embedded in their local contexts [6, 7] as boundaries between the firms and the environment have become loose [8]. Likewise, digital technologies have fundamentally reshaped the understanding of the MNC. Technology-enabled actors, also described as 'digital MNCs', do not necessarily have to employ productive assets and staff in subsidiaries abroad. By utilising for instance cloud-based platforms and business ecosystems [9], these largely virtual ventures tend to operate outside of the traditional import-export/FDI continuum. Referred to as 'born-globals' [10], these firms do not expand gradually but go global from day one. While technology can fundamentally change business models, the debate to remain in, or withdraw from, emerging markets is applicable to firms irrespectively of their degree of digitalisation. It is a matter of systemic understanding of the emerging market context, not a matter of technology. Reverting to the definition of the overarching subject, modern strategy is for the most part footed on the long-standing notion by the Harvard professors C. Roland Christensen and Kenneth R. Andrews [11] that refers to strategy as a concept that explores an organisation's internal capabilities versus the competitive environment. Correspondingly, the field of IB strategy refers to effectively and efficiently matching of an MNCs internal strengths and weaknesses (compared to rivals) with the external opportunities and threats [12] in geographically dispersed environments [13]. As such, IB strategy seeks to explain how firms generate and utilise competitive supremacy so to yield superior performance in their product-market domains [14]. It assesses the configuration, strategic orientation and leadership of cross-border enterprises and the corresponding effects on micro- and macroeconomic performance (e.g. economic expansion, productivity, workforce utilisation). Taken together, the literature on IB strategy focusses on MNCs and uses developing markets as research background to conceptualise theory [15, 16].

2.2 The enduring motives of the MNC

As outlined, MNCs play a pivotal role in IB strategy and global economic governance. There have been several explanations for their origins and existence, all offering different angles with respect to the rationales underlying international business proceedings. Major proponents include the theory of trade [17], the theory of monopolistic advantage [4, 18], the theory of transaction cost [19, 20], the theory of product life cycle [21, 22], the stage approach [7, 23–25], theory of network [26, 27] and the OLI-model refereeing to the ownership-location-internalisation triplet [3, 28–30]. The OLI framework, also called 'eclectic paradigm', presumes that production in different countries necessitates an ownership-based advantage [30]. This kind of competitive edge can have various incarnations, however, it is often manifested in the proprietary technology applications of the MNC. While the various theoretical strands are helpful in studying the roots of the foreign-invested firm, ultimately, the major reasons for exploring foreign markets refer to the accessibility of inexpensive natural resources as well as a high-skills low-cost workforce ('Ricardian' [17] argument) and economies of scale (EOS) as well as product differentiation ('Krugmanian' [31] argument). Based on these dimensions, Dunning [3] formulated several classifications of MNC motives. (1) Resource-seeking: These MNCs aim to establish access to resources like raw materials, human capital or other input factors, e.g., a UK firm sets up shop in Mainland China to manufacture and ship back to the UK and other markets. This can also entail the insurance of a stable supply of raw materials (backward or 'upstream' integration) or of product quality (forward or 'downstream' integration). (2) Market-seeking: These MNCs aim to spot and utilise additional markets for a company's goods and services. For example, in order to use excess capacity, MNCs seek to increase world market share by moving into emerging markets. It is important to consider that for specific categories of products and services, the creation and dissemination have to be simultaneous, hence, market-seeking goes hand-in-hand with other motives. (3) Efficiency-seeking: These MNCs strive to reshuffle their extant assets in order to optimise their worldwide footprints. This can entail cross-border specialisation by tapping into disparities in factor costs, to manage dependencies or to mitigate risks, as well as world-wide procurement practices to save resources and enhance cost-effectiveness by streamlining their global operations. (4) Strategic assets-/capabilities-seeking: These MNCs aim to establish a strategic presence in a foreign market in order to shield or enhance their global competitive positioning. This can entail an inorganic growth strategy based on corporate mergers/amalgamations and acquisitions (M&A) or taking control of domestic assets including research and development (R&D), expertise and staff. It can also include pre-emptive measures to prevent competitors from entering the market or acquiring local strategic assets/capabilities. The above outline shows that varied reasons have been proposed in the literature on internationalisation. These argumentations seam to be logical and have been supported by rigorous research in emerging markets. Dunning [32, 33] showed that the impetus of foreign-invested firms to operate abroad can seamlessly transform from market-seeking and resource-seeking (to utilise the extant edge over competitors) towards developing strategic assets (to defend and improve the current competitive differentiation). Notwithstanding, efficiency-seeking drivers are widely acknowledged to constitute the dominant forces of cross-border integration in the context of IB and MNC strategy. An increased focus on global sourcing has been identified by Zaheer and Manrakhan [34] as well Kotabe and Murray [35]. In contrast, Cypher and Dietz [36] see an emergence of fully aligned manufacturing networks and business models. The preceding discussion shows that MNCs are in emerging markets for motives relating to efficiency, resources, markets and strategic assets. However, these motives are subject to constant shifts and disruptions in the competitive industry, firm resources constellations and institutional environments, both in the host country and home country. In particular, the efficiency-seeking motive needs to be reviewed for its ongoing validity. In this context, MNC have been keen to maintain their ability to engage in regime arbitrage [37], a corporate practice of tapping into more favourable conditions in one jurisdiction to circumvent less favourable ones elsewhere. For instance, the controversial practice of transfer pricing poses an ongoing concern. Non-governmental organisations such as the OECD and G20 have coined these tactics as 'base erosion profit shifting' (BEPS). This criticism is echoed by the State Administration of Taxation (STA) of China which has called out the tax avoidance schemes by MNCs. Despite the institutional crackdown and public scrutiny, MNCs may not abstain from such practices anytime soon as these regimes are closely linked to the major motives to operate there in the first place.

3. The new emerging market context

Emerging markets have been the enduring raison d'être of MNCs. Having served as magnets for FDI over a prolonged period of time, these growth regions have provided MNCs with a spacious canvas to pursue their cross-border growth agendas. They offered new revenue sources and allowed MNCs to prolong the life cycle of their product segments. In return, MNCs transferred technologies, enhanced local leadership practices, created employment and upgraded China's ability to compete on the global stage. However, in the recent past, emerging markets have witnessed considerable upheaval and volatility. One manifestation of this new era has been an increasingly assertive presence by China in the global economic and geopolitical theatre. For MNCs it is helpful to understand the formative events, dynamics and risks that have given rise to these developments. Common definitions describe emerging markets as territories that feature accelerating expansion but meagre pay using elements of the free-market economy as key drivers for progress and growth [38]. This block includes the evolving economies of the Asian region, South America, the Arabian Peninsula, Africa and several post-Soviet states. One common denominator of these countries is an economy that is tightly directed by the state [39]. Emerging markets at large feature such a profile. Still, China is in a dominant position due to the country's market size and investment influx. As a matter of fact, China has attracted the 'lion's share' of FDI within the emerging market arena. Eight out of ten companies listed in the global Fortune 500 have set up operations in China [40]. Consequently, China has the utmost relevance for practicing managers of MNCs as well as academic researchers seeking to explore how economic actors interact and align with their environment [41].

3.1 The changing of the guards

The ascend of emerging markets and developing countries including China did not occur unexpectedly. It has been predicted by market observers such as O'Neill [42], former chief economist at Goldman Sachs, who published an influential analysis in which he coined a block of selected countries BRICS (referring to the Federative Republic of Brazil, Russian Federation, Republic of India, People's Republic of China (PRC) and Republic of South Africa). These economies have been credited with the prospective capacity to exert far-reaching implications for the international political economy. It has been assumed that their favourable demographics and resources endowments set them up for spectacular economic growth. Further ACRONYMs for high-potential country clusters followed suit, such as MINT (referring to the United Mexican States, Republic of Indonesia, Federal Republic of Nigeria and Republic of Turkey) coined in 2014 by asset management firm Fidelity Investments, and the Next 11 (MINT plus the People's Republic of Bangladesh, Arab Republic of Egypt, Islamic Republic of Iran, Islamic Republic of Pakistan, Republic of the Philippines, Republic of Korea and Socialist Republic of Vietnam). However, more than two decades have passed and predictions about the BRICS as the most rapidly expanding markets have not quite materialised. While China has been reporting FDI inflows and GDP in unparalleled dimensions, the economies of India, Russia and Brazil have notably disappointed by not diversifying away from commodities towards the private sector. China's GDP (>USD18tr, 2022) has been twice the other BRICS's in aggregate (<USD8tr, 2022). China's economic prowess and leadership within the BRICS illustrates the paramount importance of the country for the success foreign firms in emerging markets [43, 44]. Scholars have pointed out that the rise of China foreshadowed a 'global-Asian era' [45]. However, irrespectively of whether the forecasts have materialised or not, the BRICS movement symbolised a changing of guards in the global economy leaving the developed G7 economies in its wake struggling for relevance.

3.2 The assertive rise of China

China has been known for the utmost consistency of purpose underpinning the nation's grand strategy, which has mainly been geared towards stability. The country's focus on stability is informed by its past characterised by extreme crises during periods of turbulence (e.g. the Great Chinese Famine 1959–1961, many armed conflicts including the Opium war 1839, Chinese Civil War 1927–1950, Korean 1950–1953, Sino-Indian 1962, Vietnam 1965–1969 and Sino-Vietnamese 1979, and occupation by Western colonial powers in the 'century of humiliation' 1839–1949). Dèng Xiǎopíng, known as the chief architect of modern China, introduced a far-reaching opening-up and reform course in 1978 allowing MNCs to invest and participate in the country's exceptional development. The acceptance to join the World Trade Organization (WTO) in 2001 allowed the country to export on WTO terms, a step that turbo-charged China's drive to become a global powerhouse. This journey was supported by a relentless push to progress in the value chain cultivating proprietary capabilities including innovative technology applications. Henceforth, China has gone from being unnoticed to competing with the world's largest economies. The upward trajectory attracted the attention of foreign investors which swarmed into the Chinese market to participate in the 'gold rush'. This has led to a situation where foreign companies in China employed a workforce of 16 million individuals [46] accounting for at least half of China's exports. Foreign firms also were helpful in disseminating Western best practices enhancing China's productive capabilities. However, the long chain of crises has been a key element of the PRC's founding narrative. It also has sustained the long-standing view harboured by the Chinese Government that foreign actors are sources less of potential than of peril, uncertainty and even humiliation [47]. It is important for MNCs to understand that such thinking has shaped the country's collective social psyche. It has also been instrumental in creating today's Sino-US antagonism and regional bipolarity. One of the major triggers for the 'dragon to awake' (referring to China's rising assertiveness on the global stage), was a series of recent events that has arguably disqualified the US-led system in the eyes of China, as well as other emerging economies, as it exposed brinkmanship (not statesmanship), both in politics and in economics. The subprime mortgage crisis of 2007–2010 can be seen as a crucial juncture at which China started to openly push its superpower ambitions and the narrative that US hegemony is in decline. Under the Xí Jìnpíng administration, China switched to a more assertive brand of grand strategy. In this context, China has led the initiative to redefine the BRICS as an intergovernmental organisation to establish a parallel system to the US Dollar, as well as the Bretton Woods system of monetary management and financial agencies including the World Bank and the IMF. By doing so, China aims to champion an alternative to the Western model offering a diplomatic forum and financial system, shifting away from the US dollar as a default. The initiative is embedded in President Xí Jìnpíng's greater power diplomacy with the Chinese characteristics model. The model's manifesto is based on the four principles of (1) big powers are key, (2) neighbours [peripheral countries] are first, (3) developing nations are the base, and (4) multilateralism is the stage (dà guó shì guān jià; zhōu biān shì shǒu yào; fā zhǎn zhōng guó jiā shì jī chǔ; duō biān shì zhòng yào wǔ tái). This approach positions Chinese foreign policy in the developing world as a driver to move the global power balance. The rationale is to create 'strategic fulcrums' (zhàn luè zhī diǎn) for building Chinese influence and exporting the 'China Model' through policies. In fact, China's state media (CGTN, 2019) has positioned the BRICS as an 'antidote to the G7 and other U.S.-dominated institutions'. Alongside the BRICS, another multilateral platform has emerged in the form of the Shanghai Cooperation Organisation (SCO) which has been set up in 2001 by Russia and China. The nine-member group comprises the states of previous Soviet Central Asian as well as India, Pakistan and Iran. By courting other authoritarian regimes, China aims at countering Western control in Eurasia. Another key project along the same lines is the Belt & Road Initiative (BRI), also described as 'New Silk Road'. For China, BRI represents a new gateway to Western Europe, the African continent and the Middle East through Central Asia [48]. It also solidifies the country's new-found friendship with Russia. It has emerged since 2013 as China's geo-industrial policy and global infrastructure development strategy disrupting the previous order of regional economic integration. It involves vast capital as well as terrestrial and maritime infrastructure investments in nearly 70 countries and international organisations that help to cement Chinese influence in the many nations along these economic corridors. BRI also undermines the previous East Asian development model known as the 'flying geese pattern' (yàn hán lǐ lùn). This model by Akamatsu [49] promulgates that East Asia's economic rise has been led by Japan, followed by the newly industrialising economies of Asia (NIEs or Asian Tigers) and the members of the Association of Southeast Asian Nations (ASEAN). While being the dominant orthodoxy in the region since Japan's first modernisation drive from 1870 onwards, China has leapfrogged to a pole position bypassing the established V-shaped flight formation. By means of attracting the largest amount of FDI and know-how, China has gained competitiveness and increased the pressure on Asian neighbours to ensure that they remain competitive. The BRI has intensified these frictions as it allows China to trade overland depriving Asian neighbours along the major trade routes through the South China Sea of their share. All these forays into multilateralism—i.e. BRIC, SCO and BRI—have been designed to establishing China as a global power to challenge the US, which has not been involved in these initiatives. However, at the same time, China has become more isolated from countries and organisations in the West, as Anthony Saich [50] of Harvard Kennedy School has observed. Again, the transformation of China into a more complex and evolving country does not come as a surprise. It was predictable based on the country's sheer size, culture and work ethics as well as storied history. China works relentlessly towards becoming more confident and capable of making the goal of national rejuvenation a reality. Spearheaded by the so-called 'wolf warrior diplomacy', coined from a Chinese action movie, this approach is characterised by combative nationalism. China has moved from the more cerebral premise of 'hide and bide' (tāo guāng yǎng huì) under the leadership of Dèng Xiǎopíng to the blatant statement that the 'US is not qualified to speak from a position of strength when criticising China' [51]. The change in direction has not been an impulsive act. It is an integral part of a long-term plan, or '100-year marathon' [52]. In fact, the Chinese government is executing against a vision to outstrip the US and other economies by 2049, the centennial anniversary of the CCP-led revolution. The party also seeks to complete the long-stated goal of 'national unification' with Taiwan by the same time.

3.3 The new pressures and constraints

A high level of protectionism and regulatory complexity are characteristics of the institutional context in China, although the inflow vast amounts of FDI would suggest a more deregulated environment. In fact, China's sweeping reform and transformation process has been limited to the economy and had little bearing on the political landscape [53]. As a consequence, MNCs have been highly constrained in their pursuits to foster innovation amid the lack of basic legal certainty [54]. As a matter of fact, there have been waves of MNC market withdrawals and factory/office closures involving global players such as Yahoo, Microsoft, Adobe, Adidas and Panasonic [55]. In this context, multisport entrepreneur and publisher Dan Empfield [56] explained that 'there was a stampede into China to make bicycles beginning in the mid-1990s; and now there is a stampede out of China. Brands today are looking to make bikes anywhere ... as long as it's not China.' The damage is not limited to the manufacturing or technology sector though. In the financial services industry, venture capital firm Sequoia had to split off its China unit amid rising tensions and Beijing's crackdown on international professional services firms [57]. These high-profile cases send warnings to Western firms doing business in China. However, many departures may arguably be rooted in MNCs' skewed view of the business environment and the local institutions [58]. One indicator of firms' incapacity to adapt to the institutional context is the number of public crises that has hit numerous blue-chip companies, inflicting considerable reputational and financial harm. Longitudinal research spanning from 2000 to 2011 by the China Europe International Business School (CEIBS) found that in excess of 25% of well-known MNCs in China were subjected to public affronts [59]. Foreign market participants may have overestimated their capacity to manage and manipulate the host-country context while they may have underestimated the firepower of their host-country's arsenal of interventions. Despite the fact that the the Chinese market system is evolving, there is little doubt that China is a political economy that the local institutions can exert overriding authority over MNCs [60]. As such, doing business in China is subjected to a myriad of state interventions and political agendas [61]. Specifically, China's institutional environment has been portrayed as 'force within a cell of regulations' [62]. It also shows that ideology matters: While studying today's capitalism is important, the tenets of Marxism remain true [63]. Several political initiatives have put MNCs as a disadvantage including 'indigenous innovation' (zìzhǔ chuàngxīn) by the 2003–2013 Hú/Wēn government and 'innovation-driven development' (chuàngxīn qūdòng fāzhǎn) by the subsequent Xí/Lǐ government. These industrial strategies focussed on protectionism enacted by state procurement policies [64]. Despite the fact that stability is of fundamental importance to China, the country's institutions and policies have been altered dynamically. MNCs that want to remain in the market need to be clear-eyed about the fact that China's legal system promotes nationalistic themes singling out Chinese and non-Chinese investors [65], as manifested in regulations governing Sino-foreign joint-ventures (JVs). In the institutional landscape of China, two different types of sentiments with respect to foreign-invested players can be identified. The streams equally put China's national interests in the centre of their thinking. One group reverts to technocratic protectionism seeking to make China inhospitable for MNCs and the domestic economy more shielded. The other group favours a pragmatic market-orientation seeking to make China more welcoming for MNCs and the domestic economy more competitive. Furthermore, with respect to handling the economy, China has previously pursued a 'comprehensive well-off society' (quánmiàn jiànshè xiǎokāng shèhuì) based on a Confucian near-ideal state, and has practiced a hands-off approach to many sectors which have minted billionaires, a celebrity culture and giant companies at a breath-taking pace. However, under the current administration, China aims at rectifying perceives socioeconomic issues cultivating a 'patriotic atmosphere' for the industries, regardless of what people and companies/investors may want. The central government has launched sweeping crackdowns in many once-freewheeling sectors, including social media/e-commerce (i.e. Alibaba Group, Meituan, Tencent), online gaming (e.g. NetEase), cryptocurrency (i.e. bitcoin), education (i.e. New Oriental), online finance (e.g. Ant Group), ride hailing (e.g. Didi Chuxing), property (e.g. China Evergrande Group) and health care (i.e. unregistered cosmetics). Similarly, the government has recently embarked upon a sweeping clampdown impacting a wide spectrum of sectors creating volatility and uncertainty for newly established firms and seasoned incumbents alike [66]. China's far-reaching interventions are reportedly not aimed at choking private sector growth or decouple from the US/international system. Instead, the goal is to help consumer-facing technology platforms in fulfilling their mandate of promoting common prosperity or smoothing social disparity. This major push brings the Chinese State front-and-centre into all elements of its citizens' lives and company's strategic agendas. Major downsides to be considered by MNCs relate to China's reclassification as a political threat rather economic partner, declining public sentiment towards the country in MNC home nations, the multi-pronged regulatory crackdown on various industries (especially technology and professional services), alongside the risks related with an ageing population and associated dependency ratios and skill shortage. In addition, China is one of the most exposed geographies in terms of climate change. In terms of competition, China's local sectors have aggressively moved from a strategy of imitation to a strategy of innovation [67]. China's under-the-radar but globally competitive innovators disrupt along the entire configurational spectrum including products/services, processes and business models. The economic and institutional shifts described makes MNCs' engagement in China challenging, and potentially unfeasible. Against this backdrop, the focal point of strategic management research lies in MNCs' strategic answers to these institutional pressures.

4. The strategic (re-)orientation of the MNC

As the macro- and micro-environmental conditions for MNCs operating in China have changed considerably, many foreign-invested firms see themselves under pressure to rethink and revise their most fundamental strategic bets as well as tactical deployments.

4.1 The revised strategic imperatives

Research on MNCs has shown that major economic discontinuities in the past, such as the financial currency collapse in Asia (1998), the SARS outbreaks (2003), the subprime loan meltdown in 2008 and China's equity market crash in 2015, have tended to elicit defensive responses. Correspondingly, the exogenous shocks in recent years, including the start of the global Coronavirus pandemic (2020) and the invasions of Ukraine by Russia (2014 and 2022), have had corresponding effects. In many instances, grand strategic ambitions by MNCs have been replaced by damage limitation. Along with these economic and geopolitical ruptures, distinctive reflexes in firms' strategic responses to exterior contingencies have revealed themselves. Prior to the frictions, the unequivocal game plan of foreign-invested companies in China was to 'push the envelope' in terms of business growth often ignoring the potential performance limits that firms cannot surpass unharmed. A large proportion of the MNCs in China pursued ambitious expansion plans [68–72]. While rising competition was requiring businesses to innovate and adapt to remain competitive, potential variations in strategic orientation, organisational resources and firm performance were less decisive as organisations were growing alongside the overall market expansion. This is to say that in periods of turbulence, variations in strategy configurations may become more conspicuous as both capabilities and shortcomings are highlighted. For example, in the context of the previously mentioned disruptions, firms often revert to reflexes that can be loosely described as prospective, defensive, analytical or reactive. Utilising these conceptions as a baseline, a widely confirmed typology can utilised to further explore the peculiarities of MNC strategy in China.

4.2 The power of typology-driven theorising

Business strategy at the level of the firm has been the classical criterion for researchers in the field of strategic management. Choosing the firm as a unit of analysis, typology-driven theorising, in particular the Miles and Snow [73] typology, can be used to conceptualise the strategic orientation of MNCs in China. The major idea behind the concept of typologies is a grouping of features into generic clusters based on their level of similarity. These frameworks help to identify frequently observed characteristics of firms in order to generate overarching types which represent the different co-alignments of these organisational aspects [74]. Strategic typologies have been described as 'a form of social scientific shorthand' ([75], p. 149) and instruments to effectively explore complexity [76], both conceptually and methodologically [77]. Typologies enable scholars and practitioners to structure the organisation management in a full and integrated manner [78]. They are frequently called fields [79], modes [80], archetypes [81], generic strategies [82], gestalts [83, 84], typologies [85] or taxonomies [86] Irrespective of the terminology used, all incarnations require their members to have configurational similarity and internal consistency [82, 87]. If packaged in the form of typologies, the theory is especially practical as it can capture multiple linkages simultaneously. As such, typologies allow for a more systematic investigation of MNC strategy in emerging markets as they capture reciprocity and bidirectional cause-and-effect relationships [88].

4.3 The strategic types

The field of generic strategic typologies boasts several well-known models. Porter [82], Abell [89] and Miles and Snow [73] belong to the most prominent ones. A major difference lies in their theoretical underpinnings. Whereas the Miles and Snow [73] model entails a causal model (adaptive cycle), the designs of Porter [82] and Abell [89] lack a theory-driven approach since these typologies are axiomatic-led based on fundamental economic principles. By comparison, the Miles and Snow [73] typology appears to be better suited to examine the firm surroundings than Porter's [82] archetypes which intentionally circumvent any contextual properties [90]. The model conceptualised by Raymond E. Miles in collaboration with Charles C. Snow

(1978) encapsulates the ways that different modes of adaptive firm conduct results in distinctive organisational configurations, so-called strategic types, which can be used by an organisation to align with its context. Firms permanently face a trifecta of mission-critical obstacles which they have to deal with in an agile manner in order to reconcile both their internal capabilities as well as their external surroundings. These obstacles relate to the entrepreneurial challenge (e.g. referring to the choice of product-market domain), the engineering challenge (e.g. concerning the choice of technology) and the administrative challenge (e.g. concerning the choice of organisation and processes that translate into innovation). The framework by Miles and Snow [73] entails a quadruplet of types proposing that generic strategy commonly manifests itself in one of these forms, namely Prospector, Defender, Analyser and Reactor (P-D-A-R). The model suggests that each type seeks specific solutions to the three obstacle clusters that form the adaptive cycle. These groupings feature heterogeneity in their functional specialisation, strategic prioritisation, resources endownments, experience and economic outcomes. The **Prospector** type views the environment as unsettled, ensures manoeuvrability and draws on innovation to respond to change, frequently emerging as the trend-setter of the sector [91]. Prospector-type organisations are led by upper echelons that focus on know-how in marketing as well as innovation and constantly monitor external change in order to experiment and respond with creative solutions to novel environmental developments. The **Defender** type seeks to occupy a secure foothold in a product-market domain that is comparatively insulated from change and priorities engineering, continuous improvement in productivity and cost optimisation. At the helm of Defender-type organisations is typically a coalition of finance and production executives who often do not sense external change and who have little appetite to go out of their ways apart from conducting minor adjustments in the configuration of the organisation and process landscape. The **Analyser** type simultaneously embraces continuity and agility seeking to utilise the merits of both the Prospector and Defender modes. These organisations practice ambidexterity in a way that they dually pursue Defender strategies in certain business segments and Prospector-type strategies in different ones [73]. As such, they thrive on a 'second-but-better' positioning. Due to their dual orientation and hybrid configuration, these firms face more internal sophistication and a delicate balance between functional areas. In business area that are characterised by relative continuity, they focus on operational excellence and efficiency, in other more dynamic domains, they attentively observe the competitive landscape and engages solely in projects that offer clear potential for competitive differentiation and scalability. The **Reactor** type misses a stringent strategy and is highly susceptible to external contingencies. Firms belonging to this strategic type find it hard to cultivate a solution to the challenges of adaptation and hence are 'ill-conceived strategies' [90]. When Miles and Snow [73] and Porter [82] are compared, there is an apparent similarity between the Reactor type and Porter's [82] 'stuck-in-the-middle' classification [90]. The literature on typology-driven theorising in the strategic management and marketing field [86, 92] offers an abundance of studies on the Miles and Snow [73] framework. The conceptual and empirical soundness of this typology has been established for numerous sectors, including public services [93] as well as in emerging economies [58, 94–96].

4.4 The strategy-performance link

Firm performance, or economic validity, is the consequent of any business domain, including strategy. Broadly speaking, academic scholarship in the strategy domain seeks to explain the determinants of organisational outcomes [97]. Various research studies have examined the linkages between strategic type membership, distinctive competencies [98] and organisational performance [99]. So is there one best performing type? No, there is not. The typology developed by Miles and Snow [73] embraces the notion of equifinality [100] stating that all viable strategy types harbour the potential to yield optimum firm performance. While not directly stated in the 1978 (Miles & Snow) framework, equifinality is implicitly described [101]. None of the types, apart from the Reactor type, is associated with any performance limitations. The exception of the Reactor is based on the fact that this type has been viewed as being ill-equipped of managing the various boundaries described in the adaptive cycle [73]. When discussing research findings for MNCs' strategic type membership in China, research data surveyed in the first quarter of 2016 can be utilised. The data was collected during a time when China experienced the country's slowest economic performance since the global financial crisis 2008–2009. The empirical research was based on a questionnaire of 62 items and generated 212 responses. The data have been solidified by means of triangulated data capturing [102] including external.

third-party insights. Based on Snow and Hrebiniak's [99] framework, participating MNCs considered themselves to be Prospectors (33%), Defenders (26%), Analysers (28%) and Reactors (13%). The descriptive results were more levelled than in comparable research. For example, a study by Boyd and Reuning-Elliott [103] generated nearly two thirds Analysers (62%), close to one third Prospectors (31%), a small proportion of Defenders (7%) and no Reactors. Rugman and Verbeke [104] stated that the percentage of Reactors types is elevated in studies focussing on small-sized enterprises. Out of the study sample, 40% of firms stated that their business objectives correspond with institutional requirements, 49% view institutions to be erratic and 44% inadequately developed. Considering organisational outcomes, a substantial number of companies indicated flat or dwindling sales (39%), profits (55%) as well as market shares (57%). One statistically significant predictor of strategic type membership is volatility ($p = .028$). The level of perceived volatility corresponds (inversely) with the Miles and Snow [73] P-D-A-R continuum. Generally speaking, the more volatile the environment is perceived, the more likely the respondent shows a Reactor mode. Although the absolute figures do not immediately show: 81% of Reactors consider the environment to be volatile vs. 65% of Prospectors. Thus, the Reactor type is more likely in volatile environments. This corresponds with Tan and Litschert's [105] research in China. External volatility showed an inverse linkage with proactivity (i.e. prospective orientation) and a positive relationship with a rather passive stance (i.e. defensive orientation). With respect to the affiliation to generic strategy types, Prospectors have a positive linkage with revenue from sales (0.2998*) as well as a negative linkage with share of market (−0.4914*). On the contrary, the strategic mode of Analyser shows a positive link with share of market (0.2989) despite the fact that there is no sidak-adjusted coefficient of statistical significance. All remaining types have no sufficiently strong linkages. The Prospector and Analyser take the lead in terms of most deliberate strategic types in the Miles and Snow [73] strategy spectrum. While often described as the most aggressive [106] and boldest [107] in terms of risk-taking, the Prospector has typically been described as high-achiever. Yet, in terms of overall success, Miles and Snow [73] acknowledge that the 'Prospector seldom attains the efficiency necessary to reap maximum economic benefits from any of its chosen markets'. The time horizon of this type of generic strategy is near-term (1983). The Prospector type also appears to have a limited 'shelf-life'. This is owed to the fact that along with their successs, Prospectors seek to leverage their newly attained competitive edge to pivot into Analyser or Defender types. Moreover, some scholars found that Prospectors under-perform in emerging economies because of their limited ability to cope with ambiguity [108]. In contrast, the Analyser type has been associated with a 'second-but-better' approach championing a higher level of market-orientation as well as a stronger interaction with fellow economic actors to better understand underlying requirements [109]. In line with the analytical orientation implied in its designation, the Analysers invest more time into screening the market contenders and generate a levelled suite of both established and progressive offerings [110]. On the continuum of strategic orientations, the Analyser type is positioned in-between the Defender and Prospector type (1993). This type has proven to be effective both in constant and changing economic environments by pursuing risk-mitigated productivity [58]. They bring together a focus on cost containment and opportunistic bets, a combination that corresponds with the dynamic conditions of the Chinese market and institutional landscape. The Analyser within the Miles and Snow [73] typology is considered a highly active configuration [106] as well as a 'shaker and mover' that is surpassed only by the Prospector type [107]. Nevertheless, this type has also been perceived as a champion of incrementalism [58], a feature that can help MNCs to alleviate their 'liabilities of foreignness' [111, 112] in an economy that can be identified with dynamic conditions [113], complex entanglements [114] as well as hostile opposition [81]. In the same vein, the Defender type is often seen as a strategic type that performs underwhelmingly. This stems from the preference of this type to seal off a niche in order to compete on costs and superior engineering capabilities [109]. The Defender seeks to safeguard a relatively tight product-market segment [115]. In order to stonewall against external threats, this type tries to perfect technical details and groups around a leadership team of specialists in financial and operational management [110]. Displaying a pronounced risk-aversion [109] and muted activity level [106], this type can still yield above-average performance (profitability) in various settings and frequently overtakes Prospector entities with respect to ROI and cash flow [86]. Naturally, Defenders are more likely to do well in unfluctuating and constricted business segments than in high-powered and unpredictable contexts. Moreover, in view of MNCs motives relating to the cultivation of the Chinese market, the Defender proposition has been criticised for leaning towards being technocratic, narrowly minded, non-agile and risk-avoiding as well as too traditionalist to command a competitive edge in China [58]. Hence, Defender may not be the most fitting type for dynamic contexts as they lack experience in crafting suitable strategies and tactics [107]. As business success in China depends on the ability to handle a dynamic and contested environment while capitalising on emerging opportunities, the Defender type does not appear to be well-equipped to thrive in this context. Correspondingly, the Reactor type can be classified as a configuration that yields subpar performance since reactor firms generate outcomes below the mean. These conclusions regarding the economic validity of Reactors are largely in line with the general portrait of this strategy type. Probably for this reason, various research projects on the Miles and Snow [73] typology have deliberately excluded the Reactor proposition. This is debatable though, as using an incomplete model compromises the integrity of the overall construct. Given the premise that the key objective of foreign-invested enterprises in the Chinese market is to atain market power by tapping into the emerging business opportunities, the chance that MNCs identify as Reactors seams to be diminished [58]. Hence, it is reasonable to expect a comparatively tiny representation of Reactors in any study on this typology in emerging markets. Furthermore, this type is associated with instability, improvisation, 'fire-fighting' and short-termism. Reactors dedicate more attention to absorbing outside stress that emerges in an erratic and fleeting ways [110]. They lack both, a coherent plan on how to prevail in competitive encounters [116] and the capability to adapt to the context [106]. Hence, Reactors succumb to their environment [73]. Conant et al. [110] drew the conclusion that Reactors are eclipsed by all the other three types. Notwithstanding, different scholars concluded that this type could surpass outperform the three stable strategic types [99]. These insights have motivated scholars to propose that Reactors could position themselves in a way that allows them to exploit the absence of strategic congruity by converting it into an ability of agility and adaptability [92, 117] that is supposed to yields positive performance outcomes in ever-changing contexts. In summary, the exploration of typology-driven theorising and the review of strategic type membership of MNCs in China supports the notion that there are distinctive paths to high and low performance. The best-performing types in dynamic emerging market contexts are Prospectors and Analysers (i.e. above-the-mean). Defenders are only partially successful while Reactors performed underwhelmingly (i.e below-the-mean). Active agency strategies lean towards competing, conforming, collaborating and co-creating with institution's authority. In contrast, studies show that adopting the strategic orientation of a Defender or Reactor may not lead to the envisioned success. These strategic orientations tend to either confront, contest, circumventing or concede to institution's authority. Belligerent approaches are hardly feasible as host country institutions on a local or central level have principal impact on MNCs' business activities. Nevertheless, considering the increasingly antagonistic situation, Prospector-type MNCs may well wish to dim down their public profile, as there are multiple examples when MNCs have been scapegoated for political reasons. As the Analyser type is the most agile type, it is the one that is assumed to yield the best outcomes in the context presented.

5. Conclusion

Quo vadis? When it comes to doing business in emerging markets, in particular China, MNCs find themselves at the crossroads. Emerging economies have emancipated, and China has become a vigilant system competitor. For MNCs, it cannot be business as usual. However, the current headwinds do not *per se* necessitate firms to go backwards. The new realities may create complications for their China engagement, but it does not mean MNCs have to pack their bags and *stay foot* (i.e. stay away). MNCs need to engage in a robust reflection on the new normal in emerging markets in general, and in China in particular, and their strategic options going forward. There are very good reasons to engage and *stay put* (i.e. stay there). The discussion in this chapter shows that their primary motives and mandates (i.e. efficiency-, resource-, market- and strategic assets-seeking) appear to have shifted but in general remain valid. The pendulum has not swung from an open-door policy to a closed-door situation. However, independent of the actual status of the door, the 'house rules' may have become more strict and less welcoming. Overall, while China has become more assertive and self-sufficient, the country is not expected to enter a new phase of 'isolation and locking the country (bì guān suǒ guó). After all, the promise of economic growth and prosperity is central to the regime's on-going legitimacy. There have been discontinuities sparked by exogenous shocks and decoupling efforts between major economic blocks. However, IB does not have to mirror global political frictions. In fact, from the perspective of MNCs, the notion of decoupling from China is thorny as it entails uprooting global supply chains and rejecting the purchasing power of 1.4 billion consumers. For MNCs, the benefits continue to outweigh the hazards. While the risk-reward equation has changed, an exodus of foreign firms is not immanent. With China having become a firebrand for Western MNCs, there is a clear imperative to de-risk, that is, disentangle complex operations and balance the exposure in order to reduce the vulnerability to external shocks and systemic rivalry. A carefully crafted strategic re-orientation will allow MNCs to effectively insulate themselves from potential risks while 'keeping the lighs on' in a market that will continue to act as a powerhouse in the global economy. To do so coherently, strategic typologies, namely Miles and Snow [73], can serve as useful instruments to identify viable strategic configurations as well as modes of interactions between organisations and the environment. The exploration of strategic types showed that Prospectors and Analysers perform best, with Analysers being the most successful type in ever changing contexts including emerging economies [58]. Defenders perform moderately [86] while Reactors achieve underwhelming results. Drawing on these and other findings, one can conclude that proactive engagement and deliberate strategic choice [114] are major hallmarks of sustained performance in emerging markets. MNCs that adopt new ways of collaborating with institutions and other economic actors are best positioned to succeed. MNCs needs to prepare themselves for disclosing more details of their China business, as stakeholder including home-country policy makers may obligate them to stress-test their exposure. Embracing a proactive stance seeking strategic interaction and discourse, including corporate political activities [118] pays dividends and allows for effective risk-management. By reducing the dependency on China, MNCs can better mitigate events out of their control as well as make use of investments outside of their previous must-win market. In sum, MNCs in China face a highly volatile institutional environment and a high risk of regulation, thus it is prudent to basically expect disruption and deleveraging (i.e. a period of slower economic growth). For MNCs, this may feel like the rally is over. However, it is just the beginning of the end of naivety and the start of a more sustainable cycle. There is a fairly robust basis for continued collaboration and integration, and there is a certain level of consensus among foreign businesses to remain invested. While MNCs need to realise that the heyday of China's abnormally high growth rates has past, a diligent recalibration of their strategy and portfolio will make them continue to thrive in one of the world's preeminent economies.

List of abbreviations

ACRONYM	a coded rendition of names yielding meaning
ASEAN	Association of Southeast Asian Nations
BEPS	base erosion and profit shifting
BRI	belt and road initiative
BRICS	Brazil, Russia, India, China, South Africa
CEIBS	China Europe International Business School
CPC	Communist Party of China
EOS	economies of scale
Et al.	et alii/aliae/alia (meaning: *and others*)
FDI	Foreign Direct Investment
G20	group of twenty
G7	group of seven

GDP	gross domestic product
IB	international business
IMF	international monetary fund
JV	joint-venture
MINT	Mexico, Indonesia, Nigeria and Turkey
MNC	multinational corporation
NIE	newly industrialising economies (of Asia)
OECD	Organisation for Economic Co-operation and Development
OEM	original equipment manufacturer
OLI	Ownership, Location, Internalisation
P-D-A-R	Prospector, Defender, Analyser, Reactor
PRC	People's Republic of China
ROI	return on investment
SCO	Shanghai Cooperation Organisation
UK	United Kingdom
US	United States (of America)
WTO	World Trade Organization

Author details

Ulf Bosch[1,2]

1 Queen's Business School (QBS), Department of International Business, Entrepreneurship and Marketing (IBEM), Queen's University Belfast, United Kingdom

2 William J. Clinton Leadership Institute (CLI), United Kingdom

*Address all correspondence to: ulf.bosch@qub.ac.uk

References

[1] Peng MW. Global Strategy. Cincinnati, OH: South-Western Thomson; 2006

[2] Bartlett CA, Ghoshal S. Managing across Borders: The Transnational Solution. Boston, MA: Harvard Business School Press; 1989

[3] Dunning JH. Multinational Enterprises and the Global Economy. Harlow: Addison-Wesley; 1993

[4] Hymer SH. The international operations of national firms: A study of foreign direct investment [Ph.D thesis]. Cambridge, MA: Massachusetts Institute of Technology, Department of Economics; 1976 [1960]. pp. 1-198

[5] Gilpin R. U.S. Power and the Multinational Corporation: The Political of Foreign Direct Investment. New York, NY: Basic Books; 1975

[6] Granovetter MS. Economic action and social structure: The problem of embeddedness. American Journal of Sociology. 1985;**91**(3):481-510

[7] Hennart J-FMA. A Theory of Multinational Enterprise. Ann Arbor, MI: University of Michigan Press; 1982

[8] Mayrhofer U. Management of Multinational Companies: A French Perspective. Basingstoke: Palgrave Macmillan; 2012

[9] Moore JF. Predators and prey: A new ecology of competition. Harvard Business Review. 1993;**71**(May–June):75-86

[10] Rennie M. Global competitiveness: born global. McKinsey Quarterly. 1993;**4**:45-52

[11] Learned EP, Christensen CR, Andrews KR, Guth WD. Business Policy: Text and Cases. Irwin, IL: Homewood; 1965

[12] Stevenson HH. Defining corporate strengths and weaknesses. Sloan Management Review. 1976;**17**(3):51-68

[13] Welch LS, Luostarinen RK. Internationalization: Evolution of a concept. Journal of General Management. 1988;**14**(2):34-55

[14] Zou S, Cavusgil ST. Global strategy: A review and an integrated conceptual framework. European Journal of Marketing. 1996;**30**(1):52-69

[15] Meyer KE. Asian contexts and the search for general theory in management research: A rejoinder. Asia Pacific Journal of Management. 2007;**24**:524-537

[16] Meyer KE, Peng MW. Probing theoretically into Central and Eastern Europe: Transactions, resources, and institutions. Journal of International Business Studies. 2005;**36**(6):600-621

[17] Ricardo D. On the Principles of Political Economy and Taxation. London, United Kingdom: John Murray, Albemarle-Street; 1817

[18] Kindleberger CP. American Business Abroad. New Haven, CT: Yale University Press; 1969

[19] Buckley PJ, Casson M. The Future of the Multinational Enterprise. London: MacMillan; 1976

[20] McManus JC. The theory of the international firm. In: Paquet C, editor. The Multinational Firm and the Nation State. Toronto: MacMillan; 1972. pp. 66-93

[21] Griffin RY, Pustay MW. International Business: A Managerial Perspective. 2nd ed. Reading, MA: Addison Wesley Longman; 1998

[22] Vernon R. International investment and international trade in the product cycle. Quarterly Journal of Economics. 1966;**80**(2):191-207

[23] Bilkey WJ, Tesar G. The export behavior of smaller-sized Wisconsin manufacturing firms. Journal of International Business Studies. 1977;**8**(1):93-98

[24] Cavusgil ST. Differences among exporting firms based on their degree of internationalisation. Journal of Business Research. 1984;**12**(2):195-208

[25] Johanson J, Vahlne J-E. The internationalisation process of the firm: A model of knowledge development and increasing foreign market commitments. Journal of International Business Studies. 1977;**8**(1):23-32

[26] Coviello N, Munro H. Network relationships and the small software firms. International Business Review. 1997;**6**(4):361-386

[27] Johanson J, Vahlne J-E. The Uppsala internationalization process model revisited: From liability of foreignness to liability of outsidership. Journal of International Business Studies. 2009;**40**(9):1411-1431

[28] Dunning JH. Trade, location of economic activity and the multinational enterprise: A search for an eclectic approach. In: Ohlin B, Hesselborn P, Wijkman PM, editors. The International Allocation of Economic Activity. London: Macmillan; 1977. pp. 395-418

[29] Dunning JH. Explaining changing patterns of international production: In defense of the eclectic theory. Oxford Bulletin of Economics and Statistics. 1979;**41**(4):269-295

[30] Dunning JH. Toward an eclectic theory of international production: Some empirical tests. Journal of International Business Studies. 1980;**11**(1):9-31

[31] Krugman P. Scale economies, product differentiation, and the pattern of trade. The American Economic Review. 1980;**70**(5):950-959

[32] Dunning JH. Alliance Capitalism and Global Business. London/New York, NY: Routledge; 1997

[33] Dunning JH. The eclectic (OLI) paradigm of international production: Past, present and future. International Journal of the Economics of Business. 2001;**8**(2):173-190

[34] Zaheer S, Manrakhan S. Concentration and dispersion in global industries: Remote access and the location of electronic commerce activities. Journal of International Business Studies. 2001;**32**(4):667-687

[35] Kotabe M, Murray JY. Global procurement of service activities by service firms. International Marketing Review. 2004;**21**(6):615-633

[36] Cypher JM, Dietz JL. The Process of Economic Development. London: Rouledge; 2004

[37] Ghemawat P. Managing differences: The central challenge of global strategy. Harvard Business Review. 2007;**85**(3):59-68

[38] Rugraff E, Hansen MW. Multinational corporations and local firms in emerging economies: An introduction. In: Rugraff E, Hansen MW, editors. Multinational Corporations and Local Firms in Emerging Economies. Amsterdam, Netherlands: European Association of Development Research and Training Institutes (EADI); 2011. pp. 1-37

[39] Peng MW. Controlling the foreign agent: How governments deal with

multinationals in a transition economy. Management International Review. 2000;**40**(2):141-165

[40] Fishman TC. China, Inc., How the Rise of the Next Superpower Challenges America and the World. New York, NY: Simon & Schuster; 2005

[41] Child J, Tse KK-T, Rodrigues SB. The Dynamics of Corporate co-Evolution: A Case Study of a Port in China. Cheltenham, UK: Edward Elgar Publishing Limited; 2013

[42] O'Neill J. Building Better Global Economic BRICs. Goldman Sachs, Global Economics Paper Series, No. 66. The Goldman Sachs Group, Inc.; 2001

[43] Wilson D, Kamakshya Trivedi K, Carlson SUJ. The BRICs 10 Years on: Halfway through the Great Transformation. New York, NY: Global Economics Paper No: 208, Goldman Sachs Group, Inc.; 2011

[44] Wilson D, Purushothaman R. Dreaming with BRICs: The Path to 2050. New York, NY: Global Economics Paper No: 99, Goldman Sachs Group, Inc.; 2003

[45] Henderson J. China and global development: Towards a global-Asian era? Contemporary Politics. 2008;**14**(4):375-392

[46] Woetzel J et al. The China Imperative for Multinational Companies: Reconfiguring for Opportunity and Risk. McKinsey Global Institute; 2023. p. 23

[47] Mitter R, Johnson E. What the west gets wrong about China: Three fundamental misconceptions. Harvard Business Review. 2021;**May–June**:1173-1182

[48] Morrison J. The Global Business Environment: Sustainability in the Balance. 6th ed. Bloomsbury Publishing; 2023

[49] Akamatsu K. A historical pattern of economic growth in developing countries. The Developing Economies. 1962;**1**(1):3-25

[50] Saich A. From Rebel to Ruler: One Hundred Years of the Chinese Communist Party. s.l.: Harvard University Press; 2021

[51] Yang J. China says US cannot speak from 'a position of strength'—BBC [online] 2021. Available from: https://www.bbc.com/news/av/world-56456021

[52] Pillsbury M. The Hundred-Year Marathon: China's Secret Strategy to Replace America as the Global Superpower. New York: Henry Holt and Co; 2016

[53] Tan J, Tan D. Environment-strategy co-evolution and co-alignment: A staged model of Chinese SOEs under transition. Strategic Management Journal. 2005;**26**(2):141-157

[54] Boisot MH, Child J. From fiefs to clans: Explaining China's emerging economic order. Administration Science Quarterly. 1996;**41**(4):600-628

[55] Devonshire-Ellis C. The Strategic Reasons Behind Recent China MNC Closures. Vol. March 20. China Briefing, Dezan Shira & Associates; 2015. p. 2015

[56] Empfield D. Ventum's Metamorphosis [Online]. 2021.Available from: https://www.slowtwitch.com/Features/Ventum_s_Metamorphosis_8177.html [Accessed: December 15, 2021]

[57] The Economist. Why Sequoia capital is Sawing Off Its Chinese Branch [Online]. 2023. Available from: https://www.economist.com/business/2023/06/08/why-sequoia-capital-is-sawing-off-its-chinese-branch.

[58] Luo Y, Park S. Strategic alignment and performance of market-seeking

MNCs in China. Strategic Management Journal. 2001;**22**(2):141-155

[59] Park SH, Zhao M, Li S. From silent majority to strategic challengers: China's new stakeholders for MNCs. Financial Times. 2015;**October 13**:2015

[60] Rodrigues SB. Towards a New Agenda for the Study of Business Internationalization: Integrating Markets, Institutions and Politics. Rotterdam: Erasmus Research Institute of Management, Rotterdam School of Management; 2010. pp. 1-62

[61] Redding G, Witt MA. The Future of Chinese Capitalism: Choices and Chances. Oxford, UK: Oxford University Press; 2007

[62] Xí J. Power Within Cage of Regulations. Beijing, China: General Secretary of the Central Committee of the Communist Party of China (CPC), Plenary Meeting on 22.01.2013 of the CPC's Central Commission for Discipline Inspection (CCDI); 2013

[63] Xí J. Study Capitalism, but Marxism Remains Top. Beijing, China: General Secretary of the Central Committee of the Communist Party of China (CPC), Study Session with the Politburo on 29.09.2017; 2017

[64] Kennedy S, Johnson CK. Perfecting China, Inc.: The 13th five-year plan. Washington, DC: Center for strategic and international studies (CSIS); 2016. pp. 1-78

[65] Wuttke J. Globalisation in Retreat? Risks and Opportunities for China. In: Address by European Chamber President Joerg Wuttke at the 2016 Annual Conference on 15.12.2016. Beijing, China: European Union Chamber of Commerce in China; 2016

[66] Reuters. Factbox: How China's Regulatory Crackdown has Reshaped Its Tech, Property Sectors [Online]. 2022. Available from: https://www.reuters.com/world/china/education-bitcoin-chinas-season-regulatory-crackdown-2021-07-27/

[67] Yip GS, McKern B. China's Next Strategic Advantage: From Imitation to Innovation. Cambridge, MA: The MIT Press; 2016

[68] Bosch UT. Impact of the Asia-Pacific Financial Currency Crisis on Multinational Corporations. Stuttgart, Germany, Results of Empirical Study in Asia, Joint-Project with German Chamber of Industry and Commerce in 8 Asia-Pacific Countries. Roland Berger & Patner GmbH IMC; 1998. pp. 1-49

[69] Bosch UT. Automobildistribution in der Volksrepublik China—Eine Studie vor dem Hintergrund der zunehmenden Individualmotorisierung. Reutlingen, Germany/London, United Kingdom [B.A. Hons. thesis]. Reutlingen University, European School of Business (ESB), University of London, Middlesex University Business School; 1999. pp. 1-135

[70] Bosch UT. Stategic Challenges of Mulitnational Corporations in China. Shanghai, China: Results of Empirical Study, MNC Account China, Watson Wyatt (Shanghai) Co., Ltd; 2008. pp. 1-32

[71] Bosch UT. Strategy, Environment, Resources and Institutional Context as Determinants of Firm Performance in Emerging Markets: Empirical Evidence from Multinational Corporations in China. Hong Kong (SAR), China: Strategic Management Society (SMS) Special Conference, Contextualizing Strategic Management in Asia: Institutions, Innovation and Internationalization, Track A, Session 345—Qualitative Studies of Organizations and Governance; 2016. pp. 1-3

[72] Bosch UT et al. Market leadership through productivity enhancement—A strategy map for NetApp China [M.B.A. thesis, group project final report]. Shanghai, China: China Europe International Business School (CEIBS); 2010. pp. 1-57

[73] Miles RE, Snow CC. Organizational Strategy, Structure, and Process. New York: McGraw-Hill; 1978

[74] Miller D. Configurations of strategy and structure: Towards a synthesis. Strategic Management Journal. 1986;7(1):235-249

[75] Ragin CC. The Comparative Method: Moving beyond Qualitative and Quantitative Strategies. Berkeley, CA: University of California Press; 1987

[76] Meyer AD. What is strategy's distinctive competence? Journal of Management. 1991;**17**(4):821-833

[77] Fiss PC. Building better causal theories: A fuzzy-set approach to typologies in organization research. Academy of Management Journal. 2011;**54**(2):393-420

[78] Miller D. Configurations revisited. Strategic Management Journal. 1996;**17**(7):505-512

[79] Lewin K. Field Theory in Social Science: Selected Theoretical Papers by Kurt Lewin. New York, NY: Harper & Row; 1951

[80] Mintzberg H. Strategy making in three modes. California Management Review. 1973;**16**(2):44-53

[81] Miller D, Friesen PH. Archetypes of strategy formulation. Management Science. 1978;**24**(9):921-933

[82] Porter ME. Competitive Strategy. New York: Free Press; 1980

[83] Fahey L, Christensen H. Evaluating the research on strategy content. Journal of Management. 1986;**12**(2):167-183

[84] Miller D. Toward a new contingency approach: The search of organizational gestalts. Journal of Management Studies. 1981;**18**(1):1-26

[85] Galbraith C, Schendel D. An empirical analysis of strategy types. Strategic Management Journal. 1983;**4**(2):153-173

[86] Hambrick DC. Some tests of the effectiveness and functional attributes of Miles and Snow's strategic types. The Academy of Management Journal. 1983;**26**(1):5-26

[87] Dess GG, Davis PS. Dess, Porter's (1980) generic strategies as determinants of strategic group membership and organisational performance. Academy of Management Journal. 1984;**27**(3):467-488

[88] Delbridge R, Fiss PC. Styles of theorizing and the social organization of knowledge. Academy of Management Review. 2013;**38**(3):325-331

[89] Abell DF. Defining the Business: The Starting Point of Strategic Planning. Englewood Cliffs, New York, NY: Prentice-Hall; 1980

[90] Segev E. A systematic comparative analysis and synthesis of two business-level strategic typologies. Strategic Management Journal. 1989;**10**(5):487-505

[91] Miles RE, Snow CC. Network organizations: New concepts for new forms. California Management Review. 1986;**28**(3):62-73

[92] Zahra SA, Pearce JA. Research evidence on the Miles-Snow typology. Journal of Management. 1990;**16**(4):751-768

[93] Andrews R, Boyne GA, Law J, Walker RM. Strategy, structure and process in the public sector: A t-test of the Miles and Snow model. Public Administration. 2009;**87**(4):732-749

[94] Desarbo WS, Benedetto CAD, Song M, Sinha I. Revisiting the Miles and Snow strategic framework: Uncovering interrelationships between strategic types, capabilities, environmental uncertainty, and firm performance. Strategic Management Journal. 2005;**26**(1):47-74

[95] Peng M, Tan J, Tong T. Ownership types and strategic groups in an emerging economy. Journal of Management Studies. 2004;**41**(7):1105-1129

[96] Tan H, Weston R, Tang Y. Applying the Miles and Snow business strategy typology to China's real estate development industry: A research framework. In: Proceedings of the 12th Pacific Rim Real Estate Society Conference PRRES. Auckland, New Zealand: The University of Auckland; 2006. pp. 1-21

[97] Hoskisson RE, Hitt MA, Wan WP, Yiu D. Swings of a pendulum: Theory and research in strategic management. Journal of Management. 1999;**25**(7):417-456

[98] Selznick P. Leadership in Administration: A Sociological Interpretation. New York, NJ: Harper & Row; 1957

[99] Snow CC, Hrebiniak LG. Strategy, distinctive competence, and organizatioral performance. Administrative Science Quarterly. 1980;**25**(2):317-336

[100] Katz D, Kahn RL. The Social Psychology of Organizations. 1st ed. New York, NY: John Wiley and Sons; 1966

[101] Doty DH, Glick WH. Typologies as a unique form of theory building: Toward improved understanding and modeling. Academy of Management Review. 1994;**19**(2):230-251

[102] Jick TD. Mixing qualitative and quantitative methods: Triangulation in action. Administrative Science Quarterly. 1979;**24**(4):602-611

[103] Boyd BK, Reuning-Elliot E. A measurement model of strategic planning. Strategic Management Journal. 1998;**19**(2):181-192

[104] Rugman AM, Verbeke A. Does competitive strategy work for small business? Journal of Small Business and Entrepreneurship. 1987;**5**(3):45-50

[105] Tan JJ, Litschert RJ. Environment-strategy relationship and its performance implications: An empirical study of the Chinese electronics industry. Strategic Management Journal. 1994;**15**(1):1-20

[106] James WL, Hatten KJ. Further evidence on the validity of the self-typing paragraph approach: Miles and Snow's strategic archetypes in banking. Strategic Management Journal. 1995;**16**(2):161-168

[107] Shortell SM, Zajac EJ. Perceptual and archival measures of Miles and Snow's strategic types: A comprehensive assessment of reliability and validity. Academy of Management Journal. 1990;**33**(4):817-832

[108] Rajagopalan N, Finkelstein S. Effects of strategic orientation and environmental change on senior management reward systems. Strategic Management Journal. 1992;**13**(Special Issue):127-142

[109] Slater SF, Olson EM. Strategy type and performance: The influence of sales force management. Strategic Management Journal. 2000;**21**(8):813-829

[110] Conant JS, Mokwa MP, Varadarajan PR. Strategies types, distinctive marketing competencies and organizational performance: A multiple measures-based study. Strategic Management Journal. 1990;**11**(5):365-383

[111] Luo Y, Peng MW. Learning to compete in a transition economy: Experience, environment, and performance. Journal of International Business Studies. 1999;**30**(2):269-296

[112] Zaheer S, Mosakowski E. The dynamics of the liability of foreignness: A global study of survival in financial services. Strategic Management Journal. 1997;**18**(6):439-464

[113] Dess GG, Beard D. Dimensions of organizational task environments. Administrative Science Quarterly. 1984;**29**(1):52-73

[114] Child J. Organizational structure, environment and performance: The role of strategic choice. Sociology. 1972;**6**(1):1-22

[115] Meyer AD. Adapting to environmental jolts. Administrative Science Quarterly. 1982;**27**(4):515-538

[116] Walker OCJ, Ruekert RW. Marketing's role in the implementation of business strategies: A critical review and conceptual framework. Journal of Marketing. 1987;**51**(3):15-33

[117] Kanter RM. When Giants Learn to Dance. New York, NY/London, UK: Simon & Schuster; 1989

[118] Hillman AJ, Zardkoohi A, Bierman L. Corporate political strategies and firm performance: Indications of firm-specific benefits from personal service in the US government. Strategic Management Journal. 1999;**20**(1):67-81